RADICAL MEDIA

Rebellious Communication and Social Movements

JOHN D.H. DOWNING

with Tamara Villarreal Ford • Genève Gil • Laura Stein

Sage Publications, Inc.
International Educational and Professional Publisher
Thousand Oaks ■ London ■ New Delhi

For information:

Sage Publications, Inc.
2455 Teller Road
Thousand Oaks, California 91320
E-mail: order@sagepub.com

Sage Publications Ltd.
6 Bonhill Street
London EC2A 4PU
United Kingdom

Sage Publications India Pvt. Ltd.
M-32 Market
Greater Kailash I
New Delhi 110 048 India

Printed in the United States of America

Library of Congress Cataloging-in-Publication Data

Downing, John.
Radical media: Rebellious communication and social movements / by John D. H. Downing; with Tamara Villarreal Ford, Genève Gil, and Laura Stein.
p. cm.
Includes bibliographical references (p.) and index.
ISBN 0-8039-5698-3 (cloth: alk. paper)
ISBN 0-8039-5699-1 (pbk.: alk. paper)
1. Mass media. 2. Social movements. 3. Radicalism. I. Title.

P91 .D67 2000
302.23'4—dc21 00-008781

This book is printed on acid-free paper.

01 02 03 04 05 06 7 6 5 4 3 2 1

Acquisition Editors: Margaret H. Seawell
Editorial Assistant: Heidi Van Middlesworth
Production Editor: Astrid Virding
Editorial Assistant: Candice Crosetti
Typesetter: Rebecca Evans
Cover Designer: Michelle Lee

Contents

Preface

Common approaches to communication media are wildly lopsided precisely because they refuse to take seriously the historical persistence and geographical pervasiveness of radical alternative media. Although the extent of such media at the dawn of the 21st century CE is broader than ever before, and therefore ever more demanding of our analytical attention, radical alternative media are by no means latecomers to culture and politics. They are simply relative newcomers to the established research and theory agenda, which has a predilection for the seemingly obvious and the easily counted. By *radical media,* I refer to media, generally small-scale and in many different forms, that express an alternative vision to hegemonic policies, priorities, and perspectives.

Filling in a very significant gap is only one reason for focusing on radical alternative media. The other is related, but pragmatic rather than conceptual: the urgency of media activism in the face of blockages of public expression.[1] These blockages emerge from many quarters: powerful components within the dynamic of capitalist economy, governmental secrecy, religious obscurantism, institutionalized racist and patriarchal codes, other hegemonic[2] codes that appear natural and sensible; the insidious impact of reactionary populism, and also reflexes of all of these within oppositional movements themselves. Radical media activism is not the only response needed—media literacy campaigns, growing media democratization, scientific and technical popularization, and support for media professionals struggling to upgrade mainstream media practice are all vital—but it is essential.

How can small-scale radical media have any impact worth having? This book sets out to answer that question, but the short answer is they have multiple impacts on different levels. Let me offer two rapid examples.

In the downward spiral of the second Cold War of the early 1980s, I was only one of many Americans, Russians, and others who looked on aghast as the two camps' senile leaders, Brezhnev and Reagan, pointed ever more massive nuclear weapons against each other (with the enthusiastic backing of their military staffs and military-industrial complexes). On this issue, mainstream media followed their leaders in both camps.[3] However, in the United States and former West Germany, in particular, but also in Britain, Italy, and the Netherlands, large antinuclear movements sprang up or became reinvigorated, both against nuclear weapons and more broadly against nuclear power. Germany in particular produced a huge array of radical media exposing and attacking the nuclear arms race and the dangers of nuclear power (Downing, 1988a). In the United States, a number of antinuclear documentary films were made and widely screened, notably *Paul Jacobs and the Nuclear Gang* (1979) and *Atomic Café* (1982). These, in turn, fed the movements and ongoing demonstrations, which generated tremendous opposition to both the U.S. and U.S.S.R. leadership. A million people marched in New York City alone. This became a factor in the ability of the Soviet leadership to seize the high moral ground, but also provided an opportunity for both leaders to claim credit for stepping back from nuclear proliferation, beginning with the superpower summit in Reykjavik, Iceland, in 1987. Had it not been for these movements and their media, the possibility of mutual assured destruction—the war strategists' official doctrine—would have loomed ever larger.

This is an instance with major international impact. The Italian, Portuguese, Russian, and Polish case studies in Section 3, the Iranian case that we refer to intermittently, and the international anti-apartheid movement are some others.

On a much less dramatic plane are the little photographic visiting cards (*cartes-de-visite*) that Sojourner Truth used to sell to support herself in her later years. These little photographs of oneself, used as visiting cards and as mementos, were something of a national mania in the 1860s. Truth sat for 14 of these, all of them showing her dressed as a respectable upper middle-class woman, mostly sitting with her knitting on her lap. Over a century later, the image may seem entirely banal. But as Nell Irvin Painter (1996) points out, in context, the image made a radical assertion. Truth was not working in the field or over a wash tub (the only other visual images of her). She *was*, by contrast, a respectable woman:

> Black woman as lady went against the commonplaces of nineteenth-century American culture. But by circulating her photographs widely, Truth claimed womanhood for a black woman who had been a slave, occupying a space ordinarily off limits to women like her. She refused to define herself by her enslavement. Seizing on a new technology, Truth established what few nineteenth-century black women were able to prove: that she was present in her times. (pp. 198-199)

This instance, aside from encouraging us to acknowledge the all-important question of context, tells us something more. There is no instantaneous alchemy, no uncontested sociochemical procedure, that will divine in a flash or with definitive results truly radical media from the apparently radical or even the nonradical.[4]

In this multifarious, seething broth that we name society, what counts as politically oppositional, as personally expressive, as experimental, as embedded in the cultural present, as heralding the public's future, as reclaiming the forgotten merits of the past? For those with instinctively tidy minds, this category dilemma generates genuine pain, a real intellectual abscess. While, nevertheless, not wishing to praise fog for its own pure sake, it is perhaps precisely the indeterminacy of this seething broth that is the most important point. From such cauldrons may emerge social and cultural change in many directions, positive and negative and in between. The 1848 revolutions in Europe, the turbulence in Russia during the first decades of the 20th century, the Weimar Republic period in Germany, the Quit India movement of the 1920s through 1947, the international ferment of the 1960s and 1970s, are only a few examples.

Without such cauldrons, there is stasis—which may sometimes be preferred by reasonable and constructive people—but the issue here is not so much what is desirable as what actually happens and its relation to radical alternative media. And, simultaneously, what is at issue is the relation between (sometimes imperceptible) eddies and ferments of opinion and expression and the impact of such media. The specific question of whether any particular activity in this alternative public realm is to be considered oppositional or self-indulgent or reactionary—or some compound of these—is a matter for argument. Maybe, it will be many decades—if ever—before the significance of such events can be established. But for present purposes, it is the ferment itself that counts, as matrix to radical media.

In the original edition of this study, published in 1984 by the South End Press collective in Boston, Massachusetts, I adopted an antibinarist and a binarist definition of radical media simultaneously. I was intensely concerned to challenge a prevailing orthodoxy of the time, namely, that there were only two viable models of how to organize media, the Western capitalist one and the Soviet one. Each system had its ideologues and its counterideologues. In the West, a disturbing number of individuals on the political left could be found who were, if not advocates of sovietized media, then at least reluctant to attack them or the Soviet system, on the spurious grounds that to do so would make it easier for Western media barons and ideologues to sing the corrupt glories of their own communication media, supposedly free agents of free expression. In the East, decades of intense frustration at the absurdities and worse of their own media systems led many thinking people to yearn for Western media and to write off critical Western media researchers as smug, deluded idiots. Either way, an international consensus seemed to hold that only two models of media organization were feasible or even imaginable.

I was determined to query that consensus, and so I spent quite some time critiquing the then-contemporary application of Leninist media theory in the East, as well as underscoring the idiotic triumphalism of those who chanted (and still chant!) the unalloyed virtues of capitalist media. I also endeavored to build up the rudiments of a theory of radical alternative media on the basis of some writings by socialist anarchists, British marxist feminists of that period, and dissident marxist theorists in Eastern Europe. (And I spent time annotating typical vices of alternative media.)

So that was my antibinarism. "A plague o' both your houses!" groaned Mercutio, unfortunately with virtually his dying breath, just having been stabbed in a street fracas between Montague and Capulet braggadocios. (Not an encouraging precedent, I felt, but I went ahead anyway.)

My own binarism, however, went unnoticed, at least by myself. It came about, effectively, through my being caught up in the Cold War spiral to which I have already referred. Thus, it seemed especially urgent to try to hammer home the merits of alternative ways of communicating politically, however picayune they might appear in the first instance. Underscoring their significance, however, led me to define radical media more tightly, in strict opposition to mainstream media, to a greater degree than I now believe possible for most conjunctures in political history. It simultaneously led me to write off major commercial media as permanently part of the problem, except on rare and good days. That was my slippage toward binarism. It was only implicit, and indeed, I contradicted it at a number of points in my arguments, but it still seriously simplified both mainstream and alternative media.

Taken to its ultimate point, that position would discount any movement toward democratizing large-scale commercial media, which would let them off the hook much too easily. It would render the quite often impassioned attacks on major media from the political right and the extreme right somewhere between incomprehensible and irrelevant. It would downplay the uses that oppositional movements and groups may sometimes be able to make of mainstream media.[5] It would also flatten out the very considerable variety of radical media.

Let me sketch out then my preliminary definition of what differentiates radical alternative media from more conventional, mainstream media.

First, it must be acknowledged that to speak simply of *alternative* media is almost oxymoronic. Everything, at some point, is alternative to something else. The ever-expanding plethora of niche trade magazines or of corporate industry bulletins, although an interesting phenomenon in its own right, does not belong in the category of media studied here. To some extent, the extra designation *radical* helps to firm up the definition of alternative media, but even here, we need to make some preliminary qualifications.

For, second, radical media may, depending on the vantage point of the observer or the activist, represent radically negative as well as constructive forces. From my own angle of vision, fundamentalist or racist or fascist radical media are pushing for society to move backward into even more grotesque problems than we struggle with today. The fact remains that they are radical media. They, too, demand to be understood, even if we differentiate them by certain criteria (examined in Part II) from the media whose agendas dominate this study.

But, third, in some circumstances, the designation radical media may also include minority ethnic media. So, too, sometimes, religious media. So, too, maybe a vast mass of community news sheets and bulletin boards, depending on the issues at stake in the communities in question. But equally, the adjective *radical* may well not fit a considerable number of these ethnic, religious, or community media. Everything depends on their content and context. What might abstractly seem a bland and low-key instance could, in a given context, be wielding a hammer blow at some orthodoxy, as the Sojourner Truth example shows.

Indeed, the very intentions of the communicators themselves may turn out to be no guide at all in this maze, or at least a notably insufficient guide. History is crammed with cases of individuals and groups who had no idea, and could have had no idea, of the chain of socially disruptive events they were setting in motion.

So context and consequences must be our primary guides to what are or are not definable as radical alternative media. The edges are almost always blurred. Every technology used by radical media activists is and has always been used mostly for mainstream purposes, not theirs.

Sometimes, fourth, and maybe in a majority of cases, radical media are mixed in the depth of their radicalism, let alone in the effectiveness of their expression. An example would be the cartoons in the U.S. prosuffragist press (Israels Perry, 1994): Women were typically portrayed as inevitably virtuous, often as victims, rarely as authority figures, almost exclusively as white and well-educated, and if powerful women were depicted, it was as "Amazonian Wonder Women or allegorical figures drawn from classical culture" (p. 10). Thus, while demanding the vote for women, many of these oppositional cartoons simultaneously reiterated patriarchal stereotypes. Strictly binary definitions of these media simply bounce off their actual spectrum.

Yet, fifth, in some circumstances, when they are forced underground by systematic repression and censorship, especially in its fascist or sovietized variants, or in the typical military regime, then, such media are indeed in a binary, either-or situation. The earlier Reagan years, the Nixon years, and certainly the McCarthy era had some of that flavor for the political left in the United States, thanks to J. Edgar Hoover's FBI.

Sixth, radical alternative media are to be found in a colossal variety of formats. In the first edition, I focused almost entirely on regularly appearing print and broadcast media, the purpose being to try to understand how media activists, often unpaid or low paid, manage to keep going day by day, month by month, and even year after year. The objective was worthwhile, and indeed, the case studies in this edition are mostly of that ilk. But as a definition of the variety of forms radical media can take, it was impoverished. Such media may even find themselves within an alien media setting, as when waspish leftist cartoons nestle uneasily in conservative newspapers.

If, seventh, radical alternative media have one thing in common, it is that they break somebody's rules, although rarely all of them in every respect.

We may also say, eighth, that these media are typically small-scale, generally underfunded, sometimes largely unnoticed at least initially, on occasion the target of great anger or fear or ridicule from on high, or even within the general public, or both. Sometimes they are short-lived, even epiphenomenal; at other times, they last for many decades. Sometimes, they are entrancing, sometimes boring and jargon laden, sometimes frightening, sometimes brilliantly funny.

Ninth, radical alternative media generally serve two overriding purposes: (a) to express opposition vertically from subordinate quarters directly at the power structure and against its behavior; (b) to build support, solidarity, and networking laterally against policies or even against the very survival of the power structure. In any given instance, both vertical and lateral purposes may be involved.

Tenth and finally, there is a tendency within their internal organization to try to be somewhat more, or sometimes considerably more democratic than conventional mainstream media.

In Part I, I will endeavor to put conceptual flesh on these bones. In the rest of the book, I and my co-authors will examine a whole tapestry of radical media.

NOTES

1. There is a large literature on aspects of mainstream media hegemony, and I will refer the reader to some of it rather than try to encapsulate it here: Bagdikian (1999); Brook and Boal (1995); Curran and Seaton (1991); Dates and Barlow (1993); Entman (1989); Gitlin (1983); Gray (1995); Herman (1999); Herman and Chomsky (1988); Herman and McChesney (1997); Hertsgaard

(1988); Kellner (1990, 1992); McChesney (1996); Schlesinger (1992); Sinclair (1991); Sussman (1997); van Zoonen (1993).

2. In using the term *hegemonic,* I draw broadly on its use in the work of Gramsci. I discuss Gramsci's work in the first chapter and also in Downing (1996, pp. 199-204).

3. Although they did so completely slavishly in the Soviet bloc, whereas there were some exceptions on occasion in the West, the Soviets' public stance occupied the higher moral ground of rejecting the so-called "first strike" doctrine, that is, the strategy of initiating nuclear war. The U.S. position under Reagan was not to rule out a first strike. The Soviet position was extremely effective. It simultaneously heartened antinuclear movements in the West, gave them a stick with which to beat their government leaders, and reflected the Soviet public's very deep fear of war, ingrained from its colossal human losses in World War II. In reality, of course, in military matters as in team sports or chess, an impregnable defense makes a policy of attack all the easier to pursue because there is less fear of retribution. Describing weapons as offensive or defensive neatly skates around this reality. The Reagan administration's so-called Strategic Defense Initiative (sometimes referred to as the "Star Wars" project), the multibillion-dollar research program into computer- and laser-based weaponry, was another classic in this mystification: It, too, was claimed to be for defensive purposes only, to provide an impregnable shield around the United States to intercept any incoming missiles. Had it been technologically feasible, it would not have been simply defensive; and those of its elements that actually were feasible could be deployed in attack as well or better. The literature on the subject is enormous, but the following present useful guides: Aldridge, 1983; Lifton & Falk, 1982; Manno, 1984; Pringle & Arkin, 1983.

4. Equally, in a study of the early years of *The Cosby Show* (Downing, 1988b), I argue that in context, that seemingly cozy, even bromide-bound series successfully challenged a whole stack of racist shibboleths in and out of the U.S. television industry. In Section I, Chapter 1, and throughout Section II, we will find ourselves revisiting this question of oppositional cultures and their expression.

5. For a very helpful guide to this last issue, see Ryan (1991).

Acknowledgments

First, my thanks to Sage Publications, Inc., and particularly to Margaret Seawell, and before her Sophy Craze, for taking on this project; and thanks to South End Press for publishing the first version back in 1984. As readers of that version will know only too well—and I thank them for their loyalty to the project and their persistence—the glueing by the Dutch firm with which South End Press had contracted was entirely inadequate, and the pages fell out more or less as soon as the book was opened. This time the text is less structurally post-modernist. . . .

I have *un sacco di gente* to thank in the various media that I have studied, but before even them, I would like to thank the students in my Alternative Media classes at Hunter College and then the University of Texas at Austin for the stimulation and insights they have given me during the long gestation of this new version, constituting by my reckoning around 75% an entirely new book. Among them, I am glad to single out my co-authors of the chapters on the Internet and U.S. public access television, Tamara Villarreal Ford, Genève Gil, and Laura Stein.

For the Portuguese case study, my thanks to Fernando da Sousa, Gabriel Ferreira, João Alferes Gonçalves, Jorge Almeida Fernandes, Raúl Rêgo, Fernanda Barao, José Salvador, Fernando Cascais, Alvaro Miranda, Manuel Vilaverde Cabral, Phil Mailer, Bruno Ponte, and Manuel Braga. For the Italian case study, my thanks to Gianni Riotta,

Guido Moltedo, Angela Pascucci, Ida Dominjanni, Rina Gagliardi, Sara Maggi, Massimo Smuraglia, Stefano Fabbri, Raffaele Palumbo, Mario Bufono, Margherita Calvalli, Marco Imponente, Livio Sansone and his family, Sandro Scotto, Vito and Ombretta Conteduca, Gabriella Camilotto, Federico Pedrocchi, Biagio Longo, Paolo Hutter, Manuela Barbieri, Sergio Ferrentino, Marcello Lorrai, and Marina Petrillo. For the KPFA and Free Radio Berkeley case studies, my thanks to Vera Hopkins, Bari Scott, Ginny Berson, Eve Matthews, David Salniker, and Stephen Dunifer; and for initial insight into microradio, Tetsuo Kogawa. For the *samizdat* study, my thanks to A. J. Liehm, Jiri Hochmann, Boris Bagaryatsky, Volodia Padunov, Karol Jakubowicz, Tadek Walendowski, Witek Sulkowski, Piotr Naimski, Ryszard Knauff, Wojciech Ostrowski, Jakab Zoltan,and Szckfü Andras.

I was fortunate to receive support for the original Portuguese and Italian case studies from the British SSRC in 1980, plus a trimester leave from Thames Polytechnic (today the ESRC and Greenwich University). I received support in 1984, 1986, 1988, and 1990 from the PSC-CUNY Faculty Research Fund for my studies of antinuclear media in what was then West Germany (briefly noted in the text) and for research on Soviet bloc media (some of which touched on samizdat). I also received a travel grant in 1997 from the University of Texas to return to the Italian scene and update my case studies there, as well as a sabbatical semester from the University of Texas at Austin in 1999 to help complete writing this book. Otherwise, it has been carved out in the interstices of my daily existence, but with stimulation from terrific colleagues, staff, and students in the Radio-Television-Film Department at the University of Texas at Austin.

Thanks to Clemencia Rodríguez and John Sinclair, in particular, for some close reading of earlier drafts; and also to Dana Cloud, Jesse Drew, Bob Jensen, and some anonymous Sage reviewers for their very helpful advice on approaches to the material.

Last, on a personal note, a word in honor and love for Anneli, Corinna, Juanita, Zoë, *chetvero absolyutno zamechatel'nykh i krasivikh docheri*; in loving memory of Jamal and Stansil; and in celebration of Ash Corea, *la mia compagna dappertutto*, who as I wrote first time round, represents what this book strives to bring about.

John Downing
Austin, Texas

I

Concepts: Radical Media Intersect Media Theory

In making sense of the enormous, shifting terrain of oppositional cultures and radical media, we need sooner or later to step back a little and consider some significant and interesting thinkers' perspectives, which may help us understand these media better. Depending on readers' familiarity with some of the debates around these ideas, what follows may turn out to be a little heavy going at times, even though I have tried to write these chapters as accessibly as possible. But, perhaps, for those to whom these debates are altogether new, it may be better to roam through the rest of the book first and then return to this section to make more sense of the terrain as a whole.[1]

The topics to be explored below are approaches I have drawn together for this fairly novel purpose: popular culture and audiences/readers; power, hegemony, and resistance; social movements, the public sphere, and dialogue; community and democracy; the relation between art and media communication; radical media organization; and finally a further group of problems and issues (religion, ethnicity, the international dimension, repressive radical media).[2] What I have sought to sketch out are the launching pads for understanding radical alternative media in ways that are much more sensitive to complexity than has mostly been the case to date. However, we shall also see that the perspectives that illuminate our topic, or have some claim to do so, are multiple, sometimes overlapping, sometimes contradictory.

NOTES

1. For those familiar with the material, some footnote explanations may be otiose. Dear highly informed reader, do not thereby feel yourself offended.

2. These topics are not exhaustive. Age, gender, sexuality, ecology, and others are also relevant but in this treatment are discussed at intervals throughout.

1

Popular Culture, Audiences, and Radical Media

The argument will be as follows:

- Popular culture is intertwined in many ways with mass culture.
- We should more accurately speak of popular cultures in the plural.
- These are not automatically oppositional or constructive.
- Oppositional cultures also intertwine with both mass and popular cultures.
- Audiences/readers may be defined
  as (sometimes resistant) commercial targets;
  as the necessary "reality-check" on supposed media impact;
  as joint architects of cultural production, this being the primary sense used in this book.
- Radical alternative media constitute the most active form of the active audience and express oppositional strands, overt and covert, within popular cultures.

These are fundamental issues, inasmuch as these various radical alternative media forms are, almost self-evidently, forms of popular and oppositional cultural expression. Indeed, as we will see, a sharp division between radical media expression and other forms of oppositional cultural expression makes little sense. Yet, who makes use of these multiple forms and how—in other words, audiences and readers—is as central to their operation as it is with all other media forms.

DEFINING POPULAR CULTURE

A classic definition of popular culture is to be found in Theodor Adorno's (1975) article, "Culture Industry Reconsidered," his commentary on the famous essay Max Horkheimer and he first published in 1944, entitled "The Culture Industry: Enlightenment as Mass Deception" (Horkheimer & Adorno, 1987). Trying to rebut a charge laid by critics against the first essay, namely that it trashed popular cultural expression, Adorno urged critics to appreciate the distinction he and Horkheimer had tried to maintain between mass culture and popular culture. They had unequivocally rejected mass culture, the product of the commercial industries of advertising, broadcasting, cinema, and print media, as a spurious and implicitly even fascistic rendition of the public's needs, asphyxiating the questioning spirit. Popular culture, by contrast, was an authentic expression of the public's visions and aspirations, as in folk music and folk art, and had inherent oppositional potential.

Popular cultural forms have been quite exhaustively analyzed in the now huge literature of cultural studies. Sometimes, this has almost echoed Adorno, with a simplistic dualism that defines all popular culture as oppositional—"politically healthy"—in contradistinction to commercialized or mass culture. In one phase of his writing, a leading cultural studies analyst, John Fiske, strove[1] to identify the smallest and most fleeting flickers of audience response or shoppers' behavior as audience activism and resistance to oppressive social codes.

Tidy, but really too tidy. Jesús Martín-Barbero (1993, pp. 120-147) has rightly insisted on the interpenetrations between popular and mass culture. A major reason for the success of commercially produced mass culture, he points out, is precisely that the commercial culture industries pick up on numerous elements of popular cultural expression.

Their products and language are not simply impositions from on high.[2] He and others have correspondingly explored notions of hybridity/*mestizaje* in cultural life, examining the intricate mesh of cultural capillaries that suffuse the body of society.[3] We shall return to this notion below in the discussion of social movements.

More than being just too tidy, dualist perspectives are seriously flawed: Popular culture is perfectly able to be elitist, racist, misogynist, homophobic, and ageist and to express these values in inventive and superficially attractive forms. The negative roles of women and girls in fairy tales and folk songs constitute but one example. Racist rock groups constitute another. Neither ethnic antagonism nor misogyny are simply implanted from on high or from outside into an unsuspecting and unwilling populace.

This is not merely a passing qualification, as regards this book's theme. Popular culture is larger than oppositional culture, at most junctures in history probably considerably larger. Yet, just as popular culture and mass culture interpenetrate and suffuse each other, so, too, does oppositional culture draw on and contribute to popular culture and mass culture. A droll example was when U.S. anarchist activist Abbie Hoffman, at the height of his notoriety, persuaded a commercial publisher to entitle his mass market book *Steal This Book.* A more sober U.S. example was the 1970s television miniseries *Roots,* which depicted some of the harshest aspects of slavery to a huge mass audience. Despite its limitations, it would probably never have been made at all had it not been for the Civil Rights and Black Power movements of the 1960s. These examples are but two that underscore how these various cultural strands are typically interspersed and intertwined with each other and can only be separated analytically.

The plural *cultures* is important for further reasons. Very few nations are monocultural, and even those that are overwhelmingly so, such as Japan or postwar Poland, typically have class and regional variants of the national culture. Gender and age cultures further diversify the picture. These various cultures are in a hierarchy, with bourgeois rank, whiteness, maleness, and correct mother tongue typically given an elevated standing, often quite simply consecrated as the national criterion for being taken seriously. But given all these elements, and not least the accelerating migration from one part of the globe to another over recent centuries, multicultural nations are the norm. Thus, minority ethnic media and feminist media, to take but two instances that express the priorities and aspirations of extruded cultures, constitute an important dimension of radical alternative media.

Peter Burke (1986) has a helpful essay in which he identifies three established approaches to popular culture. One he calls media based, the second he terms society based, and a third, that of the *Annales* historiographical school, emphasizes developments in popular culture over substantial periods of time (*longue durée*). The media-based analysis reflects Adorno. The society-based approach focuses, rather, on structural and institutional changes over the past two centuries, especially relations between social classes, and the influence these changes have sparked, culturally speaking, among subordinate classes.[4] The Annales school has typically focused on premodern society and deploys quasi-ethnographic research designs. Burke pleads for a constructive synthesis of the two latter approaches, rejecting the first as threadbare. The particular point of value here is the historian's emphasis on the development of cultural forms and processes over extended periods of time, including centuries. A recurring and insidious temptation in media studies is to assess media from the singular vantage point of the contemporary moment. Both the impact and the origins of media become extremely foggy as a result. This is not least true of radical alternative media and oppositional cultures, which are already vulnerable to premature dismissal as ephemeral and therefore irrelevant.

DEFINING AUDIENCES

However, culture consists not only of texts or other artifacts, but also of their reception and use. We have already touched on the notion of audiences and readers, but once we address the question directly, we find that another central factor in this whole nexus is the kind of cultural appropriation that audiences perform on and with mass cultural products, often taking what they are offered and constructing imaginary scenarios from it, some of which have resonances with a liberating potential.

A path-breaking study by Janice Radway (1984) examined how women readers of Harlequin romance novelettes drew on them to dwell pleasurably on alternative, more satisfying types of gender relations than the ones they themselves had experienced. Her study helped to spark a huge wave of audience research that in one way or another explored the cultural activism of audiences as they use commercial media products. One instance is TV series fans' Internet use to construct discussions and interpretations of their favorite television text, as in Henry Jenkins's (1992) study of *Star Trek* fans whom, following Michel de Certeau (1984), he terms "textual poachers." Thus, mainstream media products may well draw on popular culture, as Martín-Barbero proposes, but equally, even when molded or transmuted and then "handed back" by the commercial industries, these products are still subject to all kinds of interpretive influences generated—once again—from the public's everyday cultures.

In the two terms *popular culture* and *audiences,* we also see the conceptual overlaps and contradictions mentioned above as characteristic of the array of concepts I am deploying to make sense of radical alternative media. The first term was coined in the sociology of culture, where popular culture serves as a generic category referring variously to cultural production and reception by and within the public at large. Audience serves the corporate world as a highly specific designation of enumerated groups of viewers, listeners, and readers, derived from the market strategies and discourses of film and broadcasting firms, publishers, and advertisers. For payment, media firms seek to deliver to advertisers the eyes and ears of audiences, in the sense of groups of consumers with buying power.

The two terms, used thus, raise sharply different problematics and emerge from totally distinct perspectives, even though ostensibly both are defining actual human consumers of and generators of culture. To some degree, the terms have been yoked together in the concept of the "active audience," already adumbrated just above when Radway's work was discussed, namely, an audience that is conceived as working on and molding media products, not just passively soaking up their messages. The grassroots initiative implicit in popular culture and the ineluctable question of media text reception both have a foothold in this concept. However, although more astute advertisers endeavor to refine their messages in recognition that the audience is active, in their fundamental strategy, advertisers see audiences as being there to be persuaded and seduced—if necessary by sophisticated low-key methods that do not insult their intelligence—but not empowered.

DEFINING RADICAL MEDIA

The term *popular culture,* then, focuses attention on the matrix of radical alternative media, relatively free from the agenda of the powers that be and sometimes in opposition to one or more elements in that agenda. At the same time, the term serves to remind us that all such media are part of popular culture and of the overall societal mesh and are not tidily segregated into a radical political reservation.[5] They are endemically, therefore, a mixed phenomenon, quite often free and radical in certain respects and not in others. Sadly, the record speaks for itself of many women suffragists' failures to oppose slavery, of many abolitionists' failures to support women's suffrage, and of much of organized labor's failure in relation to both women workers and workers of color. Mixed, indeed.

The popular culture frame also prods us to acknowledge two further issues central to the argument of this book. The first is that the full spectrum of radical media in modern cultures includes a huge gamut of activities, from street theater and murals to dance and song—see the Panorama section of this book—and not just radical uses of the technologies of radio, video, press, and Internet. The second is equally important, namely, what Edward Thompson (1978) described as the forgotten half of people's culture:

> [People] also experience their own experience as *feeling* [italics added] and they handle their feelings within their culture, as norms, familial and kinship obligations and reciprocity, as values, or (through more elaborate forms) within art or religious beliefs. This half of culture (and it is a full one-half) may be described as affective and moral consciousness. (p. 352)

On the other hand, the term audiences (in the plural) forces our sometimes unwilling attention toward actual users of media. It pushes us to consider the real flows of media influence, including those of radical media, and not simply to speculate concerning hoped-for flows. If audiences are redefined as media users rather than as consumers, as active rather than uncritical, and as various (audiences) rather than as homogeneous, then the term is able to be freed of much of its purely marketing baggage.

In this process, the dividing line between active media users and radical alternative media producers becomes much more blurred. It becomes more productive to envision a kind of ascending scale in terms of logistical complexity, all the way from interpreting mainstream media texts in liberating ways, à la Janice Radway and many others, through writing graffiti on billboards and culture-jamming,[6] to occasional flyers and posters, up to systematically organized and autonomous media production over extended periods of time. Juxtaposing the concept of popular culture as qualified by Martín-Barbero with this refined and not commercially driven definition of the term *audiences* offers a framework within which we can more easily understand the operation of radical alternative media.

However, we need to link the notion of audiences to two further major considerations. One is the question of time scale, the other the question of social movements.

Audience research as practiced is overwhelmingly interested in the instantaneous. Longer term impact is an extravagance in terms of commercial priorities. The notion of "slow burn," as in Peter Burke's (1986) urging that we consider the longer term in popular culture, which might have much more relevance to small-scale alternative media, is not on the agenda. If, however, the implication of radical alternative media content is that certain kinds of change are urgently needed in the economic or political structure, but the present is very clearly one in which such changes are unimaginable, then the role of those media is to keep alive the vision of what might be, for a time in history when it may actually be feasible. A classic instance here would be *samizdat* media in Russia and Eastern Europe during the Soviet era (see the Panorama section [Part III] and Chapter 22 for further details). But one might equally cite as instances some of the work of Blake or Goya, virtually unseen in their own lifetimes, but with an ongoing impact two centuries later.

Audiences, as a term, implies something rather static, typically wrapped cozily around a TV set at home. Social movements, as a term, implies something active and on the streets. We will review social movements more closely later, but it is important to grasp that audiences and movements do not live segregated the one from the other. In the ongoing life of social movements, audiences overlap with movement activity, and the interrelation may be very intense between the audiences for media, including radical alternative media, and those movements. Thus, the somewhat static, individualized—or at least domesticated—audience is only one mode of appropriating media content. Radical alternative media impact needs to be disentangled, therefore, from the often axiomatic assumptions we have about audiences.

Summary: Popular culture is the generic matrix of radical alternative media. It also intertwines with commercialized mass culture and oppositional cultures. In active, multicultural audiences, we may see the joint architects—along with textual producers—of media meanings, sometimes poaching what they want from media products and subverting the values originally intended. In turn, some of these joint architects, drawing on popular movements and oppositional cultures, may themselves become producers of radical media and, then, risk textual poaching—which is a glancing acknowledgment of one of the aspects of radical media that has been least studied and is most in need of it, namely their audiences/readership, a topic that this book only addresses at a very general level. An urgent and intriguing research terrain beckons.

But in thinking about cultural and audience processes as they relate to radical media, we need to assess them over the long term as well as in the immediate moment and to view them in relation to the dynamic of social movements. (Both these are recurring and important strands in this book's argument.)

However, we need now to add to the concepts already reviewed by exploring in more detail notions of power, hegemony, and resistance that have been implicit so far. In the preceding discussion of the hierarchy of cultures and of interactions between popular culture and mass culture, we have stepped sharply away from a common assumption about culture, which is that it simply emerges spontaneously from the bowels of society. It is naive to suppose that either culture or communication are anything so innately democratic, although their construction is certainly more emergent than it is presciently organized. In communication and culture, power processes and differentials are everywhere.

NOTES

1. See, for example, Fiske (1988), and for a very interesting study that is not hobbled by that approach, Fiske (1995).

2. Martín-Barbero's (1993) text is one in which I have found valuable confirmation and inspiration for this study.

3. Sadly, in some postmodernist writing, hybridity itself has been inflated into a mantra, with everyday life, as Tony Bennett (1992) so splendidly put it, "construed as a rich domain of the unfathomable" (p. 11). The seductiveness of all-purpose concepts is remarkable.

4. Examples include the work of Raymond Williams (1977) and E. P. Thompson (1968, 1978, 1993).

5. Lenin, in his famous strategy text, *What Is To Be Done?* (1902/1965), sought strictly to demarcate the Marxist political party press from the general run of oppositional expression, not only by its tight organizational hierarchy but also by its pristine political content guaranteed by professional revolutionary intellectuals. We will return to this topic below.

6. This term means using official cultural symbols against their intended purpose. For more on the subject, see Chapter 12.

2

Power, Hegemony, Resistance

To illuminate the relation between power and culture and, most particularly, the roles of radical alternative media within that relation, I propose to play with a mazurka of concepts drawn from socialist and feminist anarchism, Antonio Gramsci, and some other sources on subversive ploys in everyday life. Specifically,

- Socialist and feminist anarchism's identification of multiple sources of subordination beyond capitalism's directly economic dimension; what, in other words, is the full range of forces that radical media are combating?
- Gramsci's exploration of capitalist cultural hegemony and popular counterhegemony; where do radical media fit?
- Scott's examination of everyday resistance tactics; what is the relation between them and radical media activism?

THE CONCEPT OF POWER

Power is potentially one of the more vacuous concepts in social and cultural analysis. It can refer to everything from the sadistic secret police of a dictatorial regime to the diffused networks of micropower addressed in Michel Foucault's work (e.g., Foucault, 1977). In a Marxist framework, it can refer to a fusion between economic and political dominance for good (in a socialist regime) or, over the long term, for ill (under capitalism). Within a socialist-anarchist framework, power often carries a dual negative, namely, capital and the centralized state. In a right-wing anarchist framework, frequently found within the contemporary United States, the problem of power is defined as the state pure and simple, with the power of capital strangely off the map. In addition, the word may denote popular power and the power to resist as well as the competitive power struggle between corporate leaders. It may also denote positive power, the capacity to achieve something or create something (see the discussion of Macpherson in Chapter 4). Yet, everyone uses the word *power* freely and therein often lies a major problem in its discussion: the inaccurate assumption of shared meaning.

We will begin by noting an important contribution of socialist anarchism[1] to understanding the issues (cf. Martín-Barbero, 1993, pp. 13-17). A number of particular strengths in anarchist angles of vision have a bearing on radical alternative media. The one I will focus on at this point—others will surface later—is the emphasis on multiple realities of oppression beyond the economic. The tendency in Marxist thinking to focus exclusively on political economy is much rarer within anarchism, although somewhat in evidence in its syndicalist version. When reading Emma Goldman's (1970, 1974) lectures or autobiography, for instance, the breadth of her concerns is evident—the theater, women's rights, contraceptive education, sexuality, prisons, puritanism, patriotism, the positive intellectual contributions of Freud and Nietzsche—as is the fact that they are valued in their own right or denounced (prisons, etc.) for their impact on the human personality *in its entirety,* not just in terms of economic exploitation. Marxist writers often seem to have to link everything to political economy for their analysis to be validated; having made the linkage, which is predictably present at some point or points, the analysis is then considered complete.[2]

Within anarchism, however, there is a recognition, as David Wieck (1979) has put it, "that any theory that finds the secret of human liberation in something as specific as the politics of property neglects the interdependence of the many liberations" (p. 143). Defining the source of the problems we face and the nature of the power that maintains them is central to deciding how to address them. The angles of vision of socialist anarchism, historically Marxism's chief antagonist on the Left, offer a significantly wider view than does conventional Marxism.

GRAMSCI'S NOTION OF HEGEMONY

In recent decades, however, the writings of Antonio Gramsci from the 1920s and 1930s (Gramsci, 1971; see also Femia, 1981; Forgacs, 1988; Hall, 1986; Lears, 1985) have been a very influential source of thinking about power, capitalism, and culture within European, Latin American, and even some U.S. circles. Paradoxically, despite his Marxist credentials, Gramsci could be faulted for having had less to say on economic issues than they deserve, but his analyses of culture and power are remarkable for their sensitivity and precision. Elsewhere, I have offered a more detailed evaluation of his relevance to general media analysis and have suggested that a more diffuse notion of *hegemony* is probably more productive than tying ourselves to all the specifics of his *egemonia* concept (Downing, 1996, pp. 199-204). Here, it will suffice to establish some of the basics.

Gramsci's strategy for resisting and eventually overcoming the power of the capitalist class[3] in its most advanced nations, and thereby for deeply democratizing those nations, rested on his conviction of the need to challenge and displace the cultural dominance and leadership (= hegemony) of their ruling classes with a coherent and convincing alternative vision of how society might organize itself. He argued that over the two centuries of its expansion and consolidation, capitalism maintained and organized its leadership through agencies of information and culture such as schools and universities, the churches, literature, philosophy, media, and corporate ideologies. The perspectives on the wider society generated within these institutions often produced, he proposed, an unquestioning view of the world that took the status quo as inevitable and ruling class power as founded on that class's unique, self-evident ability to run the nation successfully (whatever the critiques of the class's individual members).

Thus, although the system was also powered by its economic mechanisms and shored up during political crises by the use of police, courts, jails, and ultimately the military (= the state in the classical Marxist sense), mass hegemonic institutions such as those listed were, so to speak, its first line of defense, its outer ramparts. At the same time, their cultural influence emerged over protracted periods of time, not—outside of a fascist scenario—through some centrally orchestrated plan.

A hegemonic socialist countervision of a nation's future, Gramsci argued, would be constructed over time through mass involvement—quite unlike the subordination of wage workers and small farmers characteristic in capitalist hegemony. A socialist hegemony would embrace this majority of the public, whose demands and priorities would constantly develop it further. This majority political movement would largely be led—but should never, in his vision, be manipulated or crunched underfoot—by a communist party.[4]

At all events, whatever our take on some of the specifics of Gramsci's analysis, it is reasonable to acknowledge that some forms of organized leadership are essential to coordinate challenges to the ideological hegemony of capital and to put forward credible alternative programs and perspectives. In this regard, his notion of the "organic intellectual" might almost be re-rendered as the "communicator/activist," inasmuch as for Gramsci the term *intellectual* never implied people sitting by themselves and thinking great thoughts that only they and a small circle might share. Gramsci looked forward to the role of intellectuals/activist communicators organically integrated with the laboring classes in developing a just and culturally enhanced social order, in contradistinction to those intellectuals organically integrated with the ruling classes, whose communicative labors strengthened the hegemony of capital.

Subsequently—although Gramsci himself never used the terms—notions of *counterhegemony* and *counterhegemonic* have become fairly common among writers influenced by his thinking, as a way to categorize attempts to challenge dominant ideological frameworks and to supplant them with a radical alternative vision. Many radical alternative media clearly belong within this frame. A proliferation of such media would be vital, both to help generate those alternatives in public debate and also to limit any tendency for oppositional leadership, whatever forms it took, to entrench itself as an agency of domination rather than freedom.

At the same time, Gramsci's perspective offers a fresh way of understanding such media. In a framework within which classes and the capitalist state are analyzed simply as controlling and censoring information, the role of radical media can be seen as trying to disrupt the silence, to counter the lies, to provide the truth. This is the counterinformation model (cf. Baldelli, 1977; Herman, 1992; Jensen, 1997), which has a strong element of validity, most especially under highly reactionary and repressive regimes. Mattelart's (1974, pp. 75-123, 233-267) pioneering study of radical media in the Popular Unity period in Chile from 1970 through 1973 is a classical instance. His conceptual handling of the issues was fairly rudimentary, framed mostly in terms of alternative media as devices for giving voice to the Left's political parties, given that major media were unavailable and hostile, agents of what he brilliantly characterized as a Leninist mass agitation campaign from the extreme Right (pp. 187-229).[5]

However, Gramsci's position directs our attention equally to less tense, perhaps more everyday scenarios, in which one way of describing capitalist hegemony would be in terms of *self*-censorship[6] by mainstream media professionals or other organic intellectuals in positions of authority, their unquestioning acceptance of standard professional media codes. Radical media in those scenarios have a mission not only to provide facts to a public denied them but to explore fresh ways of developing a questioning perspective on the hegemonic process and increasing the public's sense of confidence in its power to engineer constructive change.

Gramsci, however, was always at great pains to emphasize that (a) hegemony is never frozen stiff but is always under negotiation between superior and subordinate social classes, that (b) capitalist cultural hegemony is unstable and may experience serious intermittent crises, yet at the same time (c) that it may enjoy a rarely questioned normalcy over long periods.

Gramsci's approach has been attacked from a variety of quarters (e.g., Anderson, 1977; Bennett, 1992). The critique by anthropologist James C. Scott (1985, pp. 314-326; 1990) is the most interesting one for our purposes, because it raises very directly the nature of counterhegemonic resistance cultures. The issue is central in that their respective positions could be described as one in which the public mostly acknowledges the rectitude of its condition and the ability of the ruling classes to lead (Gramsci), as opposed to one in which the public is seething with systematically masked discontent (Scott). As a result, radical media could easily be read two very different ways: as necessary to build counterhegemony but only truly powerful at times of political upsurge, or as within a heartbeat of expressing deeply entrenched and disruptive mass discontent (although Scott's analysis does not address media as such, only symbolic communication).

SCOTT'S EXAMINATION OF RESISTANCE

Scott (1990) dwells at length on "hidden transcripts" and "infra-politics" (pp. 15-19, 67, 87, 111, 120, 132, 183f., 191, 200). By these, he means similar things, namely, that each social class or antagonistic group has a public statement of what it considers itself to be doing and a private one that only circulates within the group. Infra-politics, Scott (1990) argues, expresses the real, private levels of resistance and anger, typically not simply about the economic exploitation people face but also about "the pattern of personal humiliations that characterize" it, "arbitrary beatings, sexual violations, and other insults" (pp. 111-112, 21). The infra-politics of the poor hatches a variety of acts of resistance, some very subtle to the untutored gaze, some intentionally ambiguous so that even given the elite's watchful and tutored eyes, there would be insufficient grounds for reprisals. Or, in the case of the powerful elites, infra-politics meant their hidden transcript of contempt and anger at poor farmers.

In Scott's view, many, including Gramsci, are too willing to overlook "the massive middle ground, in which conformity is often a self-conscious strategy and resistance is a carefully balanced affair that avoids all-or-nothing confrontations" (Scott, 1985, p. 285), and manages thereby "to miss the immense political terrain that lies between quiescence and revolt... [and instead] to focus on the visible coastline [rather than] the continent that lies beyond" (Scott, 1990, p. 199). That middle ground is occupied by a "constant testing of the limits . . . hardly has the dust cleared before the probing to regain lost territory is likely to begin" (Scott, 1990, p. 197). Within "the continent that lies beyond" Scott locates insincere flattery, feigned stupidity, hostile gossip, malicious rumor, magical spells, anonymous threats, songs, folktales, gestures, jokes, grumbling, arson, sabotage, lateness, and failure to return to work after the midday break. He includes, too, what he terms "imposed mutuality," namely, the sanctions imposed by the group on individuals who are ready to break ranks and kowtow to the elite (Scott, 1985, pp. 241, 258-60; 1990, pp. xiii, 140).[7]

Scott's instances strongly echo the panorama of oppositional culture traced out in Part II. We have argued there is powerful reason to take into account all the levels of cultural action of which he speaks and to see them all as radical alternative communication, sometimes in media form, sometimes expressed purely through conversational networks.

Together, Gramsci and Scott have a great deal to bring to our discussion, not least their common acknowledgment of the bedrock realities of economic exploitation, political power, and social class *relations.* In some ways the difference between the two is one of focus. Gramsci was concerned with class politics in leading capitalist nations during the first third of the 20th century and often wrote more from the historian's viewpoint on long-term seismic shifts in politics and culture, such as the Renaissance, the Reformation, the Italian Risorgimento. Scott, by contrast, is concerned with a thick ethnographic description of the immediacies of micropolitical conflict, as expressed through many symbols and forms of communication, within a Third World agrarian setting in transition.

Scott does spend more time on detailing everyday resistance within this framework than does Gramsci. Yet, to understand counterhegemony in general, or radical alternative media in particular, it is essential not only to understand the dominant local class, as Scott takes considerable pains to do, but also the wider history and trajectory of the dominant classes nationally. Only armed with such understanding is it possible to comprehend why radical media are born and have sway outside an immediate locality or to evaluate their performance. Their context is not merely society, abstractly, but particular conjunctures of elite policy, as well as struggles for power—cultural, economic, and political.

MULTIPLE SOURCES OF OPPRESSION

To bring the story full circle, and also as a segue into the discussion of social movements, let us pick up again the socialist anarchist theme of the multiple sources of oppression in society. Sheila Rowbotham (1981), writing from a libertarian Marxist feminist perspective, echoes this in a way that also directly poses the urgency of lateral communication, of media of resistance:

> For if every form of oppression has its own defensive suspicions, all the movements in resistance to humiliation and inequality also discover their own wisdoms. We require a socialist movement in which

> there is freedom for these differences and nurture for these visions. This means that in the making of socialism people can develop positively their own strengths and find ways of communicating to one another what we have gained. (pp. 46-47)

The communication she means is not first and foremost a matter of having a printing press or a radio transmitter or Internet access, but it must surely include that. Sharing perceptively the gamut of issues plaguing social life, as experienced from numerous vantage points, and sharing their possible solutions, and sharing in hilarity at their daily idiocies, too, fit the potential of media far more than any other counterhegemonic institutions, such as a party, a union, or a council.[8] Resistance, in other words, is resistance to multiple sources of oppression, but in turn, it requires dialogue across the varying sectors—by gender; by race, ethnicity, and nationality; by age; by occupational grouping—to take effective shape. Radical alternative media are central to that process.

Summary: Radical media activists have very often experienced state repression—execution, jailing, torture, fascist assaults, the bombing of radical radio stations, threats, police surveillance, and intimidation tactics.[9] It is hopelessly naive to see their operation as simply part of a war of ideas conducted by Queensberry rules. The story of radical media, as Gramsci himself knew only too painfully in his own life, is all too often one of survival and tension in the face of vehemently, sometimes murderously hostile authority. Placing radical alternative media within this larger context of state power, hegemony, and insubordination is a necessary step toward understanding them. We need to be alert to multiple forms of power and subordination, often interlocking; to the centrality of culture as the ground on which struggles for freedom and justice are fought out; and to the powerful operation of microsubversive strategies. However, these strategies do not explode into life outside of a culture of resistance, social movements, and their networks of exchange and debate. Earlier, I noted how important social movements are for understanding radical media, and so it is to them that we now turn.

NOTES

1. The treasured and long-running stereotype of the anarchist as lunatic bomb-thrower is a convenient way to excuse oneself from thinking about the often searching questions raised in anarchist writing, most of which has

shunned terrorist methods. We should begin with the recognition that anarchism is not purely a philosophy. In many countries, the labor movement has been deeply influenced by it, with Spain being the pre-eminent example, but others include Italy, Portugal, Mexico, and other Latin American countries. Until 1917, the British labor movement had a considerable anarchist element. Anarchist thinking has been correspondingly diverse and multifaceted, divided not only into its syndicalist wing and its purer wing, rejecting all centralized national organization, but also into many different small groups. There is no single anarchist view on many questions—indeed anarchists have been as capable of vicious sectarian infighting as any other political tendency.

2. There is an argument, although it cannot be developed here, that it was the mistaken enthronement of Marx's (1977) *Capital* as his crowning achievement and therefore as the bible of the Marxist movement, that in turn diverted attention from his own much broader methodology, which had rather little in common with what subsequently often passed for Marxism. (See Colletti, 1972; Negri, 1991.)

3. Much of the confusion that has historically emerged over Marxist analysis of social classes has arisen from the projection—by many Marxists and many non-Marxists—of a unified political consciousness on to subordinate classes, especially wage workers. Thus, the focus has shifted tacitly but very substantively away from the leadership and direction of society supplied by capitalist classes to wage workers' class awareness and resistance. Always the most helpful way to understand how the Marxist analytical tradition (at its best) conceives of classes is to begin by focusing on the corporate sector and its policies, largely formed within national and international market competition, and on state regulations in relation to the workforce, national and global. Corporate policies are not necessarily consistent or coherent, not necessarily well-advised, not necessarily farseeing, but they exist and have repercussions and ramifications that sooner or later stretch into every corner of life. By the close of the 20th century, this corporate sector, at its most influential, consisted of huge transnational corporations, the majority ultimately based in the United States, but no more necessarily compliant with U.S. government policy at any one time than were their purely domestic corporate forebears. The responses the policies generate in the various realms of societal life in turn may spark fresh policies (be they short- or long-term, nice or nasty). Over time, the push and pull that ensues has proved to be a tremendous motor force within nations and today, increasingly, internationally.

This relational and historical concept of class is utterly distinct from the stunted one common in public discourse in the United States, where *middle class* means the vast bulk of the population. It is also sharply different from the American social science use of *class* to mean socioeconomic status (SES), which is a simple conceptual grid imposed on a nation or community at a particular point in its history to distinguish between the wealthy, the not-so-wealthy and the poor as consumers and status holders, with relative power almost absent from the picture. Finally, it has nothing to do with the lampoon version of Marxist thinking, in which there are just two social classes that will slug it out until the bigger one (the proletariat) wins and then everyone will be happy forever after. The concept of class I am deploying, I argue, is no mantra, but a way of cutting through conceptually to the bone of issues, in the cultural and media sphere as elsewhere. Its function is not to end debate but to focus it and to prompt penetrating further questions.

4. In view of the political record of many communist parties in the 20th century, although not all, this element of his vision is liable to raise acute and justified anxiety. It is important, therefore, to remember that his own year's stay in the Soviet Union was during its very early period, in a much more open atmosphere immediately following the 1918-1920 civil war and before Stalin was officially in charge or even widely known. Furthermore, Gramsci was jailed from 1926 until a few days before his death in 1937, barred from receiving information or even many visits. Thus, while his vision of the future role of a communist party may have been flawed, it was not a vision based on the historical experience that would so tragically and terrifyingly disfigure the socialist movements of the 20th century. Adamson (1987) interestingly suggests that Gramsci expressed a quasi-religious perception of the future role of Marxism in a revolutionary society, seeing it as a kind of secular faith that would serve to integrate society's goals and general culture within a socially just and democratic order. Thus, even if Gramsci might be attacked for pollyanna-ism, Stalinism was not his stock in trade. Of course, this vagueness about the future can also be attacked for paving the way, through its optimism, for ruthless opportunists to seize and wield power in the name of justice and counterhegemony.

5. Arguably, Mattelart failed sufficiently to problematize the parties of the Left, which maintained a fierce sectarian hostility toward each other even a full decade after the Popular Unity experiment had been drowned in blood under the Pinochet coup. It is also plausible that even had the parties been less obsessed with competing with each other, their instinctively authoritarian culture would have narrowed the impact of the media under their control. At the same time, the dynamism of the Right's media campaigns in that period, with energetic assistance from the CIA, does not make this a simple question to resolve. See Simpson Grinberg (1986b) and Huesca and Dervin (1994) for arguments that this dualistic phase of thinking about radical media in Latin America needed to be, and was, supplanted by more complex models.

6. Self-censorship can, of course, take different forms, one conscious, in which there is a specific decision to avoid a danger area, and the other entrenched to the point of being instinctual and unconscious. The latter is a stronger instance of hegemony in the Gramscian sense.

7. Scott's account of Gramsci tends to conflate him, without actually stating so, with Max Weber, whose concept of legitimation proposes a dualistic model in which regimes are or are not legitimated, whether in traditional terms, bureaucratically, or charismatically. There is none of the middle ground for analysis suggested by Gramsci's acknowledgment that hegemony is negotiated over time and is subject to crises and instability. Furthermore, Scott (1985, p. 314) cites the famous aphorism from Marx and Engels's (1972) *The German Ideology*—that the ruling ideas are the ideas of the ruling class—as

though this little rhetorical nugget perfectly encapsulated Gramsci's political analysis. Any reasonable reading of Gramsci, I submit, will not support this. Scott even (p. 340) refers to the notion of a hegemonic ideology as equivalent to a political theory of general anesthesia. In this, I think, he has completely misread Gramsci, perhaps confusing his work with versions of Gramsci passed through the work of Louis Althusser (1971), who defined ideology as a unitary cultural perspective solidly supportive of the capitalist order.

8. Mainstream media are conspicuously unsuccessful here, the "bare-all" TV talk-shows of the 1990s and the agony columns being pitiful caricatures of this potential.

9. See Parts II and III of this book for numerous instances. See, too, Aronson (1972, pp. 39-61), Armstrong (1981, pp. 137-159), Rips (1981), and a number of the case studies in the first version of this book (Downing, 1984), which are not included in this one.

3

Social Movements, the Public Sphere, Networks

The argument in this segment will be as follows:

- Social movements represent one of the most dynamic expressions of resistance, as contrasted with more stable and enduring institutions such as unions or parties.[1]
- Their importance for understanding radical media and oppositional cultures is enormous.
- Movement upsurges appear both to generate and to be stimulated by radical media.[2] Conversely, at times when such movements are at a low ebb, the flood of alternative media also subsides.
- However, this is not the end of the matter. Properly understood, the relation between movements and radical media is not one of base and superstructure but one of dialectical and indeed acute interdependence.
- The second related question is triangular: the connections between social movements, media (both radical and mainstream), and the so-called public sphere.

- The third question is the relation between radical media and non-media communication networks.

SOCIAL MOVEMENTS AND RADICAL MEDIA

We need to begin by clarifying what is meant by a social movement. Obvious as the term may sound, it has been variously deployed in the aftermath of the many social and political upheavals across the globe since the 19th century.

Arato and Cohen (1992, Chapter 10) offer a threefold classification of the senses in which it has been used. The earliest model was that of the rioting mob, the crowd in tumult, acting blindly and insensately, driven only by emotions wildly out of control—in other words the *perception* of mass public activism typical among those horrified alike by the French Revolution and by labor and socialist upsurges.[3] In flat opposition to this model is the second model, that of social movements as rational actors. In this view, members of the general public, because they lack property and are often impoverished, have to generate alternative resources to wield influence over the political and allocation process. These alternative resources consist of such collective actions as strikes, sit-ins, occupations, demonstrations, go-slows, and traffic blocking. So far from being irrational eruptions by crazed mobs, these actions consist of carefully considered tactics on the part of those without wealth or state power.

A third model comes from academic research on so-called New Social Movements (NSMs), namely, ecological, feminist, or peace-oriented social movements. Some scholars argue that these movements represent a qualitatively new stage in contemporary political culture, sharply marked off from the characteristics of earlier social movements, especially the labor movement. Whereas the labor movement, for example, sought to achieve specific economic gains from the capitalist class and to pressure governments into legislation and policy initiatives that its leaders felt would benefit the rank and file, NSMs had no such calculated material outcome. Rather, said these researchers, NSMs sought goals in large measure independent of what the state might concede, goals that bore a much closer relationship to a sense of personal growth and identity in interaction with the subculture of the movement. An emblematic instance of what NSM theorists had in mind would be the "consciousness-raising" dimension of U.S. and Western European feminist movements in the 1960s and early 1970s, in which small groups of women would meet together to talk through their life experiences, with the aim of exploring and thus shaking off in their own psyches the patriarchal restraints to which they had been subjected from birth—but without necessarily setting up any subsequent organized project based on this exploration. Collective identity was all.

Much of the problem with the NSM literature lies in its most eager advocates' almost messianic conviction that they have stumbled on a major new dimension of contemporary culture. Social movements that did not fit their schema, such as the labor movement, were effectively consigned to the trash can of a prior epoch, now waned. The literature was also very Western in focus: Movements in other parts of the world, such as the anti-apartheid movement in South Africa and its support network across the globe, or Afro-Brazilian political movements, or the Palestinian *intifada,* or even the nationalist movement in Québec were not on the map at all. Nor, seemingly, was the U.S. Civil Rights Movement.

Furthermore, the NSM current had a tendency to be blind to any aspects of "its" movements that did not fit its conceptual mold. Thus, those aspects of feminist movements that sought better day care facilities, or improved widows' pensions, or new legal protections for rape victims—in other words, concrete outcomes from governmental sources—simply seemed to be off the NSM analytical map. These are not the only instances of a certain programmed blindness to movement facets that evaded the model's parameters. For instance, the antinuclear movement pressed governments to close down nuclear power stations, to dismantle missiles, and to not build any more stations (or weapons). Parts of the ecological movement focused on environmental racism, attacking the established tendency for firms, with the support of local governments, to build toxic waste dumps close to minority ethnic communities. This was hardly pure identity politics.

Elsewhere, I have discussed these three approaches at greater length (Downing, 1996, pp. 18-22, 26-27, 96-102, 111-112). Here, let us simply note that each contributes something to our understanding of social movements and resistance, even the mob approach on a purely descriptive level. Political movements are a vital component of politics in many contemporary nations, not least in those where formal political processes have become colonized by the presumed demands of mainstream television on the one hand and by the colossal costs of campaigning on the other. In this situation, mainstream political parties are less and less responsive to the deepest public needs. The dynamism in the political process is, therefore, often derived from political movements operating outside the party structures, although admittedly often in some relationship with one or more political parties. Parties legislate, but they do not generally initiate or lead major movements of social opinion. This means that the political life energy and the burning issues of a nation are more often to be found in and around social movements than in the official institutions of democracy.

These movement flashpoints may be of a retrograde variety, like the anti-immigrant poison that seeps[4] out of Western nations—although not only them. Or they may be constructive, such as antinuclear or feminist movements. The fact remains, they are where the action is, and therefore, public debate, dialogue, and conversation take place around their agendas. The essential point is that in the life of social movements, there are dizzy highs and lows, dramatic moments, conflicts and splits, and generally an intense interaction with forces and subcultures on their boundaries as well as in opposition to them. Communication and media, both within their ranks and without, play a huge role in movement trajectories. Oddly, however, much of the social movement literature fails to engage in any disciplined way with the question of communication and media. For the mob approach, communication takes place by some barbaric chemistry; for the rational actor approach, by dint of demonstrations and other organized expressions of discontent; and for the NSM approach, by sustained mulling over questions of identity inside the movement itself.

It is on the edge of being weird that there is so little systematic analysis of communication or media in the social movement literature. There is now a growing communication literature on the relations between mainstream media and movements[5] and on alternative media of the movements.[6] It frankly beggars the imagination to explain how so many social movement specialists could think it feasible to analyze the dynamics of social movements without systematic attention to their media and communication.

There are, of course, counterarguments that such media have been in sharp decline, and in this case, their relative neglect would not count for much. Jakubowicz (1993) proposes that alternative media were very much a phenomenon of the turbulent 1960s and 1970s and that their proliferation should not be thought of as a permanent feature of modern media environments. Neveu (1999) writes of "the crisis of militant media" (p. 47).

The problem with this critique is to find an empirical yardstick for the claim that radical media are withering away. Almost by their nature, they often go unmeasured, uncounted, and poorly known in official circles or outside their localities. Generally—as is the argument of this book—their power is misperceived because they are not stereotypical mainstream media. Historically, however, as Part II will illustrate, such media have been a constant. Some, as the Soviet era and Portuguese examples in this book will testify, have been extraordinarily potent and wide-ranging in their impact. Obituaries for radical media, I would venture to suggest, are premature.[7]

HABERMAS AND THE PUBLIC SPHERE

At the close of their review of the three interpretations of social movements, Arato and Cohen (1992) propose that in the contemporary period, social movements constitute what they call the public sphere.[8] Here, they lock social movements together with the concept of *Öffentlichkeit* originally defined by Habermas (1962/1989) to embrace the alternative zone of freer speech and critique of monarchical government that he identified as emerging in the 18th century, especially among the intellectual elite in London's coffee- and teahouses. Regrettably, they only assert this effective fusion conceptually, without articulating further the numerous ways in which it would presumably be expressed. Nor is the problem of media on their radar. However, let us explore the concept Öffentlichkeit, and then return to their basic insight.

A whole literature has grown up around the term *public sphere*, the expression usually used to translate Habermas's term Öffentlichkeit, a word for which there is no single English equivalent that carries its range of senses.[9] Perhaps the easiest way to garner the sense in which Habermas uses the term is to consider the related but opposite sociopolitical reality, namely, the royal court. As the European monarchies gradually lost their absolute powers, a factor directly involved was the extension of the sphere of political influence and debate outside the narrow confines of the courts. Courts slowly lost their power to these wider circles. Communication and information, including broadsheets, flyers, and early types of newspapers, all of which circulated in the settings noted above, were crucial elements within this gradually widening zone of influence and debate. The virtual monopoly of the court over official politics was slowly eaten away. Thus, the openness and publicity represented by the word Öffentlichkeit were a break with the seclusion and secrecy of the royal courts. (In the contemporary era, Habermas claimed, corporate and government hegemony had ironed this public sphere out of existence.)

Admittedly, the developments Habermas pointed to were gradual and patchy and were under constraints he took for granted in his original essay. For instance, in the English setting, class and gender held sway: women were effectively excluded, along with provincial elites and indeed the great majority of the male population. In prerevolutionary France, by contrast, a few women who ran some of the famous Paris salons, which also extended political debate and influence beyond the court, were at the very heart of this expansion. Paradoxically, as Landes (1988) has shown, after a very brief experiment with further steps in women's emancipation during the French Revolution, women were then excluded from the public sphere and for some decades had less scope than previously to wield public influence.

Habermas also tended to define debate and rational exchange as activities characteristic of the public sphere. Iris Marion Young (1990, Chapter 4) has argued that this is a very masculine perception of the deliberative process. Not only is the exclusion of women passed over in silence, but the presumption is that successful discussion and review of a matter only operates, and can only operate, in a completely antiseptic rationalistic mode.[10] Yet, a number of the radical alternative media reviewed in Part II from precisely those periods in England and France show very clearly, through their use of irony, satire, caricature, cartoon, slander, innuendo, salacious public gossip, and pornography, that sober, clearly argued debate was no more victorious then, or the dominant mode of discourse, than we see it to be today. If we think of the radical Methodist chapels or the bars of 18th-century London, the radical underworld that McCalman (1988) has so vividly described, or the vigorous and sometimes scurrilous satire depicted by Donald (1996) and Wood (1994), then it is hard to envisage in those settings the orderly reasoned discourse that supposedly would have tapped its desiccated way along its appointed paths.

In a direct response to Habermas, two Marxist critics, Oskar Negt and Alexander Kluge (1972/1993), argued that in the contemporary era the notion of a *proletarian* public sphere should head the agenda. Rather than engage in Habermas's lament for the disappearance of a bourgeois public sphere, the settings in which the proletariat could debate its past, present, and future were, they urged, the really interesting question. There was a strongly doctrinaire and abstractly utopian character to large parts of their argument, but it suggested an important qualification in principle, namely, the identification of alternative zones for radical debate and reflection within present-day society.

One attempt to tie the term down to some form of relevance for radical media analysis was my own study of the antinuclear movement media in what was then West Germany (Downing, 1988a). I proposed that an alternative public sphere was empirically visible in the movement organizations and the flood of antinuclear books, pamphlets, magazines, and flyers that circulated at that time. (West Germany, Britain, the Netherlands and Italy, were then the epicenters of European antinuclear activism.) I similarly suggested (Downing, 1989) that certain forms of political activism in the United States, centering on then quite novel alternative computer uses, could be termed examples of an alternative public sphere.

Implicit was not only the notion of two types of public sphere, alternative and official, but also the variety of such spheres in and around social movements. This latter theme is precisely the subject of an outstanding essay by Fraser (1993), who writes in favor of the notion of "counter public spheres," strongly alluding to a Gramscian problematic but also recognizing the pluralism existing on the Left. She also directly involves feminist perspectives and movements in her analysis, although unlike Rowbotham, she does not address what this pluralism may bring with it or how far pluralism and fissiparity are distinct terms. Broude and Garrard (1994) provide an excellent discussion and reproductions of the dynamic impact of feminist movements on art in the United States during the 1970s, which wonderfully illustrates Fraser's argument.

So if the spatial metaphor does not require an actual agora, if the spatial dimension is overly accentuated by the terms *sphere* and *realm*, if it is the activity within locations or inside groups or particular forums that is the matter in hand, then surely the essence of what is being pinpointed in the terminology of Öffentlichkeit/public sphere is information, communication, debate, media—public conversation[11] on issues of moment. The effective fusion between public sphere and social movements proposed by Arato and Cohen (1992) injects into the somewhat static, locational sense of public sphere precisely the kinetic, contested dimension this translation of Öffentlichkeit lacks. Arato and Cohen, however, make no distinction between public sphere and alternative public sphere; for them, the public sphere is necessarily a democratic forum.

However, although we may prefer Arato and Cohen's optimism that there is a public sphere in the contemporary world to Habermas's pessimism that it is dead and gone, we must not lose sight for a moment of the fact that this public conversation within social movements is still shaped within the powerful impulses of capitalist economies, racialized social orders, and patriarchal cultures. Power, hegemony, and resistance are everywhere etched into and suffused within the institutions and practices of public dialogue and social movements, just as popular culture may be elitist, sexist, racist, and the rest.

As we pull together the threads of social movements, public sphere, and radical media, Raboy's (1984) hard-headed study of alternative and mainstream media and the nationalist movement in Québec in the 1960s and 1970s helpfully illustrates this discussion. A prevailing tendency with which I am doing constant battle in this book is to ask whether radical media have any impact at all. This leaves their status perpetually teetering on the edge of conceptual emptiness. Raboy, without ever romanticizing them, takes the opposite tack, to the point of underscoring the damaging impact that movement activists' failures to think through the problem of media and to organize effective alternative media may have on the trajectory of social movements. His study interestingly blends official and alternative public spheres by examining the relationship within the context of an ongoing social struggle between mainstream media professionals and alternative media activists. This is an issue somewhat blurred in the discussion of public sphere above, but one of considerable importance, flagged in the Preface, to which we shall need to return. Raboy also pays careful heed to the destructive impact of leftist sectarianism on movement media.

Based on his and other studies, we may provisionally conclude that radical alternative media are of considerable, if varying significance because it is they that typically first articulate and diffuse the issues, the analyses, and the challenges of the movements. They typically owe their primary allegiance to and experience their principal fascination with the movements. And although particular alternative media may get tossed aside in the impetuous, unforeseeable trajectory of a given social movement, others often rise rapidly to prominence and take their place.

Nonetheless, one reservation needs repeating. We should not let the social movement dimension, important as it is, overly frame our definition of radical alternative media. We should beware of squashing all such media into this rather effervescent model. Many continue over decades, quietly and patiently keeping issues alive and, especially, developing fresh themes in and new types of public conversation. Both phases or dimensions of such media require maintaining in focus. There can also be a process of generational resurgence, where the memory of what once was thinkable and doable is revived in new, more propitious circumstances.[12]

Thus, as already argued in the Chapter 1 discussion of audiences, a model of media influence that maintains a constant tight close-up on immediate consequences will fail to register accurately the significant long-term resonance of radical alternative media, especially if yoked only to the consideration of the moment-by-moment of social movements at their height of activity. The fact that our conscious memory does not recall everything specifically that we read or heard or saw in media does not mean that certain messages and frames have lost their sway over our imagination and sense of priorities.[13] This sense of the longer term is crucial for understanding all media. By "the longer term," I do not mean anything quite as extended as the *longue durée* of the *Annales* school, but I certainly have in mind something in the order of a three-generational scenario.

Let us add one more element to this discussion of social movements, namely, the contribution that can be made from a socialist anarchist angle of vision. Historically, the anarchist movement has always given priority to movements over institutions. Constructive social change must, in this philosophy, be built on the basis of mass activity, of self-mobilization. Effective communication within and by social movements is, therefore, a vital necessity for self-mobilization to emerge and prosper. Radical media are in no way to be dismissed as just a curious little experiment for revolutionary culture freaks.

Their linchpin role becomes all the more obvious as we face up to the tough reality of the divisions Rowbotham (1981) flags between movements and activists with different experiences and targets. Whether it is the all-too-common neglect of women's issues in labor and ethnic struggles or of racism in women's movement debates or competitive hostility between minority ethnic groups, the divisions are patent, sometimes blatant. Lateral communication between these groups, Rowbotham is totally accurate in claiming, is a first, essential, even if very difficult step, if we are not to be forever pitted one against the other. As she argues in the passage cited in the Chapter 2 discussion of resistance, our shared understanding of the dynamics of exploitation and extrusion has to grow enormously to form any movement worth committing ourselves to, let alone powerful enough to shake the power structure's hegemony.

An example of what movement building with radical media to aid us could actually look like might be taken from the women's movement's development of sensitivity to the daily immediacies and nuances of extrusion and control. This feminist awareness was a gain not only for the women's movement itself, but for everyone, and had it been more widely diffused, it would likely have matured many political projects. To cite Rowbotham (1981) once more,

> When women on the Left began to criticize this language (i.e., Fraternity, Chairman, Brothers) we were told we were just being petty. But the ideas and politics of women's liberation emerged out of precisely these small everyday moments of dismissive encounter. (p. 27)

Radical alternative media can enable people within social movements to communicate these and other insights to one another. Not with automatic success, of course. But the potential of media to communicate laterally is contained within their technology, whereas the hierarchical structure of parties and unions has been predefined for so long that they could often only operate laterally in the ideal not the real world.

Husband (1996) presents a stimulating confirmation of Rowbotham's point in relation to the public sphere notion and the question of ethnic justice. He begins from twin initial premises: (a) that a third generation of human rights entitlements is in order, beyond the first (civil and political) and second (economic, social, and cultural); and (b) that the proposal in the 1980 UNESCO MacBride Report on global communication policies about the right to communicate is one of this third generation of entitlements. Husband (1996) sees the MacBride assertion as in dire need of a complement, namely, "the right to be understood." This

> places upon us all a duty to seek comprehension of the other. It is a rejection of, and condemnation of, egocentric and ethnocentric routines of engaging with the communicative acts of others, both in-group and out-group. . . . Without the inclusion of the subordinate claim of the right to be understood the right to communicate becomes too easily a unidirectional and egocentric democracy of Babel. (pp. 209, 210)

In turn, this means very consciously defining the public sphere as multiethnic, not mono-ethnic, this latter a lapse, Hanchard (1995) argues, that has all too often disfigured academic debate around the term. The need for radical alternative media in a multi-ethnic public sphere is self-evident, and their potential roles legion.

THE ROLE OF COMMUNICATION NETWORKS

The final point to be considered in this discussion of social movements and the public sphere is the question of communication networks, that is, those webs of interpersonal communication that do not operate through media, even though they are fed by media and feed into media. Sadly, the typical rupture in communication research between media and interpersonal communication is particularly damaging to an attempt to understand the linkages between radical alternative media and social networks. Yet, these networks are essential both to such media and to social and political movements. We are dealing in this regard with a very different notion of media audience than the typical one, for it is those elements of the audience who are active members of social networks that, in times of social tumult and political crisis, are often the best-placed heralds of the new and the best-informed advisers on movement strategies to those networks. It is in those skeins that we find the key communicative linkages between radical alternative media and social movements.

Once again, however, we are confronted by overlapping terminologies. For one writer, the term will be social movements, for another the public sphere, for a third, communication networks, and for a fourth, audiences. The utility of the notion of networks is that it gets away from the notion of audiences as atomized, composed simply of individuals or households. It also underscores the internal connectivity characteristic of social movements and the centrality of that process in the mesh between media and movements. The public sphere ceases to be simply an idealized agora and becomes something tangible between members of interlocking circles, whose mutual communication engages them at many levels, not just that of rational, ordered debate. (The notion of community, to be addressed in the next chapter, partly addresses this dimension as well.)

In the Iranian revolution (Mohammadi & Sreberny-Mohammadi, 1994, pp. 35-37), we see a particularly clear instance of the operation of already existing networks in relation to media. It was through religious networks that audiocassettes with banned materials were circulated, and the values and traditions of these networks gave cohesion, sanction, and energy to the vast movement in opposition to the Shah. To appreciate radical media in that context, it is essential to perceive their interaction with these networks. The authors correctly identify a parallel with Catholic parish networks and resistance to the regime in Poland during the decades of Soviet control. Álvarez (1990, pp. 59-75) equally pinpoints the networks of Christian base communities as nodes of social movements against the dictatorship in Brazil during the 1970s.

However, although religious beliefs certainly offer a very important focus, it would be a mistake to see the relevance of communication networks to radical media operation in social movements as uniquely a religious phenomenon. Such networks are a prime dimension of all social movements and a vital audience dimension for radical media.

Summary: The relationship with movements in full flood does not exhaust the roles of radical media. To acknowledgment of their major role in that regard, to the public conversations they spark within the communication networks with which they interact, we need to add recognition of radical media's impact in periods of political quiescence and equally of how they may light a mnemonic flame that sometimes burns over decades and generations. Furthermore, the character of social movements needs accurate definition; not least, that like popular culture, they may be reactionary as well as constructive.

Öffentlichkeit—once redefined in terms of alternative or counter (Fraser) public spheres, of forums providing movements with opportunity to talk through their internal divisions and so to enrich and strengthen themselves (Rowbotham, Husband)—is a concept that directs our attention to the role of radical media in stimulating debate. Indeed, the term *conversation* has kept turning up in the review of Öffentlichkeit. In the discussion of community, democracy, and radical media that follows, we shall revisit it more closely, adding a discussion of the closely related concept of dialogue.

NOTES

1. The relation in practice between these is important and complex but would draw us too far away from our theme here.

2. Examples we will touch on in Part II and the case studies in Part III include the Reformation; the American, French, and Haitian revolutions and their reverberations in other countries; the rise of socialist movements toward the close of the 19th century; the turbulent 1960s; the growth of feminist movements during the 1970s; the 1980s antinuclear movements; and the vortex within the Soviet bloc in the late 1980s.

3. One of the earliest was Edmund Burke, whose denunciation of the French Revolution included his notorious dismissal of the public as "the swinish multitude." Radical media activist Thomas Spence named his newspaper *Pig's Meat* by way of riposte (Wood, 1994, p. 88).

4. *Pours* might be a better word.

5. Compare Halloran, Elliott, and Murdock, 1970; Gitlin, 1980; Hackett, 1991, 1993; Dale, 1996; Sampedro Blanco, 1997; Neveu, 1999. Ryan (1991) provides a very good study for movement activists on how to engage mainstream media.

6. Mattelart (1974, 1986), Raboy (1984), Goodwyn (1991), Laba (1991), and Kubik (1994) address in some measure the role of the *Solidarnosc* movement's communication processes and use of symbols. Sreberny-Mohammadi and Mohammadi (1994) address alternative media in the revolutionary movement against the Shah of Iran in the late 1970s. Thede and Ambrosi (1992) offer an edited selection of studies of alternative video use around the world. In Mattelart and Siegelaub (1983) and Kahn and Neumaier (1985), there are a number of shorter case studies of radical alternative media in relation to social movements. These edited volumes are a major resource, especially for earlier 20th-century instances in the former case.

7. As indeed the research indicates that Neveu cites in his very stimulating article.

8. A further point of importance, rarely addressed in the social movements literature, is the question of fascist and racist movements or their media. We will discuss this further in Chapter 8.

9. The root is *offen* (open), but it can be translated as publicity, public opinion (*öffentliche Meinung*), in public, public act. "To take the public into one's confidence" would be *sich in die Öffentlichkeit flüchten. Sphere* is a spatial metaphor, which does not by itself suggest the kinetic qualities enshrined in the term Öffentlichkeit. The spatial metaphor does, however, have the merit of

prompting the empirical question, Where and what is the public sphere? An extraordinary amount of toner has settled on to paper in referring to this term and precisely, sad to say, because it is one of those concepts whose academic vogue is directly proportional to its ample measure of the vague. For the two best collections of essays on the concept, see Calhoun (1993) and François and Neveu (1999).

10. Habermas's (1984/1987) later emphasis on the "ideal speech situation", although intended as a yardstick against which to measure social reality, has the same implied ratiocinative character.

11. The word *conversation* has its own limits: It implies a relaxed chat between friends, whereas in Öffentlichkeit, the debate is likely to be noisy, rancorous, and pungent, at least from time to time—a long way from Habermas's vacuum-packed vision of communicative bliss. But we need to theorize the actual, not only to set up abstract yardsticks by which to judge it. In Chapter 4 on community and democracy, we will return to this topic.

12. One of the more notable examples in the later 20th century was how a number of the young intellectual rebel communicators of the Soviet "thaw" era of 1956-1964 became leaders for a while of the *glasnost* process in Soviet media in the late 1980s (until they, too, were mostly swept from influence in the final collapse of the Soviet Union). In the deadening intervening years of Brezhnev's period in office, they had bided their time, but their memories were fresh (Downing, 1996, p.121, note 3, p. 226, note 8). A complementary example is the role of the daughters of U.S. leftists of the 1940s and 1950s in the genesis of the internationally influential U.S. women's liberation movement in the 1960s and 1970s (Evans, 1979).

13. The question of political and historical memory and media is a vast one. One of the most crippling obstacles to the development of constructive social movements is the absence of public memory of the struggles of past decades. In Argentina, the Mothers' of the Plaza de Mayo struggled for over 20 years to keep the horrors of the 1976-1982 military junta from lapsing into a cozy silence (Kaiser, 1993). In Stalin's Russia, painstaking steps were taken to iron the past out of both history books and news photographs (King, 1997), and one of the most pivotal moments in the collapse of the Soviet system in the later 1980s was when this history began at last to be made available for public discussion (Davies, 1989; Nove, 1989).

Yet, without state censorship of such materials in many Western countries, a voluntary political amnesia seems often to be in force there. In the United States, the Palmer raids, unemployed workers' marches, McCarthyism, two World Wars, continued interventions in Latin America and the Caribbean, the Korean War, the Vietnam War, civil rights struggles, labor history, and women's struggles seem only to resurface as obscure flotsam and in no way shape or form as moments and movements that almost indelibly stamped American culture. Moreover, although the United States is often thought of as having an exceptionally ahistorical culture, this is not much more true than it is of many European countries. Political amnesia typically benefits the ruling order, dropping a thick, hushed blanket of sparkling snow over somber and jagged landscapes.

Throwing conventional understandings of the past into question with the aid of social and labor history can often be a hugely subversive act that provokes substantive re-evaluation of the present.

In addition, radical alternative media may serve to disarray a second vital component of collective memory by challenging the mnemonic categories iterated by mainstream media, which enable axiomatic slotting of each day's whirl of new information into a hegemonic frame. This may be done by media critique and media literacy columns and programs or by humor and irony. Even, occasionally, within the framework of mainstream media, a classic example being the media skits in BBC television's *Monty Python's Flying Circus.*

4

Community, Democracy, Dialogue, and Radical Media

- Radical media are quite often referred to as community media and as democratic alternatives to media monopolies. However, both *community* and *democracy* are potentially fuzzy words, a mere heartbeat behind *motherhood,* typically signifying a "generally good thing." They urgently need anchoring by definition and critique to make them in any way useful.
- Some significant recent writers on democracy are reviewed to underscore the frequent failure to connect media to strong definitions of democracy. C. B. Macpherson's work is noted because his definition of developmental, counterhegemonic power helps ground radical media in a unifying concept.
- The discussion of *conversation* as the leitmotif of democratic process is resumed, reaching more closely into the everyday role of media in the United States and to some observations of Bakhtin and Freire on the term *dialogue.*

THE FUZZY CONCEPT OF COMMUNITY

The term *community* has been widely used as a catch-all. It has had a localist sense (this community stands firm on the issue of . . .), a world politics rhetoric (the international community's stance against terrorism), a professional sense (the scientific community), a politics of sexual frankness usage (community standards of decency), and a nostalgic sense hearkening back to a supposed era of harmony (we need to recover a sense of community). *Community* also commonly turns up as a way of attributing lock-step homogeneity of opinion to minority ethnic groups (*the* Black community, *the* Jewish community).

The term has also been used as a populist way to refer to subordinated social classes while avoiding the use of leftist jargon. It has also been used to avoid singling out any particular group among the poor. Thus, the designations *community radio* and *community access television* have been ways of defining these media as institutions responsive to demands and priorities from below (the working class plus[1] women plus minority ethnic groups plus lesbians and gays, plus . . .). Implicit in this use of community is the assumption that mainstream media are at the service of power (how that is so is variously conceptualized).

Often, many of these latter uses imply a seamless social tissue that is local and therefore healthy, in contradistinction to a wider governmental reality that is foreign and unhealthy. This can easily slide into a right-wing version of anarchism and even forms of xenophobia. It also makes quite idiotic assumptions about the absence of class and other serious social rifts within the local tissue. It is, therefore, exceptionally hard to give the term community a lucid and exact sense.[2] Yet, when the word is used as convenient verbal shorthand for the spectrum of the relatively dispossessed, or local realities, it is hard to think of a replacement.

Whichever way you cut it, the term persistently raises many more questions and dilemmas than it answers. Using it in relation to radical alternative media demands that its meaning be carefully defined to avoid the production of endless and pointless fog. Perhaps a viable meaning, pinpointing something genuinely important in social life, can be constructed through combining the inclusive populist meaning of the word with a sense of social connectedness over at least a generation, indeed, with the local communication exchange and networks that have grown up over time.[3] But we must repeat: This connectedness is but rarely egalitarian or democratic on the local level. It may only seem so relative to transnational corporate power, or the national state. Terms such as *community* media or *grassroots* media may easily conceal more than they reveal. They are stronger in what they exclude—mainstream media—than in what they signify.

MODELS OF DEMOCRACY

Democracy, as a term, knows only highs or lows: the mellifluent highs of political theorists, and the lows of shabby practice, of procedure mongering and procedure flouting, vote fixing and vote interpreting, trash can manifestos and demagogic politicos, tens of millions spent on TV blitzkriegs and secret polling.

Yet, junking actually existing democracy rather than struggling to improve it is self-evidently no option. So our central question for the remainder of this segment of the discussion is what roles do radical media play in democratic processes? Especially, beyond formal democratic procedures at the national or regional level, how do they strengthen democratic culture in everyday life?

If we examine the huge political science literature on democracy for guidance, we find an immediate paradox. Quite often, even those in favor of struggling to improve democratic processes have little or nothing to say about communication or media, except by silent implication or occasional throw-away reference. Let us take as examples three U.S. contributions to debate on democracy.

Held (1987), in an exemplarily lucid dissection of 10 different models of democracy, explicitly intends to encourage a broadening of democratic process, but he only begins to draw near to the issues of communication and media at the close of his book (pp. 283-289) when he addresses what he argues as the pressing need for a "double democratization," that is, of both the state and civil society. Even Barber's (1984) very searching analysis of how to strengthen democratic life, which centers on communication issues, barely touches on media as such.

Touraine (1994), too, underscores the urgency of extending democratic culture to rescue us from the destructive centripetal tendencies he argues are driving us into a technological and market-driven instrumentalism, on the one hand, and spurring retreat into a closed world of communalist[4] cultural identities, on the other. He takes on some of the most difficult problems for democratic practice, such as majority-minority rights, the status of immigrants, women's equal participation, even the ramifications of the global North-South split. He adopts, indeed, the immigrant as emblematic of modern society's acute dilemmas of inclusion and extrusion. Like Rowbotham and Husband, Touraine insists that the only solution to so much fissiparity is democracy, because that

> is where dialogue and communication take place. . . . What measures the democratic character of a society . . . is the intensity and depth of dialogue between personal experiences and cultures different from one another that are, moreover, responses, all of them specific and limited, to the same common quests (concerning human purposes). (pp. 315-316)

Yet, he, too, has just four pages (pp. 247-250) on the need to reconstitute the public sphere, in which he nowhere suggests how this might be done in practice with actual media, mainstream or alternative.

The unfortunate aspect of the political science literature's lacuna in the area of media and communication is that it is often those most committed to democracy who seem to wander forever in a media-free desert. Some of the worst, admittedly, do scrabble around in media and elections, to the point in some cases of offering themselves as spin merchants to career politicians, which ranks as one of the more egregious forms of academic prostitution. But most just never get to the point at all.

It is absurd. It is as though the democratic process were conceived, as I have suggested elsewhere when discussing the standard tropes of political science (Downing, 1996, Chapter 1), as being composed of astute but entirely mute chessboard pieces, anticipating each other's moves and forging countermoves in total silence. In other words, the majority of political analysts' models of democracy, because they are without communication, are without humans, too. Does this not risk caricaturing the simplification inherent in model construction?

I do not mean to say that such theorists have nothing at all for us. It merely means that their obsession is with structures and issues, laws and institutional procedures, all of which are certainly important, but—in the absence of communicating actors and groups—their models resemble the machine without even its ghost. Patently unrealistic: For how, in a large-scale society, does democracy communicate without also using media? If, however, all this quite inexorably present communication process is not discussed simply for the reason that it is automatically oiled and glistening, nonproblematic, and, therefore, a trivial dimension for professional political scientists, why will they not tell us where lies this magic transparent land so we can all go see how it works?

There are a few voices within political science that address media seriously. Dewey and Lippmann did so (see Hardt, 1993), although their perspective receives a needed corrective in the work of Raymond Williams (see Sparks, 1993). Dewey and Lippmann judged media in general as providing the necessary information and communication opportunities for effective deliberation to take place. Williams also argued that media, once freed from their overwhelming subjection to private firms or the state and opened up to mass participation, could stimulate and sustain a common culture and a lively democracy. Particularly important, he took the issue beyond straight information, as in the rather ratiocinative focus of Habermas, Dewey, and Lippmann, and wrote very tellingly of the need to embrace fiction and the imaginative realms of culture, the "structures of feeling" (Williams, 1977, pp. 128-135) that are integral to a nation's or a community's public conversation.[5] In Chapter 5's discussion of art and radical media, and in some of the chapters in Parts II and III, we will venture further into this theme.

The difficulty with even these three thinkers is that although they state very attractive positions concerning communication and democracy, they do not address the messy world of actuality. They do not engage closely with the tiresome and daunting problems of trying to democratize actually existing mainstream media. So although that goal remains one of immense importance, until or unless there is substantial movement in that direction, the role of radical alternative media of all kinds will continue to be extremely significant.

This is not to say that mainstream media contribute nothing at present to democracy. That would be an ill-considered and lumpish distortion. The organized far Right in the 1980s and 1990s, in the United States and elsewhere, has made great play of denouncing mainstream media as leftist pulpits, so that it would be a huge error for the Left simply to contribute to a "media-attack culture" without, simultaneously, very noisily indicating fierce opposition to the extreme Right's project to wipe out all expression of dissent to its left.

We still must face up to the fact that mainstream media make no pretense of offering themselves up to any form of public control, short of consumers' letters or consumers' refusal to buy them or switch them on. As means of public leverage or democratic influence, these various responses are either feeble or indiscriminately blunt. In small communities, they may be used to some effect, but not in nations with a large population. Indeed, when these levers are pulled, it seems likely to be by tightly organized extreme Right fundamentalists putting pressure on a firm to pull TV advertising from a program they hate.[6] Consumer sovereignty, often blazoned as a democratic fix-all, bears no relation to practical media realities.

Can we say that, by contrast, radical alternative media are the chief standard bearers of a democratic communication structure?

The argument here is yes; that, although flawed, immensely varied, and not necessarily oppositional, many such media do contribute in different degrees to that mission, and more truly than the mainstream media, in ways that are often amazing, given their exceptionally meager resources.

MACPHERSON AND DEVELOPMENTAL POWER

It helps to support this judgment to reflect on C. B. Macpherson's (1973, Chapter 3) analysis of the basis of democracy, even though he has nothing directly to say about media at all. His concepts nonetheless provide a pivotal schema by which to interpret the roles of radical media. He has proposed, as central to our understanding of the basic purpose of power in a democracy, developmental power, the opportunity for members of the public "to use and develop [their] capacities" (p. 42). Developmental power represents the positive possibilities for human achievement inherent in cooperative social life, which, up to the present, the construction of economic and political life most often sidelines.

Macpherson's (1973) low-key and apparently innocuous language is actually much more momentous and challenging than it appears at first blush. It has as its ground his conviction that the public's "capacities" to create viable societal arrangements are infinitely more capacious than cynics and elitists will allow, but also that the public's ability to activate them is widely shackled. The shackles may include, most obviously, malnutrition, homelessness, and illiteracy, but also lack of access to the means of production as a result of the division of power between capital and labor. The obstacles also encompass lack of protection against arbitrary attack on one's body or one's liberty (for further explication, see Macpherson, 1973, pp. 59-70).

Macpherson uses the term *extractive power* in the opposite direction, to denote both the power of capital over labor and the very concepts of power customary among modern philosophers and resonant with the capital/labor relationship. These theorists almost universally define power as the ability to impose your agenda on other people. Democracy, in this light, is then best understood as far more than a set of agreed procedural rules of debate and negotiation, important as those are; if Macpherson is correct, democracy, at its best, entails a cultural, political, and economic setting in which developmental power flourishes. The concept of developmental power may be used to build on the notions of counterhegemony and alternative public spheres, and it has an easy symbiosis with the hallmarks of many social movements.

Radical alternative media serve as developmental power agents in a number of senses. Without idealizing them (some of the case studies later in the book militate against that), they are much more central to democracy than commentators bemused by the easily visible reach and clout of mainstream media will typically acknowledge.[7]

First, radical alternative media expand the range of information, reflection, and exchange from the often narrow hegemonic limits of mainstream media discourse. This is accomplished, in part, by their very number. Second, they frequently try to be more responsive than mainstream media to the voices and aspirations of the excluded. They often have a close relationship with an ongoing social movement and thus fairly spontaneously express views and opinions extruded from mainstream media, or ridiculed in them. They are quite often in the lead in addressing issues that only later get noticed by mainstream media. Third, radical alternative media do not need to censor themselves in the interests of media moguls, entrenched state power, or religious authority. Fourth, their own internal organization is often much more democratic than hierarchical, as we shall see in a series of the case studies. And last, some of these media fulfill the innovative role that Raymond Williams (1977) ascribed to what he termed "formations; those effective movements and tendencies, in intellectual and artistic life, which have significant and sometimes decisive influence on the active development of a culture, and which have a variable and often oblique relation to formal institutions" (p. 117). Putting these elements together, it makes every sense to see radical media as agents of developmental power, not simply as counterinformation institutions, and certainly not as a vapid cluster of passing gnats.

To be blunt, however, we are faced with a key problem still, or rather two. One is the level of abstraction of these concepts, for although they are a necessary stage in understanding the roles of radical media, they are not sufficient. We need to link these overall angles of vision with more immediate practicalities. Later, we will address these in significant measure, but the second problem we need to re-examine more closely is equally practical, namely, public conversation, dialogue, talk, communication networks, popular culture, all of which have much to do with democracy and a democratic culture.

However, the contributions we will examine to help us do this also do not address radical media but rather focus more generically on the relation between public communication and developmental power. Nonetheless, it is the argument of this book that what media could be is often much better realized in alternative public spheres, so the fact that these writers do not themselves address radical media does not particularly matter.

RADICAL MEDIA AND DIALOGUE

Two major writers who directly focused on the notion of dialogue, with definite implications for the democratic roles of radical alternative media, are Freire (1970, 1972, 1974) and Bakhtin (1981). Their contributions are on quite different but ultimately complementary planes.

Freire, primarily concerned with literacy education for public empowerment, put oppressive structures and political engagement against them at the center of the communication process (McLaren & Lankshear, 1994). In his concept of *conscientizaçao*[8] he emphasized eliciting students' intelligence and perceptions rather than delivering "superior knowledge" to empty subjects. Thus, in teaching literacy, he insisted on using the everyday language and images of the students (poor farmers or city dwellers), and rejected pre-packaged language and images pulled from the scholar's authoritative shelf. This was to engage in a dialogue from the start with the learners' reality, to encourage their expression of opposition to their exploitation and material poverty. Freire saw literacy as a technique enabling students not to fit into the world as it is but to change it: It would help students to challenge the history of their own shaping. He readily acknowledged, too, the opportunity for the educator to grow in this process as well as the student.

Freire solely and entirely concentrated on face-to-face interactivity and never extended his vision further to encompass media (De Lima, 1979, p. 98). However, if for dialogic educator we read radical media activist, Freire's pedagogy can serve as a core philosophy within which to think through the nature of the activist producer/active audience relationship.[9] It proposes a democracy of the communication process, once more acknowledging the audience as joint architects with the media producers, radically unlike the "they watch it so we must be giving them what they want and need" ideology of commercial media. Whereas Freire tended not to differentiate different groups among the oppressed (Weiler, 1994), Findley (1994) proposes that the learning processes Freire championed can, nonetheless, be an important means for social movements "in their struggle to achieve and maintain common understandings of the problems they intend to address, and thereafter to work toward continually renewed consensus on strategies, tactics, and procedures" (p. 118). The role for radical media in this process is obvious, underscored by Rowbotham and by Husband in Chapter 3's discussion of the public sphere.

Bakhtin, focusing on novels[10] as a vital form of popular, even subversive, narrative communication in the modern era, particularly stressed the competing discourses and voices *(heteroglossia, raznorechie)* represented in them. His observations, perhaps seeming not contentious to the casual reader, were penned during the depths of Stalinist repression in the Soviet Union, when enormous pressure was applied to public expression to force it into a deadening ideological uniformity. *Raznorechie* was a notion in deep disfavor, and indeed, Bakhtin wrote his essay during a 6-year political exile in an obscure little town far away from the Kremlin in the wilds of Kazakhstan. (Some of his close intellectual associates perished in the camps.)

It was within that stifling context that Bakhtin (1981, pp. 297, 342-348, 369-371) critiqued the limitations of poetic discourse, authoritative discourse, and mythological thinking, in favor of "internally persuasive discourses." By this, he meant the day-to-day language and voices of the general public, emerging from the public's experiences and their great variety. His commentary on the raunchy marketplace language in

Rabelais' novel, *Gargantua and Pantagruel,* which we shall discuss in Chapter 5, is a strong example. He urges that the novel should always give these internally persuasive discourses pride of place against official, uniform speech issuing from on high. He writes,

> In the history of literary language, there is a struggle constantly being waged to overcome the official line with its tendency to distance itself from the zone of contact [i.e., everyday life] . . . the internally persuasive word is half-ours and half-someone else's. Its creativity and productiveness consist precisely in the fact that such a word awakens new and independent words . . . It is freely developed . . . it enters into interanimating relationships with new contexts. (p. 345)

Bakhtin's emphasis on this dialogue of voices within the novel (or the soap opera) could equally be applied to radical media as a dialogic, democratic public sphere within popular culture. Furthermore, his angle of vision on this art form underscores a recurring theme in this book's argument, already noted in the discussion of popular culture and of Iris Marion Young and Raymond Williams: the centrality of emotion and imagination in radical media, the peril of seeing their role as informative in a purely ratiocinative sense. A democratic culture cannot only subsist on rational argument, a theme that will be taken further in Chapter 5 on art and aesthetics.

Both Freire and Bakhtin provide support for a dialogic vision of radical alternative media, embedded in the push and pull of everyday life, not sectarian, at their best engaged with audiences at their most active, producing as well as receiving media content.

COMMUNICATION AND DEMOCRACY

Barber (1984) argues for a series of procedures that can be undertaken to strengthen the democratic process and, in so doing, nails his colors very firmly to the mast on the subject of communication.[11] "At the heart of strong democracy is talk" (p. 173), he says. Indeed, he is quite lyrical on the subject:

> Politics . . . would ossify completely without its (i.e., talk's) creativity, its variety, its openness and flexibility, its inventiveness, its capacity for discovery, its subtlety and complexity, its eloquence, its potential

> for empathy and affective expression, and its deeply paradoxical . . . character. (p. 174)

In line with some of the other thinkers already cited, Barber stresses that "strong democratic talk" requires listening as well as uttering, that it is affective as well as cognitive, and that its linkage to intentions draws it out of speculation and into the realm of real-world practice. "Listening is a mutualistic art that by its very practice enhances equality . . . [talk] can build community as well as maintain rights and seek consensus as well as resolve conflict" (pp. 175, 177). He proceeds (pp. 178-212) to define nine functions of what he terms *strong democratic talk.*

However, there are two absences in his argument, arguably related to each other—media[12] and democracy beyond the locality. He sees media technologies as aids toward effective public debate in neighborhood assemblies. Media, for him, seem to be technical channels rather than social institutions. In his final chapter (pp. 273-281, 289-290), he explores a little gingerly how democratic activity might deploy local television, videotex, electronic balloting, and favorable postal rates for informational print media. But he does not grapple at all with national realities outside neighborhoods, let alone with the international media dimensions of a functioning democracy.

Communication theorists Carey (1995) and Schudson (1997) have presented opposing views[13] on the question of *conversation, talk,* and *democracy.* For Carey, drawing heavily on Dewey and somewhat on Habermas, spontaneous conversation about policies and politics is the very kernel of democracy. By the close of the 20th century, however, Carey argues, a culture of political conversation is more or less extinct because mainstream media have almost ceased to prime the public's conversational pump. Political polling and manipulated television spectacles have largely replaced politics. Hence, democracy itself is withering on the vine. He does not address the question of social movements, although it seems from the music of his argument that it would naturally flow in that direction. Nor does he address alternative media.

Schudson's (1997) critique is concerned to inject a certain sour realism into Carey's impassioned call. He suggests, with corroborative evidence from both New England town meetings and the American Constitutional Convention, that although conversation in general is the very stuff of society, democratic debate is a specific form of conversation that needs to be procedurally based to work. Thus, it cannot evince the quality of spontaneity that Carey sees as its soul. Furthermore,

Schudson proposes, democratic debate typically results in printed media (a petition, a notice, a law), rather than being sparked by them.

Their disagreement is apposite to this phase in our discussion of public sphere, social movements, community, and democracy. It addresses exactly the intersection between the social, the political, and the communicative (three conceptual categories that have heuristic value only up to the point at which they are not reified). Schudson wins the argument so long as we accept that the formal structures of democracy are its core. Yet, although we certainly cannot pretend that such structures are not there or that they are irrelevant or purely oppressive, a democratic culture is a necessary part of the democratic infrastructure. A democratically organized economy would be just as much so.[14] Without that culture, congressional proceduralism may entirely replace the rules of debate, and indeed, the polling management and public relations manipulation that Carey deplores may easily be victorious. That is precisely why the energy of popularly based social movements—not manipulated jacqueries[15]—is central to democratic culture and why the media of such movements are at the core of the process. It is a pity Carey did not address them.

Valuable further insight is provided by Friedland (1996), who primarily discusses specific U.S. case studies of Internet use in the democratic process.[16] His conceptual starting point is an interesting combination of civic engagement and social capital theory with network theory. In the course of his argument, Friedland underscores the very important point that the purpose of democracy is not only deliberation but also governmental action, whether on the national or the local level or a combination.

With this in hand, Friedland (1996) stresses that democratic conversation consists not only of people sitting around talking politics (Carey) or of legislators deliberating policy (Schudson) but also of engaged citizens combining in a variety of roles to review what they may achieve with a given project—and then carrying out the project, often debating and modifying it as they go. Those combined roles may, in the United States, be those of federal, state, city, or county legislators; civil service workers at any level of government; staff at large or small think-tanks and academic research institutes; community and movement activists, and netizens or media activists. There may be serendipity in debate and policy execution, or the reverse.

This conversation/deliberation is not abstract, unbundled from everyday practice; it is both national and local, and especially—

Friedland stresses this point—it centrally involves ongoing relationships of reciprocity and trust.[17] This links straight back into Chapter 3's discussion of communication networks. Thus, Friedland's approach to the issues suggests a rich and complex integration of levels and aspects of talk/conversation, democratic culture, media technology, and political action.

To wrap up this discussion, let us examine a very interesting argument from what Rodríguez (in press) describes as a nonessentialist feminist position. She specifically takes up the question of praxis and democracy in relation to radical media. She argues that we need to break away from "a modern understanding of citizenship as expressed by voting and protesting ... [and] from thinking of political actions and social movements as linear, continuous, and conscious processes toward a common goal." Instead, based in part on her own research in Colombia and Nicaragua and partly on the theoretical work of Mouffe (1992a, 1992b) and of McClure (1992), she proposes that we reconceptualize the impact of alternative media in terms of their impact on the participants' sense of themselves and their potential as human beings. She summarizes what may happen as follows:

> It implies having the opportunity to create one's own images of self and environment; it implies being able to recodify one's identity with the signs and codes that one chooses, thereby disrupting the traditional acceptance of those imposed by outside sources; it implies becoming one's own story teller . . . ; it implies reconstructing the self-portrait of one's own community and one's own culture; it implies exploring the infinite possibilities of one's own body, one's own face, to create facial expressions (a new codification of the face) and nonverbal languages (a new codification of the body) never seen before; it implies taking one's own languages out of their usual hiding place and throwing them out there, into the public sphere and seeing how they do, how they defeat other languages, or how they are defeated by other languages. (1996, p. 2)[18]

THE PRICE OF PARTICIPATION

The final, very basic topic to include under the democracy heading is cost. Access to media is governed, over and above the codes mainstream media lay down for the public's participation (talk shows, game shows, opinion poll results, establishment "experts"), by how expensive media technologies are. In early 19th-century Britain, for instance, the Stamp Tax, described by its opponents as "a tax on knowledge," lifted the price of a daily newspaper to seven pence, far beyond anything a worker could afford, and was clearly designed to price workers out of the public realm.

At various periods in time, print technology has been fairly cheap. Until, for example, the outset of the 1840s, the United States boasted a considerable number of labor newspapers in the incipient industrial centers of Boston, New York, Philadelphia, and Baltimore (Schiller, 1981). The advent of the rotary technique brought with it machinery costs that mostly crushed the labor press. It would be fair to say that the spread of photocopiers since the 1970s has worked in the opposite direction (cf. Enzensberger, 1974). Indeed, the very strict control of access to them within the old Soviet Union reflected rather exactly the then political elite's anxieties about the uses to which dissident communicators could put them.[19] The rise of cheap video cameras and cassette recorders had a similar trajectory, although in their earliest, most expensive phase, print was still necessarily the format of choice for low-cost radical media. Public access television is one result (see Laura Stein's Chapter 20, this volume). The expanding uses of the personal computer and the cheap modem since the mid-1980s are a further case in point, as Chapter 17 by Ford and Gil demonstrates.

However, there are also radical formats that are not technologically driven and expensive, such as graffiti, buttons, T-shirts, song, street theater, performance art, many of which we will discuss in Part II. If the public is not to be priced out of communicating via media, then low-cost formats become all the more crucial for democratic culture and process.

Summary: We have examined the rather fluffy notion of community and some approaches to expanding the democratic process. Oddly, the wing of political science that favors a deepening and strengthening of democracy rarely addresses the role of media in the cultural and procedural mesh that would be needed, including Barber, who examines communication up to a point but does not really engage with media. Even those who do, such as Williams, rarely engage with the messy world of everyday praxis, and Keane (1991), who follows Williams's basic diagnosis, similarly offers only rather implausible proposals for implementing mainstream media change.[20] Carey and Schudson's debate about the role of conversation in the democratic process is resolved to a considerable extent, although he makes no specific reference to it, by Friedland when he links together deliberation, policy action, and the question of ongoing reciprocity, reviewing roles that may be played by Internet communication in this linkage. Obviously, the notions of counterhegemony, alternative public sphere, and dialogue, which we have already examined, are in their various ways also addressing these problems, and they ultimately all center on what Macpherson would term the expansion of developmental power.

In the next chapter, we will layer into our analytical framework approaches to the exceptionally important relation between art, media, and communication. Too often, these three are written and spoken about as though each were an entirely separate realm. The high-art/low-art distinction, which strictly segregates art from media, is really quite extraordinarily tenacious. We shall examine some approaches that do not fall into the trap of segregating information, reasoning, and cognition from feeling, imagination, and fantasy, thereby focusing our attention on how media may enhance developmental power.

Dance, street theater, cartoons, posters, parody, satire, performance art, graffiti, murals, and popular songs or instrumental music are, as we shall illustrate fully in Part II, only some of the most obvious forms of radical media whose communicative thrust depends not on closely argued logic but on their aesthetically conceived and concentrated force. For easily understandable political reasons, in the analysis of radical media, tremendous weight has often been placed on their role in transmitting to the public information that has been systematically censored, distorted, or dismissed in mainstream media. This information/counterinformation model (cf. Baldelli, 1977; Jensen, 1997) is an important one, but it has sometimes overflowed into a purely logocentric definition of alternative media: lies/truth, cover-up/facts, ideology/reality.

We need to begin by acknowledging that part of the 19th- and 20th-century background to this issue is the long history of ultradogmatic alternative media, associated with leftist political currents of one stripe or another, whose rhetoric was only too often dipped in concrete and judged by its Leninist/theological exactitudes, or similar pseudo-religious jargon named for some revolutionary figure (Kropotkin, Trotsky, Mao Ze-dong, Che Guevara, etc.). A language of lead and an incantation of enshrined phrases were the result, inordinately reassuring to the faithful and somewhere between sophomoric and soporific to those outside the magic circle: Capitalism is in its death-agony . . . The proletariat, under the wise guidance of the party . . . Stormy applause greeted the General Secretary's speech . . . The heroic struggles of the people . . . Imperialism, as comrade Lenin so brilliantly observed . . . The USSR is a degenerated workers' state. . . The renegade revisionist clique . . . Communism will win . . . The masses . . .

Thus, the liveliness and zest that ideally should be synonymous with radical media have been conspicuous by their frailty within the highly influential Marxist and Leninist political tradition over the past 150 years.[21] For this reason alone, it is essential to recuperate the urgency of artistic flair in planning or evaluating radical media projects.

NOTES

1. The effort becomes more and more tortured, as though the working class were composed entirely of straight white males.

2. Also, see Downing (1999a) on community in cyberspace.

3. See Putnam (1993) for an extended argument in this direction, based on Italy.

4. I am using the word here in the sense in which it was used in public debate in India in the later decades of the 20th century, to denote the destructive focus on the supposedly homogeneous and embattled interests of particular segments of the nation. In India, it was a matter of religio-political identities (Hindu, Muslim, Sikh), but the particular labels and cues vary from nation to nation.

5. See similarly Edward Thompson's assertion that "fully one-half of culture . . . is affective and moral consciousness," noted in Chapter 1.

6. The history of this tactic on the part of the extreme Right goes back at least to the *Red Channels* saga of the McCarthy era (Barnouw, 1990, pp. 121-28).

7. Kellner (1990, pp. 207-222) is a notable exception.

8. Roughly, evoking a critical perception of reality. A term Freire used in his earlier work, *mutismo,* later rendered in his writing as "the culture of silence" (of the poor), which he perceived as "rooted in the favorable spoils of Latin American land tenure" for the rich (De Lima, 1979, p. 117), is unfortunate in that it implies still the need for the outside intellectual to arrive to start people thinking. James C. Scott's (1985, 1990) work raises serious questions about

this perception. Nonetheless, Freire maintained a mixed attitude on this score, insisting, for example, that clay dolls and popular songs were as much culture as internationally famous artworks (De Lima, 1979, p. 125). His contemporary compatriot Glauber Rocha's beautiful 1962 film *Barravento* evinces much of the same dualism of perception. I am grateful to Cacilda Rêgo for advice on interpreting Freire's work.

9. See Huesca and Dervin (1994) for a utilization of Freire's notion of "theoretically guided and self-reflective action," which requires "a synthesis of local process and global referent through reflective practices" (p. 63). This "untamed terrain" as they term it (p. 65), enables, they claim, the entrenched opposition in much social theory and analysis between structure and agency to be transcended, with great benefit to the understanding of alternative media. A transition "from the conceptual to the practical world" (p. 64) seemingly compels, or at least enables, this to happen. Yet, although they correctly note (pp. 65-67) that Latin American alternative media theory, up to the date of their article, did not engage very much with the question of how communication has its effect, their own focus on praxis equally constitutes a claim, not an actuality.

10. We perhaps tend to think of the novel as "frozen" communication, radically distinct from the unpredictable process at the heart of Freire's work, but that, in turn, implies that the author's intentions lock the novel's readers into a single interpretation of it. The discussion of Janice Radway's (1984) work in Chapter 1 suggests that to be a very inadequate understanding of how audiences operate.

11. Barber's proposals approximate Held's (1987) two final models of the democratic process, the participative and the democratic autonomy models (pp. 254-264, 289-299).

12. Barber's (1984) only fleeting references to media in the body of the book are slighting ones to mainstream media, to the danger of letting specialists such as journalists do our democratic communicating for us (p. 193), or to the inevitable degeneration of language into an instrument of elite rule once we hand it over to "the media, the bureaucrats, the professors, and the managers" (p. 197).

13. I am indebted to my colleague Chuck Whitney in the Journalism Department at the University of Texas for drawing my attention to this debate.

14. A serious discussion of what this might mean in practice is beyond our scope here.

15. The Rush Limbaugh phenomenon in the mid-1990s was an instance of what I mean here. I repeat, the wider question of fascist social movements and populist ultra-Rightism will be addressed later.

16. Besides Chapter 17 on radical Internet use, the case studies on cyberdemocracy in Tsagarousianou et al. (1998) are well worth reviewing.

17. Putnam's (1993) study of civic engagement in Italy interestingly puts this latter dimension in a long historico-cultural framework, far beyond individual lifetimes.

18. See Huesca and Dervin (1994) for a very comparable argument about the centrality of praxis in the analysis of radical media and Huesca (1995) for an

empirical study of Bolivian miners' radio stations from that perspective (although in the second piece, he uses the term *process* instead of praxis).

19. See the discussion in Chapter 22 on *samizdat* media in the former Soviet Union and Soviet bloc, not least the success of Polish oppositional movements in evading photocopier controls.

20. See, for example, the review of his book by Scannell in *Media, Culture & Society* (1992).

21. For a further evaluation of Leninism and alternative media organization, see Chapter 22.

5

Art, Aesthetics, Radical Media, and Communication

- Art and media: critique versus capitulation?
- Expressionism, dada, surrealism, the Situationists
- The elusive but ultimately productive notion of aura in the work of Walter Benjamin
- Bertolt Brecht, radical theater, and cofabulation

It is interesting to note how difficult it is even for a politically committed writer and artist such as John A. Walker (1983), in his stimulating and lucid discussion of the relation between art and mass media, to concede anything to media in the process. Walker effectively defines art—not all art, he makes very clear, but politically committed art—as the only form of radical alternative media left to us. Indeed, for him, fine art's role in the present era must include the critique of mass media representations, so as to enable media consumers to distance themselves from the deluge of deadening images and narratives poured out through those channels. He writes that fine art continues to be essential because it "is distinguished . . . by its greater degree of independence, individuality, personal expression, and handwork" (p. 90).

Walker's tendency simply to dismiss media as the problem facing us practically dismisses alternative media uses and projects as well (although along the way he does passingly acknowledge radical and community video). He also fails to address the potential for audience users to create their own dissident readings of mass media texts, nor does he mention culturally subversive elements in mainstream media. Willy-nilly, then, as the only substantive version of radical communication still standing, critical artwork will be destined to reach a rather small choir. This is often true of small-scale oppositional media, as well, but it seems perverse to neglect them and thereby shrink the authentic world of radical communication still further. Walker's argument risks, despite his patently expressed wishes to communicate with as many people as possible, being a left-wing pitch for a political ghetto. It would be much more productive to consider how the kinds of political art he discusses might feed into alternative media content and how a stimulating dialogue might be mounted over the long term between politically committed artists and media activists.

THE RELATION BETWEEN ART AND MEDIA

There is, after all, a rich history to be considered here. Emerging out of German Expressionism, the dada movement, surrealists, and Situationists have variously conceived the relation between art and media. All three formations, in Williams's sense of the term, foregrounded art as a form of public, political communication, and in certain ways, although very distinct, each formation was heir to the previous one. Walter Benjamin and Bertolt Brecht, both of them influenced by the Berlin dada movement, also contributed interesting perspectives to the discussion.

None of these can be understood outside the context of the millions slaughtered for nothing in World War I, the turbulent years of the Weimar Republic, the Nazi era, and Stalinism, although for Situationists, the post-World War II era was the most immediate context. Expressionism, an artistic current with a long history in German art from Max Ernst through to the films of Fassbinder, seemed in the early period of the First World War carnage to speak through the harshness of its imagery to the horrors of the trenches. As the war ground interminably on, gorging itself on hundreds of thousands then millions, some artists—and vast numbers of others—became galvanized by the desire to communicate their impotent scream of outrage, their total rejection of the unending mass slaughter. To some in that frame of mind, even Expressionist art seemed to have become passive and futile.

Enter dada. For the dada movements, art was "shit." Art itself had to be exploded, both as a category and as an institution, because its modes of expression had either helped pave the path to the war or were totally irrelevant to its understanding. Dada, possibly derived from a French children's term for rocking horse, instead generated art objects that until then had been considered totally irrelevant to art. Examples included so-called "found objects," everyday products such as shoes or bricks or rusting iron or a toilet-bowl, which were made part of formal art exhibits. Berlin was one of the dada movement's several centers, along with Zürich, Paris, and New York. Berlin dada was marked strongly by support for socialism and the early Russian revolution and was greatly influential on the work of Grosz and Heartfield (discussed in Chapter 14), as well as Brecht and Benjamin. In the end, this attempt to dismantle conventional art ended by being absorbed into the canon as a school, and as much a commodity as any other.

Surrealists by contrast, such as Breton, Cocteau, Magritte, Dalí, Aragon, Césaire, and Lam, largely operated from the get-go within artistic and literary conventions, subverting them from inside rather than struggling to dismantle them entirely. Their work sought to defamiliarize the public with what seems self-evident, most easily taken for granted: hegemonic visual and verbal reality. They focused on "the eruption of the marvellous into ordinary experience . . . [they were] searching for the means to express all that is unexpected, fresh, awesome, and vertiginous" (Plant, 1992, p. 48). For both dada and surrealism, public shock and scandal by means of art—although dada ferociously rejected the title, thereby seeking to blur the art-media distinction—was their primary objective. Some of the leading French surrealists were pro-Marxist, although most kept their distance from the organized Left.

The situationists (Andreotti & Costa, 1996; Marelli, 1998; Plant, 1992; Wollen, 1989) were deeply knowledgeable in and influenced by the historical currents of both dada and surrealism. It makes sense, therefore, to leap ahead a moment in time to discuss them here, before returning to Benjamin and Brecht. Their definition of post-World War II consumer society or sovietized nations in Eastern Europe as a huge, mystifying spectacle and of the public as constrained only passively to spectate (cf. Marcus, 1989, p. 99) led them to urge the creation of provocative counterspectacles. These were typically mounted on behalf of rather than by the public and, like dada and surrealist expression, were designed to scandalize, to disrupt the cozy alienation of First World[1] capitalism. The most famous verbal examples were from the social explosions of May-June 1968 in Paris, not all of them directly authored by situationists, but often influenced by a situationist aesthetic (Viénet, 1992). Some of the slogans give the flavor: "Beneath the cobble-stones, the beach,"[2] "Put imagination in control!" and "Humanity will not be happy until the last bureaucrat has been hanged with the guts of the last capitalist."[3]

Situationism, unlike Marxism, had no sense that human history was moving toward victory for subordinate classes. There was a permanent dualism in its adherents' view of recuperation, namely, that the ruling class could twist every form of protest around to salvage its own ends. The situationists' enthusiasm for what they termed *détournement* (Plant, 1992, p. 86; cf. Andreotti, 1996, pp. 26-30) suggests that by this term they meant something akin both to subversion and diversion. In terms of the spectacle of everyday life, détournement particularly operates by redeploying official language but can also employ official visual imagery to subvert the established order.[4] It is the revolutionary counterpart to recuperation, a subversive plagiarism that diverts the spectacle's language and imagery from its intended use. When we come to examine in Part II the impact of dada on graffiti, public and performance art, street theater, and culture jamming, a number of these dadaist, surrealist, and situationist themes will recur. The notion of détournement, in particular, will be seen to have had great influence even without being cited as such. These varying historical and conceptual attempts to fuse artistic and media expression—and to declare en passant the destructiveness of their mutual segregation—are of abiding interest.

BENJAMIN AND THE NOTION OF AURA

Let us now return to two of the most influential writers on the art-media relationship. Walter Benjamin (1973), in his by now interminably discussed essay on artworks in the era of technical reproducibility,[5] vigorously argued that art and media should not be separately categorized. McCole (1993, pp. 180-205) offers perhaps the best discussion of Benjamin's reasoning on this issue, and I shall rely on his exposition here.

As opposed to those who saw mass media technologies as bringing about a continual debasement of culture and communication, Benjamin joined ranks with the Soviet constructivist artists of the early 1920s, along with filmmaker Sergei Eisenstein and photo artist Aleksandr Rodchenko, in celebrating the combined political and aesthetic potential of these then-novel technologies. Benjamin saw film, says McCole (1993, pp. 190-191), as fostering a critical testing stance toward experience through bringing the images and sequences filmed right up close, so that they were almost tactile, as distinct from the sacral, "auratic"[6] quality of traditional art's distanced, reverential modes of exhibition and contemplation.

This immediacy and virtual tactility, Benjamin proposed, would stimulate audiences to adopt for themselves the camera's actively constructing posture rather than one of contemplative passivity before the divinely inspired—or genius inspired—painting or sculpture. Rather than genuflecting, audiences would reach out, grasp hold, and engage. The ability of the camera operator to focus on movement and to change both angles and location, together with the editor's ability to create a montage of close-ups, distance shots, and scenes, fostered, he argued, a new and much more intensively analytical mode of seeing into contemporary culture, one with the sensual closeness of touch rather than the distance of vision.

Benjamin also argued that this gradual, even imperceptible expansion of people's perceptual thresholds through familiarization with cinema, together with the collective mode of film reception and its pleasurable dimensions, were decisive steps forward in artistic awareness enabled by the new technology. In other words, these then-new media technologies held ample possibilities for the cultural empowerment of vast numbers of people, for energizing popular culture.

At the same time, as Cooper (1996) is at pains to point out, Benjamin's celebration in this essay of the death of the aura of artwork hails the democratization of a contrived aura, one that mystified artwork and reserved it for a small elite. Indeed, Cooper argues (p. 165f.) that aura in a different sense is still a positive term for Benjamin. He instances Benjamin's (1973, p. 190) description of aura being experienced to the highest extent (in his essay, "On Some Motifs in Baudelaire") in the dialogue process between two individuals who return each other's gaze—or even between an artwork and its beholder, when struck by it and engaging critically with it, rather than approaching it reverentially as sacral: "to perceive the aura of an object we look at, means to invest it with the ability to look at us in return." In the technical reproducibility essay, (Benjamin, 1973, pp. 224-225) by contrast, the aura Benjamin attacks is one that underscores the hierarchical distance between the perceiver and the object.[7]

Benjamin's positive and negative notions of aura, intensely suggestive but also elusive, may be taken as his attempt to articulate the impact of art and of media. Not only that, but to define the impact in terms of interactivity, of a dialogical "looking" and interrogation rather than a hegemonic relationship. Benjamin directly continues, in his Baudelaire essay, with an initially delphic illustration of his point that is, nonetheless, worth unraveling, an illustration drawn from his interpretation of Proust's fascination with unexpected flashes of memory (*mémoire involontaire;* see McCole, 1993, pp. 259-279) that he seeks to develop in a fresh direction.

Benjamin picks up on Proust's observation that memory surfaces spontaneously and then can be reflected on—or not—depending on the alertness of the individual. For Proust, this operated principally within the realm of individual biography, whereas Benjamin is at least if not more interested in engaging with the public's history and memory. In this re-reading, the present can be reflected on to debate with a collective past, and in the process, aspects of the past that were previously unremarkable or obscure may suddenly come to make sense and have meaning in relation to the present. There are, in other words, artwork and media moments in which people may find themselves unexpectedly addressed, challenged to intense reflection on how historical forces have shaped them and the political conjuncture. Freire's conviction that education must seek to stimulate critical reflection—*conscientizaçao*—is couched in different terms but to the same end, a process of critical engagement with and against hegemony.

BRECHT AND RADICAL THEATER

In Bertolt Brecht's work, we see the same commitment, albeit expressed in different terms, to understanding and using art and media dovetailed. Dramatist Erwin Piscator was part of Berlin dada. Brecht was somewhat younger but initially worked closely with him. Together, they injected a series of new dimensions into theatrical performance during the 1920s (Mueller, 1989, pp. 5-21). These included

> [the] use of banners and placards, division of the stage by colorful curtains, simultaneous scenes, short scenes, montages of scenes, use of songs, dance and pantomime, and emphasis on rhythm, movement and body language. Spoken language was not required to comply with the acceptable standard of stage language; instead, actors were encouraged to retain their dialects and individual characteristics . . . the cabaret style . . . is the epic style par excellence, in that episodes, events and "numbers" are only loosely strung together, an ideal structure to accommodate epic breadth and volume. (Mueller, 1989, p. 8)

The connections between Berlin dada and Russian artists in the early Soviet period, such as Mayakovsky, Meyerhold, Eisenstein, and Tretyakov, have already been flagged. In various ways, the Berliners found in the Bolshevik revolution's initial years a huge opportunity to experiment with novel artistic forms.[8] Brecht's and Piscator's work in part drew as well on amateur theater work done in Germany at that period. From film in particular, they not only drew versions of montage for the stage but even imported screenings into their plays. A rendition of the satirical antimilitarist Czech novel, *The Good Soldier Schweik,* for example, included filmed tracking shots of Prague streets and an animation film designed by Grosz. This was a period in which alternative media production in both Germany and Russia was at the cutting edge aesthetically as well as politically.

The theatrical communication strategy for which Brecht is most renowned is his effort to engage the audience actively rather than luring them into passively soaking up the play's narrative. A favorite comparison he drew was with people watching sports. Just as members of the crowd at sports events or watching them on TV will comment, sometimes boisterously, on their approval and disapproval of the action and will readily voice their judgments on particular turns of play, so Brecht wanted theater audiences to be equally engaged. He did not mean to produce plays whose scenes and characters were mechanically constructed to be "bloodlessly noted and weighed up" by detached spectators (cited in Mueller, 1989, p. 64). The mainstream theater strategy he attacked was, rather,

> the obsession with coercing the spectator into a one-dimensional dynamic where he is prevented from looking left or right, up or down . . . the reduction of an infinite variety of emotional as well as intellectual responses to one single mode of reception, namely empathy—the single act of identification with the hero . . . [where] the interdependence of audience and performance acts as a vicious circle, one reinforcing

> the other to disfranchise the spectator completely. (cited in Mueller, 1989, pp. 65, 64, 62)

Instead, he argued for what he termed *cofabulation*—akin to joint architects of production (the term used earlier to describe the active audience)—which in his view would leave "the spectators free to agree with, disagree with, or change any of the parts presented on stage" (Mueller, 1989, p. 94). They would compare the play with their own experiences and stories and so would import their own narratives into the production. Shades of Freire once again—although Augusto Boal, whose theatrical work will be discussed in Part II, moves a further step beyond Brecht.

Brecht enunciated this art/media dialogism (Brecht, 1983) less intensely but with exemplary clarity in his well-known remarks on the potential of radio to be a gigantic interactive transmission system, as opposed to its vertical one-to-many utilization. Between World Wars I and II, the worker-photography movement in Europe and the worker-documentary movement in the United States also endeavored to activate the democratic and participatory possibilities in visual media technologies, albeit inevitably with varying success (Alexander, 1981; Mattelart & Siegelaub, 1983, pp. 174-181).

Now, admittedly, Benjamin and Brecht were writing at a time before film production and distribution had become such a gargantuan international enterprise, and one that is so profoundly commercially driven, as it is today. Naturally, they were aware that these media technologies were not simply, or even mainly, in the hands of the public. They were not writing out of technological triumphalism, but rather out of desire to grasp all the media that the public could access to foster counter public spheres to try to combat the fascist tornado. We need to recall their context in other respects: the riveting socialist experimentation in film, photography, and theater being undertaken in Russia and Germany; the root-and-branch obliteration of confidence in civilization seared by World War I into many survivors' consciousness; and the urgency of effective communication to large masses of people if Europe were not to be engulfed by the even more monstrous avalanche of Nazism and fascism. This was the stark agenda of their struggle: to communicate against the impending crisis.[9]

The agenda continues to be to address ways in which all radical media, from paintings to video, from flyers to computer games, can convey aesthetic impact and stimulate alternative dialogue activity, not simply provide counterinformation. Interaction between artists and alternative media producers, and overall the kind of intense media interactivity of which Benjamin and Brecht wrote, are central to the future of radical media. Alexandra Juhasz (1995), in her study of oppositional videos on AIDS in the United States, has made this point particularly forcefully:

> It is precisely this openness of the alternative AIDS media, as opposed to the bounded and closed nature of so much mainstream television, which I celebrate and applaud: a forum as rich, open, and malleable as are the individuals and communities who have been scarred by AIDS and scared into action against it. For the AIDS community, in all its diversity, as for minority populations around the world, access to media production allows us to express our needs, define our own agenda, counter irresponsible depictions of our lives, and recognize our similarities and differences. (p. 73)

Summary: Moving beyond Walker's constrained definition of media, the history of dada, surrealism, and situationism suggest very lively scenarios for radical media, even if as artistic movements they ended by partial absorption into the canon they had struggled so hard to explode. Benjamin's reflections on art and media technologies with respect to radical media focus on (a) the impact of aesthetic content, (b) the intensely interactive character that should denote such media—compare Brecht's cofabulation and the notion of joint architects of production—and (c) the possibilities opened up by mass access to media technologies. At the dawn of the 21st century, this interactive access is especially visible in terms of computer technology, and Chapter 17 by Ford and Gil at the close of Part II explores that theme in some detail.

In some ways, this discussion of aesthetics and alternative media brings us back to some of the questions of audiences and readers, of resistance, and of the public sphere, that we examined earlier. It does so with a new twist, injecting into the analytical framework the necessity of creativity in interaction. Difficult as Benjamin's notion of aura is to grasp, it serves to address the mysterious power of those moments in which our active intelligence and emotional perspicacity are engaged by, and engage with, a communication, an interaction, that we denote as artistic. Despite its imprecision, it captures the process—I would argue—much more effectively than empiricist audience studies have been able to do. Benjamin's dissolution of art into media does not evacuate art of its punch.[10]

We must now move from the absorbing question of radical media aesthetics to the intensely mundane but absolutely unavoidable question of radical media organization. This is a jump-cut only because we are used to notions of art as the lofty work of the lone genius.[11] Some of the longer case studies in Part III examine this aspect of radical media at length, both because the issue must be addressed head-on and not be skirted and with a view to making sure that the wheel does not have to be reinvented by every new radical media project. For a number of the more short-run radical communication examples in Part II, these questions are of less relevance, but for ongoing radical media, they are intensely significant.

NOTES

1. In fact, they generally wrote as though the affluent nations in which they lived were the only ones that existed, and if they did break their silence to speak of Vietnam or Cuba, it was often as a convenient metaphor for revolt.

2. Perhaps the most famous of them. The reference to cobblestones is to the form of paving of Paris' streets in some areas at the time; to the fact that they were dug up during the May-June upsurge to hurl at the police, whose brutality against protestors was merciless; and to the fact that simultaneously with driving off the forces of repression, the earth beneath emerged to view and suggested, in a sideways slippage, sunning and enjoying oneself "doing nothing" at the seaside. The fusion of protest and pleasure was exactly symptomatic of situationist philosophy.

3. This one has a long history. A version was popular in radical London taverns by the close of the 18th century.

4. Instances cited by Plant (1992, pp. 86-89, 148-149) include altering comic strips, creating public provocations such as installing an unofficial Santa Claus in a department store at Christmas to give out free gifts, and altering public notices with interspersed graffiti.

5. As Walker (1983, p. 70) among others has pointed out, the translation in *Illuminations* of the title words of Benjamin's essay—"technischer Reproduzierbarkeit"—as "mechnical reproduction," fogs the sense of his essay. He was not writing about art and industry in general.

6. The term aura was common at that time in the many German literary circles influenced by the art-for-art's-sake poet Stefan George but carried a foggy mystical and spiritual sense, almost like the notion of *numen*. Benjamin used it differently, as we shall see, and not always consistently.

7. The example he draws from the contemplation of peaceful nature (a mountain range, a branch casting its shadow over the onlooker) has perhaps suggested, inappropriately, that this kind of aura is a positive one.

8. The finely illustrated catalog edited by Antonowa and Merkert (1995) provides a whole series of essays examining the multiple artistic links between Berlin and Moscow in particular, during the first three decades of the 20th century. They were years of extraordinary political and cultural ferment in both nations and especially in both capitals. The essays trace the interconnections between the Expressionist and dada movements, constructivism (as interpreted in both locations), and still other artistic currents and phases. One of the signal features of the connection in both countries was the frequent overlap between politics and art. Another was the conscious interpenetration of artistic forms, not only between traditionally separate disciplines such as architecture and theater design but also between established art forms such as painting and sculpture, and technologies that were simple to access, new or old, from still photography to woodcuts. All this was in considerable measure the matrix from which sprang much of Benjamin's thinking about art and communication, reviewed in Chapter 4. (For a review of Berlin's socialist and communist cultural activity in the 1920s, which traces its influence over Brecht's work, see Bodek, 1997). The implications of the period in terms of *agitprop* art and the dynamics of socialist evangelism was taken up in Chapter 6. But as I noted earlier in this chapter, the ebullience of radical alternative cultures in Germany was not strong enough to withstand the murderous onset of Nazism, nor could the dynamism of Soviet cultural experiment survive the descent into Stalinism. The later essays in Antonowa and Merkert's (1995) volume address these grim histories.

9. And in retrospect, a tragedy beyond description, not least in view of the horrors befalling Soviet Russia only a year or so following Benjamin's 1926-1927 visit to Moscow.

10. I am not a boxing or martial arts enthusiast, but readers finding the metaphor distasteful might recall that these performances are highly interactive and, at advanced levels, quite the opposite to pugilistic.

11. An older English expression—"from the sub-lime[y] to the gor-blimey"—expresses the irony in the character of this transition. But the connection must be forged and held on to tenaciously.

6

Radical Media Organization: Two Models

- The Leninist model and its influence: context, strengths, perils, and its absolute corruption
- The self-management model, socialist and feminist anarchism, and prefigurative politics

The best-known radical media organizational model of the 20th century, regrettably, was the Leninist one, often characterized as the transmission-belt model because it served solely and simply to transmit the party elite's priorities and perspectives of the moment. Its regrettable character derives not so much from all of its inherent characteristics as from the fact that it was enshrined in international communist party lore through much of the 20th century as the definitive, scientific form for both pre- and postrevolutionary media. Had communist parties not undergone the transition to taking state power and clinging on to it,[1] the model's longevity could simply have stood as a monument to inertia, but historically, it had huge and altogether malign political and cultural consequences.[2]

Nonetheless, the origins of the model need understanding. Its original baking was under tsarist political repression, in which oppositional media activists who did not choose to operate clandestinely and with a certain level of organizational discipline to communicate against the regime were ripe candidates for prison life in Siberia, or worse.

Now, to neglect those realities as regard the Leninist model is only to commit a historical faux pas. But to ignore that certain regimes harshly punish the expression of dissent, let alone its organization, is pure idiocy. Under those conditions, something approaching the Leninist model, whatever it may be called, approaches common sense. My example of choice to support this argument is the highly conservative Polish Catholic hierarchy during the decades of Soviet domination. Parish organizations in those days were under the strict and unique control of the parish priest, precisely to avoid their infiltration by the secret police. As a general model of religious organization for all situations, the Polish Catholic Church was distinctly antidemocratic. But, in that particular context, this rigid hierarchy was valuable, a defensive necessity. Examples from Argentina, Chile, Bolivia, China, and other nations that have experienced shorter or longer periods of dictatorship vindicate this argument.

AGITPROP AND THE LENINIST MODEL

One further comment is in order on the Leninist model, namely, on agitprop—an abbreviation for the combination of short-term information tactics to bring immediate abuses and problems to public notice (agitation) and longer-term political communication strategies (propaganda) to shape the hearts and minds of the public in a coherently Marxist-Leninist direction. People who grew up within the Soviet or Chinese Communist experience generally had an almost emetic reaction to agitprop, both as a word and as a practice. Its grossly manipulative and contrived characteristics required a very strong stomach to tolerate, especially year after year.[3]

However, it is important to try to see past the huge and systematic corruption of this approach over the decades of the Soviet era and to realize that the original basic insight has validity for crisis situations, moments in which an either-or situation is widely acknowledged as inescapable. In Chapter 12, for example, we review the work of ACT-UP in organizing in-your-face demonstrations and posters to force attention to the AIDS crisis. The extreme urgency welling out of that movement resonated strikingly with the intense urgency of those convinced and self-sacrificing socialist activists who risked their freedom and their lives against the tsar, against Hitler, against Mussolini, against Franco, against Stalinist dictators, against Salvadoran death squads, against the apartheid regime in South Africa. The commitment to act, to risk everything, if necessary, to persuade as many as possible to join the movement before time runs out, before the opportunity is lost, can be (and was) manipulated, was an opportunity for macho heroics. But, at the same time, it stands for some of the most magnificent political instincts and priorities history offers for our consideration. The 29 years South African leader Nelson Mandela spent in jail will stand as an instance.

For Lenin, activists' involvement in immediate struggles was only a stage along the way to realizing his vision of a comprehensive revolution under scientific Bolshevik control. To us, with the 20th century behind us, his tightly unified vision seems somewhere between simplistic and alarming. But the positive dynamism of developing movements for change, the communicative agitation work involved, need not be harnessed to a rigid formula for unified global change. It does make every sense, however, for radical media to be organized within at least a provisional overall strategy and not to be purely and simply the product of instantaneous emotion. In that carefully restricted sense of *agitation* and *propaganda*, it is worth rescuing the categories, if not the words themselves, to guide our thinking concerning roles for radical alternative media.[4]

THE SELF-MANAGEMENT TRADITION

A radically different model of organizing such media is offered by the self-management tradition, namely, one where neither party, nor labor union, nor church, nor state, nor owner is in charge, but where the newspaper or radio station runs itself. Simpson Grinberg (1986b), in a review of Latin American alternative media experience, urges careful consideration of this alternative to the received Leninist model. The structures of democratic self-governance in these media vary widely, however. Let us examine them further.

Perhaps one of the best known instances internationally in the latter part of the 20th century was the French daily newspaper of record—certainly not a radical alternative outlet—*Le Monde*. Another French newspaper, which later moved to a typical organizational hierarchy among mainstream media but began as a self-managed entity in the hectic aftermath of the 1968 turmoil in France, was *Libération* (Samuelson, 1978).[5] Germany's *Die Tageszeitung* is yet another case in point (Downing, 1988a, pp. 172-175). The detailed Italian, Portuguese, and *samizdat* case studies in Part III provide further instances.

Media run on this model are much more likely to be small-scale than large, for perhaps obvious reasons. There is a standard danger that, although they may be highly democratic internally, they may become politically insulated from the ongoing push and pull of social life, a little self-sustaining oligarchy. Jakubowicz (1993) rightly critiques the notion of media self-management as an automatically democratic form, noting that ownership of a newspaper or radio station in collective hands only guarantees the expression of that collective's positions, not those of the entire public. For self-managed media to evince a fully democratic character, it is indeed vital for their internal democracy to be constantly responsive to the democratic trends and movements in society at large. That interrelation is very complex, as our case studies will often demonstrate. Furthermore, the definition of what constitutes internal democracy is sometimes taken as axiomatic, and this, too, we shall see was a problem in a number of instances. Nonetheless, some notions of self-governing media structures have much to commend themselves as a strategy for radical alternatives.

A SOCIALIST ANARCHIST ANGLE OF VISION

Let us explore some issues here a little further, once again with the aid of a socialist anarchist angle of vision. A point at which anarchism raises vital issues bypassed by Marxism, and once more with a direct bearing on media democracy, is the related questions rather of intellectuals, culture, education, and the Marxist-Leninist political party. In his Marxist critique of Soviet bloc society, *The Alternative,* Rudolf Bahro, for years a political oppositionist in sovietized East Germany, cites the anarchist Bakunin, who wrote as early as 1873 about the results of Marxist theory if put into political practice. The result will be, said Bakunin,

> a despotism of the governing minority . . . But this minority, say the Marxists, will consist of workers. Certainly . . . of former workers, who

> however as soon as they have become representatives or governors of the people, cease to be workers and look down on the whole common workers' world from the height of the state. They will no longer represent the people, but themselves and their pretensions to people's government . . . a new privileged scientific political class. (cited in Bahro, 1978, pp. 40-41)

Bakunin had an extraordinarily prescient understanding of Marxism's potential to be harnessed as an ideology of a new elite, ruling in the name of the exploited and claiming the mantle of science. Its scientific political supremacy constituted its right to dictate, based on that effortlessly "transcendent correctness which Leninism implies" (Rowbotham, 1981, p. 47) and which enshrines the Leninist definition of alternative media as transmission belt for the party elite's "correctness."

However, the correctness phenomenon is not only enshrined in Leninist parties but also may emerge in self-managed radical media. As we shall see in Part III, divisions often play themselves out, sometimes very destructively, between media-activist staffers with considerable formal education and cultural capital, often possessed of the great self-confidence and verbal skills these bring, and the technicians, printers, bookkeepers, receptionists, and secretaries who are also essential to the operation. On top of these class divisions, gender quite often enters the picture, in that the lesser jobs are often a women's preserve. To cap off the problem, these sources of stress quite often go unaddressed within self-managed media collectives, rendering the divisions more destructive still. Jo Freeman's (1975, pp. 199-129) famous observations of "the tyranny of structurelessness"—describing the emergence of potent hierarchies in feminist discussion groups in the shadow of the denial of hierarchy—might have been framed with many self-managed radical media in mind. The central issue is that, whatever egalitarian ideology they espouse, and whichever gender is theirs, intellectuals' class experience often leads them to assume they are destined to lead.[6]

A final aspect of anarchism's angle of vision that I wish to discuss here is prefigurative politics, the attempt to practice socialist principles in the present, not merely to imagine them for the future. Self-managed media represent one such project. Wieck (1979) puts it this way:

> Anarchism proposes the *continuous realization* of freedom in the lives of each and all, both for its intrinsic and immediate values and for its more remote effects, the latter unpredictable because they depend on

> the unpredictable behavior of persons not known and of non-personal historical processes. (p. 144)

Porter (1979) adds to this the following dimension:

> Any liberated areas, however limited, are a challenge to the capitalist order. The challenge lies in their visceral resistance to and struggle against the system, and in their offering time and space for potentially less sublimated behaviors. . . . Such zones sustain the energies of militants. (pp. 223-224)

As Rowbotham (1981) puts it, the vision of a just and culturally enhanced society "cannot be separated from the process of its making" (p. 17), and politics must in some measure provide staging posts along the way, moments of transformation, however small.[7]

For anarchism, however, it has normally been enough to attempt to create little islands of prefigurative politics with no empirical attention to how these might ever be expanded into the rest of society. Example has often been considered sufficient. What is needed is a recognition of the many areas of life that are political (as opposed to conventional Marxism's privileging of the economic), together with the most painstaking, unremitting search as to how prefigurative politics can expand beyond its islands (as opposed to anarchism).

Summary: There are important reasons why radical media cannot simply preach correct principles, enable needed debate, expose hidden operations of the power structure, defend against abuses, and be aesthetically stimulating. They also need to be organized in ways that promote developmental power within their own ranks, that develop participation in all decisions by historically extruded groups, so that thereby on every level, they help the islands become an archipelago. This is not to say there is a simple, single, or uniquely successful model of self-management for radical media. We shall see a great variety of models at work in Parts II and III. But the democracy of social movements has to be expressed in the democratic organization of radical media, at the same time that they bring a completely realistic approach to the practicalities of bringing out a daily newspaper or organizing a radio station that broadcasts 24 hours a day. Sifting the benefits of professionalism from its retrograde mystique—journalistic objectivity, film-editing principles, editorial rules—is an important component of this task.

Not easy on low wages and long hours, as we shall see. But amazingly yeasty.

NOTES

1. This transition, and the role of artists during it and in some instances working to achieve it, is a very important one to grasp. There were continuities as well as ruptures between the "wild" phase of art in the Soviet Union from some years before the 1917 revolutions and during the 1920s, and Stalinist socialist-realist state art. Taken together, the willingness among Western leftists to attribute utopian achievements to the early Soviet Union, and the early Soviet artistic avant-garde's equal readiness to see itself as at the pinnacle of artistic achievement (with a kind of mystical claim to a proletarian-revolutionary seal of approval), combined with its undoubted distance from popular cultural forms, all served to confuse the issues at stake tremendously. In that fog, the actual downward slide toward Stalinism became obscured to many artists and activists. For example, Soviet constructivism shaded into reverence for industrial technology as such and then gradually, in the case of some of its proponents, into commitment to Stalin's 5-year plans for industrialization, with the indescribable treatment of many tens of millions of peasant farmers as the plans' inexorable condition. Artists' distance from the public became an excuse to harness that public forcibly to the Soviet state's priorities. Meanwhile, in the West, loyalty to the Soviet Union became pivotal to the Left's fragmentation and its consequent weakness in the face of fascism—and these struggles were fought out among the Left in the artistic arena as well as in the street. The artistic realm did not cause these defeats, but nor did it really succeed in transcending the issues or pointing to other credible options. The issues are a great deal more complex than this short summary: see Koljasin (1995), Chochlowa (1995), Gregor and Klejman (1995), Graeve (1995), Hoffmann (1995), and Adkins (1995); Gleason, Kenez, and Stites (1985); Fitzpatrick (1978); Guérin (1965); Orwell (1952).

2. Simpson Grinberg (1986b) and Huesca and Dervin (1994) both note the widespread influence of the model in Latin America from the 1960s through the 1980s.

3. Socialist-realist art, laughable from a distance, was a part of agitprop. At the same time, there is an argument that the Soviet authorities were not interested in persuasion so much as setting clearly defined and inescapable markers that warned potential dissidents from articulating their thoughts (Benn, 1989, pp. 42, 84, 172; Sinyavsky, 1990).

4. As Strigaljow (1995) has noted of the 1910s and early 1920s,

> Agitprop developed a specific artistic language that in many respects was common to German and Russian artists: dynamic, of great expressiveness, rich in contrasts, poster-based—plain and straightforward, in order to provoke, indeed even to shock, the spectator. Agitational

> art had a great influence over the character and language of the whole of 20th century art . . . through the bold use of technical formats (photography, photomontage, typography, film, radio and others), through startling syntheses of new and traditional artistic genres, the active alliance of representation and text, the elevation of works constructed for a fleeting purpose and of one-time artistic engagements to the ranks of works of art. And finally through the creation of a gigantic fund of utopian projects, plans, ideas, etc. (p. 117)

Strigaljow's observations should be read in conjunction with my remarks on art and alternative media above, and the discussions of Brecht (Chapter 5) and of Grosz, Heartfield, Kollwitz and others in Chapter 14.

5. The official policy of self-management in former Yugoslavia, which also extended to media (Robinson, 1977), was often taken as a hopeful beacon for a nonauthoritarian governance model within the Left at that time, mostly in naive ignorance of the ways in which the League of Communists—the title of the communist party—called virtually all the shots that were worth calling, as opposed to the self-management councils. The monstrous ethnic cleansing policies by the Serbian and Croatian governments during the 1990s were precisely enabled by the ruthless authoritarianism inherent in the former Yugoslav state structures that they turned into separate regimes.

6. To be one of Gramsci's organic intellectuals demands much more in self-awareness than simply the words.

7. The notion of "anti-politics" formed by Polish, Czech, and Hungarian activists in opposition to their sovietized regimes during the 1970s and 1980s was analogous; namely, the establishment of alternative public spheres in which people behaved normally, that is, as though they were not living under repressive legislation that choked off their right to speak or organize politically against the regime. Although on one level the notion was abstract and utopian, in practice, it gave direction and legitimacy to their struggles (cf. Downing, 1996, p. 23).

7

Religion, Ethnicity, and the International Dimension

We have far from exhausted the issues that need weaving into a satisfactory framework for analyzing radical media. We could address many such with profit, not least how these media relate to such deep divisions as language, gender, age, sexuality, ecology, but for now, we will leave these to further research. Those we will begin to grapple with in this chapter are the religious, the ethnic, and the international dimensions of the topic, a rich enough diet for the moment.

RELIGION

Without claim to comprehensiveness, we will examine

- Radical media expression of explicit religiously based challenges to the political order
- Subterranean religious contestation of the status quo
- Attacks on religious endorsement of an unjust order

In religiously saturated cultures and subcultures, the impact when popular struggles claim divine endorsement is hard to overestimate. From millennialism[1] to self-defense,[2] from land rights[3] to the very forms of religious expression itself, the sense that there is a morally superior force that acknowledges the truth of your plight and its rank injustice discourages despair and sometimes encourages resistance. Marx is often cited as referring to religion as "the opiate of the people," but critics and followers alike typically forget that in the very same paragraph he also describes it as "the heart of a heartless world."[4] E. P. Thompson (1993, pp. 106-114), in his remarkable study of the context of William Blake's radicalism, has an absolutely brilliant discussion of the radical implications of the antinomian heretical culture of Blake's day.

Let us review two instances of the explicitly religious framing of political injustice and its articulation via radical media. They are drawn from the English Civil War of the 1640s and the revolutionary movement against the Shah of Iran in the 1970s.

Some of the worst fears of the ruling classes in regard to the vernacular Bible were fully realized during the English Civil War. Although the eventual outcome of that revolutionary period ended with satisfaction for the gentry and the merchants, various groups such as the Diggers, the Ranters, and the Levellers, vociferously advocated an economic system that would favor poor farmers and a political order that would embrace justice. They repeatedly used the Bible to justify their rage against the despotism of landowners and their government. In 1649, we find Gerrard Winstanley, one of their leaders, writing a pamphlet that echoes today's liberation theology:

> If you would find true majesty indeed, go among the poor despised ones of the earth . . . These great ones are too stately houses for Christ to dwell in; he takes up his abode in a manger, in and amongst the poor in spirit and despised ones of the earth. (cited in Hill, 1975, p. 38)

Still more trenchant was Abiezer Coppe, one of the Ranters' leaders, who, speaking in God's name, addressed this indictment to the powerful:

> Thou hast many bags of money, and behold I (the Lord) come as a thief in the night, with my sword drawn in my hand, and like a thief as I am—I say deliver your purse, deliver sirrah! deliver or I'll cut thy throat. I say (once more) deliver, deliver my money . . . to rogues, thieves, whores and cutpurses, who are flesh of thy flesh, and every

> whit as good as thyself in mine eye . . . Have ALL THINGS common, or else the plague of God will rot and consume all you have. (cited in Hill, 1975, p. 211)

Sreberny-Mohammadi and Mohammadi (1994) have studied in detail the role of alternative media and religion in the 1979 overthrow of the Shah of Iran, through a popular revolt led in large part by Shi'ite fundamentalists such as the exiled Ayatollah Khomeini.[5] Khomeini's sermons from exile on audiocassettes[6] were effectively diffused through pre-existing religious networks inside Iran. The message in them was basic and binary: "Death to the Shah!" and "Bring Khomeini home!"[7] The Shah stood for corruption, not only in his unashamed public luxury but equally in culture (his pro-Western stance); his followers were "tie-wearers," infatuated with the West; and his secular Marxist opponents, considerable in number, were bluntly written off as "godless." In contrast, Khomeini was portrayed as ascetic, ready for martyrdom for the sake of Islam and Iran, and consistently radical. Islam, rather than socialism, was seen as offering true democracy and justice. Political commitment to these goals was every Muslim's religious duty, if need be to the point of martyrdom; the aim was to install an Islamic republic (Sreberny-Mohammadi & Mohammadi, 1994, pp. 114-115). The low levels of literacy and the absence of any tradition of public debate under the Shah or before him made it all the easier to mobilize masses of people through these audiocassettes with their intensely simple, religiously validated messages.

We may well have more sympathy with the revolution that failed in 17th-century Britain than with the one that succeeded in 20th-century Iran. Nevertheless, the religious content of radical media was a vital aspect of the process in both cases.[8]

Examples of the more subterranean expression of contestation in religious terms are to be found after the colonization of the Americas, from both Africans and Indians.

Enslaved African Americans transformed traditional Christian teachings. According to Genovese (1975, pp. 161-284), two such trans formations are visible. One had a clear relation to millennialism, namely, the fusion that often took place between the figures of Moses, a secular liberator, and Jesus, a purely other worldly liberator (his role within the canons of orthodox Christianity). Thus, implicitly, future redemption not only was spiritual, it also bespoke the end of slavery. Closely related in ideological terms but drawn from separate and very ancient African roots was the absence of the doctrine of original sin.[9] This is nowhere a tenet of traditional African religions, which are generally world affirming, but in the Americas, its absence among African Americans was particularly significant. Beginning with St. Augustine of Hippo in the 5th century CE, who formally codified the doctrine of original sin, Christian theologians repeatedly used it as an explanation and thus justification of slavery (Davis, 1970, pp. 104-108, 187-209, 221-235). Their reasoning was that the institution of slavery, like other tribulations of social existence, was a divine punishment for Adam and Eve's first sin.

Thus, without fanfare, an African reverse colonization of Christian doctrine emerged, one that disputed the very foundations of the religious endorsement of slavery. This is not to say the process was organized or universal in scope. Many black preachers were forced under extreme duress to urge their congregations to obey and honor their masters. Some may have been ready to do so anyway. Others provided different messages in public and in private. Nonetheless, a religious framework widely presumed by the planter class to justify the status quo was frequently transformed into its opposite (cf. Levine, 1977, pp. 5-80; Sobel, 1979).[10]

A more contested instance of transformative processes may be seen in the history of the figure of the Virgin of Guadalupe in Mexico and the southwestern United States (Lafaye, 1985; Rodriguez, 1994). This devotion[11] closely merges Indian and European traditions of Mary's representation. On the one hand, devotion to the Virgin Mary was a direct cultural import of the Spanish conquest. At the same time, many of the features of the picture at the center of the cult are distinctively Indian, not European. Not only is the shrine located at the precise point where Tonantzin, the Náhuatl mother goddess, had her shrine before the conquest, but the dress and facial appearance of the woman portrayed either are Indian or have even been altered over time in the direction of Indianizing—or re-Indianizing—her. Examples of original or added features include the dark skin of the face and the Virgin's hands, which are in an Indian style of offering rather than poised and clasped in the standard Catholic mode; those fingers have also been shortened to approximate more closely Indian finger size. The Virgin has a small flower beneath her belt tassle, which was a Náhuatl symbol for the sun god and a feature of the Aztec calendar. Furthermore, the stars, the sun rays, and the moon in the picture all allude to Náhuatl lore, as does the turquoise color of her mantle.

Obviously, these changes were made by the Spanish colonial hierarchy, not by mestizos or Indians, albeit in response to a need to legitimize their rule. They represent in a certain sense a dialogue between colonizer and colonized. However, determining with any precision what these elements have signaled over the centuries to the Virgin's adherents is virtually impossible. Rodriguez (1994) found that, with the single exception of her skin color, many contemporary Mexican American women were unaware of most of these features—but skin color is no small point of identification, politically ambiguous as it may be. Some analysts would argue that Tonantzin was more colonized in the process, more eviscerated of her original significance, than the Virgin Mary. Others would incline in the opposite direction. It may be, too, that the figure has had a shifting significance. Certainly, her picture has been carried in political demonstrations. These fused images leave open a series of possibilities for audiences to explore, not a fixed and final imprint of the supremacy of Spanish religious culture, of the Spaniards' understanding of the sacred.[12]

Antireligious expression in radical media also needs some comment in this discussion. When religion, as so often happens, is used to endorse the status quo, blasphemy may be a radical political contestation, not merely a fart in the face of the faithful. Wood (1994) notes how at the outset of the 19th century, the British and Foreign Bible Society was founded to diffuse popular pamphlets to bring about "*the sterilization and control of the Bible* [italics added] for consumption by the lower orders . . . a sanitized version of the scriptures which would encourage obedience and trust in the existing Establishment" (p. 107). At that time, the British ruling class legally equated blasphemy with sedition, so that the Bible Society's efforts represented a preventive ideological strategy, supplementing the court's purely punitive approach.

One of the British establishment's most persistent critics in this regard was William Hone, who was possessed of a "radical hatred for the Church in its role as an organ for state control of the poor" (Wood, 1994, p. 110) and who produced a huge array of parodies of religious and political hypocrisy. An example of the former is this version of the Pater Noster, directed at members of Parliament:

> "Our Lord who art in the Treasury, whatsoever be thy name, thy power be prolonged, thy will be done throughout the empire, as it is in each session. Give us our usual sops, and forgive us our occasional absences or divisions; as we promise not to forgive those that divide

> against thee. Turn us not out of our places; but keep us in the House of Commons, the land of Pensions and Plenty; and deliver us from the People. Amen. (cited in Thompson, 1968, p. 792)[13]

A different example, not authored by Hone, was the public attack in pamphlets and flyers on the "arsebishop," that is, the then Archbishop of Canterbury, who had been accused of sexually molesting some boys (McCalman, 1988, p. 213). The lines between pornography, politics, and, no doubt, homophobia were blurred here, but it represents nonetheless a clear example of the determination to go for the jugular in the attack on reverend hypocrites whose chief function was as servants of power and who used that power to try to cover up their misdeeds. The discussion of pornographic radical media in Part II illustrates this point further.

Summary: Religious dimensions of power, therefore, have had and will continue to have considerable practical import for radical media. Secular research that is blinded by its secularism into neglecting this leaves a significant lacuna. Reduction of the problems confronting radical media to a capitalism-state dyad makes for a damaging oversimplification.

ETHNICITY

Again without claim to comprehensiveness, we will address:

- Ethnicity and racism: defining the terrain
- Minority-ethnic media: their multiple dimensions

Ethnicity is an overdetermined zone. Historically speaking, ethnicity has served as a shifting signifier whose reach, destructiveness, and tenacity in racialized social formations are in no way softened—indeed, sometimes made more effective because adaptive—by this instability. Ethnicity often acts as a pivotal element in the formation of radical media and the communication of resistance, but like religion, its roles have sometimes been sidelined. Simpson Grinberg (1986b) explicitly challenged this sidelining in the Latin America context: "The problem is to capture the social communication reality of a continent that is peasant and pluricultural" (p. 180). His observation was especially pertinent given the overwhelming tendency within the Latin American Left of the

1950s through the 1970s to homogenize Latin Americans as uniformly Latin, not indigenous or African, and as a virtual proletariat mystically unified in opposition to U.S. imperialism, economic and cultural.

The latter decades of the 20th century, with their accelerating transfer of farming families to metropolitan areas, often across national borders and even continents, have led to an explosion of what might be termed ethnic media (cf. Riggins, 1992). Yet, such media circulate within at least three different sectors, namely, indigenous nations and communities, recent migrants as in the example cited, and settled subordinate ethnic groups. Examples of the first sector would be indigenous Americans from the Mapuche to the Inuit; Berbers in northwestern Africa; Australian aboriginals; and tribal peoples in India, Russia, and the Nordic nations. Of the third, Asian, Caribbean, Jewish, and Arab[14] communities in Britain; Turkish communities in Germany; Algerian communities in France; people of African heritage in the United States and Brazil.

Determining the radicalism of media that emerge from or address these publics must be done case by case, and doing so may require contextual information. For example, Seubert (1987) points out that Native American videos concentrating on cultural issues—apparently apolitical—are totally misunderstood if divorced from their context, in which cultural survival is a desperate political priority.[15] By contrast, in research on Spanish-language media in New York City during the 1980s (Downing, 1992), I found that they were mostly owned by profit-oriented Anglo firms, the major exception to this rule being a weekly newspaper ultimately controlled by a Korean ultra-rightist religious empire (Reverend Moon's Unification Church). Certainly, none of these media seriously set themselves the task of voicing the economic or other demands of the immigrant Latino communities that constituted at least a quarter of the metropolitan region's population, many of them among its most desperately poor communities. By contrast, again, Rodríguez (1999) discusses the role of "TV Spanish" on *Noticiero Univisión*, the main U.S. Spanish-language TV news and suggests that in shedding identifiable accents (Mexican, Caribbean, Central or South American) to appeal to the widest audience, it is perhaps slowly fostering a certain pan-Latino ethnic identity within the United States.

These three instances give some notion of the complexity of minority ethnic media. To add to the brew, we should consider musical cultures and forms of religious expression specific to minority ethnic groups (e.g., Khosrokhavar, 1997; Limón, 1992). These may, along with language and dialect, act as a media force somewhere between shock absorption and psychic validation in the often fraught atmosphere between the ethnic majority and ethnic minorities. Use of VCRs by recent immigrants, whether by Asians in Britain (Husband & Chouhan, 1985) and the United States or by Turks in Germany or by many other comparable groups elsewhere, to watch films and news of the homeland has a similar role. At the same time, as Gillespie (1995) found in her study of London Asian teenagers and as Lloréns (1994) found with teenage children of recent Quechua migrants from the Peruvian interior, the cultural conservatism of such media often fails to meet the needs of a younger generation with shallow roots in their parents' birthplaces. The second category—of recent migrants—inexorably leaches over time into the third, the settled subordinate group.

In short, the sprawling and expanding world of minority ethnic media—properly speaking, most media are ethnic—offers an array of examples that are as diverse as mainstream media. Radical instances are only one facet within the category, and even then, as we have seen, the content may well need contextualizing if an ethnic outsider is to grasp its subversive import. Furthermore, the import may be counterhegemonic in one direction, locked into the prevailing hegemony in another.

An illuminating example of this split direction is the Afro-Brazilian glossy magazine *Raça,* which took black Brazilian readers by storm when it first appeared in 1996, doubling its sales from 100,000 to 200,000 in the first week, despite its high cover price. It was the first such magazine specifically to address itself to Afro-Brazilian readers, and in a context in which the assertion of Africanity had been officially despised and even actively repressed except within a strictly religious, traditionalistic framework (cf. Hanchard, 1995; Stam, 1998). *Raça* offered a long overdue media endorsement of an Afro-Brazilian identity and status. At the same time, its photography and advertising policies were similar to *Ebony*'s, featuring light-skinned models and promoting hair-straightening and skin-lightening products.

Summary: Of course, there are many examples of much more assertive and radical minority ethnic media that have promoted rights, reclaimed histories that had been officially obscured, and exposed and attacked racist abuses. But given the tenacity of racism and ethnic discrimination, the radical media counterattack generally takes a variety of forms and operates at a variety of levels. All of them need analysis and debate (See, among others, Barlow, 1999; Berry & Manning-Miller, 1996; Downing, 1990a; Noriega, 1992; Watkins, 1998).

GLOBAL DIMENSIONS

This signifies radical media communication across national frontiers, not the comparative dimension.

- Clandestine media
- Combatting transnational media hegemony
- Cross-frontier migrant media
- International human rights campaigns

Examples of clandestine radical media operating across frontiers are numerous, including radio in Algeria's anticolonial insurgency, the audiocassettes smuggled into Iran to feed the movement against the Shah, books and cassettes smuggled into the former Soviet bloc countries, or in earlier centuries in Europe the smuggling of vernacular Bibles and Protestant literature or of critiques of the monarchy in the build-up to the French Revolution. In Part II, we shall return to all of these, as well as noting the cross-Atlantic communication networks of African sailors during the slavery era.

This clandestine activity represents only one international dimension of the issue. Jakubowicz (1993) argues that the explosion of transnational media corporations makes the contemporary task of achieving a democratic communication system in any given nation all the harder. Drew (1995) offers an analysis of how international communication strategies among labor groups have developed in the era of transnational corporations. Simpson Grinberg (1986b) critically reviews the tendency within radical media debates in Latin America to focus too intensively on the need to combat the transnational U.S. media onslaught, as though once a successful counterattack were launched, democratic media would prevail. This, he argues, understates the domestic forces in favor of media hierarchies.

Appadurai (1996), linking this topic and the previous one, offers a global framework within which to conceptualize international migrant media and argues that they are serving to refashion the world in unprecedented ways. Migration, now prominently including the "brain drain" as well as the transfer of more traditional agrarian, industrial, and service skills, has created vast numbers of people whose experiences have had to adjust to global as well as primordial realities. They have created numerous "diasporic public spheres" (pp. 21-23), especially within the brain-drain sector of labor (pp. 195-197). Appadurai stresses here the powerful fusion of media and interpersonal communication flows among migrants and between them and their communities of origin. He has the merit of having suggested a global framework within which to understand the migrant media phenomenon, although he does not pursue the radical dimension except in relation to diasporic support for insurgencies, such as the overseas Sikh campaign for a Sikh state, Khalistan, independent of India.[16]

A further dimension of radical international media is communication about human rights issues and abuses. Probably the most significant, decades-long international communication campaign, whose story to date has only been written in small part,[17] was in support of the struggle against apartheid in South Africa, which reached a watershed moment with the election of Nelson Mandela as South Africa's president in 1993. But our attention may also focus on the campaign against nuclear power, on the struggle for power in the last year of the Chilean Popular Unity period before the Pinochet/CIA coup, on the trampling of Palestinian territorial rights, on Mexican *maquiladoras*,[18] on the international traffic in human organs and in prostitution, and a whole host of other issues.[19]

Ford and Gil's Chapter 17 reviews international Internet uses by the Zapatista rebels in the state of Chiapas, Mexico, during the 1990s. The Zapatistas not only communicated for their own solidarity and self-defense, but also injected more general political issues into international debate concerning neoliberal and structural adjustment policies in parts of the Third World, questions of democracy in Mexico, and North American Free Trade Agreement/Tratado De Libro Comercio (NAFTA/TLC) policies. The Internet has opened up new possibilities for radical international media, although at the time of writing, affluent metropolitan nations still enjoy the greatest freedom of access to it.

Summary: The common image of radical media as local needs correcting. Neither historically nor currently does it stand scrutiny. Radical media have been, and are, a global as well as a local or regional force. At the same time, as Winseck's (1997) thorough review of international communication policies and paradigms clearly indicates, the World Trade Organization and other international agencies have framed legal and administrative scenarios in such a way as to disadvantage citizen media communication and to promote corporately organized media communication. Radical media, besides sometimes being global, also face organized global obstacles to their effective operation.

There remains one highly important dimension of radical media that demands separate attention, namely, media of the ultra Right. Their consideration amply demonstrates one of the theses of this book: the power that small-scale media can wield and the extreme folly of dismissing them. That the power such ultra-Right media wield is destructive and poisonous does not render it any the less potent.

NOTES

1. The belief that the world has become so unremittingly evil that God will very shortly intervene in outrage at the wickedness of his creation and call a final halt to the present world order. The rich and powerful will at last meet their just deserts, and the subjugated will be freed from their yoke. Some of the first expressions of this heavily politicized theology were seen in Judea nearly two centuries before the Christian era, when the Maccabees' guerrilla force rose up against Syrian and later Roman rule. Other examples have surfaced in the English working class movement in the later 18th and early 19th centuries (Thompson, 1968, pp. 52-55, 127-130, 420-428, 877-883), in the so-called cargo cults of colonized Melanesia after World War II (Worsley, 1968), and elsewhere.

2. A reading of *The Autobiography of Malcolm X* (1968) makes clear the extent to which, via the Nation of Islam in African American communities in the 1950s and 1960s, the Qur'an's endorsement of the right to self-defense was a vitally important message, given the caution and passivity of many (not all) black churches in the face of racist attacks and the general system of white supremacy.

3. In El Salvador in the 1980s, Catholic Bible study groups were one of the few locations in which issues of economic justice, land rights, and political rights could be addressed. It was not very long before these, too, became targets for military and extremist political forces, and violent retribution began to be meted out against farmers who took part in them. This repression also extended to the bishop of San Salvador, Oscar Romero, who one day after calling on the military to stop the killing was gunned down at the communion rail during Mass; to four American nuns and churchworkers, ambushed, raped, and murdered; and to six Salvadoran Jesuit priests, their housekeeper, and her

teenage daughter, who were liquidated by U.S.-trained commandos in a dawn raid on their presbytery in San Salvador.

Herman and Chomsky (1988) contrast the huge U.S. media attention to the brutal murder of a political activist priest in Soviet-era Poland with the virtual silence on the scores of clergy, nuns, and religious workers in Latin America liquidated during the same decade. The disparity they quantify indicates that the Polish Catholic priest, in the judgment of U.S. media executives, was 100 times more worthy and noble and thus newsworthy than his fellow sufferers in Latin America. General Al Haig, Reagan's first secretary of state and a dedicated Catholic, was content publicly to opine that the four American nuns raped and murdered in El Salvador had probably foolishly run a roadblock (Gettleman et al., 1981, 139-46). Politics clearly overwhelms piety or even plain honesty among such distinguished public servants.

4. "*Religious* distress is at the same time the *expression* of real distress and also the *protest* against real distress. Religion is the sigh of the oppressed creature, the heart of a heartless world, just as it is the spirit of spiritless conditions. It is the *opium* of the people." (Marx, 1975, p. 175)

5. The Shah was the ruler of Iran, installed in power following a CIA-sponsored coup in 1953 to protect access to Iran's cheap and plentiful oil supply. His combination of ostentatious and profligate spending, ruthless secret police, and avidly pro-Western policies led to massive alienation, which came to be voiced especially through the sermons of the zealot-scholar Khomeini, diffused from his exile home in France via audiocassettes to the Iranian public. (An ayatollah in Iranian Shi'ism is a scholar of Islam who has come to acquire major public renown for his sermons and writings.)

6. The role of audio- and videocassettes in the latter decades of the Soviet bloc will be noted in Chapter 22.

7. Darnton (1995) draws an analogous judgment on political agitation in France leading up to 1789.

> Instead of splitting the issues into hundreds of fragments, the pamphlets of 1787-88 simplified them. They presented the situation as a radical choice: for or against the government.. . . They provoked the drawing of lines; they helped to polarize public opinion . . . the great majority . . . reduced the issues to a single theme: despotism. (p. 245)

8. Even Methodism, now one of the more heavily respectable brands of Christianity, was once upon a time seen as dangerously subversive by many in positions of power. At the turn of the 18th into the 19th century, a number of British political dissidents were to be found under its banner, such as Robert Wedderburn, the Devil's Engineer. A fiery preacher of African and English descent, Wedderburn ran one of the dissenting chapels of the period in London. It was relatively easy to get a license for these chapels, because, for the authorities, there were no clear means of differentiating between purely religious chapels and politically active ones. This reflected the fact that these chapels were not fronts for secular political activity but public spaces in which heterodox religious beliefs and radical politics were inextricably intertwined (McCalman, 1988, pp. 128-151). "Their rhetoric," McCalman comments, "drew

heavily on allusive traditional symbols, motifs and beliefs, disregarding most literary sources or authorities apart from the Bible" (p. 140).

9. The doctrine teaches that humans have universally inherited an inescapable proclivity to commit wrongdoing from the supposed misdeeds of Adam and Eve, the mythical forebears of humanity.

10. The rich examples from *vodun, santería, camdomblé, umbanda* in the Caribbean and Brazil are powerful testimony to this process, although there is no space to explore them here.

11. Its contemporary prevalence was underscored to me by a friend in the Communication Department at the Instituto Tecnológico in Monterrey, Dr José Carlos Lozano, who humorously characterized Mexican religious culture by saying "we are Guadalupan atheists."

12. See further the illuminating discussion in Bonfil Batalla (1996, pp. 132-144), who proposes that Indian cultural priorities, although seemingly submerged, are far more dominant in Mexican life than many Mexicans would acknowledge.

13. Unusually among his contemporaries, Hone was very keenly informed of a whole series of Levellers' and Diggers' tracts from the time of the Civil War. He represented an important element of continuity in the British political tradition.

14. For some readers, the inclusion of Jewish groups in this list may come as a surprise. If so, they should interrogate their own understanding of racism. Even if Jewish communities in Britain are generally fairly comfortably off, and some of their members occupy distinguished positions throughout the professional, artistic, and business worlds, the Nazi Holocaust and the history of racism in general proves that no one—no one—is definitively secure. The constant desecrations of Jewish graves are only one pointer to the thinness of the ice.

15. For an extended and absorbing treatment of this question, see Leuthold (1998).

16. By the time of writing, this movement had subsided, but for a period during the 1970s and 1980s, it was extremely active and led to enormous violence, including the explosion of a passenger plane in mid-Atlantic, the bloody storming of the most sacred Sikh shrine in Amritsar, and the assassination of the Indian prime minister, Indira Gandhi, in retaliation.

17. Molete (1992) addresses radical video inside South Africa in the later 80s; Tomaselli and Louw (1991) and Switzer (1997) deal, respectively, with the radical press in the final era of apartheid and in earlier decades; and Schechter (1992) discusses the work of Globalvision, the New York-based video project, which regularly conveyed video documentaries to the world about the struggle against apartheid in the latter years of the regime.

18. Industrial centers close to the border with the United States that employ mostly women, in wretched conditions and for very low wages, in producing for the U.S. market.

19. Within the United States, some major distributors of these include California Newsreel in San Francisco, Facets Video in Chicago, and Documentary Associates in New York.

8

Repressive Radical Media

A significant issue so far left untouched is that of radical media in the service of repression. Some examples: in the Iranian revolution, the anti-Shah communiqués and audiocassettes, which did not merely denounce the Shah's regime but prepared the ground for Khomeini's; the big-character posters that Mao Zedong's legion of young supporters splashed over city after city, propping up his failing authority; the Nazi propaganda campaigns in the period before they were elected to power; the Ku Klux Klan's hate media; violent pornography. And what of the mass[1] of radical media that seek to propagate religious obscurantism (Kintz & Lesage, 1998), white racism, misogyny, homophobia, xenophobia, anti-Semitism, fascist or reactionary violence—using the Internet, computer games for young people, and shortwave radio among other media (Hilliard & Keith, 1999; Latham, 1999)? Do they simply mirror everything we have been talking about, but in reverse, repugnant and reactionary modes? The right methods and the wrong messages?

One prior counterquestion has to be posed: For those whose political home is in the center, equating radical media on the far Left and the ultra-Right represents a quick and easy political strike for themselves and in principle, therefore, flatulent fence-sitting, the cheap, automatic superiority of avoiding two extremes[2] and thereby any political engagement or risk for constructive change.

We will begin to address this disquieting issue with reference to

- The relevance of Macpherson's approach to power for defining these media
- Divergences among ultra-Right political movements
- The relation between the ultra-Right and the state
- Fascist social movements and authoritarian populism
- Stalinist radical media
- The edgy question of overlap and difference between democratic radical media and repressive radical media

Let us begin with the easiest and most obvious point distinguishing repressive radical media from democratic radical media. Macpherson's (1973) definition of developmental power, discussed in Chapter 4 as a hallmark of democracy, has a central place in evaluating ultra-Right media. Such media not only fail to enhance but actually maim the public's ability to develop its powers. Neither critical reflection nor any genuine increase in personal or collective freedom are on the radar screen of such media. This is fundamental.

VARIATION ON THE ULTRA RIGHT

The second point is also important. Neither the ultra-Right nor its media should be homogenized. Throughout the 19th and 20th centuries, and undoubtedly in the 21st, we see religious, racist, reactionary, modernizing, elitist, and populist trends within the ultra-Right. Between each current, the capacity for vicious infighting is at least as well developed as on the far Left. To take one example within the ultra-Right that shows how carefully we need to understand it, the Unification Church of the Reverend Moon has long emphasized the transcending of all racial and ethnic boundaries within its ranks. It offers no foaming claims of Jewish conspiracies, no genocidal tirades against African Americans and Mexican Americans.

To those focused on the Ku Klux Klan and its ilk, this may come not only as a surprise but as a relief ("they're quite mild, relatively")—but a relief only so long as class and environmental exploitation and oppressive religious dogmas are not also thought to be lethal dangers to the common good. And so long as, by not thinking the issue through very carefully, we equate the ability of Moonies to learn not to be racist to each other with a campaign against institutionalized racism.

The third point restates a vexed question, namely, the nature of the relation between ultra-Right movements and groups and the power structure. For some, the ultra-Right is a stalking horse for the power structure. For others, it is a Trojan horse that the power structure welcomes at a time of crisis because it mistakenly thinks it can control it (a standard interpretation of the rise of German and Italian fascism). For others again, to focus much on the ultra-Right is a diversion from the real threat, that is, the repressive power of the state, its policies, police, and prisons. For still others, the energy and terrorist capacity of the ultra-Right, quite often with strong international supporting links, is disturbing in itself. We cannot solve this dispute here, but I would suggest that much of it is situationally derived. Often, those who adhere to one or other view have a specific situation at the back of their mind that most closely fits their opinion, whereas in actuality, the history of the ultra-Right provides grist to all four of these mills.

FASCISM AND RADICAL MEDIA

Fourth, the question of fascism and authoritarian populism[3] is an important one for analyzing radical media, because the factor that distinguishes fascism from military dictatorships and other autocracies is precisely that it began with a strong social base. It often expressed itself precisely as a social and political movement in the period before, during, and even after its assumption of state power. Both Italian and German fascism, in their earlier periods, had a quasi-socialist platform.[4] Repugnant as fascism is, our analysis can no more omit its social movement dimension than we can assume all radical media are somehow positive forces for good.

Now, it may be argued that fascism in the Italian, German, Spanish, and Portuguese versions of the period 1919-1975 is a dead duck and that a future fascism would look very different to the Nuremberg rallies and the Italian *squadristi.* Yet, although we may say *future,* the fact remains that there continues to be a strong populist current within the ultra-Right. It is also the case that in nations with a European-descended majority, white racism continues to be a powerfully unifying populist force, especially in situations of economic dislocation. Obvious illustrations during the 1990s were the success of Le Pen's *Front National* in France and Jörg Haider's Freedom Party in Austria. Regional autonomy movements such as the Northern League in Italy in the 1980s and 1990s, or the terrorist wing of the Basque movement in Spain in the same period, had very noticeable elements of mass support at times for their deeply xenophobic stances. Repressive Christian fundamentalist movements in the United States in the latter part of the 20th century have enjoyed equally substantial popular support. In Chile, as we noted in the Chapter 2 discussion of Gramsci, certain media—radio stations, comics, women's magazines—were used intensively by the ultra-Right in the latter period of the 1970-1973 Popular Unity government to develop mass opposition. As Mattelart (1974, p. 216f.) put it, this was Leninist mass agitation—by the ruling class.

Thus, in analyzing repressive radical media, we are compelled to give an account that engages with the vitality of authoritarian populism (Betz & Immerfall, 1998). Such political movements often appear to side with the underdog and, indeed, to portray themselves as the underdog. Mussolini used to rail against the plutocracy. Using everyday media, low-cost media, and simple forms of communication is a tactic embraced, not despised, by such movements. It is not a question of defining ultra-Right and far Left social movements or media as a unitary category, as mirrors of each other. It is, however, the need to understand all of them better, a question of reviewing those factors and mechanisms they happen to share and what it is that divides them. And this point is not merely a formal one, of comparing seemingly similar tactics. Given the numbers of communists in Germany and Italy in the 1920s who switched to the fascist side, 1990s French *lepenistes* who were formerly communist party members, and those of the 1980s Italian far Left who turned to terrorism in the Red Brigades, maintaining a vigilant lookout for commonalities is a necessary step toward self-critique for those social movements we deem constructive.

STALIN AND A MEDIA MODEL

This leads directly to the fifth point, which is that Stalinist radical media—as noted in Chapter 6's discussion of radical media organization—have to be acknowledged as skeletons in the far Left's closet. Evgenia Ginzburg (1967), caught up in Stalin's purges in the 1930s, ran into Klara, a German communist, in one jail:

> Klara lay down on the bed, turned over on her stomach and pulled up her skirt. Her calves and buttocks were covered with deep, hideous scars, as though wild beasts had been clawing at her flesh. Her lips tight in her swarthy face and her gray eyes flashing, she said hoarsely: "This is—Gestapo." Then she quickly sat up again and, stretching out both her hands, added: "This is NKVD." The nails of both her hands were deformed, the fingers blue and swollen . . . Klara, the ex-victim of the Gestapo, assured us that the [torture] implements used here must have been imported from Hitler's Germany. (pp. 154-159)

Ginzburg ran into an Italian communist in another jail: "I heard clearly, in the midst of the wailing, the words 'Comunista Italiana, Comunista Italiana!' So that was it! No doubt she had fled from Mussolini just as Klara, my cellmate at Butyrki, had fled from Hitler" (p. 224). Not that historically it makes sense to label every single communist party newspaper or activity Stalinist, or that common or garden parliamentary parties do not use some of Stalin's lesser tricks at times to discipline their members. But nonetheless, the far Left has not been immune from the instinct for repression. There is no safe haven in human history.

With these more general considerations in mind, let us consider further certain other commonalities, although less unnerving ones, between rank and file ultra-rightists and the far Left that can easily be found in their media. The radical distrust of mainstream media found on the far Left can certainly be found in spades on the ultra-Right. Political paranoia, an instinct to credit conspiracies, and the psychic superiority of being an underground minority that alone really understands the world—all stances beloved of some on the far Left—are equally attractive to many on the ultra-Right. The far Left's conviction that the ultra-Right is lacking heart and compassion, with no values worthy of the name, is mirrored in currents within the religious ultra-Right's view of the Left.

We should also note that there are often elements of a hunt for justice and dignity even in ultra-rightist movements,[5] manipulated and overridden though they are by unscrupulous leadership—not that unscrupulousness is the sole preserve of the Right, or indeed of leaders. We might instance tax revolts from among those whose income is steadily declining, opposition to abortion rights from among those whose own dignity and purpose as human beings are rarely acknowledged, rage among ordinary Germans at the punitive conditions of the post-World War I Versailles Treaty.

THE ULTRA RIGHT VERSUS THE FAR LEFT

Does then the ultra-Right, as a bloc or in some of its strands, use radical media in ways akin to the far Left? It must be said that, formally speaking, it quite often does. The ultra-Right is ready to embrace commonplace, simple means of mass communication, although it is always important to remember that this is alongside their access to mainstream media: For on a number of hot-button issues—especially race/ethnicity/immigration, women's rights, and homophobia—some mainstream media are happy to propagate many of the ultra-Right's positions, although not necessarily by giving them access in person to their columns or studios. The far Left has no such channel multiplicity or wealth. The ultra-Right, as noted, is often very successful at portraying itself as frozen out by the establishment, and the Left as in control and malevolent. In the Chilean example cited, the ultra-Right and the CIA used the fact that the Popular Unity government gained votes in its second election not as an indication of its legitimacy but as a way of demonizing it as a more serious threat than ever. The explosion of ultra-Right AM radio talk shows in the United States during the Clinton presidency, denouncing it as a leftist menace—a comic accusation, had it not been so widespread—was another instance.[6]

One point at which ultra-Right media most sharply diverge from the far Left—although not a Stalinist-style Left—is their easy acceptance of manipulative tactics, of demagogic slogans, as opposed to challenge and debate. They particularly like to present themselves as crying out for the right to free speech, a free speech they would cheerfully refuse to any opposition, were they in power. They especially like to present groups who are beginning to assert themselves—women, ethnic groups, lesbians, gays—as actually already in full and almost despotic control, calling every shot that can be called. Whether Hindu ultra-Right media in India that feast on defining the mostly poor Muslim minority as dominating the country, or ultra-Right media in Russia that gorge themselves on anti-Semitism, or ultra-Right Australian media that wallow in the trough of defining aboriginals and Asians as running the country, the phenomenon is pretty well universal.

But a thriving, diverse, radical media culture, one that can sit lightly to government or corporate or religious oversight, one responsive to and critical of constructive social forces, is a very different phenomenon and a major stimulus to democratic outcomes, to an increase of developmental power in Macpherson's (1973) sense.[7] Brecht, in theory, even if his own plays did not really have the effect he wished, saw this sparking of debate as the acid test of radical media in the struggle against the mindlessness with which otherwise people would readily swallow fascist propaganda or capitalist hegemony.

I would add that a problematic criterion of the difference between far Left and ultra-Right radical media is the scope given to slightly more than half of the public, namely, women's voices. It is problematic on a number of grounds, because the far Left was male-dominated, and quite often by unreconstructed chauvinists, until the advent of the modern feminist movement. It is also the case that women have been ultra-rightist activists, including in the Ku Klux Klan (Blee, 1993; Cochran & Ross, 1993), and as is very evident, in anti-abortion rights campaigns. However, there is no overlap between radical media that embrace a feminist orientation and ultra-Right media. Ultra-Right media may well adopt certain women as icons, endeavor to mobilize them, and give them a carefully channeled voice,[8] but they pursue a sharply different tack to media that women organize for themselves.

DEMOCRATIC VERSUS REPRESSIVE MEDIA

And last, a key difference is media that are self-governing. For the ultra-Right (aside from the anarchist ultra-Right), a comprehensive future of self-governing media is simply not imaginable because—and here, there is very substantial unity on the Right—hierarchy is its deepest principle. How it believes in hierarchy, what consequences it draws, which hierarchy, all vary, but not the underlying commitment to the principle. We shall see in the case studies in Part III how self-managed media have had to struggle to realize internal democracy and to dissolve hierarchy, and the compromises they have often found themselves forced to make between these goals and their effective functioning. The radical alternative path they have pursued has often been an extremely difficult and taxing one. But their democratic goals, and the very fact they have had fierce struggles over them, are absolutely unimaginable on the ultra-Right.

And, decisively, respect for these goals strengthens a democratic culture. The ultra-Right can operate within formal trappings of democracy accompanied by media-supported authoritarianism and its culture.[9] The far Left, operating from the principle of a huge swarm of self-governing media, is virtually impossible to co-opt into that frame unless it slides into Stalinism, forgetful of its immense atrocities.

Summary: For all the reasons cited, the consideration of repressive radical media cannot simply consist of a self-gratifying denunciation from the moral high ground. Their roles are too pervasive, their variations too significant, their historical practice in the 20th century in the name of socialism, too terrifying. And they particularly exemplify the power of micromedia, in this case, the lethal power.

NOTES

1. For a chilling survey of some leading cases of the role of such media around the world, including genocide, see the collection of essays in Reporters Sans Frontières (1995), which addresses Rwanda, Burundi, Niger, Israel, Palestine, Egypt, former Yugoslavia, Romania, the Crimea, and the Transcaucasus (Chechnya and Nagorno-Karabakh). See also Kellow and Steeves (1998).

2. As Kaiser (2000) shows, the favorite method of evading the issue of military repression in Argentina's Dirty War (1976-1982) was to refer to the "two demons"—the extreme Right and the extreme Left. This disregarded entirely that the murders by the extreme Left, which did take place, were a handful compared to the 30,000 disappeared people at the hands of the junta.

3. *Populism* is one of those maddening words that tends to elude definition. Here, I use it with adjectives such as *rightist* or *authoritarian* to indicate social movements whose leadership purports to offer radical solutions for popular ills, but whose strategies for the solution of those ills involve the public not as joint architects of solutions but only as cheerleaders for the leadership—and quite frequently as instruments to repress political minorities on the leadership's behalf.

4. *Nazi* is an abbreviation of National Socialist; Mussolini used, for as long he found it expedient, his credentials as former editor of the socialist party's newspaper.

5. Both here and in the discussion that resumes on this issue at the close of the chapter, I have found Saponara (1997) very illuminating.

6. A fascinating example was the campaign against "political correctness" in the 1990s, which succeeded in portraying the Left as rampantly seeking control of free thought on campus and in the media. Those leftists who recalled from their younger days the extreme anxieties effortlessly induced in them by conservative senior faculty and editors, who made no bones about rejecting candidates and publications because they thought their views insufficiently conservative, could only lift an ironic eyebrow. Equally ludicrously, the ultra-Right trumpeted public radio and TV and the National Endowments for the Arts and Humanities as left-wing colonies.

7. For some Americans, the First Amendment represents the crystallization of this impulse in official public policy. Would it were so, but the realities are much less encouraging (Downing, 1999b).

8. For example, the American World Church of the Creator, which grew rapidly during the latter 1990s and came to widespread notoriety in July 1999 when one of its members shot dead two people of color and wounded 12 others, ran a strong drive to recruit and promote women.

9. Examples include war campaigns, such as the Malvinas/Falklands war of 1982 or the 1990-1991 war in the Persian Gulf, or the trend, virtually unchallenged in mainstream media, toward national central banks' autonomy from democratic accountability.

9

Conclusions

We have drawn on a considerable variety of perspectives, all of them framed by different questions and problems, to begin to make sense of the radical media phenomenon and potential. The journey we have undertaken has not led to a tightly wound, smooth conceptual conclusion. There are a number of rough edges and discontinuities, but perhaps that better corresponds to the messy nature of social being than a series of perfectly oiled axioms.

We will recapitulate them in a moment, but before we can do so, there is one dimension of current media theorizing that must first be addressed. It is the position, especially identified with an early phase of U.S. media research (Katz & Lazarsfeld, 1955; Klapper, 1960), that media are weak social agents. If this view were to hold, it could be devastating to the argument here about radical media. If large-scale media are thin and insubstantial entities, what interest could there possibly be in researching small-scale radical flimsies?

It is my contention not only that the weak effects model is wrong about mainstream media, but also that the serious study of radical media helps show why. For the weak effects school, media seem always assumed to be an either-or. Either they are autonomous agents, shown by their measurable power and distinctive functions—like, say, the family, or schooling, or religion—or they are woven so imperceptibly into the social fabric that their influence is virtually impossible to detect.

The problem in this argument arises from the implicit comparison of media to other social institutions, which then ends up by making their particular cultural roles almost invisible. The family and the other institutions mentioned have a set of roles unique to each of them. We, for the most part at this point in history, do not expect religious institutions to nurture babies, or schools to propagate religion, or the family to broadcast the news. Media, however, are lifelong and universal in a way religion no longer is, even in theocratic states. They are multiform, from news to fiction, from sport to religion, from comedy to kid stuff, from music to computer games, from discussion to databases.

Their influence, therefore, I would argue, issues normally and overwhelmingly from a molecular, symbiotic strength in their very connectedness to other social forces and processes. We are not segregating physical elements, nitrogen from oxygen from hydrogen, but studying media as what they are, perhaps the most universally—globally, throughout the life cycle, graffiti to Internet—enmeshed social institutions of all. Their power stems precisely from combination, from embeddedness, not even necessarily or generally in parasitic dependence but in dialectical mutuality over time. Like enzymes such as yeast, media cannot operate without co-enzymes (minerals, vitamins, proteins) and without the amino acids that operate as their bodily carriers.

I would, therefore, conclude that the study of radical media and their impact, whether by the array of concepts defined and discussed above, or in the empirical tapestry that follows in Part II, acts to highlight this combinatorial reality. Popular culture, audiences, social movements, democracy, developmental power, hegemony, resistance, artwork, public sphere, and radical media are sometimes complementary, sometimes conflicting angles of vision; on another level, inasmuch as each captures something of social reality, they are each other's matrices. In media research, even more than family or state or social movement research, the hunt for sole agents is condemned to futility.

The concepts and issues we have discussed evince certain continuing strands: power relations, political, cultural, and economic; the relation between information, emotions, humor, art, dialogue, and democracy; the usefulness of concepts of public sphere and alternative public sphere and their relation to social movements. We also shook the kaleidoscope and examined ethnic, religious, and global dimensions of radical media and the shadow case of repressive radical media. And, not least, we explored last century's two leading organizational directions for the daily pragmatics of radical media.

I would conclude by suggesting that maybe the metaphor of the yeast enzyme might actually help to focus our understanding of the cultural and political operation of radical media. All inanimate analogies for animate processes are flawed, yet, if we consider the generative power of this microscopic enzyme, its capacity to alter its environment, perhaps we will not be so trapped by our instinctive skepticism concerning small-scale and often ephemeral media. Whether we take social movements, artworks, radical media, democracy, and the rest as political commitments or as concepts that shed light on different facets of oppositional activity, or just dispassionately as enzymes and co-enzymes, it is polymorphously perverse to dismiss the historical and contemporary impact of rebellious cultures and their media. The chapters of the next two Parts argue why that is so.

Radical Media Tapestry: Communicative Rebellion Historically and Globally

The tapestry that this section will weave is drawn from practically every strand of radical communication, whether using media as conventionally defined or not. For example, Chapter 1 includes a study of the body as a medium of radical communication in dance, and Chapter 8 addresses the Internet.

The purposes of assembling this tapestry are multiple. On one level, these examples give a historical and global sense of the excitement, the flavor, and the sparks of radical media activism. On another, they demonstrate the amazing—especially if the subject is new to the reader—multiplicity and richness of radical media past and present. On a third, they illustrate, are clarified by, and also tease out the concepts discussed in Part I. And finally, they suggest that the radical media tradition has been a vivid and core dimension of the international history of popular movements against tyranny, mystification, exploitation, and official hypocrisy. Their impact has sometimes been instantaneous, sometimes tantalizingly slow. But to neglect them is to amputate at the hip our understanding of popular struggles.

In the 1984 version of this book, I took my examples from highly organized instances of radical media, on the ground that they were the hardest to sustain over time and, therefore, their problems and successes were the most interesting to analyze. They were also the most important to understand, I thought, so as not to have first-time media activists perpetually reinventing the wheel. The detailed case studies in Part III still largely reflect that priority, but in this section, ephemeral media forms receive plenty of attention as well.

This is because ephemeral media have been a presence throughout modern history, constantly bubbling up all over the place. Furthermore, as Sreberny-Mohammadi and Mohammadi (1994) and Martín-Barbero (1993) particularly emphasize, and as the exploration of popular culture, resistance, and art in the previous section argued, the interconnections between various forms of media are central to their impact. And, ephemeral media address social memory differently.

There is no space here to develop this third proposition systematically, so I will leave it as a hypothesis to be fleshed out at a later date. Nonetheless, there is reason to consider that ephemeral media tend to lodge themselves in conscious memory more readily because of their one-shot concentrated pungency. Stephen Dale (1996), in his discussion of Greenpeace activism and mainstream media, cites a term coined by one activist: "'mind bombs': influential, sometimes archetypal images that can cut through the hypnotic drone of the day-to-day babbling to reach people at a deeper emotional level . . . it is the force of impact that counts, not the number of media hits" (p. 134). Conversely, ongoing media (of all kinds) tendentially operate to set up mnemonic frameworks that allow incoming information to be effortlessly, unconsciously, sorted into those defining categories. The number of media hits is also important, but in the sense of refreshing and sustaining those mnemonic frameworks. Both media operations have significant impacts, but in different ways.

I will devote this section, then, to surveying the extensive spectrum of radical media, historically and comparatively. Whereas the previous section may have been difficult to read because of its sometimes intricate conceptual arguments, it may be unwise to try to read this one at a single sitting because of the sheer richness and variety of the material. Examples are mainly drawn from the United States, Britain, Germany,

Italy, and France, but others are from Algeria, Argentina, Bolivia, Chile, China, El Salvador, Iran, Ireland, Mexico, Morocco, Nigeria, and Russia. This is by way of drawing on the widest sources readily available to me. I have, however, quite often dwelt on African American and German examples, for reasons I will now explain.

A number of the African American instances were chosen precisely to illustrate the extraordinary communicative tenacity and versatility of human beings under the most extreme circumstances, namely, centuries of enslavement and its aftermath in the Americas. African American radical media are heuristically illuminating, humbling, and heartening.

German experience is highlighted for two reasons. First, the rich traditions of 19th- and earlier 20th-century German cultural and political radicalism were enormously influential among radical media activists internationally throughout the 20th century. Yet, the unprecedented Nazi genocide has so indelibly engraved itself on our consciousness since then—and the mnemonic engravure of genocide is essential[1]—that often we do not know this making of our radical media heritage. Second, however, a most sobering consideration: That very strong oppositional culture was still not sufficient in Germany itself to withstand the tumbling descent into World War I or the gigantic tidal wave of Nazi repression. That failure is an extremely chilling universal warning for the politics of liberation. No casual optimism is warranted for radical media. Both African American and German experiences particularly demonstrate, in Nelson Mandela's (1973) words, that there is indeed "no easy walk to freedom."

In organizing what follows, I have mostly categorized examples by format and/or technology. This poses certain disadvantages, especially in cases of multiple or hybrid format media activities, and it certainly risks deifying technologies and genres rather than focusing on their common uses and integration. The alternative was to divide the material up by specific topic, or chronologically, or by nation or ethnic group, all of which would have distorted it in other ways, probably worse ones. But, at various points, I have departed from this rule. For example, I have treated all of ACT-UP's work, including its posters, under the street theater/performance art heading, and I have grouped graphic art and print media in adjoining segments, not in one.

One final introductory point, building on the argument already made concerning the interconnections between radical media: To grasp the full spectrum of radical alternative media forms, it is first necessary to shed the restrictive implication of the term *media,* which tends to rivet our gaze too much on broadcasting and newspapers, or perhaps cinema. The social base underlying radical media is radical communication, and it is from that base that we must begin. The linkages between communication in general and media communication would probably already be much better understood than they are, were it not for the wasted effort that has been poured into mind-numbingly scientistic research into interpersonal communication, especially within the United States, and the consequent divorce between that focus and a focus on media. (The contemporary development of Internet applications renders that divorce even less tenable.)

Thus, if the blurring of *communication* and *media* in what follows seems strange, readers should ask themselves why it is so strange to them. We will proceed to review, as radical media, public speech, jokes, dance, and song; graffiti and dress; popular theater, performance art, and culture-jamming; print media; mind bombs (woodcuts, prints, flyers, posters, photomontage, murals); radio; film and video; and, with the help of Tamara Ford and Genève Gil, the Internet.

NOTE

1. The massive Holocaust Studies literature is pivotal in this regard, notwithstanding some of its contributors' attempts to hijack that unspeakable experience in defense of indefensible Israeli government policies of colonizing and repressing Palestinians.

10

Public Speech, Dance, Jokes, and Song

- Moroccan women street traders
- Bakhtin, Rabelais, and marketplace humor
- 19th-century African American public festivals
- The Mothers of the Plaza de Mayo, Buenos Aires
- Radical pre-Emancipation communication networks among African American mariners
- Stalin-era Russian poet Anna Akhmatova and *Requiem*
- African American dance in the era of chattel slavery and afterward
- The blues
- Song in the German labor movement through 1933

The most accessible and most fundamental mode of radical expression is speech for public purposes (i.e., even if clandestine, uttered within one or more publics) and, not least, ironic and satirical speech. Close to it are dance and song. The instances below, including the "high-art" poem *Requiem*, exemplify many of the issues raised in the conceptual discussions in Part I: notably, the rebellious strands in popular culture and the importance of nonmedia networks in alternative public spheres. Many, particularly aspects of German labor movement songs, also exemplify the typically impure, irretrievably mixed character of oppositional expression. At the same time, Benjamin's aura, the interactive aesthetics of radical communication, is evidenced at almost every turn. Last, many of the illustrations below are drawn from radical cultural expression in the face of a repressive power structure, from New World slavery to Stalinism and military dictatorships, including masculinist cultures that strictly regiment women.

MOROCCAN WOMEN STREET TRADERS

Deborah Kapchan's (1996) study of Moroccan women market traders nicely introduces us to some of the fundamentals, in this case, the subtle but powerful erosion of patriarchal codes, in a way reminiscent of Scott's (1985, 1990) analysis of everyday resistance.

Let us begin with context. In 1980s Morocco, for women to act as traders in the public marketplaces rather than as shoppers was a very new phenomenon, unknown 20 years earlier. How, then, did these women communicate in public to casual passers-by, generally unrelated to them, males as well as females? How did they manage to assert themselves, to be insistent in calling shoppers' notice to the merits of their wares, and yet stay unsanctioned, remaining within—while simultaneously stretching the bounds of—what was considered acceptable for women?

Kapchan (1996) presents a detailed analysis of their selling patterns that evinces an impressive capacity to negotiate and erode patriarchal codes without sparking a damaging condemnation or retribution. One of these market women, trading in herbal medications, actually spoke out loud in the marketplace about male impotence and sexual intercourse. But to legitimate her candor to her largely male audience, she wove into her speech reference to sayings in the *Qur'an* or familiar proverbs and aphorisms, which established her piety. Statements such as "God bless the parents" normally required a repetition from the hearers, so that inclusion of the statement and its answering echo were also ways of bringing the hearers along with her. She might even affect extra piety, saying "I didn't hear you all say, 'God bless the parents,'" and they would feel duty-bound to repeat the saying more loudly (Kapchan, 1996, pp. 103-137).

A different example comes from a conversation in which a male customer was insistently trying to bargain a woman trader down. He told her he would go buy the item from the store (where prices were rarely negotiable), and she responded, "Well, offer a price, sir, and buy. It's not shameful. We're just like the store. What's the matter with us [women vendors]? Aren't we all Muslims?" "No, no," he replied, "we're all Muslims, one people" (Kapchan, 1996, p. 58).

What she was doing here, Kapchan explains, was to respond to his dismissive comment on her female trader status—stores were still owned by men—by pulling him into agreeing with a pious statement, one generally used in Moroccan conversation to call for harmony between Arab and Berber men. She extended it to apply to male-female relations, as a way of pressuring him into a degree of respect for her and continuing the negotiation on her terms.

Here were subtly subversive communications, bending the limits of the possible for women, gradually altering the contours of Moroccan women's freedom of public expression. They involved no expense, no collective organization, only the elaboration and deployment of rhetorical skills in conversation, sometimes very finely tuned, and the necessary degree of emotional determination not to be inhibited from self-assertion. Yet, these are the communicative stances from which radical alternative media are ultimately derived and with which they interact.

A related example is offered by various kinds of verbal humor, not particularly as expressed by professional stand-up comedians, but rather in everyday situations. Humor is multifaceted, and so, it is important not to infer it is always beneficial or always subversive.[1] Nonetheless, in many situations, humorous comments or actual jokes directed against employers, against bureaucrats, against clergy, against hypocritical and corrupt authorities, against colonial invaders, against racially defined superiors, serve to puncture the pretensions of those on high and to reduce the legitimacy of their authority. The more these comments and jokes diffuse out along conversational networks, the more purchase they achieve. Women's ironic discussions among themselves of males constitute a universal example of subversive speech communication. Once more, in the strictly gender-segregated cultures of North Africa, both the flat rooftops in cities, where washing is hung out, and the women's bathhouse are locations where only women congregate and thus where this freer talk is possible, a kind of women's alternative public sphere (cf. Fraser, 1993; Said, in press). The Moroccan market women made ample use of humorous comment. But there are many further examples, some cited later in this section under the heading of satirical cartoons and political pornography.[2]

RABELAIS AND THE MARKETPLACE

A notable example comes from Mikhail Bakhtin (1984), who in his now famous book about 16th-century French writer François Rabelais addressed the way in which Rabelais' notoriously raunchy novel, *Gargantua and Pantagruel,* focused so much attention on its characters' belching, farting, urinating, defecating, sexual release and proclivities. He argued that Rabelais had reproduced the standard speech of the town or village marketplace, a language far removed from the stilted purities of the court, the intelligentsia, or the clergy, a language full of vitality and force, far more vibrant than "correct speech." Bakhtin[3] proposed that particularly underlying Rabelais' novel was the deep folk tradition of many, many centuries that addressed hierarchy, power, repression, and fear, with mocking laughter:

> Laughter . . . was not only a victory over mystic terror of God, but also a victory over the awe inspired by the forces of nature, and most of all over the oppression and guilt related to all that was consecrated and forbidden. . . . It was the defeat of divine and human power, of authoritarian commandments and prohibitions, of death and punishment after death, hell. . . . Through this victory laughter clarified man's consciousness and gave him a new outlook on life. This truth was ephemeral; it was followed by the fears and oppressions of everyday life, but from these brief moments another unofficial truth emerged, truth about the world. (Bakhtin, 1984, pp. 90-91)

The collective expression of this irreverent laughter in late medieval Europe was confined to locations such as the town and village markets and intermittent carnival festivities and fairs, which were quite frequent throughout the year. Common days for such festivals included Shrove Tuesday and the feast of Corpus Christi. Perhaps the most extreme instance was All Fools' Day, when all the solemnities of religion and authority were ritually inverted and mocked. Excrement was used instead of incense in the mock mass in the church, and priests riding in carts tossed dung at passers-by. Men and women cross-dressed, and kitchen utensils were pressed into use as musical instruments.

In contrast to the rollicking forms of subversive communication reviewed by Bakhtin, Fabré (1994) notes the much more sober public speech at annual African American festivals in the 19th century:

> African Americans . . . were using the power of the imagination to invent, visualize, and represent themselves in roles they had always desired. . . . Feasts . . . marked the passage from various forms of subordination and enslavement to a "season" of change which could ultimately bring complete emancipation and liberation. (p. 75)

There would be "fairs, parades, picnics, banquets, and dances . . . the ringing of bells, burning of powder, display of banners" (p. 85).

Besides this prefiguration of the future, there was also a rehearsal of key moments in the recent past of Africans in the Americas. The mnemonic aspect of radical communication, as we will see again and again, beginning with the Mothers of the Plaza de Mayo, the poem *Requiem,* and African American dance in this chapter, is one of its critically important aspects. One such festival was the Fourth of July, when the wider ideals of 1776 could be restated but when black insurrectionist Nat Turner's attempted slave rebellion was also memorialized. Not only Turner: Crispus Attucks in Massachusetts; in Baltimore, the Haitian revolution; a local leader of the Underground Railroad known popularly as Jerry Rescue in Syracuse. Another such festival in New York and Philadelphia was January 1, used in the early 19th century to celebrate the 1808 legal end to the right of U.S. citizens to buy new slaves from Africa. At that point in U.S. history, it was both a sign of change and a push to still further change that such events came to be part of the open public sphere rather than clandestine.

Radical speech events of these kinds—to recompose Habermas's (1984/1987) terminology in favor of something perhaps less precise, but certainly less aseptic—are sometimes downplayed as brief and harmless safety-valve occasions, helping to stabilize an unjust social order. James C. Scott (1990, pp. 178-181) takes important issue with this view. He suggests that even when these communicative events are sponsored from on high, the fact that elites want them to act as a safety valve does not mean that they do so. He notes how often elites are preoccupied with the potential for serious disturbances in connection with such festivals. Scott's observation also reminds us how we need constantly to steer between dismissing radical communication as trivial and overstating its impact. Furthermore, as several times emphasized in Part I, the time frame over which we assess the question of radical media impact is also decisive in assessing it accurately.

MOTHERS OF THE PLAZA DE MAYO

A further example, this time of radical public speech in demonstrations,[4] and especially of their relation to keeping political memory alive, is provided by Susana Kaiser's (1993) study of the communication strategies of the Mothers of the Plaza de Mayo.[5] This was a group of mothers and grandmothers among the very few who publicly protested the systematic tortures, murders, and disappearances perpetrated by the Argentinian military junta of 1976 to 1982. Any form of opposition at that time, however mild, brought the risk of being defined as subversive, which in the junta's language meant being officially marked out for bestial repression. As many as 30,000 citizens may well have perished in this process. The media were silent, "normality" reigned, if the junta and the media could be believed, and protest virtually evaporated.

The Mothers, regardless, met every Thursday in the Plaza de Mayo and demonstrated, wearing diapers as head scarves to communicate graphically their own maternal identities and the absolute legitimacy of their questions about their own disappeared children. They held aloft placards with enlarged photos of their children, including their names and the last date they were seen alive. The Mothers continued, too, year after year, even after 1982, when the junta had collapsed, and when the political class wanted nothing more than to turn the page and forget the atrocities—when the Mothers were written off in many quarters as just a bunch of crazy obsessive old women.

Finally, however, some 15 years after the junta had fallen, a few individuals formerly involved in the repression began to come forward and confess to some of the crimes committed. In due course, some mainstream media began to address the issue, sometimes poorly, but at long last, it was on the public agenda. Some of those responsible were indicted for kidnaping; they and others were the object of angry denunciations in the streets and restaurants when they were spotted and of *escraches,* demonstrations outside their houses, to the point where they were barely able to circulate, a virtual form of citizens' house arrest (Kaiser, 2000).

Finally, in 1998-1999, some of the most vicious members of the former junta found themselves jailed despite the amnesty that was supposed to ensure their impunity, on the ground that they had ordered the kidnaping of children, namely, the infants of those they had executed, some born in their torture cells. Kidnaping was a crime not covered under the amnesty. And, then, in Chile in 1999, some of their counterparts from the Pinochet dictatorship, who had the same blood on their hands, found themselves in jail on the same charge, while Pinochet himself was detained under house arrest in Britain facing extradition to Spain under European Union human rights law. The crazy old women's communication strategy had flowered.

Keeping political memory alive, therefore, was at the very center of the Mothers' message and successful strategy. It is important to note how their public speech also took nationalist, religious, and military themes and used them in a form of *détournement* against the ruling powers. At the time of the Malvinas/Falklands war, when the junta desperately sought to prop up its popularity by retaking the islands from Britain, the Mothers chanted in the square, "The Malvinas are Argentine—and so are our children!" They spoke in public in other ways, for example, kneeling at the altar rail and before the priest delivered the communion wafer to them, announcing out loud for all to hear: "I accept this Host in the name of [X.Y.], my daughter, who was last seen alive on the [day/month/year]." Given the Argentine Catholic hierarchy's deep complicity with the junta's crimes, such public statements were a communication against church and state alike. Once the captain of a detachment sent to scare them out of the square told his troops to train their rifles on the Mothers and rapped out "Take aim!" A number of the Mothers spontaneously shouted back "Fire!"—with their colossal courage rendering his terror tactics threadbare.[6]

Clandestine speech and networking have also been of great political importance in many repressive situations. Let us examine some further examples from African American history and one from 20th-century Russian history.

NETWORKS AMONG AFRICAN AMERICAN MARINERS

Bolster (1997) has described how African American mariners played a very significant radical communication network role in the period before and during the Civil War:

> Voyaging between the West Indies, Europe, and the American mainland enabled enslaved seamen to observe the Atlantic political economy from a variety of vantage points, to subvert their masters' discipline, and to open plantation society to outside influences . . . situated on vessels connecting all corners of the Atlantic world, black seafaring men were newsmongers central to the formation of black America and a multidimensional racial identity. They broadcast accounts from Blacks' perspectives regarding the Haitian Revolution, the movements to abolish the slave trade and emancipate slaves, and the debate over decolonization that centered on the question of whether people of color would remain in the United States. (pp. 26, 36)

Bolster similarly notes how the first six black autobiographies published in English before 1800, each of them an opening salvo in the media war against slavery, were written by sailors. One of the main slave rebellions in the United States was led by Denmark Vesey, also a former mariner.

A further example of the mixture between oral and media modes of radical communication networks is offered by African American David Walker's *Appeal to the Colored Citizens of the World*, published in Boston in 1829. This pamphlet, a devastating attack on Africans' enslavement, was considered pivotal in the antislavery campaign by a whole chain of leading African American activists of the 19th and 20th centuries, including Frederick Douglass, Maria Stewart, and W. E. B. DuBois, as well as William Lloyd Garrison (Hinks, 1997, pp. 112-115).

In this case, we see an absorbing instance of media/network interplay. The pamphlet found its way to Savannah, Richmond, Wilmington, Charleston, and New Orleans as a result of a network of individual distributors, the initial links in the chain being coastal mariners (both black and white). From there, the copies fanned out through urban freedmen and -women, mobile nonplantation slaves such as riverine mariners, preachers, (including some white Methodists), and runaways in some of the marshy coastal regions of the South where small Maroon communities persisted. Plantation slaves, who generally could not read because learning to do so risked brutal punishment, had it read to them despite the surveillance of their masters (Hinks, 1997, pp. 116-172). As a result of the Georgia plantocracy's panic, which recognized the pivotal role played by mariners in this communication network, the legislature put a 40-day quarantine on all ships with black sailors aboard that docked in Georgia ports (Bolster, 1997, pp. 197-198).[7]

POETS OF THE STALIN ERA

As our final example of radical speech communication in conditions of extreme repression and its potential power despite the huge odds against it, let us consider how the leading Russian poet, Anna Akhmatova, at the depth of Stalin's terror, composed her long poem *Requiem.* Several pages long, it was about her son's jailing and the terror imposed by Stalin, but she never wrote it down in case it should be found and used against her or him. Instead, she had a series of closely trusted friends each memorize one portion in case she should herself be liquidated. Astoundingly, its impact gradually overflowed from the tiny, brave circle in which it was first committed to memory. Over the years, *Requiem*[8] became a powerful talismanic statement, committed to memory in its entirety by many as a flame of determination to withstand and survive the Stalin regime's monstrous repression.

COMMUNICATION IN DANCE

We switch now to consider dance and the body as a mnemonic communication instrument subverting a strategy of cultural extinction. It is perhaps hard for many people to think of dance as a mode of communication. If they reflect on it at all, they think of dance as something people do at parties to relax and get sexy, or as art (= classical European ballet). How can dance be communication when no words are spoken, and sometimes no music is played?

These responses are littered with hidden assumptions. We see the assumption that percussion has to involve drums and probably even that drums are percussion, not music. We see the assumption that art is one thing, communication another. We see the assumption that body language is not communication. We see the assumption that pleasure and relaxation and sexual expression are not enmeshed with art.

Dance, among African Americans during the centuries of their enslavement, was a particular kind of alternative medium of communication. Sometimes performed for the slave holders but also performed clandestinely,[9] it was for many reasons a particularly important form of communication. It constituted the continuation of a culture denied, a culture that over the centuries drew further and further away, but which, even after African languages had been banned and then nearly forgotten, spoke of a time before enslavement. It was the bodily celebration of a different era, before the totalitarian unfreedom of the Americas. It was an enactment of political memory.

This leads to a second point, namely, the mode of dance traditional within African cultures, where the body's fulcrum when dancing is the hips, unlike European dancing, where the fulcrum is generally the sternum. Abrahams (1992, pp. 94-95) notes that African dancing also embraced patting one's body; snapping one's fingers; clapping one's hands; using one's feet as percussive instruments; involving hips, legs, arms, and hands, sometimes operating separately from each other according to different counter-rhythms and cross-rhythms. Each part of the body also held a symbolic meaning. This represented an intensely powerful mnemonic expression because it engaged the entire person, demanding all the body's and all the mind's attention. And, needless perhaps to underscore, African dancing's aesthetics were powerfully interactive. There was no gulf between performers and audience, except the plantation masters, on the occasions they demanded a show.

Third, because the laws said the enslaved Africans' bodies were owned by the plantocracy, this expression of their own body culture represented a certain reclamation of their being. Their bodies were moving to their own pace and demands, not the slave driver's. Having, often, to perform traditional dance at the planters' festivities obviously cut into this self-assertion, but from contemporary accounts, it would seem that many Africans could retain their sense of validation and excitement and were able not to be engulfed in alienation at being part of a "command performance."

After the Civil War and Emancipation, Tera Hunter (1997, pp. 168-186) has noted, dance continued to be important. Urban dance halls became very popular among working class African Americans, despite being denounced as immoral by both the white authorities and the emerging black professional class. In the black neighborhoods of Atlanta, dance was to be found everywhere, at picnics, house parties, and especially in some of the churches. Music and dance styles were similar in both secular and religious settings, a reality abundantly evident in the entire history of blues, soul, gospel, and other African American musical genres. Dancing in religious services, however, was deemed by polite society, black as well as white, to be on a par with the city dance halls. Nevertheless, Hunter writes,

> The blues and dance were developed with a fierce sense of irreverence—the will to be unencumbered by any artistic, moral or social obligations, demands or interests external to the community which blues and dance were created to serve. . . . The feelings of self-empowerment and transcendence emanating from the blues and dance were evident. . . . The complex rhythmic structure and driving propulsive action endowed participants with the feeling of metaphysical transcendence, of being able to overcome or alter the obstacles of daily life. (pp. 183-184)

Dance in this context, then, during slavery and afterward, was a form of communication principally directed within the community, not as a communication from the community to those outside it. As Clemencia Rodríguez's remarks cited in Part I underscore, radical communication may direct itself to strengthening those to whom it is addressed, to validating their dignity and renewing their cultural identity. It need not necessarily be a programmatic or propaganda endeavor, nor need it be a protest framed explicitly against those in power.

SONG

Song has been another familiar alternative medium. In the segment in Part III on Soviet Russia, we shall see how both guitar poetry and rock music played an important role there from the 1960s onward. But we could equally cite the political street ballads of 18th-century Paris or London, African American work songs and religious songs, the history of blues music, the role of *nueva canción* in Latin America in the 1960s and later, the *rembetiko* music generated in the 1920s by Greek refugees from Turkey, the Mexican and Mexican American *corridos,* protest songs of the labor movement in Germany and elsewhere, antiwar songs from the Vietnam war era, antinuclear lyrics, reggae, punk, rap, and many other instances.[10]

Here, I will focus on just two: the blues and song in the German labor movement around the turn of the 20th century.

The blues provide another opportunity to consider religious elements in radical media, and another illustration of time's importance in assessing radical media impact. The linkages between religious and secular expression in the blues were always extremely tight (cf. Barlow, 1999; Harris, 1992; Keil, 1966; Levine, 1977, pp. 190-297; Sobel, 1979).[11] Patently, the melodies, stylistic elements, sometimes the instrumentation, and most certainly the intensity of expression and feeling all bear testimony to this truth. The point is that even in secular versions, the existential intensity of the musical expression derives in significant measure from its spiritual connotations—even, I would suggest, when the lyrics are not merely secular but also somewhere between sexually suggestive and downright bawdy. For while the preacher might wish to sanitize the devil's best lyrics, his satanic majesty's best tunes often found their way straight into the gospel churches' hymns.[12]

The fundamental point is that there was a huge communicative charge to the musical sound, in principle almost independent of the lyrics. This is one of the hardest, most elusive elements to describe or discuss in music, and yet, most everyone will admit its centrality. Harris (1992) cites Thomas Dorsey[13]:

> Blues were really born shortly after slaves were free, and they were sung the way singers felt inside. They were just let out of slavery or put out, or went out. . . . They poured out their souls in their songs . . . blues is a digging, picking, pricking at the very depth of your mental environment and the feelings of your heart . . . It's got to be that old low-down moan and the low-down feeling; you got to have feeling. (p. 98)

Thus, over time, gospel blues voiced the wrenching decades of slavery, of sharecropping, of Jim Crow, of lives uprooted in the urban North, of relentless racism, and of life's more everyday trials and tribulations. They also searched for consolation by acknowledging the American nightmare and by fastening on to anciently rooted modes of generating hope through the expression of spiritual anguish. For a while in the 1960s, this music was often judged defeatist and passive by black political activists, and, indeed, as blues music at about that time embraced the electric guitar and heavier percussion and branched out into fusion with newer forms of rock music, it spoke a more directly assertive and defiant message.

In a sense, this argument about the blues was about whether radical media should be directly defiant or should help people handle defeat so that they can accumulate the strength to fight another decade. The time frame for judging the roles of radical alternative media shows itself once again as an important dimension in judging radical media's impact.

The German song example nicely illustrates the issue of *mestizaje* in popular culture and the frequent difficulty in identifying in what senses its strands can be termed oppositional. In Germany from the 1840s onward, song anthologies with a labor dimension were published, but explicitly socialist songbooks only began to emerge in the 1860s (Lidtke, 1985, pp. 102-135). There may have been no less than 250 such songbooks published between 1870 and 1914, reflecting the dramatic and seemingly inexorable growth of the German Social Democratic Party,[14] a growth that, as Lidtke demonstrates in considerable detail, brought with it a mass of cultural activities, daily newspapers, women's newspapers, quarterly theoretical journals, workers' festivals, poetry and drama clubs, and all kinds of study programs. The German party was the envy of similar parties across the world at the time, many of which could only marvel at its numbers, organization, and presence throughout every aspect of working class life.

Songs were to be found in two basic categories: the standard political songs, which could be sung at a variety of occasions and whose wording was set, and the strike songs, which might have had a common core but whose wording was changed to suit the specifics of the occasion. Some traditional songs were included, but not if they had nationalistic or religious lyrics. Sometimes, however, if these were easily replaceable by, for instance, references to freedom, then these changes were made in the text. Lidtke (1985) notes that "the labor movement was a singing movement" (p. 108) and that workers who had never read a word of the Marxist classics had probably often sung such songs in company with others in the movement's clubs. He suggests that

> in song, and especially in group singing, one simultaneously enjoyed the companionship of other people, expressed some ideological tendencies (often vague, to be sure), and could also find gratification by participating in simple artistic performances. Songs encourage an infinite repetition of ideas, and for that reason consciousness can be more deeply affected by song texts than by speeches that are heard once. . . . Words and phrases that seem trivial when judged by the standards of high theory may nonetheless take on considerable meaning when understood as part of an informal matrix of sentiments and aspirations. (pp. 108, 114)

At the same time, Lidtke draws attention to some rather mixed dimensions of song in the German labor movement. The lyrics were typically written for, not by, workers themselves, and addressed them in exhortation. The actual melodies were often well-known tunes to patriotic songs, such as *Deutschland, Deutschland Über Alles.* Even though the Social Democrats changed the words, and even though in the 19th century the song was patriotic rather than imperialist—Germany "before" everything rather than "over" everything—the tune still carried a hegemonic referent. And last, these songs did not change very much over the decades in response to changing trends in society. To that extent, Lidtke (1985) suggests, those singing them "declared not so much *what* they believed, but *that* they believed and that they *belonged*" (p. 135).

The songs did not then, probably, carry the racination of the blues or their depth of sentiment. They were an assertion of pride in workers' place in and contribution to society, a rejection of their exclusion from political power at the official level nationally—but they were not necessarily an expression of either their own deepest yearnings or of a clearly defined political agenda that could become hegemonic over time.

Summary: We have repeatedly seen how visible have been questions of resistance, counterhegemony, the public sphere, and the push for a democratic culture. So, too, has been the aura, the interactive aesthetics of these examples of self-expression, whether directed internally as in African American dance or German labor movement songs, or externally as well, as with the Mothers of the Plaza de Mayo or Moroccan women traders. At the same time, the *mestizaje* has often been apparent of oppositional, popular, and hegemonic elements. Last, the element of time has been very obvious: We would be blind to the impact of these radical communication activities if we assessed them only over the short term.

NOTES

1. See Charles Husband's (1988) important essay on racist humor.
2. See, too, the extended discussion of enslaved African Americans' humor in Levine (1977, pp. 298-366).
3. In Stalin's Soviet Union, his book was itself a veiled denunciation of the stifling status quo.

4. The street demonstration is frequently written off as a passé form of radical communication and only effective if picked up by mainstream media—indeed, to be an artificial media event. Writing shortly after the tremendous impact of the demonstrations against the World Trade Organization in Seattle, Washington, in November 1999, this "higher political cynicism" looks distinctly threadbare (http://www.speakeasy.org/citizen). Favre (1999), in a valuable sociological analysis of the demonstration, notes among other things that the police are required to report on all demonstrations to the civil authorities, meaning that media inattention has no correlation with whether or not a message is delivered to the power structure. The police habit of publicly underestimating the numbers at demonstrations does not mean they do so in private communications as well.

5. May Square, in the center of Buenos Aires, with the president's official palace at one end.

6. Shooting down unarmed mothers in Argentina's main square would hardly have hushed up the regime's crimes, nationally or internationally.

7. Another fascinating example of clandestine speech and political organizing is provided by Tera Hunter's (1997) study of African American laundrywomen in Atlanta in the decades following the Civil War (pp. 67-68, 74-97). They secretly organized as the Washing Society and called a strike in July 1881, tactically timed for 2 to 3 months before the International Cotton Exposition, the first-ever world's fair in the Southern states. It was the largest and most wounding of all the strikes in Atlanta in those years and led to many later forms of self-help and self-defense network organizing.

8. English translations of the poem, neither of them entirely satisfactory but still useful, are in both the W. W. Norton and the Penguin Books editions of selections from Akhmatova's works. For poems as radical alternative communication, see Alan Bold (1970), *Penguin Anthology Of Socialist Verse.* See, too, Cronyn, McKane, and Watts (1995), as well as African American and antiwar poetry broadsides of the 1960s (Sullivan, 1997, pp. 27-87) and John Brentlinger's (1995, pp. 197-214) absorbing and sensitive account of the politics and practice of poetry during the Sandinista period in Nicaragua.

9. There was a tradition of "steal aways" at night for the Africans to celebrate and continue their cultures. The sound would be contained by holding a large inverted cooking pot up above the heads of the speakers and singers.

10. See, for example, *Blues in the Mississippi Night* (1946/1990); *Greek-Oriental Rebetica* (1991); Limón (1992); Marcus (1989); Mattern (1991); Potash (1997); Seeger (1992).

11. This is not to say that African American religious expression was musically homogeneous. Harris (1992) devotes much of his study to the transition process in the 1920s whereby respectable, mass-attendance northern churches gradually shed their leaderships' deeply held assumption (cf. Tera Hunter) that blues music was culturally retrograde and morally suspect. The same supercilious attitude was evident at the posh dance clubs, although it was a standing joke that people with that attitude who attended rent parties

where blues were played would pretty soon drop their propriety and start to throw down, too.

12. This is not unique to African American culture. Some of Johann Sebastian Bach's most famous religious chorale melodies are versions of tunes with originally quite spicy lyrics. The hybrid quality of which we spoke in Part I takes many, many forms.

13. A pivotal figure in the development of gospel blues (not to be confused with Tommy Dorsey, the music tycoon portrayed in the film *The Godfather* as terrified by the Mafia's slaughter of his favorite racehorse into releasing the young Sinatra from his contract).

14. At that point in time, the standard designation of a Marxist-inspired workers' party. It was the German party's majority endorsement of the move to war in 1914, leading to over 4 years' of mass slaughter of the working class—German, French, British, American, Russian, to name only some—that poses one of the harshest questions as to how effective are radical media and oppositional culture.

11

Graffiti and Dress

Many of these instances relate to previous chapters in terms of the mixture of popular and oppositional cultures, directness of aesthetic impact, low-cost accessibility, and their function in tightly repressive situations (Soviet-era Moscow, military dictatorship, the slavery era). They are public sphere interventions that spark the very conversations and interactions, even if surreptitious, that feed social movements, and a movement toward democracy or toward a more strongly democratic culture. Women's agency is very visible again, as it was in Chapter 10.

- Young people's graffiti in Moscow before the collapse of the Soviet Union
- Nigerian students' political graffiti under a harsh military dictatorship
- African American dress styles
- Maya dress in Guatemala during the decades of military repression
- Under military rule Chilean women make *arpilleras*
- Quilting as clandestine communication
- Pins and lapel-buttons
- Bumper stickers

Graffiti are an aspect of popular culture generally thought of by respectable people as visual pollution, often obsessed with the obscene or the racist, sometimes consisting of incomprehensible territory markers between rival youth gangs. And indeed, all these are aspects of graffiti. Yet, they have a significant counterhegemonic dimension, too, and are very easily accessible. Susan Phillips (1999), in her discussion of 1990s black and Latino gang graffiti and of hip-hop graffiti, argues,

> All community-based graffiti are political if viewed from the inside. They are manipulations of group and individual relationships, representations of internally focused ideologies, power plays that negotiate position and define identity . . . people write graffiti to create or utilize windows of change. (pp. 53-57)

YOUNG PEOPLE AND GRAFFITI

For example, as John Bushnell (1989) has described Moscow of the 1970s and 1980s, some young people were active in writing up on the walls of the gloomy, massive apartment blocks the names of their favorite football teams and rock groups. So far, nothing exceptional, readers may think. But the context made them strong statements. Often, the graffiti about rock were written in English, and this was not just a quirk. The Soviet regime at the time defined rock music, just as it had previously defined jazz, as a decadent and unhealthy foreign influence on Soviet youth. Little Western rock music, especially from its centers in Britain and the United States, was permitted into the country, and rock concerts were rare and frowned on. Instead, the regime regarded Russian traditional music, or after a time, Russian rock music (at that time, generally a weak echo of the real thing), as the only wholesome fare for "honest Soviet youngsters."

Thus, the use of English in these graffiti simply but very directly challenged the bureaucrats' stultifying cultural policies. It said, in telescoped terms, that Western rock music was dynamic, that defining it as imperialist and corrupting was absurd, and that the authorities' cultural isolationism and manipulative trumpeting of wholesome Russianism were so much hooey. The graffiti neatly and effectively blew off core Soviet propaganda and invited passers-by to do so, too. The radiant Soviet future—its young people—were blowing the regime a radiant raspberry.

Political graffiti in 1991 in a Nigerian university's men's toilets, during a long period of intensive government repression, similarly served the function of allowing radical conversation to be registered for wider publics (Nwoye, 1993). Surveillance of students, generally perceived by the government as dangerous subversives, was widespread. Conversation about politics was carried on only under people's breath and among trusted friends and family members. The frequent brevity of the graffiti reflected the anxiety of being discovered in the act of writing them and the harsh punishments entailed. At the same time, the graffiti writers pulled no punches.

In the following excerpt, Dele Giwa and Gloria Okon were two political dissidents the military had ordered murdered, IBB signified the then-President's initials, and the SSS were the secret police:

> Who killed Dele Giwa?
> Are you asking me?
> Ask IBB.
> Ask SSS.
> If you know who killed Gloria Okon, then you know who killed Dele Giwa.
> Drug barons in government know the answer.
> If you keep asking, you will be blown up like Dele Giwa.
> So you are one of them?
> SSS is everywhere on campus.
> Even in this toilet?

Other contributions varied from Marxist slogans to denunciations of the university administration to obscenity as a mode of political attack. One exchange ridiculed the president, an army general, as militarily incompetent and, into the bargain, as impotent and/or sterile. In answer to a question (dated before Nelson Mandela's release from prison) about who would liberate South Africa, the following exchange ensued:

> Who will lead the High Command, IBB?
> No, he can't even shoot.
> Does he fire blanks?

Both the Nigerian and the Russian examples illustrate the way graffiti can establish a rudimentary alternative public realm. We have already noted the radical use of humor, and in subsequent chapters, we will review murals and political pornography, both of which have links with graffiti. In the meantime, let us register their rightful place in the radical media panorama.[1]

THE MEDIUM OF DRESS

Dress is another absorbing subject within the discussion of radical media communication. Very often what is being communicated is wealth, official status, gender, sexual orientation, the wearer's side in the battlefield, sometimes avant-garde fashion taste—but equally, dress may be counterhegemonic. In the United State beginning in about 1980, wearing a baseball cap backward was a signal of rebellious youth. For black youngsters from the 1960s through the end of the century, hairstyles were often a message, varying from dreadlocks to shaved skulls to bushy Afros to patterns and symbols cut out to the scalp, such as the letter X (for Malcolm X). As each style became more widespread, it often simply signified being in fashion, but at the outset, each style was generally a form of self-assertion against the majority ethnic rejection of young black men. Certainly, among many white people, the hair styles were read as a "Don't risk treading on *me*!" message.

In the 1930s and 1940s in the United States, something of the same combination of resistant attitude and macho self-assertion could be seen in the zoot suit: a very long jacket, down to the knees; baggy pants, with the crotch cut much lower than usual; and often, a long slim gold chain, elegantly draped from an inside pocket near the shoulder and sweeping down in a deep loop to the knee and then back up to the pants pocket. In Los Angeles in 1943, this form of self-assertion by young black and Chicano men led to a savage street attack by white soldiers in uniform, in the bloody "zoot suit riots" as they were termed.[2] In Harlem and Detroit, black zoot-suiters were physically attacked. The garb was a symbol of potency and self-assertion that the young white men who attacked—and the white police who stood by watching—felt they had to stamp out.[3]

OTHER TEXTILE MEDIA

There could be many instances cited of dress and textiles as radical political communication. In contemporary Guatemala, many brilliantly colored Maya textiles—usually not those designs available for sale—carry deep cultural and political meaning. In the context of the history of colonial repression and Maya resistance, the former bloodily resurgent in the 1970s through the 1990s and costing 150,000 overwhelmingly Maya lives, Maya women weavers were reasserting both their historical origins and their contemporary identity rights: "wearing and weaving Maya dress is an artistic observance of, and a demand for, sociocultural liberty" (Otzoy, 1996, p. 150).[4]

A different textile format was deployed for about 15 years in Chile, melding the simplest form of radical media with international communication against savage human rights abuses. During the repressions carried out from 1973 onward by the Pinochet military dictatorship, in which about 10,000 dissidents or suspected dissidents were seized, tortured, and then "disappeared," small embroidered rectangles of burlap sacking were one of the very few modes of communicating their plight available to their families (Agosín, 1987). The mothers of the detained and the disappeared painstakingly sewed these little *arpilleras*, each one taking at least a week.

Initially, the objective was to stretch the family income, especially if the husband had been the one seized. As time went on, the women began to use them to express their own grief and their determination to see justice done on behalf of their family members, who could not communicate either because they were jailed or more probably murdered. An oppositional popular culture emerged. Some arpilleras directly portrayed arrests, beatings, bodies being buried in haste at night, empty chairs; one cited by Agosín showed a woman's disappeared brother and the words "Truth and justice for the detained-disappeared." Others, however, carefully avoided explicit political comment.[5] The workshops where the women made the *arpilleras* became places where they nurtured each other's strength and developed an extraordinary solidarity and spirit of struggle: "Here they are next to me, sometimes trembling and sometimes laughing, so fragile in their innocence, and searching. Then all of a sudden it seemed as if I was speaking with giants" (Agosín, 1987, p. 11).

The military dictatorship banned these *arpilleras* from being sold within Chile, but solidarity activists quite often used them in other countries in lectures and exhibits as a way of maintaining international attention on the Chilean junta's crimes. Successive Catholic archbishops of Santiago, in sharp contrast to the despicable complicity of nearly all the Argentinian bishops during the 1976-1983 dictatorship on the other side of the Andes, permitted this communicative work to go unhindered despite the controlled press's venom against the burlap scraps and threats the junta issued to try to frighten off those active in the distribution network. The Vicaría de la Solidaridad set up by the Catholic hierarchy provided the materials, bought the finished products on a monthly basis, sold them overseas, and then redistributed the proceeds to the seamstress-artists. As we keep noting, religious institutions have a significant relationship in some cases to radical media.

Quilting, it transpires, was also a form of radical communication in the slavery years in the United States (Tobin & Dobard, 1999). The colors and patterns on quilts have long attracted attention, and in the early 1990s, a huge AIDS quilt was created from numerous single quilts made by women across the United States. But quilts were also used to advise enslaved Africans how to escape north, first to the northern United States and then, following the Fugitive Slave laws that permitted them to be captured and returned, to Canada. Seemingly insignificant details, such as the stitches, the knots, and their arrangement in relation to each other, were signals to the initiated. Quilts would be draped out in public, ostensibly to air, but actually as a series of up to 10 different designs to communicate clandestinely advice such as the most propitious periods of the year for escape, routes to follow, locations of safe houses, or a zigzag line of flight that would throw pursuers off the track. Some considerable part of the symbolism used in the quilts was drawn from much older religious design traditions from Africa.

PINS, BUTTONS, AND BUMPER STICKERS

Buttons (pins, lapel badges) were another form of dress popular in the latter half of the 20th century to convey a myriad of messages, among them political ridicule (If Mrs. Thatcher is the answer, it must have been a really silly question), support for a political leader who tells the truth (Tell them, Boris!), cross-racial solidarity (*Touche pas à mon pote*), and political opposition (No nukes).[6] Like most of the examples cited in this chapter, pins and badges were very cheap, and in urban settings, they could be displayed to many people in a single day. They also represent an individual commitment proclaimed by the person standing next to you and an invitation to political engagement, both of which lend them immediacy. They can easily spark political conversation and thus expand the public sphere.

Bumper stickers in the late 20th century occupied a status somewhere between buttons and flyers. They were used for every conceivable political message, from anti-abortion to pro-choice, from far Right to far Left, in a kind of public realm argument. They have also been used intertextually: a cut-out metal fish sign attached to the back of a car, for example, sometimes with the word *Jesus* or the Greek characters for the word *fish* (ιχθυσ/ichthus), was much favored by Southern creationists in the United States in the 1990s. Those who saw fundamentalism as dangerously retrograde retaliated by putting the word *Darwin* inside the sign and attaching a couple of small feet to the bottom of the fish, symbolizing evolutionary science. There were even fish signs with the word *gefilte* inside.[7]

Summary: Perhaps the primary lesson of the examples in this chapter has been the low-cost accessibility and easy spatial diffusion of these particular examples. A series of issues have also surfaced—radical humor, street communication, interactive art, the impurity of oppositional cultures, the alternative public sphere, the long-term impact of radical media, their low-cost accessibility. These will be further, and differently, illustrated in the next chapter.

NOTES

1. Perhaps one of the most provocative and witty of the graffiti seen by this writer was a large, white-painted lesbian separatist slogan on the side of a house near an open market in Dalston, east London, in the late 1970s. It read "A woman needs a man like a fish needs a bicycle." Graffiti may also be used to deface and comment on public advertisements, rather like the *détournement* discussed in Part I and the culture-jamming discussed in Chapter 12. A famous example from London in the late 1970s was a huge billboard advertising a new Fiat car, with the statement "If this car were a lady, she would get her bottom pinched." In large letters, the size of the ad's graphics, feminist activists wrote on it: "If this lady were a car, she'd run you over." In 1991, in Austin, Texas, home by then to a public that valued good beers and loathed the tasteless chemical muck most widely sold as beer, Lite Beer put up a large billboard, which it then removed in a distinct hurry. The billboard had blazoned Lite Beer as "It's it, and that's that!" Some beer-loving prankster promptly scaled a ladder at night and added *sh* to *it*. See also Schlecht (1995) for a study of the

depoliticization of graffiti in postdictatorship Brazil and Chaffee (1989, 1990) for studies of political graffiti in Buenos Aires and in Paraguay.

2. Moments in the clash are reconstructed in early scenes in the films *American Me* (director, Edward James Olmos, 1991), and *Zoot Suit* (director, Luís Valdez, 1981). The use of extra material during wartime rationing for making the suits was read as disloyal by the marines, notwithstanding the many African Americans and Chicanos serving in the military.

3. See White and White (1998), for an absorbing study of African American dress and body styling through the 1940s.

4. In the late 18th and early 19th century in England, pocket handkerchiefs with political prints on them were popular clothing items among men (Donald, 1996, p. 187). In the furor in Britain in 1767 over the government's banning of issue 45 of political critic John Wilkes's *North Briton*, buttons and brooches were stamped with the number 45, and even men's wigs were popular for a while made with 45 curls in them (Wood, 1994, p. 54). These examples may seem to sit oddly with each other, but together they serve to underscore how communicating opposition to injustice, on whatever levels, needs a commonality, not an apartheid.

5. Agosín's (1987) description of the gradual coming together of these women is reminiscent of Anna Akhmatova's description of the lines of women outside Leningrad's jails when she was searching for news of her imprisoned son: "They got to know each other as they inquired in prisons, police stations, detention centres for their family members, or they met in places where they went to ask for aid because their husbands were out of work" (p. 44). Akhmatova was asked by one such woman waiting in line whether she could possibly describe in writing the horror they were all facing; she replied, "I can." *Requiem* was the result. Pinochet, however, brazenly trumpeted his coup d'état as essential to prevent a communist dictatorship. However, despite the hideous actions of his torturers against women defined as leftist activists, the patriarchal Catholic ideology suffusing the Pinochet regime fortunately made it harder than it was for the Stalin regime to move with systematic violence against peacefully protesting mothers.

6. Mrs Thatcher was British premier from 1979-90, notorious for her contemptuous ironclad dismissal of Irish hunger strikers, striking British miners, the unemployed, the homeless, and, indeed, anyone who disagreed with her. Boris Yeltsin, although later widely reviled as first president of Russia, was amazingly popular in the late 1980s as someone who dared to pinpoint in public the failures of the Soviet system. Touche pas à mon pote [Hands off my buddy] was a popular button directed against racist attacks in France at about the same period; it defined people of color as the wearer's friends, not as aliens. "No nukes" was a long-running favorite during the decades of nuclear confrontation between the United States and the Soviet Union and did double duty as a statement of opposition to nuclear power stations.

7. The Greek characters are an acronym from the first letters of the words *Jesus Christ, Son of God, Savior,* and the fish was a common clandestine symbol in the Roman catacombs in the period when Christianity was a persecuted

faith, literally underground. The term *gefilte* refers to a popular East European Jewish delicacy made from two kinds of fish, ground together, and formed into patties; its use in this context crisply deflated the portentousness of the fish symbol at the hands of humorless fundamentalists.

12

Popular Theater, Street Theater, Performance Art, and Culture-Jamming

Popular theater and street theater are a further type of radical communication that we must include in this tapestry of rebellious cultural expression. Their medium, ultimately, is once again public speech and the body, as in dance, but sometimes with stage effects added. They have as long or longer an alternative history as any of the other media forms examined here, and they also have important linkages with radical radio and video. Performance art and culture-jamming are some of their offshoots. At the same time, we will see how varied, in some instances, are the levels of political opposition expressed (e.g., anti-Vietnam War theater) and begin to address organizational problems in composing an alternative public sphere (e.g., British radical theater).

- British radical theater 1960-1990
- *El Teatro Campesino*
- Political theater against the U.S. war in Vietnam
- Augusto Boal and street political theater

- Performance art: the Art Rebate/*Arte Reembolso* event
- ACT-UP street events
- Culture-jamming

BRITISH RADICAL THEATER

The British example is in part a tribute to Brecht's influence in the drive to render the audience active and in other ways an interesting commentary both on the problems of organizing radical media and on the issue of their long-term influence. Kershaw (1992) says the British alternative theater activists' "starting point was the nature of their audience and its community" (p. 5). They

> aimed both to de-mystify the art form, especially to strip it of the mystique of professionalism, and to promote greater equality between the stage and the auditorium . . . for example in the form of adaptations of interactive techniques drawn from . . . pantomime and music hall . . . comic-strips, film animation, cinema and television . . . through the adaptation of . . . fun-fairs and festivals to produce the sensory, wrap-around effects of psychodelic spectacles; through the physical participation of the audience in the action. (p. 103)

The results of this cofabulation were frequently a wild mixture of celebration and social criticism, of carnival and satire.

Typically, these performances took place outside conventional theater settings and often before first-time theatergoers, whose reluctant and ambivalent attendance had to be won. One of the central insights, at least for some theater groups, was how important for the impact of the play was what happened to the audience before and after the performance. In the theater activists' view, the play was not a separate sacral moment for an intellectual audience to switch out from life and on to high culture, but an artwork whose purpose was to engage with people's ongoing lives. The linked themes of art, radical media, and interactivity surface once more.

Despite many tenets held in common, however, the radical theater movement was as fissiparous as alternative media tend to be anywhere:

> The movement was awash with fluidity and fission. Groups transmuted from one constitution to another with remarkable frequency, often changing names in the process. Breakaway companies were formed out of disagreements, dissatisfaction, and the desire to cover new theatrical or social or political ground. (Kershaw, 1992, p. 47)

Inevitably, too, the experiments did not all work. Sometimes, regard for the audience dissolved into cheap and easy gimmicks to keep its attention, the commitment to egalitarianism produced a politically "holier than thou" stance by some activists, and petty despotism flourished in spaces opened up by participatory democracy (cf. Freeman, 1975).

From a longer perspective, however, Kershaw (1992) argues that the movement was a typical formation (in Raymond Williams's sense) in the alternative public sphere counterculture of those decades, "testing and suggesting developments of their oppositional ideologies through the concrete medium of performance projects" (p. 253). He also suggests, with good evidence, that radical theater had considerable ramifications within mainstream theater, in mainstream media, and in school drama. Not least, it was influential within the social movement of the 1980s against Prime Minister Thatcher's administration: That movement, in turn, sparked many local councils' community-oriented cultural programs, which created alternative public spheres where dialogue and conversation could thrive and hatch challenges to Thatcherism's destructive social policies. Looking for radical media impact may often, as emphasized already a number of times, mean following apparently circuitous trails such as this through a whole generation and its informal communication networks.[1]

RADICAL THEATER IN THE UNITED STATES

A notable U.S. example of radical street theater was *El Teatro Campesino,* The Fieldhands' Theater (Broyles-González, 1994). The sources of this theater movement were many. Most immediate were the labor struggles of Chicano and migrant Mexican farmworkers on huge California plantations in the 1960s, often led by the United Farmworkers of America (UFW), the unofficial union founded in 1962 by César Chávez, Helen Chávez, and Dolores Huerta. Earlier centuries of struggle by poor farmers, *peones,* slaves, and seasonal day laborers were another more diffuse but powerful source, whether they worked in Mexico or the southwestern United States.[2]

Popular oral traditions of commentary, protest, and ridicule based on these grievances fed into the productions of El Teatro Campesino. So did a well-established popular Mexican theatrical form, the traveling *carpa* (tent) performance, whose performance space was, literally, a collapsible tent, taken from site to site on a truck or even a mule cart. It had brightly painted backdrops, often a single naked electric lightbulb, and plain benches for the audience, and it offered live music, dance, and a series of comic sketches with both earthy and fantastic subjects. As in the earlier instance of African American dance in the era of slavery, the performers' use of their bodies as a communication instrument was especially important, sometimes almost more important than the words themselves:

> To these audiences, understanding a performance meant a great deal more than a semantic de-coding. It entailed an apprehension of tone, of silences, of body movement, of images, of sounds in all their variety . . . the performance aesthetic capitalized on mime. (Broyles-González, 1994, p. 18)

Both in carpa theater and El Teatro productions, the script was an approximate guide, discussed in common beforehand but not memorized; rather than a legislated performance, the show was intensely interactive: "Improvisation [depended] most notably on . . . audience response and participation. . . . Essential to this process is each individual's split-second timing and capacity to think on one's feet" (Broyles-González, 1994, p. 17). A key character in carpa was the underdog, *el pelado/la pelada*: irreverent, ribald, irrepressible, at one and the same time truculent and scared, winner and loser, scruffily dressed, a trickster figure combined with man/woman of the people.

Commentators have often suggested the influence of Brecht and other radical theater exponents on El Teatro Campesino, but Broyles-González insists, without discounting such influences, on the very strong indigenous roots of the company. Its members drew in considerable detail on Mayan and Aztec religious cultures in developing a theater philosophy anchored in a philosophy of existence (Broyles-González, 1994, pp. 79-127). Rejecting the segregation between performance and personal life frequent in mainstream theater culture, or between political activism and religion common in the United States, its performers sought to develop a single interpretive basis both for their training and their vision of El Teatro Campesino's contribution to Chicano communities' struggles. Accounts of El Teatro's work often stress their support of the UFW in the protracted grape-pickers' strike of 1965 or their lead in the revival of Chicano awareness in literature, history, the arts, and politics but regrettably omit their endeavor to revalorize the core native component of *Mexicanidad*.[3]

Thus the El Teatro Campesino intriguingly illustrates the frequent importance for radical media of engaging with local popular cultural traditions, including theatrical and—not least—religious ones (cf. the Iranian case). It shows how important is spontaneity in radical theater and how all these elements interlocked in this instance with political support to the labor movement.

THE VIETNAM WAR ON STAGE

The Vietnam War plays Alter (1996) discusses were staged in the United States, the former West Germany, France, Austria, Britain, and Vietnam itself. As the U.S. war escalated, these plays formed an active ingredient within the counterculture. Their denunciations of the war had certain things in common, such as an intentional one-sidedness to counterbalance the pronounced one-sidedness of mainstream media support for the war[4]—or at least lack of official support for the Vietnamese—but their actual points of emphasis varied, and their national contexts shaped the form of protest they voiced. A consideration of these plays sharply demonstrates how all the standard terms denoting dissent—alternative, radical, oppositional, counterhegemonic, resistance—essentially beg the further question of how deep and how focused is that dissent.[5]

Some plays, for instance, primarily promoted nonviolence. In many, the Vietnamese were there as objects, pivotal symbols of wrong done to the helpless, not as agents in their own right. Black and female roles sometimes expressed the same syndrome. Vietnam became a metaphor rather than an actual place, speaking of the fatal nexus between masculinism and technology, or becoming (in the German play) an illustration of capitalist imperialism. In France, Austria, and Britain, the Vietnam war was principally used to reflect on each nation's postcolonial role. The French play compared France's two former colonies of Vietnam and Algeria. The Austrian and British plays seemed to propose a postcolonial moral high ground role for their respective nations—that is, that they should lead international condemnation of the war—as a way to retain their presence on the world stage. Only the Vietnamese play presented the Vietnamese themselves at center stage, but that work was mainly a vehicle for the Vietnamese Communist Party's line.

Thus, although any opposition to a monstrous war was to be welcomed, these plays' tendency to use its horrors as a symbol rather than centering them provides an important corrective reminder that radical media projects may not have any compelling interest in the viewpoints of those repressed, or even in their resistance.

THE CONTRIBUTIONS OF BOAL

Some of the most dynamic and radical forms of popular theater have been pioneered in Latin America, where the name of Augusto Boal has particular resonance in this regard.[6] Boal's theater is not for the stage and has no three-act structure or conventional audience. His work is designed for the street and other public places and as a provocation. His goal is to engage the audience existentially and politically within the physical space of their everyday terrain and preoccupations. His work especially illustrates the importance, for radical media activists, of not limiting themselves to providing counterfacts, central as that exercise is, but developing ways to give their media bite. Boal's book *Theater of the Oppressed*, after Freire's *Pedagogy of the Oppressed*, has been something of a bible to a whole generation of street and community theater activists in Latin America and elsewhere. Forced into political exile from several Latin American countries as they underwent military dictatorships, in 1978, Boal finally sought political asylum in France and pursued his theater work there and elsewhere in Europe.

A description of one quite elaborate piece, scripted to confront sexual harassment on the Paris Métro and performed three times, will give the flavor of his work (Boal, 1997, pp. 28-31). Aside from the high-voltage theme, what stands out is the intense immediacy and interactivity between performers and audiences. It closely mirrors Benjamin's notion of aura, of the reduction of art's distance from the public and the intensification of interaction between artwork and public. The piece also involved activists of both genders and different ethnic groups.

A group of actors would board the Métro at Vincennes on the long Vincennes-Neuilly commuter line: There would be two women who stood talking near the central doors, another woman sitting, a Tunisian man sitting next to her, a mother and child sitting a little farther off, and other actors scattered through the car. For the first two stops, everyone behaved normally, reading the paper or passing the time of day with other passengers. At the third station along the line, a further actor (the Groper) would get on the train. He would sit down by the seated woman or stand next to her. Soon, he would begin to push his leg against hers. She would immediately start to complain loudly. The actor would say it was an accident. Not once did a passenger come to her defense.

Then, a little later, the man would not only push his leg against her leg but would ostentatiously run his hand over her thigh. She would object loudly, but again with no support from her fellow passengers. She would get up and stay standing. At this, the Tunisian actor would take a moment to voice support for the Groper.

At the fifth station, another actor would get on, young and particularly handsome, and almost immediately the two women standing chatting would start to comment very loudly on what a fine specimen he was. Then, one would ask him the time, he would tell her, and she would ask him when he was getting off—to which he would react with some irritation: "Look, I didn't ask you that, what do you mean?" She would answer, "Well if you'd asked me, I'd've told you: I'm getting off at République, and if you'd like to get off there too, we could have a great time together." While saying this, she would begin caressing him. He would try to move away, but she would grab him and say, "You know, you're a real hunk. Shit, I'd love to jump on your bones." Again, he would make as if to flee but would find himself trapped between the two women. Those within earshot would hear them insisting it was their right to get up close and personal with him.

At long last, passengers would speak up. Often, against the women. The Groper would defend the young man, and then, the actress he had groped would loudly object that no one had come to her support just a few minutes earlier, so why was it wrong if a woman sexually harassed a man? Then, all three women would turn on the Groper and badmouth him, and he would shortly afterward leave the scene.

To be sure that no one in the car had missed what took place, the mother would ask her young son what had been going on. He was chosen for his very piercing voice, so no one could fail to hear what had happened.

Some astonishing conversations were sparked. One old lady said, "Well that girl was right, he was quite a hunk." One man said, defending the Groper's aggression but not the women's, "Look, it's human nature." Another opined that "it's always women who start that stuff going." One of these males speaking in defense was sitting next to his wife, so the Tunisian actor immediately went on the attack: "You think so? You think men have the right to rub up against women in the Métro?" "Yes, I do." "OK, well excuse me, that's exactly what I had in mind to do to your wife." And made as if to stroke her. The husband instantly exploded in fury, and a major fracas was only averted by the actor apologizing profusely and leaving the car at the next station.

In one performance, the discussion became so heated and noisy that the train was halted, and all the passengers in the other cars left their places to see what was going on in the performance car.

Boal acknowledges that for real impact, rather than three performances of such a piece, 50 such groups should perform it 500 times over. The greater flexibility of theater over mass media, the possibility for actors "to update their message from day to day" (Alter, 1996, p. 21), "to develop especially subtle ideological negotiations with audiences" (Kershaw, 1992, p. 66), is offset in other ways by the reach of contemporary media. But this instance of Boalian street theater also underscores his principal objective, namely, that radical theater should engage with people, push them to discuss with vigor and passion by what principles they intend to live out their lives in future.

PERFORMANCE ART

The minimal costs of this theater, its freedom from the typical constraints (stage, lighting, costumes, makeup, a paying audience, a formal division into acts or scenes), its conviction that although some can act better than others, everyone can act, its selection of "hot-button" topics to provoke discussion, its engagement in dialogue with the audience, are all distinguishing marks of a theater brought directly into everyday life. This is not to say that more conventional theater has no constructive role to play,[7] only that in considering radical media we need to appreciate the full spectrum of low-cost and direct-impact possibilities. Street theater can be much simpler than this Paris Métro example. For instance, in attempts to spur solidarity with Central Americans faced with U.S.-backed terror during the 1980s, some U.S. student groups would stage a plainclothes police swoop in a university cafeteria, hauling someone out of a chair at gunpoint, and then would break the action and start a discussion about repression in El Salvador, Guatemala, and Honduras.[8]

Performance art is closely allied to street theater. Two particularly pungent illustrations follow, one from San Diego, California, the other from the AIDS campaign ACT-UP.[9] Both suggest fresh approaches to radical media aesthetics. Both emphasize the street as a crucial component of the alternative public sphere.

Arte Reembolso

San Diego is the largest U.S. urban center on the Mexican border, historically a highly conservative naval base city where hostility to Latino workers without visas and labor documents runs high. A local poster and performance group wished to highlight the dependence of California's economy on these men and women's cheap labor power and the fact that many also pay taxes deducted at source from their pay packets.[10] So they put on *Art Rebate/Arte Reembolso* in 1993 (Pincus, 1995), in which they distributed $10 bills to such workers in locations where they typically gathered to be picked up for work. The recipients were required to sign a sheet that said in bold letters, "This $10 bill is part of an art project that intends to return tax dollars to taxpayers, particularly 'undocumented taxpayers.' The art rebate acknowledges your role as a vital player in an economic community indifferent to national borders" (Pincus, 1995, p. 48). The money in question came from the National Endowment for the Arts, the San Diego Museum of Contemporary Art, and the Centro Cultural de la Raza.

A political firestorm erupted. The symbolism was immense of giving away the sacred American dollar publicly to undocumented Latin American workers and of connecting that cash directly with the tax revenues that arts institutions redistribute, mostly to politically safe "high art" institutions and projects. The potency of this artwork was proven by the disproportion between the tiny total amount distributed, a mere $4,500 to just 450 recipients, and the purple apoplexy that ensued. Having this action defined as art seemed to be the final goad, given the basic conservative axiom that art—or science, or journalism—must have zero linkage with contemporary oppositional politics. The National Endowment for the Arts, panic stricken, asked for the return of its part of the money. One of the pleasing effects of such art, however, is precisely to precipitate such reactions, which in their turn may serve to draw much wider attention to the work and the questions it raises.

ACT-UP

The other example of performance art from the United States was undertaken over a 5- or 6-year period by the group ACT-UP, standing for AIDS Coalition to Unleash Power, formed in 1987 (Crimp & Rolston, 1990; Meyer, 1995). The most widely seen of their works was the Nazi-era pink triangle[11] on a black background with Silence = Death, which appeared on posters, buttons, stickers, and T-shirts—although the group inverted the Nazi pink triangle as a resistance statement. ACT-UP also disrupted the stock exchange on Wall Street, and a Mass at St Patrick's Cathedral in New York. The most active performance art group within the coalition was an anonymous collective entitled Gran Fury,[12] a group of professional and part-time artists.

When they demonstrated on Wall Street in 1988, they printed up small handbills with images of dollar bills on one side and trenchant commentary on the other. The reverse side of the $10 dollar replica read, "White heterosexual men can't get AIDS . . . DON'T BANK ON IT." The $100 reverse side said, "FUCK YOUR PROFITEERING . . . People are dying while you play business." The group disrupted a Mass inside St Patrick's Cathedral in 1989 to protest Cardinal O'Connor's continual denunciations of condom use and of homosexual lovemaking. One demonstrator dropped a consecrated wafer on the floor, an action that aroused mainstream media horror and condemnation.[13]

In other instances, Gran Fury targeted *The New York Times*, the Food and Drug Administration, New York's City Hall, its Department of Health, and Grand Central Station; members sometimes sat down and blocked the city's road traffic. One of their most pungent posters (Crimp & Rolston, 1990, p. 135) had in flaming red block letters against a pale pink background **KNOW YOUR SCUMBAGS.** To the right were two photographs, one of Cardinal O'Connor, the other of a condom. Underneath the condom, in smaller upper-case black, was THIS ONE PREVENTS AIDS.

What stands out about these and other examples of performance art of this period is the direct fusion of political, media, and artistic activity. The international movement *Reclaim The Streets*, which began in Britain in 1998 and rapidly grew into coordinated street protests and dances in major downtown centers of London, New York, and other cities, is a further example.

CULTURE-JAMMING

One version of this mixture, developed in and around Austin, Texas, and elsewhere[14] in the mid-1990s, was what some of its practitioners termed *culture-jamming.* Given the preponderance of rightist religious radio stations with a largely talk-show format in the South, some activists began phoning in to the shows claiming to be devout fundamentalists and filling up the airtime with lengthy statements that began to edge further and further away from religious verities and closer and closer to taboo sexual or political issues until—usually—they were cut off the air after the talk-show host woke up to what was happening. Some talk-show hosts showed themselves to be remarkably gullible—or just slow off the mark. Some of the culture-jammers had extraordinary talents at mimicry and would sound on the air as if they were elderly, slightly confused and disorganized, but nonetheless firm in their obscurantist prejudices, by all of these tactics disarming the hosts' suspicions—yet all the while insinuating improprieties.

It is hard to convey the riotous flavor of some such calls. One culture-jammer, calling himself Melba and appearing to be a pensioner, actually managed not to be cut off during a long, rambling phone-in during which he/she suddenly squawked loudly in feigned pain and shock "*OW*! my *pussy*!" and then excused him/herself by saying "I'm real sorry to make all that noise, but I just done dropped my hot tea on my pussy"! Another time, posing as minister of a fundamentalist tabernacle, he managed to get the talk show host genuinely intrigued by a book he claimed to possess that purported to show how the Vatican had been specially training attack baboons to help invade the United States and set up a one-world government (a favorite paranoia of the loony Right in the United States).[15]

We have already spent some time on "mind-bomb" media/artworks, such as song, graffiti, buttons, and carnival, and will return to them when we discuss poster art, satirical cartoons, political pornography, comics, and various other instances of politically active art. What is noticeable is that the situationist impulse, even if not specifically claimed, seems to be alive and kicking in many of them. Radical media with spice.

Equally noticeable in the examples above is their interaction with movements of resistance: feminist, labor, ethnic, socialist, gay, antiwar. The dialogue and conversation they sparked and enabled drew much of its juice from the movements in question and in turn helped to empower the movements. This was a form of democracy a long way removed from the formal democracy of intermittent big-money elections. At the same time, as the plays framed against the Vietnam war indicated, the counterhegemonic process operates at differing depths, and as British radical theater demonstrated, it is never or only rarely free of internal strife. This latter is an issue that will be ventilated in much more detail in some of the case studies in Part III.

NOTES

1. Charlotte Canning's (1996) marvelous treatment of feminist theater in the United States in the dynamic period 1969-1986 came to my attention too late—an ironic by-product of our both working on a campus some 20,000 bodies bigger than the town I grew up in as a teenager—for discussion here. Her account of both the organizational dynamics and longer-term impact of the projects she surveys extends and strengthens the case Kershaw makes, and enriches considerably an understanding of women's agency as radical communicators, of social movements and their alternative public spheres, and also of the complex interethnic dynamics of progressive projects.

2. California, Arizona, New Mexico, and parts of Colorado and Nevada constitute fully four ninths of the original Spanish colonial territory, ceded as a result of the 1846-1848 U.S. war against Mexico. Texas had already been seized in a white settler revolt in 1836. The U.S.-Mexican border is a historical-cultural fiction in certain senses, with continued cultural and economic flows exposing its reified character; in other ways, it is a harsh, heavily policed reality. See Fox (1999) and Dunn (1996). See further the Arte Reembolso case study below.

3. For an analysis of Mexico's culture that underscores its continuing indigenous base, see Bonfil Batalla (1996).

4. This issue has been contested for years, with military and conservative opinion contending that U.S. media eroded the public support necessary for crushing the Vietnamese, and their critics arguing that this is a wildly overblown reaction that masks the comprehensive failures of U.S. military strategy, the official lies disseminated about the war, and the war's basic illegitimacy. See Hallin (1986).

5. An interesting case study, although not from the theater, is the newspaper *PM*, founded in 1940 in New York City to provide a voice in support of the more leftist policies of the Roosevelt administration. It was perpetually torn between reflecting popular discontent and loyalty to Roosevelt. See Milkman, 1997. Chicago's labor-oriented radio station, WCFL, which ran from 1926

through 1978, illuminates a number of the same issues of hegemony and counterhegemony. See Godfried, 1997.

6. Boal's projects have taken Brecht's attempt to revolutionize theater several steps further. He has consciously distinguished himself from Brecht, claiming that the latter sought to put theater at the service of revolution, whereas in his view, theater is an integral part of revolution (Boal, 1997, p. 20). Admittedly, each is using *revolution* in different senses. Brecht, during the struggle against fascism in the 1930s and 1940s, saw the Soviet-led revolution as the only game in town (although in the 1950s he retracted that view). As a strategy against fascism's and capitalism's seductiveness, Brecht emphasized that spectators must learn to distance themselves from theater and spectacle. This was the purpose of his famous term, *Entfremdungseffekt* (usually translated alienation effect). Soviet Russian artists and playwrights of the period, committed to building the Soviet experiment, did not follow a Brechtian approach, but instead tried to enthuse people, concerned lest they should distance themselves (Mueller, 1989, p. 13). Boal, writing from the 1960s onward, defined revolution in terms of continuing popular struggles, without any reference to things Soviet. Whereas Boal's approach is equally based on helping the spectator to be transformed into a political and social activist, he argues that even Brechtian theater, in the final analysis, is cathartic, that is to say, it purifies / suppresses tendencies in the audience that might lead to their challenging the status quo.

7. We need only think of Henrik Ibsen, Samuel Beckett, Arthur Miller, Dario Fo, Athol Fugard, Wole Soyinka, Ngugi wa Th'iongo, David Edgar, Caryl Churchill, Vaclav Havel.

8. Thanks to my colleague Cathy Echols in the University of Texas Psychology Department for this example.

9. For two useful critical surveys, see Felshin, 1995, and Lacy, 1995. I am grateful to Laura Saponara for bringing these two sources to my attention.

10. California's imfamous Proposition 187, passed some years later, denied health and educational services even to those undocumented workers who had been paying taxes for many years.

11. The Nazis forced concentration camp inmates interned for their sexual orientation to wear a pink triangle differentiating them from the Jews, who were required to wear a yellow star. It is unknown how many homosexuals perished, but estimates are at least half a million.

12. The collective's title was taken from the brand-name of the powerful Plymouth car used by undercover New York police.

13. No such media fury was aroused by members of New York's finest who, outside the cathedral and not even in holy Christian response to sacrilege, dragged one of the street demonstrators into a store doorway and repeatedly kicked him in the groin. For the instances cited in this paragraph, see Crimp and Rolston, (1990, pp. 46-51, 130-140).

14. See, for example, the magazine *Adbusters* and the website (http:// www.adbusters.org), produced in Vancouver, Canada.

15. Examples include the following compact disks: *Brother Russell's Radio Jihad;* and *Melba Comes Alive*: Vinyl Communications, P. O. Box 8623, Chula Vista, CA 91912 (http://www.vinylcomm.com).

13

The Press

The overriding theme here is the powerful role of the alternative and underground press in social, political, and cultural change in Europe and the United States since the 1500s. Here, we see some of the most significant historical illustrations of the power that radical media may exert despite their small size and sometimes their very gradual transformation of the status quo. In the earlier examples, we see the force of religious elements in subverting official culture, in later examples, both the use of pornography and the subversive implications of even the most decorous of respectable women's media. In between, we can observe earlier examples of international radical media flows. Concluding comments on comics and graphic novels illustrate the priority of how to make the political accessible and how visual imagery can dovetail with verbal address and narrative to intensify aesthetically counterhegemonic communicative force.

- The *Flugschrift* war of the 1520s
- The vernacular Bible
- International publication centers in the Reformation
- Radical media in the French Revolution
- Politically dissident pornography

- The radical press in the United States from the Revolution to the present
- The novel and the 19th-century conduct book as alternative media vehicles for women communicators
- Comics and comix

MARTIN LUTHER AND THE PAMPHLET WAR

Martin Luther is often cited as saying that the printing press was the latest and greatest of God's gifts, and, indeed, he himself was certainly catapulted into tremendous prominence through his leading role in the so-called pamphlet *(Flugschrift)* war of the early 1520s.[1] Yet, his general view of the printing press was much less positive; he was often deeply distrustful of a growing volume of publications that he claimed misled rather than enlightened the public (Gilmont, 1990a, pp. 9-12). His violent hostility to the radical Anabaptist movement in the Peasants War in Germany is noted in Chapter 14's discussion of woodcuts. And the pamphlet war itself was not widespread in the Reformation era as a whole in Europe or throughout every part of Germany.

Nonetheless, although the role of print media in the Reformation movements can be and has been exaggerated, it was still significant.[2] Diffusion of the vernacular Bible was clearly far and away the most significant force in disrupting established religious and political authority, but a mass of other Protestant publications were also circulated, to the point where in France, for example, to try to combat them, Catholic theologians found themselves compelled to write countertreatises in French rather than Latin. The religious public sphere was clearly being forced to expand, although the expression of dissident views could be lethally dangerous for printers. Hans Hergot was executed in Leipzig in 1527 for having twice published a pamphlet, *On the New Direction of a Christian Life* (*Von der newen wandlung eynes Christlichen Lebens),* which proposed that goods, including land, should be held in common (Flood, 1990, p. 41).

CRADLES OF HERETICAL PRINTING

An absorbing dimension of the process was the international role of particular cities as cradles of heretical printing. They were, so to speak, forerunners of the *tamizdat* publications of the later Soviet era[3] and early instances of radical media's global dimension. During the Reformation, the leading print cities were Antwerp, Strasbourg, Basel, and Venice. Although they held in common the advantage that they were not subject to the same reprisals from the authorities faced by heterodox printers in France or Italy or many other countries,[4] other reasons for their playing this role differed from city to city. Antwerp and Venice were major commercial seafaring centers, where the dynamic of trade and the multicultural quality of the citizenry and its merchant visitors served to mute ideological absolutism (Johnston & Gilmont, 1990; Rozzo & Seidel Menchi, 1990). Venice was also Europe's leading print center in the first half of the 16th century. Antwerp's presses published in Dutch, English, French, Spanish, Italian, and Danish, not to mention Latin, Greek, and Hebrew. Strasbourg was a self-governing city located exactly between France and Germany, and Basel not only was self-governing and similarly located, it also was a center of Protestant activism and home to one of Europe's leading universities during that period (Bietenholz, 1990; Chrisman, 1990).

The penalties enacted against the local distributors of these publications, whether they were booksellers or itinerant vendors, ranged from severe to terminal. Their printers, even in these protected locations, could also face sanctions, inasmuch as once they were identified as a heterodox source, any of their publications might be automatically confiscated from vendors and summarily burned. As a result, the name of the author and the printer, including the latter's address, were typically left out, the font and format were designed to make the book look like a standard devotional work, and the titles were selected to avoid arousing suspicion. The size of the publications also reflected these major concerns, with the small octavo size increasingly favored so that it could be concealed in someone's clothing or baggage or deep within a consignment of larger books. Once the Counter-Reformation and its Inquisition took hold, moreover, both Antwerp and Venice were compelled under maximum duress to close shop as publishing centers for books of this kind.

MEDIA IN THE FRENCH REVOLUTION

The comparison is notable between these small-format books and similar dissident uses of easily concealed audio- and videocassettes both in the former Soviet bloc and during the build-up to the 1979 Iranian revolution. Furthermore, the role of radical print centers outside the government's reach was paralleled in the build-up to the 1789 French revolution. In the latter instance, Darnton (1995) notes,

> Dozens of publishing houses sprang up all around France's borders. Hundreds of agents operated an underground system, which brought the books to readers . . . they circulated in a society that overflowed with gossip, rumors, jokes, songs, graffiti, posters, pasquinades,[5] broadsides, letters, and journals. (pp. xx, xxii)

He concludes with this summary of the effects of radical media in fomenting the French Revolution:

> [They] molded public opinion in two ways: by fixing disaffection in print (preserving and spreading the word), and by fitting it into narratives (transforming loose talk into coherent discourse). (p. 191)

An interesting feature, however, of this later period (certainly as contrasted with the Reformation) was the use of pornography as a weapon against the high and mighty. Darnton (1995, p. 165) appropriately flags the cultural context of the time, one in which many French people believed that scrofula could be cured by simply touching the king's body. It followed that exposing the most intimate aspects of royal and even noble or clergy personages' bodies to ridicule and shame was a pungent, Rabelaisian form of political critique. In a deeply phallocratic culture, the links between alleged sexual impotence and incompetence in ruling, which we already observed in Nigerian political graffiti, went beyond correlation to virtual equation.[6] Claiming that the king could not achieve an erection, or possessed a minuscule phallus, was equivalent to laughing him off the political stage.[7]

In reverse, claiming that his mistress, the Comtesse du Barry, had to go to the servants' quarters to achieve sexual satisfaction also validated the sexual, and thus political credibility of the *sans-culottes.* For bishops and monks to be portrayed as fixated on flagellation suggested that their readiness to warn others of the perils of hell was bound together with their own morality in a distinctly unholy embrace. Merely seeing such material in print ate away at the edifice of reigning ideology among the literate, for even though it attacked individual monarchs' and prelates' unworthiness, it also implicitly questioned the very system that allowed such grossly negative individuals to wield authority.

PORNOGRAPHY AND POLITICS

This linkage between pornography and politics has been examined in some detail in a collection of essays edited by Lynn Hunt (1993). It is interesting to note how the political impulse in pornography seems to have been relatively common in Europe up until the early 19th century, at which point the straightforwardly titillating dimension appears to have supplanted its political bite. But in the earlier period, as Findlen (1993) notes in the conclusion to her chapter on post-Renaissance Italy, a mix of the "voyeuristic, subversive and highly philosophical, pornography quickly became the preferred medium through which to vent one's outrage about the ills of society while, at the same time, making a tidy profit" (p. 108). This tradition seems to have spread from Italy to other parts of Europe until, as noted, its early 19th century demise. In a different place and time, the graphic sexual statements pervasive in the U.S. youth underground press of the 1960s, read in the context of the puritanism endemic in official U.S. culture of that time (Jezer, 1982; Peck, 1985), probably demonstrate an enduring truth: entrenched sexual repression may make irresistibly seductive the temptation to set the cat among the pigeons with politically angled pornography.

Hunt's contributors do not really address the connection between medieval marketplace ribaldry, as celebrated by Rabelais and analyzed by Bakhtin, and this political dimension of 16th- to 18th-century pornography. But (a) this pornography's bite effectively extended the targets of marketplace scatology from ordinary people to the very apex of society and its ideologies and (b) politicized pornography's impact was greatly enhanced by the very fact of its appearance in print, taking its place, however outrageously, within letters, even able to stand side by side on a bookshelf with authoritative, canonized texts.

THE RADICAL PRESS IN THE UNITED STATES

The Revolutionary Years

In the American Revolution, more or less contemporaneously with the outpouring of fierce antipathy to George III within England itself, which continued long after 1776, flyers, pamphlets, and newspapers contributed a major form of yeast to the political ferment. Tom Paine's 1776 pamphlet *Common Sense,* in which George is described as "the Royal

Brute of Great Britain," is perhaps the most celebrated of those that circulated, but there were many, many more. Print materials also circulated defending the monarchy, just as Catholic publications circulated in Europe defending Rome against the Reformers, but in both instances, the pro-status quo publications had the disadvantage of not being enmeshed in an energetic social movement. It seems, however, that the main spate of these broadsides was in the decade before 1776 and that once British control had been shaken off, it subsided (Sullivan, 1997, p. 17).[8]

As the 19th century developed, so did radical alternative publications in both the United States and Britain. The Chartist movement in early 19th-century Britain was distinguished by the obduracy and courage of many printers and vendors who went to jail for shorter or longer terms, some repeatedly, for publishing and selling radical newsheets whose price did not include the government's Stamp Tax on newspapers, which would have put them beyond the budget of the general public. The unstamped, as this determined alternative press was collectively described, were a vital force within the political insurgency of the Chartist movement's decades (Hollis, 1970). In the United States in 1800 to 1850, the first labor press, the first minority ethnic newspapers, the first women's suffrage publications, and the first Abolitionist press all saw the light of day.

Abolition and the Media

The complex relation between minority ethnic and radical media, and their degree of overlap were discussed in Chapter 7. Suffice it to repeat for now that within the context of an overwhelmingly European majority population whose public policies were axiomatically racist, and whose mainstream culture was exclusionary, the very act of instituting a publication dedicated to and written by people of color was virtually a radical alternative step in itself. Self-evidently, the Abolitionist press, whether Frederick Douglass's *Northern Star* or the books published by formerly enslaved mariners that we noted earlier, offered a revolutionary platform against economic dependence on forced labor based on race.

The Labor Press

Labor newspapers, too, flourished in the United States in the period before the advent of the rotary press. However, it would be erroneous to assume that they vanished from view from that point onward. With the arrival of increasing numbers of migrant workers from the 1880s through 1917, the year the United States finally entered the First World War, the foreign language press flourished, including many publications of a socialist or labor hue. In addition, weekly or monthly English-language socialist and anarchist publications emerged, whether J. A. Wayland's *Appeal to Reason*, the widely distributed weekly published from 1895 through 1922,[9] or Emma Goldman's anarchist newspaper, *Mother Earth*. One of the liveliest radical alternative newspapers in the United States early in the 20th century was *The Masses* (Jones, 1993; Zurier, 1988). *The Nation*, published throughout the 20th century, was already an established presence.

From the latter part of the 19th century onward was an era in which socialist and anarchist movements grew apace across the globe, and labor unions blossomed even more, as traditionally harsh working conditions now came to combine with larger and larger units of production, whether factories, mines, shipyards, railroads, or docks. In this situation, especially in Germany, as already noted, radical publications were more and more numerous; in the United States, radical media played a large role in encouraging political action. They also made the authorities increasingly anxious that their enormous industrial workforce expansion might, indeed, as Marx had cheerfully forecast, produce the very gravediggers of capitalism.

Although from our vantage point at the beginning of the new century, it is simple to see that the immediate fears of ruling circles were exaggerated, as were the corresponding hopes of the revolutionaries, it would be mistaken to conclude that it was all a storm in a teacup. Lives were lost; political activists were blacklisted, jailed, and badly beaten; they and their families suffered greatly in consequence; yet, very haltingly in consequence of these struggles, but still step by cautious step, the United States moved toward forms of protection for labor and some freedom of operation for unions. Admittedly, in the process, labor union leadership quite often became integrated in negative ways with corporate strategies, but unions' basic freedom of operation was a major gain. The history since then, in some respects one of serious reverses for labor, is much too complex to review here, but suffice it to say that radical print media were absolutely integral to this earlier process, just as radical media will be equally integral to the next major wave of labor activism, this time necessarily on a transnational scale.

Civil Rights and the Media

The whole gamut of such media in the period since then constitutes a large terrain for study in the United States alone, far larger than can even be summarized here. Especially the 1960s and 1970s, with their huge political turmoil over civil rights, Black Power, the Chicano and the Native American movements, the new feminist movements, and not least the opposition movement to the war in Vietnam, both at large and within the military itself, provided the combustion for wildly proliferating alternative media (Armstrong, 1981; Aronson, 1972). The nationalist and leftist political turbulence in Québec in the same period also led to a profusion of alternative print media there that played a major role, such as *Parti pris* and the *Bulletin* of the Québec Free Press Agency (Raboy, 1984). Dickinson (1997) gives a very lively and insightful account of the underground press in Britain, including the north of England, during that time (cf. Fountain, 1988; Nelson, 1989). The turmoil of those years was not only seen in North America, it stretched from Brazil to Poland, from Japan to France, from Australia to India, from Senegal to Portugal. It was a period of turbulence in which radical print media were often at the eye of the storm.

THE NOVEL AS A MEDIUM FOR WOMEN

Two other print formats, the novel and comics, need to be examined.

The novel, an early vehicle for women's voices, illustrates the necessity of focusing closely on context if the text's radical implications are to be perceived beneath its surface quietism. Because of the novel's association with high culture and its enthronement as elite art in connection with such names as Margaret Atwood, Jane Austen, Miguel Cervantes, Honoré de Balzac, Fyodor Dostoevski, Nadine Gordimer, Günther Grass, Naguib Mahfouz, Murasaki Shikibu, and Virginia Woolf, its role as a radical medium seems implausible. Even the fact that these particular novelists stabbed hard at the pretensions of power elites, the image of the highly literate, leisured reader—as opposed to the mass audience—might render many skeptical of the novel's capacity to act as a mass political force. Literature (especially when enunciated as LITTruhchuh) does not appear to have the ethos of political challenge.

Yet, as Bakhtin (1981, pp. 3-41) argued with more than half an eye on the Soviet regime, the novel from the very outset challenged authority, and frequently, the power structure returned the compliment by denouncing the novel as subversive. The novel did not require clergy or other authority figures to interpret it and often could be read without knowing classical literature. It drew on popular literary genres, such as letters, diaries, folktales, travel stories, tracts, and chapbooks. Throughout its history, it was endemically in a process of change, questing for new possibilities. In particular, it appealed to individual responses from readers and encouraged readership as an independent social activity outside the shackles of established religion or political surveillance. In other words, not simply individual novels but the novel as a format acted as a radical alternative form of communication within an imposed collective culture.

In particular, women's activity as novelists has been one of the most significant forms of radical media activism, although often not recognized as such. Whether in Japan or the West, women have been exceptionally prominent in this regard. Beyond their success in breaking the silence historically imposed by patriarchy, especially within the modern public sphere, the content of what they wrote often subverted patriarchy. As Virginia Woolf (1975) puts it, "Thus towards the end of the eighteenth century a change came about which, if I were rewriting history, I should describe more fully and think of greater importance than the Crusades. . . . The middle-class woman began to write" (p. 69). Granted, her dating of the process and her comparative reference point are European and American, not Japanese, where women began to write earlier still, but her point is historically fully attested.

Writing on this theme has been voluminous since Elaine Showalter's (1977) *A Literature of Their Own* and has developed in several different directions. Two, however, are particularly stimulating for our definition of radical media and their impact. The first is the exploration of the full contextual significance of seemingly hegemonized, pro-status quo novels by women writers. The other is the acknowledgment of the importance of now-forgotten novels and other publications that may have long lost any literary cachet they once had, but nonetheless played a significant role in shaping reflection and discussion in their day—and thus played an important part in shaping the world we have inherited.

Contextual Issues in 19th-Century Fiction

Examples of the importance of close attention to contextual issues are offered by Tompkins (1985), in her analysis of American sentimental fiction of the 19th century, and by Poovey (1984, pp. 143-207), in her commentary on Mary Shelley and Jane Austen. Tompkins (pp. 182-185) argues that the chilling conclusion of one such novel (Susan Warner's *The Wide, Wide World* published in 1851), which has the heroine finally experiencing happiness only once she has learned to expel the last vestige of self-regard (except for insisting on the importance of Bible reading), is entirely misunderstood if read in the context of feminist consciousness-raising of the 1970s. If, however, placed in the context of the biblical Job narrative, which saturated the surrounding culture at the time the novel was written, is a rather stunning tribute to the power of women to withstand everything thrown at them and a ringing affirmation that in the truest, ultimate order of things, they richly deserve reward. Despite its surface content, the novel is not calling for women's spiritual annihilation but rather describing heroic passage through ordeals.

Poovey (1984), likewise, proposes that even in Mary Shelley's final novels, which appear to hymn women's self-denial, the "crippling" (p. 170) ideology of respectability they and similar novels expressed nonetheless had its dialectical reverse: "As Proper Ladies, and acting in the name of duty, the very women who had initially been instructed to regulate their own passions eventually became the wardens of men's desires, authorized to punish the men society set over them." Revenge was possible, then, and "morally justified" anger was probably sweet.

The patriarchal cultural sickness of the context and of these "solutions" to women's repression is perhaps one of the more striking illustrations of Marx's aphorism that we make history but not in circumstances of our choosing. Unlike the surreptitious codes African Americans employed to refer to whites during the centuries of slavery, or the obscure words Gramsci deployed to evade the prison censor, such novels use a seemingly secure bed of patriarchal cotton wool to muffle women's rights and needs—but nonetheless contrive to address them. Much more immediately sympathetic today are those few women writers who consciously set out to reframe patriarchal fairy tales, myths of American frontier life, the supposed warm cuddliness of family support (Walker, 1995). But they were a minority within a minority.

Conduct Books

Surprisingly, the radical media significance is also considerable—once we stop assuming media impact must be instant to be effective—of now-obscure conduct books that became a major publication field for women writers in the early 19th century (Armstrong, 1987, pp. 59-95). Although these works are far from being the most dramatic examples of women's writing, Armstrong argues that nonetheless, their early 19th-century development enabled a huge shift away from aristocratic notions of women's nobility and from previous conduct books' typical focus on men's ideal comportment, both of these self-evidently being unattainable by the vast majority of women. The new, effectively radical message, reiterated endlessly, was that—admittedly with the noble justification of being desirable to the proper men—women required an education. Women writing to and for women thus constituted a substantial force for opening up educational and cultural possibilities hitherto regarded by men as otiose for, and possibly even damaging to "their" women. That the education available was generally crimped and ideologically saturated did not prevent its bounds being stretched and sometimes burst by scores of millions of women over succeeding decades.

A study by Pearson (1999) of women's reading habits in Britain in the period from 1750 to 1835 serves to underscore some of these points. It is quite likely that by the close of the 1700s, the majority of readers were female. Pearson observes how ambivalent many men and even some women commentators were about women's reading, defining it now as potentially seditious, now as the mark of a woman earnestly dedicated to improving her domestic contribution. Some parents tried to prevent their daughters from reading; others condemned it as a sign of laziness. Inevitably, certain books and themes were regarded as especially dangerous: those dealing with political, religious, and sexual deviance from established codes. In the 1790s, a period of cultural and political repression in Britain in response to the American and French revolutions, surveillance of women's reading preferences became much more intense:

> It seems there was hardly any crime, sin, or personal catastrophe that injudicious reading was not held to cause directly or indirectly—from murder, suicide, rape, and violent revolution, through prostitution,

> adultery and divorce, to pride, vanity, and slapdash housewifery. (Pearson, 1999, p. 8)

Pearson stresses that this overheated response also typically homogenized the woman reader. However, anxiety was often particularly marked about the reading habits of women of the industrial and rural working classes. "Circulating" (i.e., lending) libraries, of which there were nearly 400 in Britain by 1800, a third of them in London, were regarded by many official commentators as dangerous—"an evergreen tree of diabolical knowledge" according to one source cited by Pearson (1999, p. 163)—because they made books available at low cost to large numbers of people. Although we may rightly be amused at the hysteria of some of these responses, just as in the 1980s intelligent Russians laughed at their bureaucrats' panic at the prospect of young people enjoying themselves at a rock concert, there is also a glimmer of realism in the responses we ridicule. However mistily these crusted reactionaries see the future, they see that it is a future without them. These media toll the bell for them.

Now, such aspects of the novel and women's writing and reading are hardly as dramatic, certainly not as spicy, as other forms of radical media surveyed in this tapestry. Nonetheless, they raise acutely the critical question of the power of radical media, stretching out the time frame for impact over decades and viewing it as a molecular process, an almost imperceptibly rolling snowball, quite the opposite to the instantaneous punch on the jaw that the mind-bomb type of radical media constitutes.

COMICS AND COMIX

Last, let us examine a print form often dismissed as unserious, or sometimes even held up as emblematic of cultural decay and danger. Comics (Sabin, 1993, 1996) in the 1960s and 1970s became a significant force among young adults in the United States and also in France and some other European countries; *manga* have consistently been popular in Japan across all age groups. In the United States and Britain, the term *comix* has been popularly used to distinguish this later generation of work from its predecessors. Particularly in the United States in the 1980s and 1990s, a number of comics were developed targeted specifically to adults. In the 1990s, there was even an upscaling maneuver to define certain lengthier comic-strip works as *graphic novels.* Outstanding examples of the latter, constituting a radical alternative within the merely alternative, would be Art Spiegelman's (1987, 1992) *Maus and Maus II* about the Nazi Holocaust or Keiji Nakazawa's (1989) *Barefoot Gen* about the atomic bombs dropped on Japan, although not many engage with issues such as these.[10]

Indeed, as with all other media genres, the majority are not radical thematically. Comix convey the standard values of many other mainstream media, although, like video and computer games, some are much more unabashedly violent, sexist, and ethnocentric than most mainstream media. At the same time, some are heir to the satirical cartooning tradition examined in Chapter 14, and in a number of cases, they overlap with film and video animation.[11]

A radical U.S. version of the genre[12] is *Hothead Paisan, Homicidal Lesbian Terrorist,* published starting in the early 1990s.[13] Its writer-designer, Diane DiMassa, calls it a comic-zine, putting it midway between comic and *zine,* the related genre that operates both in print and on the World-wide Web.[14] It is exceptionally hard to do justice to the zip, pungency, and straight laugh-out-loud-*and-rocks* caliber of *Hothead,* the name of a scrawny, hyper-feisty young dyke wrapped up in her relationship with older, wiser superbutch Roz, and Hothead's very savvy cat Chicken, with whom she has an almost 100% perfect intuitive communication. Hothead acts out and spews her rage at patriarchy's pervasiveness and power, yet, she is vulnerable, funny, and prone to delicious fantasies of revenge. As irreverent, no-holds-barred radical media go, *Hothead* merits a special place in the pantheon, for both drawing and wonderful comic brilliance.

A different example is provided by the punk-influenced Hernández brothers, Jaime and Gilbert, who portray varying facets of urban Chicano life in *Love And Rockets*[15] and a series of later works. Women were given important roles in their work and assigned multidimensional characters. Some of the stories are like *telenovelas,* everyday human interest sagas; others focus more on the roller coasters of teen life. These works make use of flashbacks and different perspectives on the same event, evincing exceptional story lines and characterization.

Summary: In social movements from subversive Protestantism to radical lesbianism, from labor activism to the American and French Revolutions, from political pornography to women novelists—and in many examples in Chapter 14, as well—print has served numerous ends for radical media communication. Its counterhegemonic impact has varied from the imperceptible—especially out of context—and the long-term, to the instantaneous shock of humor and outrage. Radical print media have overflowed borders, clothed themselves in the external pieties of patriarchy and religion, and still repeatedly brought down retribution on the heads of the activists who produced and distributed them—and even on the heads of those who were merely found reading them.

In Part III, we will examine in some detail the roles of other radical print media, including *samizdat*[16] in the former Soviet bloc, the newspaper *República* in the transition from fascism to democracy in Portugal, and the long-running leftist daily *Il Manifesto* in Rome.

NOTES

1. Historian H.-J. Köhler defines a *Flugschrift,* at that juncture, as "a printed publication consisting of more than one page, independent, occasional, and unbound, directed to the general public" (my translation), in his essay "Die Flugschriften. Versuch der Präzisierung eines geläufigen Begriffs," (cited in Flood (1990, note 109).

2. For a comprehensive overview revising much earlier historical commentary, see Gilmont (1990b).

3. The term *tamizdat* meaning "published (over) there," that is, books published in the West and smuggled back into the Soviet bloc, was modeled on the term, *samizdat,* which is the subject of Chapter 22.

4. With the well-known exception of Germany and the interesting exception of Poland (Kawecka-Gryczowa & Tazbir, 1990), whose extensive landed nobility was something of a law onto itself. Books were burned in Poland but never their authors or vendors, an altogether pleasant contrast with the savage repression of radical media activism in much of the rest of Europe.

5. *Pasquino* was the word used in late medieval Rome for any statue on which people hung satirical lampoons.

6. Sembene Ousmane's marvelous political novel and film satire *Xala* (1974, available with English subtitles in video and 16mm film formats from New Yorker Films in Manhattan), pivots precisely on this theme as a way of discrediting neocolonial governments in Africa in the first decades of independence. The businessman/nightclub owner is represented as suffering from the same political affliction in *La Vie Est Belle* (1987, director, Ngangura Mweze & Benoît Lamy, available with English subtitles in video format from California Newsreel, San Francisco).

7. Weil (1993), in a discussion of this theme as it was applied to England's Charles II, suggests that the imagery could cut a number of ways, with the royal phallus also sometimes standing in as a symbol of rape and despotism. In some instances, the king was equated with a dildo as well as with Priapus, thus creating a fused image of both despotism and dependence: "The joke, of course, is that a dildo is also a woman's tool. The association of Charles with both a priapic god and a dildo is thus a savage jibe at the ambiguous character of tyrannical power" (p. 151).

8. See Rosenfeld (1997) for an absorbing account of the Philadelphia's *Aurora,* a newspaper that repeatedly accused President John Adams of planning to declare himself king of the new United States and suffered serious repression in consequence.

9. Shore (1988) provides an excellent history of this foolishly neglected newspaper, a hugely significant voice from 1895 through 1912. From 1918 until its closure in 1922, its new owners retitled it *The Appeal,* largely to distinguish their editorial stance in favor of U.S. entry into World War I from the previous owners' root-and-branch condemnation of the war.

10. *Maus* has been critiqued, however, for presenting all Poles and all Germans as homogeneously vicious.

11. The consistently brilliant work of Steve Bell, who produced *Maggie's Farm* and *If . . .* as a regular cartoonist for *The Guardian* newspaper, and of Terry Gilliam, animator for the BBC television series, *Monty Python's Flying Circus,* are some leading cases in point.

12. Sabin (1996, pp. 177-215) excellently describes and excerpts a number of these from the 1980s and 1990s, placing them within their contemporary genre context.

13. Published by Cleiss Press Inc., Pittsburgh and San Francisco.

14. A zine is a kind of mini-magazine, with its own luxuriant crop of subgenres such as fanzines for the aficionados of TV series.

15. Fantagraphics, Seattle, WA, 1982. I am grateful to Lizzie Curry Martínez for bringing their work to my attention.

16. The term means "self-published" in 180-degree contradistinction to *gosizdat,* state published. Awkward as the translations sound in English, they signaled, then, the vast difference between a media system monopolized by the Soviet state and publication "from below" outside the censor's control—although never immune from political repression—and for horizontal distribution.

14

Mind Bombs: Woodcuts, Satirical Prints, Flyers, Photomontage, Posters, and Murals

When we step into the print world of woodcuts, prints, flyers, and posters, and then still further into photomontage and murals, we are operating within another whole level of radical alternative media. Not that these technologies and formats have exclusively been used for such purposes. Like all media forms, their more common use has always been in the service of classes in power or immediate money-making ends, or both. But the use of these artistic techniques and genres for protest, and especially for the purposes of caricature and satire, has a rich and fascinating role in the history of social movements. Sometimes, these media were incorporated in books and newspapers; at other times, they stood by themselves as pictures or flyers. Their technology has mostly been easily accessible, as has their point. Along with graffiti, performance art, street theater, and song, among the forms we have already reviewed, they have lent the vitality of the imagination to alternative public spheres, have made those spheres exciting as well as informative, and have sent public conversation flying.

Here, I have cast them together as mind bombs because they aimed to make a potent statement in one short space and thereby to lodge themselves in people's conscious memories, although of course they were reproduced, sometimes on a mass scale. And I am using the metaphor *bomb,* as I said in the Introduction to Part II, to signify the unanticipated disruption of settled patterns of thought, not the obliteration of thinking. On the other hand, it would be an error to assume all these artworks expressed unalloyedly constructive oppositional passions. They illustrate the *mestizaje* of the popular and the oppositional, even of the hegemonic, a hybrid quality argued in Part I to be characteristic of many if not most radical media.

- Woodcuts and political critique, from Albrecht Dürer to Käthe Kollwitz
- French political cartooning—Honoré Daumier
- Satirical prints in 18th- and 19th-century Britain—William Hogarth, James Gillray, George Cruikshank
- Political satire in 19th- and 20th-century Germany—*Kladderadatsch, Simplicissimus, Der Wahre Jakob,* and Georg Grosz
- Photomontage as radical media—John Heartfield
- The political poster and the *dazibao*
- Political murals—Chile's Popular Unity period, the "Great Wall" of Los Angeles, the Northern Ireland "troubles" 1969-1999

WOODCUTS AND POLITICS

We will begin with one of the very cheapest and most accessible technologies for reproducing images: the woodcuts. One of the earliest instances of their deployment as radical media was in Germany in the aftermath of the brutal suppression of rebelling farmers—supported by Martin Luther—during the 1515-1525 Peasant Wars. Dürer, Deutsch, the Petrarch Master, Tirol, and Lucas Cranach the Elder were among those who used the medium to denounce the repression (Philippe, 1982, pp. 12, 83).

Wood-engraving would continue to have its place right up to the early 20th century, when Käthe Kollwitz's (1867-1945) extraordinary talents permitted the world of official art to acknowledge the medium as art as well as merely communication. She, indeed, made an early "conscious choice to work with graphics because of their accessibility" (Lippard, 1981, p. viii). Her first woodcuts date from 1919 in the traumatic aftermath of the war. She wrote in 1916 that"genius can probably run on ahead and seek new ways. But the good artists who follow on after genius—and I count myself among these—love to restore the lost connection once more" (cited in Lippard, 1981, p. vi). This is an insight of great interest for analyzing radical alternative media. Some commentators tend to wish to choose between accessibility and diffusion as touchstones of radical communication media, rather than including originality. Kollwitz's observation suggests that a longer time frame makes more sense, a time frame in which both types of talent make complementary contributions.

Kollwitz first came to a certain notoriety in 1898 when a work of hers on a famous 19th century weavers' strike was awarded the gold medal at the Great Berlin Art Exhibit, only for the honor to be vetoed by the Kaiser. Her most active period, however, especially in woodcuts, was in the 1920s and 1930s. In 1929, she was listed in a public poll as one of the three German artists who best expressed workers' aspirations. Her works dealt with the situation of women, inflation, unemployment, abortion, gay rights, and peace issues. She was always a pacifist but never a Marxist. Unlike some radical media such as *Simplicissimus*, "Kollwitz managed to portray victims in a manner that endowed them with strength" (Lippard, 1981, p. ix).

A paradox that requires comment is that some of her works were used by the Nazis, without attribution, for their propaganda purposes. For several decades, she was also the most popular foreign artist in the Chinese Communist regime. This raises complicated questions about imagery and its uses. For someone like photomontagist John Heartfield, to seize an image and pitchfork it into a totally new set of related images to make a particular point raises no real problems regarding the continued meaning of the original. But the use of imagery designed and generally interpreted as liberating to control seems acutely paradoxical.

One basic question is why both these regimes felt inclined to use her work. A part of the answer assuredly lies in their wish to use a certain level of radical populism, a show of being in favor of everyday people, shoring up their own political power. There is an appeal in dictatorship, sadly, one it would be pleasanter to skate over, but which helps to explain how they function. Brutal and violent as such regimes are, their repression is often targeted, and their propaganda to the majority promises stability, direction, and national independence—even may offer new affluence for a time. Mussolini used to attack "the plutocrats"; Hitler and Goebbels isolated the Jewish people for demonization to avenge Germany's humiliation; Idi Amin did the same with Ugandan Asians; Mao signaled an end to warlords and foreign interventions; the murderous Chilean Pinochet regime and the even more murderous 1976-1982 Argentinean military junta promised political and economic stability: Dictatorships do not only work by means of terror.

A further question is what these manipulations of her work meant to German or Chinese publics unaware that her work had been forced into service by their regimes. Yet, just because a propaganda effort tries to harness imagery to its ends does not automatically guarantee that perspectives and ideas will be sparked that mirror those ends. The message of repressive political regimes is that they alone can solve people's problems—but if the public resonates with the depiction of the problem and not the proffered solution, then the message effectively fails. Also, undoubtedly, the more basic the image, the easier it is for a variety of forces to invest it with different meanings.

Prints, especially satirical prints, were immensely popular at various junctures in the 18th and 19th centuries.[1] They were important before the era of mass literacy, in that the words were often few, the pictures graphic and easily recognizable lampoons[2] of well-known public figures, and the prints were displayed in city store windows where passers-by could stop and examine them. Sometimes, gales of laughter would emanate from the crowds standing around peering at a new print just displayed. Their store window display was an important balance to their relatively high price, so that whereas owning one was expensive, viewing one cost nothing.

French governments, in particular, were made extremely nervous by them. The minister of trade in 1835 denounced them, saying "there is nothing more dangerous, gentlemen, than these infamous caricatures, these seditious designs [which] produce the most deadly effect"; and a government deputy in 1822 warned that "as soon as they are exhibited in public, they are instantly viewed by thousands of spectators and the disturbance has taken place before the magistrate has had time to repress it" (Goldstein, 1989, pp. 1, 3). Even in 1880, another deputy is quoted as saying,

> A drawing strikes the sight of passers-by, addresses itself to all ages and both sexes, startles not only the mind but the eyes. It is a means of speaking even to the illiterate, of stirring up passions, without reasoning, without discourse. (Goldstein, 1989, pp. 4-5)

We need not share the last speaker's clear contempt for most of his fellow citizens to recognize that, nonetheless, he had understood the print's impact. For these reasons, successive French governments banned caricature of political figures in 1820-1830, 1835-1848, 1852-1870, and 1871-1881, even restoring the ban during World War I (Goldstein 1989, p. vii). The press, for most of that period, was not systematically censored, only these lethal drawings.[3]

DAUMIER AND POLITICAL CARTOONS

Probably the most famous were by cartoonist Honoré Daumier (1808-1879), an immensely versatile artist who, in his lifetime, created about 4,000 lithographs, along with wood engravings, oils, watercolors, black chalk drawings, even clay models. He contributed work especially to *Le Charivari*, a daily, and to the weekly *La Caricature*. His first real political campaign as a cartoonist was against King Louis-Philippe; for this, he was fined and jailed in 1830. In 1832, with his father's sickness, he became sole provider for his parents and two sisters. His skills as caricaturist then proved vital for the family income: "What earned him his daily bread in the 1830s and 1840s was his power to draw cartoons that could be instantly understood by everyone, whether their targets were political or social" (Laughton, 1996, p. 11).

Indeed, much of his work was social. He cartooned lawyers very effectively but also did many portraits of regular working class life from the Île St. Louis, then a mixed-class neighborhood in which he lived. A dispiriting feature of his work, however, was that he frequently lampooned women, should they venture to be assertive, with socialist women and women writers as cases in point (Ramus, 1978, p. xv). As is amply evident from the history of radical alternative communication, constructing a binary drama in which such media or media activists are unequivocal heroes does violence to both history and common sense. The scenario was, and is, mixed.

SATIRICAL PRINTS IN BRITAIN

Although the art of caricature[4] began in Italy and was associated with such luminaries as the multitalented Bernini, it was in England that, as Diana Donald (1996) has proposed, artists "shaped the budding naturalism and earthy exuberance of the medium" (p. 1).[5] This was connected partly with the relatively freer political restraints during much of the 18th century in Britain as compared to the exceptionally tight reins on political expression in continental Europe. The key figure in caricature's introduction and popularization was William Hogarth (1697-1764), who habitually fused together classical motifs and popular lore and thus expanded the audience for the medium. In this manner, he paved the way for his successors James Gillray (1757-1815), George Cruikshank (1792-1878), and others.[6]

In Britain, these prints were typically issued on single sheets, not within newspapers:

> Graphic satire was . . . highly visible. Distributed to overflowing print shops and boisterous coffee houses, pinned up in cluttered street windows, scattered across crowded shop counters and coffee tables, and then passed from hand to hand, or hung and framed in glass, or pasted in folios bulging with other graphic images—the satiric print was . . . a ubiquitous feature of . . . urban life. (Hallett, 1999, p. 1)

Prints were not only diffused widely in London. There is evidence that they were frequently purchased in the provinces by mail order, where their arrival represented the latest, "hottest" news from the big city, an occasion to invite gentry neighbors over to join in admiring the latest acquisition. They traveled around, too, carried by the large floating population that spent part of the year in the metropolis and part of the year in the countryside. There were also a few provincial print shops. Reduced versions of particular prints turned up on handkerchiefs, fans, cards, and even playing cards, on ceramics and in woodcut versions, the latter now nearly all lost. Their themes were recycled in the large-format broadsides and in street ballads, and pirated copies were common. Furthermore, satirical prints had an international circulation, being very popular in other European countries because of their frequently merciless attacks on royalty. Thus, copies reached as far as Germany, the Netherlands, France, and Spain.

It would be an exaggeration to term them mass media. Not until the diffusion of wood-engraved prints in the next century, especially in the period following the Peterloo massacre[7] of 1819, would this medium truly become a mass phenomenon. Nonetheless, their impact needs to be judged within the constraints of the time. Capital cities such as Paris and London, then even more than now, were a world apart. Short of armed insurrection, governments were much more concerned with metropolitan reactions, both from disaffected sectors of the elite and from what the elite thought of as the mob, than with sentiment out in the provinces. They were also often more alarmed by the prospect of successful propaganda against their rule than by plots to overthrow them. Anything that bridged the cultural gap between the elite and the more general city public, as many of these prints succeeded in doing, was viewed as potential dynamite, not only in France, as we have seen, but also in Britain. Some of the more sophisticated prints would not have overcome that cultural gap, but many did.

There are absorbing features to consider in these satirical "squibs" and "drolls" (terms then in use) and the way they developed over time. Among them is the transition from emblematic and often cryptic depictions of those lampooned to allusion and parody, Gillray having been a major architect of this shift. From Hogarth onward, the targets of satire had included the mores of high society and low society, as well as the shenanigans of the royals. As the 18th century continued, a more and more popular target was the commercialization of society, expressed in the airs and graces and decadence of the rich (although, interestingly, wealth as such was not a target). At the same time, the caricature became "urbane and self-conscious . . . not so much an affront to high culture as a playfully antithetical form which confirmed its hegemony" (Donald, 1996, p. 74).

This observation of Donald's (1996) should give us pause. Whether the prints did, in fact, simply confirm high culture's hegemony or whether their impact was more mixed is a very difficult judgment to make, but an important question to consider. For example, attacks on King George III were at least as rife in British prints as they were in the 13 American colonies during the 1770s and thereafter. One cited by Donald, for example, shows someone farting at the king's picture (p. 162).

Yet, on the other hand, it was common to see patronizing depictions of the Scots and the Irish, very heavy-handed satires on the supposed French and Italian addiction to fashion, invitations to gasp in scandal at what was thus presented as the feminization of male manners in those nations, and the consequent risk of emasculating English men miserably ensnared in the vogues of contemporary fashion. In parallel, any signs of women's assertiveness were trenchantly attacked, such as the comportment of those women who ran the Parisian salons in the decades before the French Revolution. Also, in those instances where aristocratic license was under fire (usually as a way of ridiculing aristocratic authority), aristocratic women's sexual improprieties were much more viciously castigated than men's. Hallett (1999) has proposed, in an intriguing intertextual analysis of prints as a whole in Hogarth's era, that the more radical satiric strategies began as challenges to the London elite's earnest pretension to define itself as "polite" society, and the prints that celebrated that claim ended by being absorbed into that project, merely registering discrepant features of London's increasingly commercialized life rather than critiquing it root and branch.

A further mixed feature of political printmaking in Britain later in the century was that with the coming of the American and French Revolutions and the consequent turbulent political mood in London, the prints of the 1790s barely reflected the widespread street protests and agitation which caught up a wide assortment of artists, printers, pamphleteers, dissident ministers, and political activists, such as William Blake, Thomas Spence, Robert Wedderburn ("the Devil's Engineer"), and Thomas Evans (McCalman, 1988; Thompson, 1993; Wood, 1994). This near silence may partly or even mainly be explained by the heavy penalties, especially harsh during the years 1795-1803, for public expression of pro-Revolution sentiment. Because the individuals and their circles conducted much of their political activity in tavern debating clubs, the groups involved were small enough to make it hard for the many spies the government put into service to escape detection. By contrast, prints had to be seen, had to be paid for, and their sources, both printers and artists, could easily be identified.[8] This was especially true for the most fashionable print shops.[9] The cheaper shops, however, typically produced pamphlets and woodcuts rather than prints. The conclusion is also plausible that the more fashionable the print shop and its stable of artists and journeymen, the more cautious its own radicalism, in part because of its greater proximity to the power structure.[10]

Interpreting the situation during these successive decades demands considerable subtlety, because the satirical print depictions of the British crowd during the 1790s also generally emphasized its freedom and independence, its collective vitality, often drawing contrasts with the more subjugated publics of continental Europe. John Bull, already a symbol of the British public, was repeatedly portrayed by both Gillray and Cruikshank at this time as the target of energetic propaganda from those for and those against the French Revolution and as a force that "like Aristophanes' Demos is ever ready to destroy his creators" (Donald, 1996, p. 162). Given the French Revolution's pendulum lurch from the establishment of democratic governance to the Terror, the sources of this imagery are understandable; yet, was not the depiction of the tough John Bull a little more than simply flattery?

Thus, an analysis of these radical alternative media in Britain during this period illustrates, as a number of cases we have examined also do, the ambiguity and negativity of their contents, sitting cheek by jowl with their more insurgent messages. Not least, the definition of what constituted radical at that time needs bearing in mind throughout. Patricia Anderson (1991) has rightly emphasized how "working people's taste embraced every level of cultural expression: literary, lurid, radical, religious, respectable, morbid, moralistic, serious, sensational, salacious, educational, escapist" (p. 180). Similarly, McCalman (1988), in line with Bakhtin and the political pornography we noted in Chapter 13, argues that "humour, escapism, sex, profit, conviviality, entertainment and saturnalia should be admitted to the popular radical tradition, along with the sober, strenuous, and heroic aspects which are more customarily described" (p. 234).[11]

POLITICAL SATIRE IN GERMANY

Germany's radical media tradition offers some interesting examples of satire and caricature in the later 19th and into the 20th century, further elements in the alternative political culture already mentioned in the discussion of labor movement songs. Indeed, one could almost draw a line from the newspapers *Kladderadatsch*, *Simplicissimus*, and *Der Wahre Jakob*[12] through to Expressionism, Berlin dada, Georg Grosz, the pioneer photomontagist John Heartfield, and—to one side—Käthe Kollwitz, all of whose work had tremendous influence on other political graphic art all over the world throughout the 20th century (see Allen, 1984; Lewis, 1971; Hinz, 1981; Evans, 1992; De Micheli, 1978). However, at no point was this a simple success story. There were flaws, sometimes severe and on occasion abysmal, in most of these radical media.

Kladderadatsch had sales of 50,000 in 1890, *Simplicissimus* 86,000 as of 1908, and *Der Wahre Jakob* toward 250,000 in the latter year, rising to nearly 400,000 by 1912 (Allen, 1984, p. 3; Rothe, 1977, p. xiv). Copies also passed through quite a number of hands. The genre had international influence as well,[13] known as *Witzblätter*, usually translated as "comic papers," except that *Witz*, like *wit*, has a sharper, more attacking sense than the word *comic*. The glaring contradictions in Germany in that era were a heavenly gift for satirists and cartoonists: a dynamic industrial sector that every year generated a larger and more organized labor movement, juxtaposed with the pitiful idiocies of the semifeudal Kaiser regime. "Emperor jokes" (*Kaiserwitz*) were part of these newspapers' stock in trade. Potential penalties, however, included fines, imprisonment, exile, and loss of one's livelihood.

Kladderadatsch used language, including satirical verse, *Simplicissimus*, cartoons as well. *Kladderadatsch* focused on the royal court's lackeys and their political antics, whereas *Simplicissimus* included the impact of those antics on the working classes. An example of the former's approach is the description of an onlooker rushing forward to salvage a cigarette butt from the horse manure into which the Kaiser had discarded it, and "gladly" licking it clean. An example of the latter is one cartoon's depiction of savage military discipline, a soldier lying nearly dead on the parade ground from his flogging.[14]

Kladderadatsch's critiques, however, were within tighter bounds than *Simplicissimus*. The paper was anti-labor union, thought German colonialist adventures were merely an error of political judgment, and evinced increasing distaste for new artistic trends. *Simplicissimus*, by contrast, took pains to stay on the artistic cutting edge and campaigned for a coalition between centrist and labor political forces. However, its cartoons tended to present workers as downtrodden, half-starved, illiterate victims deserving of pity rather than solidarity. Despite its lampooning of traditionalist patriarchy, it still portrayed British suffragists "with undisguised disapproval" and educated women "as a strange, slightly humorous phenomenon" (Allen, 1984, pp. 168, 177). It depicted Balkan peoples in ethnically disparaging terms and was even prone, despite its several leading Jewish staff writers, to represent Jews as themselves responsible for sparking anti-Semitism. Ironically, the paper was often perceived as "typically Jewish" because of its subversive critiques of religion and the established order (Allen, 1984, pp. 131-132, 188-194, 215-216).

Came the First World War, however, and both papers doughtily swung behind the Kaiser. During the postwar Social-Democratic regime, many traditional targets were missing, and the writing seemed to lose its bite. When Hitler came to power, he was initially defined by both papers as a passing fad, and then, both actually swung into line behind the Nazi regime. These terrible conclusions to their history are important to bear in mind, for they illustrate more than simply the corruptibility of journalists or the fear inspired by the Nazis. They also remind us how satirical humor can become its own pure rationale.

A different example of the achievements and the limits of satire is the immensely influential political artist George Grosz (1893-1959), a great admirer of Hogarth, Goya, and Daumier, who often said he had no trust in or affection for the general public. He simply shared a hatred of their common enemy, the bourgeoisie, and in particular of militarism (Lewis, 1971, p. 67). His fierce paintings of the rapacity of the German capitalist class and his depictions of the blood-drenched heartlessness of the country's military caste during the First World War occupied a middle ground between the roles of attacking journalist and attacking artist. His Berlin dada context constituted a fertile location for this fusion of roles. He illustrated a substantial number of books printed by Berlin's newly founded Malik Verlag publishing company, set up as an independent leftist venture without any party sponsorship. Of 36 books issued by the firm in from 1919 to 1921, 18 were illustrated by Grosz, three consisting of his portfolios. Over the next 10 years, eight books of his own artwork would be published by Malik Verlag.

Unlike Daumier, who ridiculed to produce ironic humor, Grosz produced what Beth Irwin Lewis (1971) has called "cruel, painful, and biting derision [of] . . . the essential naked ugliness and sad reality of men" (p. 122). Exposés of official hypocrisy and lies were his forte, yet, like *Simplicissimus,* he never depicted any opposition. He mostly portrayed workers as resigned to their lot. Thus he never really went beyond his searing visual invective directed at brutal generals and money-obsessed businessmen, some of whose representations found their way into cartoons and illustrations around the world throughout the 20th century.[15] From the mid-1920s onward, he became very famous and his work very popular in Germany, but his drawings were increasingly devoid of any political edge.

John Heartfield (1891-1968) and Georg Grosz initially worked very closely together. Both were involved with Malik Verlag, which had been started by Wieland Herzfelde[16] in part to publish Grosz's drawings. Heartfield and Grosz had already been involved in a series of radical magazine projects, spurred by the 1919 murders of Marxist leaders Karl Liebknecht and Rosa Luxemburg.[17] Their first magazine, *Jederman* (Everyman), instantly banned after the first issue, set out "to drag all that the Germans have loved up till now into the mud and to expose all the German ideals to fresh air" (cited in Lewis, 1971, p. 70). Other magazines followed, some also banned, but the one for which Heartfield is particularly and justly famous is the *Arbeiter-Illustrierte Zeitung* (Workers' Illustrated Newspaper). In the 1930s, through Hitler's accession to power in 1933, it sold about half a million copies weekly. It then was forced to move to Prague, where many fewer could be sold, and then again to Paris in 1938, following the Nazi seizure of Czechoslovakia. Heartfield subsequently crossed the English Channel and placed his services at the disposal of anti-Nazi propaganda efforts there.

HEARTFIELD AND PHOTOMONTAGE

His contribution was in photomontage. Within the Soviet Union in its earliest years, and within Germany itself, this technique of pasting together excerpts from still photographs had already begun, but Heartfield took it to a new level. One of the practical challenges pushing him in this direction was that the Workers' Photography movement, a German Communist Party-led effort to put communication technology in public hands, had achieved rather patchy results.[18] Ideally, the best photos taken by the workers themselves would have appeared in *AIZ*, or in a previous magazine, *Der Knüppel* (The Cudgel), which Heartfield and Grosz edited from 1923 to 1927. However, in the absence of sufficient material of quality, Heartfield took to using pieces out of mainstream photos, placed together in a montage, to rework into socialist meanings and critiques (compare the situationists' notion of *détournement*, and culture-jamming).[19]

One of his best-known montages shows Hitler as a puppet in the hands of top industrialist Thyssen. It exactly copied a drawing by Grosz of postwar chancellor Ebert (under whose authority Liebknecht and Luxemburg were murdered) in the hands of Stinnes, yet another tycoon.

But the use of the photographs, especially, perhaps, given the relative newness of photography at that time, gave a new twist to the image, a new force probably drawn in significant measure from the public's powerfully ingrained perceptions of realism. Heartfield also created montages across a double-page spread and sequences of montages from page to page. He also colored parts of his montages for heightened effect. His works often drew on fairy tales, proverbs, and famous or notorious sayings by powerful figures of his day.

Grosz's international influence since then on political poster art has been extraordinary. In Germany, one of his most brilliant followers in the 1970s and 1980s was Klaus Staeck (1985). The poster art of ACT-UP in the period 1987-1992 owed much to Heartfield's work (Crimp & Rolston, 1990). Just as Grosz drew on Hogarth, Goya, and Daumier, so, too, was he a source of inspiration along with them for British print caricaturists such as Ronald Searle and Steve Bell and their U.S. counterparts such as Al Hirschfeld, David Levine, Sue Coe, and Sara Schwartz (Heller & Anderson, 1992, pp. 40-52, 100-102, 104, 149). Film and television animation equally owes a massive debt to these forebears. The "claymation" techniques developed by Britain's Roger Law and Peter Fluck in the 1980s TV satire *Spitting Image* and *Kukly* (dolls), a Russian TV satire program modeled on the British series, created brilliant, splendidly pungent versions of these earlier traditions.

POLITICAL POSTERS AND MURALS

Posters effectively date as a mass medium from the latter part of the 19th century. From the outset, they have often been used as radical media and have been quite intensively analyzed (cf. Gallo, 1974; Paret, Lewis, & Paret, 1992; Philippe, 1982; Quintavalle, 1974). A particular example of radical poster use that demands commentary is the *dazibao,* usually translated "big-character posters," in China in the period 1978-1979 (Chen, 1982; Sheng, 1990; Widor, 1981). In this saga, a mixture of political forces, some of them highly reactionary, is evident once again, confirming the importance of making careful distinctions when analyzing radical media.

China's Dazibao

Dazibao had been a notable feature of revolutionary mass communication in China for much of the 20th century. They could be anonymous—very wise in view of likely punishment—had no graphics, and were cheap, quickly assembled, and effective. The recent background to the dazibao of 1978-1979 was the Cultural Revolution (1964-1976), in which Mao Zedong was struggling to regain his personal ascendancy. For a while, he incited the teenage generation in revolt against his enemies in the Communist Party leadership. They dutifully posted masses of dazibao, denouncing the "capitalist-roaders." Mao even had the constitution amended in 1966, in part to legitimize the posting of dazibao, but then to his cronies' chagrin, the posters came to be used intensively against them in 1976 during a pivotal mass demonstration in Tien An-Men Square.[20] That demonstration was drowned in blood but left an indelible imprint in people's minds in Beijing.

Two years later, in the winter of 1978, the government proclaimed that the 1976 demonstration should not have been repressed, and imprisoned demonstrators were freed. The following day, a 200-yard brick wall in Xidan to the west of Tien An-Men Square became the location to post a new wave of dazibao critiquing many aspects of contemporary Chinese life, even Mao's legacy, and soon thereafter his successor, Deng Xiao-ping. It quickly became known as the Democracy Wall[21] and attracted many readers as well as open-air public discussions and speeches. Some of these dazibao were very long, consisting of numerous sheets, equivalent to a very lengthy journal article or even a small book, such as perhaps the most famous of them all, Wei Jing-sheng's[22] call for democracy. One very popular dazibao, however, was extremely short, a poem consisting of a single character for the word *Net*, which condensed into this one image the sense of being hemmed in at all points and the frustration deeply felt by young Chinese in particular.

These new dazibao quickly spread to other urban centers in China as well and simultaneously prompted a flood of unofficial journals and non-poster publications, some of them campus-based. Chen (1982), who counted over 130 such publications, also notes,

> It was a fresh start, heartily embraced. The excess of demand over supply, proof of the journals' popularity, was too striking to be ignored by

> the authorities. Though they were inferior to the official journals by being mimeographed, often illegible and roughly bound with poor editing and often poor writing, nevertheless their ample variety of content, bold approaches to sensitive subjects and, most of all, prompt response to current events and to readers' demands outweighed this. (pp. 1, 65)

When we examine the history of *samizdat* in the Soviet bloc in Chapter 22, we shall see a similar pattern of media content far outweighing the technical deficiencies of its production.[23] On the other hand, Soviet samizdat was clandestinely circulated, and its writers, at least of the secular material, were typically from the top intelligentsia, whereas many dazibao contributors were from humbler backgrounds. A certain parallel definitely exists, however, with the role of certain official Soviet newspapers as voices for reform factions in the Soviet leadership, both in the period 1956-1964 and later, during the second half of the 1980s.[24] Deng's intention in permitting these dazibao and the free journals was, like Mao's, to try to dislodge his political opponents. When the free expression of opinion overflowed the bounds he had set for it, he promptly banned the journals,[25] imprisoned many media activists, and had the constitutional right to publish dazibao deleted—rather in the same way that Mao banished his teenage battalions from the cities once they had served his purpose (although this was done ostensibly so they could "learn from" the farmers in the remote countryside).

As Sheng (1990, p. 235) comments, the 20th-century history of dazibao is in significant measure the history of struggle in China over the public sphere and for free speech.

Muralists in Chile

Political murals effectively present a spectrum from something fairly close to graffiti through permanent artworks, such as those by Mexican muralists Orozco, Rivera, and Siqueiros.[26] Among many interesting examples of murals as radical alternative media, Kunzle (1983) vividly describes the work of the Ramona Parra[27] brigades in Chile through the murderous U.S.-backed coup of September 1973. Composed mostly of teenagers, some in their very early teens, these brigades produced work that was strictly collective for the most part. In the run-up to the 1970 elections at which the socialist coalition won a plurality, they worked in groups of 10 to 12, largely at night and at high speed to avoid police reprisals or clashes with muralists from conservative political parties. Part of what they did was simply fighting for communicative space with the other parties, often painting out and then over each others' slogans. Public sphere struggle yet again.

After the Popular Unity coalition won, its advocates no longer needed to worry about the police, but the war of the walls continued. They only used city walls without further ado, however, always taking care in villages to request local permission. They did not paint over or deface billboards advertising U.S. products, and they entirely avoided the walls of churches and schools. Some of their work continued to be short slogans or statements, one of the most popular being that of the internationally renowned Chilean poet Pablo Neruda in response to the election victory, *Me has dado la patria como un nacimiento* (You have given me the fatherland like a quickening into life[28]). Other work, such as the 10-foot-high by 400-foot-wide Rio Mapocho mural in the center of Santiago, which took 30 people 15 days to complete and which traced the modern history of Chile, was awash with symbolic representations, a number drawn from Siqueiros, Rivera, Picasso, and pre-Columbian artistic sources. At their height, up to 150 Ramona Parra brigades were in operation.

The Great Wall of Los Angeles

Thus, just as Russian icons and religious painting elsewhere were often dedicated to communicating religious truths to an unlettered public, so the painting of murals was a form of accessible political communication but especially a reclamation of social truths typically denied in hegemonic discourse.[29]

Baca, Neumaier, and Angelo (1985) describe the origins and making of the Great Wall of Los Angeles, a mural that runs for over a third of a mile along the concrete-lined former path of the Los Angeles River. The most extensive example of the murals, which became a very visible part of the cityscape from the early 1970s onward (especially in East Los Angeles, historically a Chicano zone), the Great Wall sought to portray the many cultural strands that made and continue to make the city what it is: Chicanos, Oklahoma Dust Bowl refugees in the 1930s, African Americans, Koreans, Japanese Americans interned during World War II, and many more.

For this mural, as for the Chilean examples cited and for many other political murals, collective labor, not only in execution but also in conceptualization and design, is a major hallmark of their production process. At the same time, these accounts emphasize the division of labor involved in collective activity. Kunzle (1983) notes the central role of the gifts of the *trazador* tracing out the initial letters 8 to 10 feet high, which will then be filled in by others, whereas Baca and her colleagues (1985) talk about "orchestrating people's best skills, using their better abilities, putting them together where they match; it's geometric in proportion; it multiplies the power that you have by taking the best" (p. 73).

Murals in Irish History

Rolston (1991) provides an absorbing account of three kinds of political murals in the struggle over the public sphere in Northern Ireland.[30] The traditional Loyalist Protestant murals that had been in place for many decades defensively rehearsed certain tenets of that version of Irish history, such as King William's liberation of Ireland from the threat of papal domination in 1690.[31] Catholic Nationalist murals were a much later development, at their height in 1980-1982. Unlike their Loyalist counterparts, they typically addressed immediate issues, particularly the agonizing deaths of Bobby Sands and nine other political hunger strikers in 1981-1982, as a result of Prime Minister Thatcher's refusal to respond to their demand for political rather than criminal prisoner status.[32] There was a huge mobilization to support the hunger strikers, and the murals were integrally part of that campaign, often put up at very high speed to be timely. A number were paint-bombed by Loyalists or British soldiers but then quickly repainted. (The third type of mural was sponsored by the British government, although without much effect, as one tactic in its attempt to normalize local political life in Northern Ireland.)

Some of the insurrectionary nationalist murals were in Irish; some fused religious themes with political ones, such as the figure of Jesus watching over a political prisoner in solitary confinement; some made links to Palestinian and anti-apartheid struggles; some portrayed past and present heroes of the nationalist movement; some depicted armed guerrillas in action; and some outlined the history of British repression in Ireland. In the period after the hunger strikes, the political party, Sinn Féin, took more control over which murals were painted, and at that point, the predominant theme became armed struggle against the British. Other issues, such as women's community activism or prison conditions in general, took a back seat. The Provisional Irish Republican Army's (IRA's) long obsession with an elitist militarism seemed to be winning out against the new forms of community activism simultaneously being developed at that time by Sinn Féin, its political wing. By the mid-1980s, the nationalist mural movement had subsided, perhaps a victim of struggles within the wider political movement.

Muralists and other public artists, like the theater activists cited earlier, redefine artwork audiences; instead of addressing a tiny knot of fellow artists, critics, and curators, they reclaim the streets, the public realm, an interactive, counterhegemonic sphere:

> It is not art for public spaces [*as such*], but art addressing public issues. This art is dependent upon a real and substantive interaction with members of the public, usually representing a particular constituency, but not one that comes to art because of an identification or connection with the art world. Such work must reach those for whom the art's subject is a critical life issue. This work deals with audience first: the artist brings individuals into the process from the start, thus redefining the relationship between artist and audience, audience and the work of art . . . [It] recognizes that art is made for audiences, not for institutions of art. (Jacob, 1995, p. 54)[33]

Summary: We have noted throughout how the pungency of all these mind-bomb examples is frequently meshed with their mixed and contested politics. The alternative public sphere is not a secluded convent in which only the purest of radical thoughts circulates. These examples also quite often contain more levels of meaning than one would suppose, perhaps in significant measure because of their compression of so much into so little. At the same time, they do provide suggestive evidence for the argument I have made earlier, that—like some other forms of radical communication we have examined—their particular contribution within and at the edges of social movements and alternative public spheres is on the level of conscious memory, as distinct from more ongoing media, which tend to feed unconscious memory in the form of definitions and frameworks. This very combination, as Sreberny-Mohammadi and Mohammadi (1994) more generally argue, has had a great deal to do with the power of radical media.

NOTES

1. From France comes the term *silhouette,* named after the very unpopular Étienne de Silhouette, appointed controller general of finances in 1759. Outline sketches of him began to appear in Parisian windows. Philippe (1982) observes,

> Man reduced to a mere outline no longer inspired the same restraint. Prints were freed of many constraints by this graphic simplicity . . . An over-inquisitive parliamentarian would have a mouse's snout . . . [another] would be graced with the cruder olfactory organ of the pig. (p. 14)

2. The origins of this word are a little obscure, but may derive from a word meaning to gulp down alcohol. In vino veritas.

3. An official working for arch-reactionary Lord Sidmouth, leading government minister in George III's final years, publicly described political caricatures as a "deadly weapon" (cited in McCalman, 1988, p. 176).

4. The word comes from the Italian *caricare,* to overload, and thus in this context, to exaggerate.

5. There is a particularly rich recent literature on this and related aspects of 18th- and 19th-century British life. See Anderson (1991), Donald (1996), Hallett (1999), McCalman (1988), Thompson (1993), Wood (1994). Parody is a closely related genre. For an outstanding illustrated catalog of parodic art by young Argentineans, addressing the deep traumas of the 1976-1982 dictatorship and the subsequent refusal to come to terms with the disappearance of up to 30,000 people, see Mari Carmen Ramírez, 1999.

6. Donald (1996, p. 17) suggests, moreover, that many of those involved in printmaking, whether designers, tradespeople, or hawkers, may have been women. Clearly, there is a further story to be told one day if sources permit. The profession, although relatively well-paid, generally operated on the margins of society, so perhaps the standard exclusion of women from public life was less in force.

7. In which 11 peaceful protesters were killed and hundreds wounded in the ruthless suppression of a mass demonstration at St. Peter's Fields near Manchester, retitled "Peterloo" after the bloody Battle of Waterloo against Napoleon 4 years earlier, to underscore that the British state had moved into war against its own people. The violence of the repression catalyzed enormous popular hostility to George IV and the government in general.

8. It is, however, hard to put all the weight on this explanation or to escape the conclusion that the difference in behavior had something to do with English interpretations of the American colonists as fortunate in being able to shake off autocracy and yet as being no military threat to England, whereas with the French, it was easy for the British authorities to summon up past history and evoke a military specter. In the later years of the Revolution, the Jacobin Terror made the latter ploy all the simpler. Numerous prints depicted its atrocities and denounced the French for their barbarism (Donald, 1996,

pp. 150-155). When the United States signed an alliance with France, however, it dissipated some pro-U.S. public sentiment.

9. Philippe (1982) takes this point still further and asserts,

> Unlike wood-engraving, [intaglio engraving] remained strictly in the service of the rich and powerful. No doubt it was used by one faction against another, and doubtless it was also used for propaganda, but always by a social group that could finance the artist and his work . . . Expression of popular cries for justice is not to be sought for in the sphere of metal engraving. (p. 113)

His use of the term *expression* is too narrow, implying that only the most direct articulation of a grievance would fit his definition. He also overlooks the extent to which the factions to which he refers might, in the course of pursuing their political campaigns, identify up to a point with the grievances of the poor.

10. With this context in mind, the attacks at the time and since on Gillray for having accepted money at one point in time from Pitt (and thus pro-George III) forces to draw anti-Fox caricatures seem to have lost sight of certain realities. Far from having deserted Fox and his campaign, as though he were simply part of a political machine, Gillray was merely doing what many artists in need of money habitually do, namely, taking needed money from a patron. Whether, too, Fox was simply the representative of angelic forces is also highly disputable.

11. Belchem (1996, p. 5) urges that there has been overmuch "fusion" between liberal and radical political philosophies in the analysis of popular political culture in this period of British history. Although it certainly makes sense to distinguish between the various currents and positions, the actual process seems generally to have been much less tidy and therein lies its fascination. In this discussion, we need to keep in mind the contributions of Bakhtin.

12. *Kladderadatsch* (meaning Crash! or Boom!) was founded in Berlin in 1848; *Simplicissimus* (Simpleton), in München in 1896; and *Der Wahre Jakob* (The Real Jacob, a term signifying someone astute, quick-witted. and verbally adroit, like poor old Esau's brother), also in München in 1884. They represented, respectively, a critical bourgeois, a leftish liberal, and a socialist perspective. Stuttgart's *Der Süddeutscher Postillon* (The South German Postillion), which often took an even sharper line, sold about 100,000 copies at the height of its success (Rothe, 1977, p. xiv).

13. *Simplicissimus* could reckon not only on its German readership but also on the inspiration it gave to similar newspapers in other lands (Allen, 1984, p. 228), such as the French *L'Assiette au Beurre* (The Easy Job), the American *Liberator,* and the Russian *Zhupel* (Brimstone).

14. A traveling Russian nobleman, on being brought a copy of *Simplicissimus* along with the rest of the day's papers, kicked the hotel clerk violently in the stomach, causing him very severe injuries. The judge observed in extenuation of the nobleman's brutal action that the paper was indeed "a shameless rag" and fined him a paltry 1,000 marks. Seemingly, the paper had been equally relentless in its attacks on the tsars, and thus, the worthy judge

felt impelled to stand as firm as he was able in defense of imperial dignity and against the dissident press's outrages. In 1910, the war minister issued an order requiring all officers to sign a pledge not to read *Simplicissimus*(Allen, 1984, pp. 74-75, 89, 119).

15. It could be argued that, in later decades, Grosz's images backfired. The image of the fat, cigar-smoking, top-hatted, bulbous capitalist that leftist caricaturists reproduced ad nauseam may later have served more as a stereotype of Marxist obsessions than as critique. Effectively, however, it was radical but not Marxist, in that it identified individual capitalists' greedy attitudes as the source of exploitation and war, rather than the comprehensive dynamics of the capitalism.

16. John Heartfield's brother and collaborator. John's switch from Herzfelde to Heartfield was a World War I protest against German militarism. Grosz, similarly, turned his last name, Gross, into a Polish-looking version, playing off—and against—the frequent contempt Germans expressed for Poles. The cultural and political background of the Malik Press is described in detail by Maier-Metz (1984).

17. These murders took place with the support of the post-Kaiser Social Democratic government. They represented a huge watershed, politically, in that Liebknecht and Luxemburg, both leading Social Democrats before and during the war and fierce critics of the Social Democratic leaders' endorsement of Germany's engagement in war, had led a failed insurrection in 1919. When this was crushed and its two famous leaders were extrajudicially liquidated, it meant not only the final collapse of any hopes for a socialist victory as then conceived but also the final absorption of the Social Democratic leadership into the logic of state power in Germany.

18. For further information on this movement, see the essays by Höllering (1983), Hoernle (1983), and Münzenberg (1983).

19. The contemporary corporate obsession with intellectual property would have had him fined and imprisoned.

20. This took place at the funeral obsequies for Zhou En-lai, widely perceived at the time as having been a voice of restraint and moderation. The enormous cultural and political significance of this huge square in the center of Beijing, rendered even deeper by the tragic events surrounding the pro-democracy occupation of the square in 1989, is well described by Schell (1994, pp. 15-30).

21. See Barmé and Minford (1989) for an excellent anthology of the writings of Chinese democratic oppositionists and critics from this period.

22. Wei, an electrician, was imprisoned in 1979, was briefly released by the authorities in the hope that it would help them win international approval to hold the Olympic Games in 2000, and, when this did not ensue, was rejailed. He was finally released and allowed to migrate to the United States in 1997.

23. Indeed, the concessions made to the *Solidarnosc* movement in Poland in those years were widely covered in Chinese media and regarded as inspirational by many dazibao activists (Chen, 1982, p. 35).

24. See the discussion of *samizdat* in Chapter 22 for further explanation of some of these details.

25. As Chen (1982, p. 32) makes clear, their editors repeatedly requested official permission to publish and never received a response. This makes abundantly clear the short leash on which the Deng faction wanted them to operate.

26. A couple of the murals painted by Rivera and Siqueiros within the United States aroused a political firestorm. Rockefeller commissioned one from Rivera and then had it destroyed because it depicted Lenin and included an image equating capitalism with syphilis; the Los Angeles city fathers had Siqueiros's mural painted over because it portrayed a crucified Chicano as well as a *mestizo* shooting at the American eagle. Within Mexico itself, however, murals by Rivera, Siqueiros and others are politically much less challenging, even hegemonic:

> The Indian presence as depicted in murals, museums, sculptures, and archaeological sites . . . is treated essentially as a dead world. It is a unique world, extraordinary in many of its achievements, but still a dead world. . . . It is the glorious past of which we should feel proud, which assures us a lofty historical destiny as a nation. . . . Through an adroit ideological alchemy, that past became our past, that of the Mexicans who are not Indians. . . . However, it is an inert past. . . . It has no real connection with our contemporary reality and our collective future. (Bonfil Batalla, 1996, p. 55)

27. A young woman activist, assassinated in 1949.

28. A somewhat free translation, but it comes across with more strength in English than the literal "birth."

29. The writer recalls being thrown out of the office of a loan officer in the giant Williamsburg Bank building on Brooklyn's Atlantic Avenue in 1981 because he asked the officer whether the bank "red-lined" certain neighborhoods (i.e., refused to grant mortgage-loans because the inhabitants were people of color). Four blocks from the bank was a mural covering the whole side of a house, the centerpiece a particularly vicious-looking eagle hovering over city streets, with a capitalist sitting astride it and carefully drawing a red line around certain blocks. The mural, later blotted out when the vacant lot was built on, daily spoke and insisted on the truth of the matter.

30. In the final chapter to his book, Rolston (1991) also provides a helpful survey of political mural work around the world.

31. In fact, the pope of the day celebrated a Mass of thanksgiving for the Dutch Protestant king's victory. The idealized history does not address such complications.

32. Only when the hunger strikes had been discontinued did the British government stop requiring political prisoners to wear prison uniforms, which had been a form of criminalizing their political beliefs and actions. The uniform issue had been the source of extensive protest inside and outside Northern Ireland's jails. The lives of 10 hunger strikers would have been saved had this concession been announced immediately. A sense for some of the issues

involved is given by the feature film, *Some Mother's Son* (Castle Rock Entertainment, 1995), directed by Terry George, and starring Helen Mirren and Fionulla Flanagan.

33. Steven Dubin's (1992) *Arresting Images* provides a helpful survey of the controversies of some public art and "shock" art in the United States during the later 1980s and into the 1990s.

15

Radio

The story of radio's radical alternative uses is hugely important, for in the second half of the 20th century, the technology has the profound advantages of cheapness and, since the transistor radio, of easy portability. In nations with substantial illiteracy, including major nations such as India or Brazil, radio has predictably played a more important role than the press. Even in the United States, people over 12 spend 44% of the time they devote to media to listening to radio—more than to any other single mass medium[1]—although the programming options are extremely limited by international or even earlier American standards. Internet radio, in its beginnings at the time of writing, offers extraordinary possibilities for national and global diffusion of radical interactive audio.

Radio's accessibility has been crucial to its radical uses, whether we are considering micro-radio in Japan in the early 1980s (Kogawa, 1985), ethnic minority radio in the United States (Downing, 1990a), or the famous miners' radio stations in Bolivia (Gumucio Dagron & Cajías, 1989; Huesca, 1995; O'Connor, 1990), an important beacon for the whole of Latin America. The Algerian, Italian, and French experiences summarized here are particularly selected to illustrate the national impact some radical radio projects and movements have achieved, in situations where the state jealously guarded its monopoly control over broadcasting—although the examples far from exhaust the spectrum of experience of radical radio.[2] The three cases we focus on in a moment also illuminate in different ways the complicated relationship between oppositional and hegemonic vectors in popular culture and the relationship between social movements and radical media.

In Part III, we will take the study of radio further, reviewing in some detail Pacifica station KPFA in Berkeley, California, and Free Radio Berkeley; Controradio in Florence and Radio Popolare in Milan, Italy; Radio Renascença in Lisbon, Portugal, during the struggle to consolidate a postfascist and anticolonialist Portugal in 1974-1975; and, more fleetingly, the roles of Radio Liberty and Radio Free Europe during the final 20 years of the Soviet era.

- Frantz Fanon and *The Voice of Fighting Algeria*
- Political movements and free radio in Italy in the 1970s
- The free radio movement in France, 1977-1985

FANON AND THE VOICE OF ALGERIA

We will begin with Frantz Fanon's (1968, pp. 51-82) classic description of how radio's role expanded from narrowly hegemonic to counterhegemonic over the course of the 1956-1962 Algerian uprising against French colonial rule. Algeria, however, let us be quite clear, constitutes much more than a case study with high drama or a vivid illustration of a counterhegemonic social movement. Together with Vietnam and some other colonies,[3] Algeria bore the brunt of military repression in the global struggle against colonialism after World War II. The ability of the majority of colonized territories to achieve a measure of independence without significant bloodshed owed a great deal to the message these armed insurrections sent to the colonial powers, who were forced to accept that if such revolts were to increase in number and take place simultaneously, they could not be quelled.[4] Radical radio's contribution to the Algerian revolution had global consequences.

Fanon describes how, until the 1950s, the vast majority of Algerians saw radio solely as an expression of French cultural hegemony and how radio was shunned for its alien program content, which was at loggerheads with the Algerian family's hierarchical codes. The cost of a set was a further disincentive, but even a sharp price reduction would not have increased set sales in this ethnic group. For the colonial settlers on their farms and in the cities, by contrast, radio programs served to confirm daily that the colonial order was in place, that France was in full and confident control, and that they, the listeners, were indeed denizens of "Overseas France."[5]

In the late 1940s, with the rise of radio stations broadcasting from Egypt, Syria, and Lebanon, Algerians' radio use began to change. Especially when nationalist confrontations heated up in neighboring Morocco and Tunisia, the need for information about them, information that was totally absent from French colonial radio, began to be felt intensely. As the Algerian struggle itself began to gather momentum, the few somewhat more independent local newspapers began to be censored and/or to censor themselves.[6]

Fanon describes how this virtual vacuum of information led, among other things, to a highly elevated role of rumor, the so-called "Arab telephone," which at times produced weird happenings such as individuals running down the street screaming that the colonizers had been militarily crushed and driven out. These individuals were typically captured and tortured by the French police, then often shot "while trying to escape," and yet they had no authentic information or guerrilla connections: Such occurrences served to heighten the climate of tension sharply on all sides.

Into this vacuum finally arrived the *Voice of Fighting Algeria,* the rebels' own station. Algerians virtually overnight shed their decades-long refusal to own a radio. Buying a set meant acquiring for the very first time a sense of the progress of the liberation struggle. Entire families would be glued to the set. Buying a radio was like paying a tax to become part of the newly self-defining nation. Broadcasts in all three languages of Algeria (Arabic, Berber, and French) sought to emphasize national unity against the colonial power.

When the French authorities began jamming the frequency, the guerrillas encouraged the public to listen for 2 to 3 hours at a time, so that once one frequency was jammed, they would switch to another, which the listeners would have to discover by working their way through the positions on the dial, their ear flattened against the speaker. The French soon banned battery radio sales (only affluent neighborhoods had electricity), and battery chargers were taken off the market.

In army raids on homes, radios were seized as a matter of course. Nonetheless, through devious channels and via Tunisia and Morocco, the equipment continued to be available to some degree. Even the crackle and static of the jamming were read as a confirmation that the resistance was still alive and fighting (or why block its messages?).[7]

The other cases we shall examine have not been literally life-and-death affairs (1 million Algerians died in the war by the time independence was won). Nonetheless, they have been quite intense, although sometimes with a hilarious side. All across Europe, the 1970s were a dynamic period for radical radio, even though any radio project that sought to be independent inevitably challenged the state's broadcasting monopoly, either its ownership or its licensing power, and therefore provoked police action to repress the challenge.

The leading instances were as follows. In November 1973, Greek students occupied Athens Polytechnic and briefly succeeded in setting up their own radio station to broadcast opposition to the military junta then in power. It was the first serious challenge to the fascist colonels since they had seized control in 1967, and their regime fell apart within the year. In April 1974, Portugal's fascist regime, in place since 1926, was overthrown, and two radio stations were taken over by the Left, Radio Renascença and Radio Clube Português in Lisbon. Both played a pivotal role over the next 2 years in consolidating the transition to democracy (see Chapter 18). With Spanish dictator Franco's death in 1975 and the explosion of long-suppressed political freedoms in Spain as well, creating alternative public spaces on the airwaves appeared quite intoxicating. And it was. Italian radical radio began in earnest in 1975 and became legalized the next year. French experiments with radical radio began soon after, and smaller German projects at about the same time.[8] Even the *Solidarnosc* movement in Poland (see Chapter 22) endeavored to gain access to the airwaves as early as 1981, and following the military clampdown in December 1981, a Radio Solidarité station was soon set up in Paris to broadcast into Poland.

RADICAL RADIO IN ITALY

The largest radical radio movement short of a revolution was Italy's from the mid-1970s to the early 1980s.[9] Continuously since the end of World War II, the conservative Christian Democratic Party—with more than its fair share of archreactionaries and even mafiosi in its leadership—had run the government and maintained a numbing monopoly over broadcasting. From the outset in the struggle to open up the airwaves, there were two sharply contrasted forces at work. One was the huge political movements of labor, youth,[10] and women that roiled the country from 1969 through the early 1980s. The other was aggressive corporate ambition to make money from the airwaves, and indeed the Constitutional Court's 1976 decision that the state had no monopoly over local broadcasting was pronounced in favor of a case brought by a conservative station in Parma. However, the politically intense atmosphere in Italy generated a huge crop of leftist radio experiments, as well. Taking all such independent broadcasters together, in 1977, about a quarter were broadcasting 24 hours a day and half between 14 and 19 hours a day. In 1978, it was estimated that there were well over 2,000 independent radio stations and about 500 independent TV stations as well (Trasatti, 1978).

The most notorious of the radical radio stations was Radio Alice in Bologna in 1977. It was quite short-lived and certainly not typical within the spectrum of leftist radio in Italy, but during a period of pitched confrontations between police and students at Bologna University in March, in which one student was shot dead, the station became for a moment the nerve center of the highly militant national student movement.[11] The station was, however, as much a public realm for poetry and political imagination to flourish as an organizing center—in all respects, quite unlike the conventional image of a radio station. Over the days of the campus battles, open discussion ranged over Italy, global issues, cultural politics, gender, socialism, anarchism, and university life. In an image that reverberated across Italy when the police eventually stormed the station, the confrontation went out live, including the students shouting "We have our hands up! Don't shoot!"

The range of alternative stations went all the way from little groups of friends in someone's apartment with a pile of discs, a microphone, and a small transmitter, to dyed-in-the-wool sectarians giving the correct line to save the world, to student movement activists using broadcasting as an organizing and debating alternative public sphere, to still other formats, some particularly fresh and original in context, for example, giving voice to housewives or gay activists. There was even a short-lived federation of 70 or more free radio stations, whose Italian acronym was FRED, the Federation of Democratic Radio Broadcasters.

By the later 1980s, with the decline of movement politics, the number of progressive radio stations had decreased considerably, and in the meantime, commercial vultures such as Berlusconi's Fininvest[12] had grabbed radio and television frequencies for their own lowest common-denominator programming. And even though the most active phase of the movement came to an end with a sudden enormous release of heroin to the streets at the very end of the 1970s,[13] and with the appalling degeneration of some leftist groups into terrorist tactics (the Red Brigades, Prima Linea, etc.), many of the most committed activists began to switch their energies into Italy's growing environmentalist and antinuclear movements, into new counterhegemonic public spheres. The longer-term impact of radical media activism can be seen to take many forms.

Some of the radical radio stations persisted, however, as we will see in Chapter 19. The period was one of very rich radical media experience. Particularly, the interaction between the wider movement democracy and the internal democracy of movement media was played out in many different ways. Meanwhile, the Italian radio stations were acting as a beacon to radical media activists in other nations, not least in France.

FREE RADIO IN FRANCE

In France, the state had consistently held a very tight leash on broadcasting.[14] Widespread public frustration had been engendered: with the liberation of France in 1944, a national broadcasting service had been proposed, but in practice, it had quickly become governmental. Successive French presidents assumed it was theirs. By way of illustration, soon after the May-June events in 1968, when first French students and then 11 million workers went on strike, a number of broadcast news staff who had joined the strike were fired by the government or were transferred to the provinces, once the tumult had spent itself. The director of broadcast news was always a frequent visitor at the Ministry of Information. Nor did the other political parties ever think of challenging this process, always hoping that with a switch in government, they might enjoy its fruits, as indeed several had for brief periods in the less stable years from 1945-1958. The French Communist Party's line was consistently that breaking up the state's monopoly would mean handing the channels over to commercial interests, but the problem was that the party leadership's own eyes were on the eventual prize of a single broadcasting monopoly for itself and its allies. It simply wanted to switch ownership, not to democratize it.

The era in which radical and not-so-radical independent stations challenged the state's monopoly on radio broadcasting ran from March 1977 through summer 1985. Cojean and Eskenazi (1986) provide a lively account of the numerous twists and turns of the saga and portraits of a number of the stations, especially in Paris. As is so often the case, these short-lived projects act as a reminder of what is needed and what could be achieved in broadcasting and, by contrast, what a state-dominated or corporate media system will not permit.

Cojean and Eskenazi (1986, pp. 43-47) describe one of the most famous instances, Heart of Steel Radio in Longwy, Lorraine, in 1978, founded in the course of resisting a disastrous steel mill closure that heralded the town's economic devastation. The station gave the local community a sudden voice and also showed itself quite independent of the communist labor union[15] that was leading the strike against closure, forthrightly condemning, for example, the 1979 Soviet invasion of Afghanistan, and sympathetically reviewing the *Solidarnosc* labor movement in Poland. Transistor sets were priced down by the town's single retailer, who also gave 10% of his profits to the station. The sets were to be found everywhere. At one juncture, steelworkers and their families even fought physically with the police to keep the station open.

Cojean and Eskenazi (1986) also describe stations that addressed the repressions of the state typically passed over by France's mainstream media, such as prison brutality and abuses, confessions by former soldiers of how they had tortured Algerian rebels in the 1956-1962 war, statements by serving police officers about how their training psyched them up for violence and even sanctioned murder. Cojean and Eskenazi also list stations that broadcast messages to prisoners, that gave voice to gay issues, that gave a voice to Muslims, as well as stations that were strongly conservative in bent.[16]

Both the conservative and then, from 1981, the Socialist Party government had the stations systematically jammed (on the colonial Algerian model of just a few years previously), but only until the end of the evening shift, about 10:30 p.m., after which the illegal stations had free play. An exquisite touch was when one rebel station, Vertigo Radio (known in the movement as "the pirates' pirate"), actually succeeded in broadcasting for 4 months from right inside the very headquarters where the jamming signals were emitted, operated by a technician totally disillusioned with his work as a jammer (Cojean & Eskenazi, 1986, pp. 87-88).

In the end, the pressure to revoke the state's broadcasting monopoly was overwhelming—but so, too, was pressure to finance the new stations through advertising. This last was a major sticking point for many in the socialist government. The 1981-1984 Socialist Party Premier Pierre Mauroy was deeply hostile to both advertising and giant media corporations and was a passionate believer in the volunteer spirit, which he saw as the ideal dynamic of independent radio stations, if they were to be permitted. Many in government also found the Italian radio scene at the time totally disorderly and reprehensible. Other leftist deputies looked with some anxiety at the Chilean experience during the Popular Unity period, in which radio was used effectively by the far Right, along with other media, to help destabilize the leftist government. They feared that French public opinion could be alienated by these means from the then-socialist majority in power.

In some sense, the Italian and French winners of this long drawn-out battle, it is true, were the major corporations, which moved in on radio and especially television[17] in a big way, once advertising was permitted and professional commercial broadcasting became the norm (Mignot-Lefebvre, 1984). The Berlusconi story is only the most egregious example of what happened.

Summary: Despite the degeneration of the Algerian postrevolutionary regime, the meteoric rise of Berlusconi, and the commercialization of French broadcasting, it is important not to slide into a knee-jerk fatalism. The key issue from this book's perspective is the very explosion of radical radio that took place during those years, covering topics normally way outside the limits of either the government's or the major political parties' permitted discourses. The experience demonstrated just how many Italian and French citizens did want access to media, not exclusively and not all the time, and maybe not in their own hands but at least in the hands of media activists tuned to the public's wavelengths rather than the parties' or the state's or the churches'. The fact these citizens largely lost out by the end of the process should be a stimulus to develop fresh ways to operate public access media, not a tocsin for the pointlessness of political activism. The need has increased, not vanished.

Furthermore, some stations survived and maintained significant alternative broadcast programming. We will review two of these in Part III. The global community radio scene, evident in considerable measure in the periodic AMARC conferences (see World Association of Community Radio Broadcasters website at www.amarc.org), was greatly encouraged and influenced by these major upsurges in alternative radio use, relatively short-lived as they proved to be in their own countries. The government's monopoly was broken, even if corporate oligopolies took its place. There are indeed many levels of radical media impact. Just as radical British theater led to many kinds of activism over time, so these bold radio ventures cannot be declared null and void because they themselves did not last. Would it really be better for the French still to govern Algeria, for the corrupt and reactionary mafia-penetrated Christian Democrats still to run Italy, for the Gaullists still to have a lock on France?[18] Radical radio alone did not lever these political regimes out, but it did amplify and encourage the movements against them in very considerable measure.

NOTES

1. Arbitron Radio Market Reports, Summer 1996.

2. For an overview, see Dunaway, 1998, and for an excellent collection on radical radio projects around the world, see Girard, 1992. In the Girard book, I would especially point out the chapters on radio in Africa; on Radio Soleil, Haiti; on Peru's feminist radio collective; on the Wawatay Radio Network in Canada; on multicultural stations Marconi (Amsterdam), Radio Centre-Ville (Montréal), Co-op Radio (Vancouver), and Radio Gazelle (Marseille); and, not least, on low-power radio in Argentina. For feminist radio, see Mitchell, 1998. For the U.S. micro-radio movement, see Sakolsky and Dunifer, 1998; and Soley, 1999, pp. 71-111, 119-139. For audiocassette use in Brazil, see Kouloumdjian and Busato, 1987. For a very lively and impassioned account of Radio Venceremos, the station of the guerrilla insurgents against the merciless Salvadoran oligarchy and its military—and the U.S. government—during the 1980s, see López Vigil (1994); and for a collage of memoirs of Radio Rebelde, the station of the Cuban rebels during the 1956-1959 insurgency, see Martínez Victores (1978). Garitaonandia (1988) analyzes the uses of radio by the Popular Front (and the fascists) before and during the Spanish Civil War. Jankowski, Prehn, and Stappers (1992) offer a variety of instances from Western Europe in the 1970s and 1980s. Soley and Nichols (1987) review clandestine radio broadcasting. Vargas (1995) examines indigenous radio stations in Chiapas, Mexico. Garofalo (1994) and Stevens-Fernández (1995) discuss radio stations belonging to communities of African descent on Colombia's Pacific coast. Godfried

(1997) studies the history of Chicago's long-running labor union radio station, WCFL. And all these cases are only the tip of the iceberg.

3. Also leading the list were South Africa, Namibia, Zimbabwe, Palestine, and to a lesser extent, Malaya, Kenya, and Cyprus. Cambodia and Laos were sucked into the Vietnam war, with especially hideous consequences in the former case (Hersh, 1983).

4. Indeed, had it not been for U.S. financial and military support, the French would have been driven out of Vietnam well before the climactic battle of Dien Bien Phu in 1954.

5. The laughable term the French government uses even today to denote continuing colonies such as the Caribbean territories of Guyana, Martinique, and Guadeloupe.

6. Certain French metropolitan newspapers (such as *Le Monde*) provided at least a measure of the truth, but they could only be bought at kiosks. When Algerians asked for these papers, there were increasingly ugly confrontations with the French vendors. These latter interpreted any inquiry for such papers as a prime index of anticolonial sentiment and would announce that "the assholes' papers didn't come in today" or get personally abusive. When people started sending their children to buy the papers in the hope of avoiding such confrontations, the vendors soon began to refuse to sell them to minors.

7. The subsequent abuse of radio as a mechanism of control by the postcolonial Algerian government over the next 30 years, culminating in the terrible repressions and bloodshed of the 1990s, represent an intensely depressing aftermath. They cannot expunge, however, the remarkable role played by radio in the anticolonial struggle, given Algeria's pivotal role within the movement.

8. For the German free radio experience up to 1981, with additional information on Switzerland, Austria, Belgium, Sweden, and some other countries at that period, see the self-published text by Münster Free Radio's Christoph Busch, 1981, *Was Sie Schon Immer Über Freie Radios Wissen Wollten, Aber Nie Zu Fragen Wagten* [What you always really wanted to know about free radio stations, but never dared to ask]—a play on Woody Allen's film, *Everything You Always Wanted To Know About Sex But Were Afraid To Ask.* See also Network Medien-Cooperative (1983), and Bischoff (1978).

9. For further detail, see my *The Media Machine* (Downing, 1980, pp. 200-218) and also Collectif A/Traverso (1977), Macali (1977), Siliato (1977), Hutter (1978).

10. The status of student in Italy at that period was not a full-time temporary one typically lasting from one's late teens to one's very early twenties: study was likely to be part-time, composed of vast mass lectures and absentee professors and not much else, so that young people remained students for up to 10 years before graduating, often worked part-time for a living, and were largely responsible for their own educational process.

11. For activist accounts from the time, see autori molti compagni (1977) and Collectif A/Traverso (1977); for retrospective assessments, see Bascetta, Dominijanni, and Gagliardo (1997) and Grispigni (1997).

12. With political assistance over a number of years from the highly corrupt Italian premier Craxi (who fled to Tunisia to avoid jail), Emilio Berlusconi rapidly came to own all three national commercial channels in Italy. For a brief period, he was also premier himself, which meant he had control ultimately over the three public TV channels as well. See Ruggeri and Guarino (1994).

13. Because heroin had never been a component of youth culture in Italy, its widespread appearance out of the blue inevitably led to speculation that corrupt conservatives in Italy's power structure had colluded with American mafiosi to release it in mass quantities onto the streets to defuse the threat of Italy's growing militancy. Although this is certainly plausible, given the amoral and ruthless qualities of one wing of conservative leadership in Italy, it still leaves the other term of the equation out of focus, namely, what it was about so many young people's political style that allowed them to experiment with heroin in the first place. The Left needs the same critical frankness applied to itself as it applies to the power structure.

14. For the period before the French airwaves went commercial, see De Tarlé (1979).

15. Historically, the French Communist Party had always been militantly pro-Soviet, in sharp contradistinction to the Italian party. The station's political openness showed beyond doubt that it was primarily under popular control, not party control.

16. Indeed, as in Parma, Italy, in France, one of the first stations to challenge the state's broadcasting monopoly was Blue Thread Radio, sponsored by Montpellier dignitaries of the then-president's own party.

17. Most of these corporate heavy-hitters were even more interested in television than in radio. In the late 1950s, United Kingdom media magnate Roy Thomson had opined from his own experience that a commercial broadcast license was "a license to print money."

18. For France, see Collovald and Neveu (1999), and see Dauncey and Hare (1999) for commentary on the increased political and cultural openness of French broadcasting, despite typical commercial excesses.

16

Film and Video

Walter Benjamin's 1936 commentary on the rapidly growing accessibility of media technologies, which we examined in Part I, proved ever more prescient in the final years of the 20th century. The cost of high-quality cameras and editing equipment plummeted, while public engagement with audiovisual media continued at a very intense level. In the first edition of this book (Downing, 1984), I gave scant attention to film and video because of my overriding concern with low-cost access. Twenty years later, this no longer makes sense.[1] Computer developments ensured that these features of the culture will continue in force farther than the eye can see. TV penetration in the Third World, with the aid of satellites, rose sharply toward the close of the 20th century, although camcorder and VCR penetration, while also rising sharply in the latter 1990s, initially took some time to follow suit. Video activists in minority ethnic communities in the First World and in many Third World settings began using the technology at roughly the same point in time.[2] The scope for further research and evaluation in this field is simply enormous and growing all the time.

The examples below give a brief sense for how film and video were deployed as part of social movements that were variously—and sometimes overlappingly—pro-labor, antinuclear, and black, addressing people with AIDS and HIV, empowering low-income inner-city communities, and combating communalism in India. Their counterhegemonic and alternative public sphere dimensions will by now be self-evident, as will their role in fostering developmental power. In Chapter 20, Laura Stein's detailed study of U.S. public access television takes this analysis of radical video a very important step forward.

- Documentary film and political critique
- Political video in the United States since the 1960s
- AIDS videos
- The problem of national distribution for radical film and video
- TV Maxabomba, Rio de Janeiro
- Anand Patwardhan and zero-budget documentary in India
- Britain's black film and video movements in the 1980s

Popular video is often seen as a dramatic new development, and technologically that is true, but historically, it is not. For although cheap micro-videocameras and VCRs have tremendously extended access to visual media-making, the access pioneers were those radical media activists in still photography and 16mm and 8mm film who saw and seized the opportunity to place communicative power in the public's hands.

DOCUMENTARY FILM AND POLITICAL CRITIQUE

Earlier, in Chapter 14's discussion of John Heartfield and radical photomontage, we noted the workers' photography movements of the 1920s and 1930s. Growing out of them in the United States were the films on labor struggles produced by Nykino and the Workers' Film and Photo League during the 1930s (Alexander, 1981) and films produced in the 1960s and 1970s by Newsreel, later Third World Newsreel.[3] Albeit feature filmmakers and not documentarians, independent African American filmmakers, beginning with William Foster and his 1910 film *The Pullman Porter* and continuing through such luminaries as Oscar Micheaux and Spencer Williams in the 1920s and 1930s, are a key related part of this history and its very earliest American chapter. The 1954 drama, *Salt of the Earth,* portraying a Chicano miners' strike demands mention, as do major 1980s documentaries such as *Atomic Cafe, Four Corners: A National Sacrifice Area?*, and *El Salvador: The People Will Win.*

These latter, addressing, respectively, the nuclear threat, the clash between mining corporations and ecological survival, and U.S.-backed repression in El Salvador, are the tip of the tip of the 1980s iceberg of radical documentaries. They represented the radical formation in the independent film movement, with experimental uses of film (Adams Sitney, 1979) and low-budget features (Levy, 1999), some of which also had a radical focus, constituting its other formations. The influence on this radical wing of Jean-Luc Godard's political films, of Joris Ivens' and Chris Marker's work, of Italian neo-realism, and of the radical neo-realist so-called Third Cinema (Solanas & Getino, 1969/1983; García Espinosa, 1969/1983; Gabriel, 1982; Willemen, 1989), were all considerable.

Video, like independent cinema and like unofficial photography, represents a wide spectrum, from family document and personal expression through artistic experiment or political intervention. The term *video* has come to be used in the United States in large part to refer to the difference between how TV technology is used in broadcasting and cable and how it is generally used for alternative purposes. To some degree, the term also signifies differences in the reception setting, namely, that video is typically viewed via a home VCR, or in a classroom, or in an art installation, or as part of a political mobilization.

The trouble is that the use of two different terms for the same technology risks enthroning a certain fatalism about the destiny of television. Although this may have a rhetorical payoff as a spit-in-the-face at the corporate networks, it may also lend itself to letting commercial television off the hook regarding its public responsibility. Britain's Channel 4 was commercial, not public, yet, nonetheless, it is widely credited with many achievements: There is no absolute law that all commercial TV must be of poor quality,[4] even if the advertising spots are so.

Independent video's history in the United States (Boyle, 1997; Gever, 1985; Drew, 1995; Anderson & Goldson, 1993) is distinctly checkered and repeatedly manifests a tension between cultural and technical innovation as a stimulating end in itself and radical media's use of these as instruments of debate and critique of the established order. The narrative of early independent video in Appalachia, which Boyle recounts (pp. 48-54, 96-104, 139-145) reveals many of these strains, whether between building community by giving everyone a voice to tell his or her story (up to and including fundamentalist snake-handler sects) or drawing attention to political and economic ills (such as strip-mining), or becoming video-ethnographers contracted by foundations, universities, and museums.

There are many, many instances of politically pointed and artistically excellent independent videos. It is impossible to convey their richness here in short referential sentences. Videographer Eden Véliz's depictions of Mayan life in Guatemala, Victor Masayesva, Jr.'s portrayals of Hopi life, Sylvia Morales's 1985 narrative film *Esperanza* about undocumented migrant workers in California, Joy Shannon's 1987 documentary *Till the Last Stroke* on elderly African American women artists in Washington, D.C., are only randomly selected moments from a treasure chest of work that simply cries out for distribution (cf. Downing, 1990b).

AIDS VIDEOS

Alex Juhasz (1995) has described the U.S. trajectory of a particularly important category of independent video, namely, AIDS videos. Just in the years 1987 an 1988, hundreds of such videos were produced, and she analyzes certain key instances. These videos filled a crucial gap, in that many were made *by* people with AIDS for people with AIDS. As a result of homophobic discrimination, or because AIDS also spread rapidly among black and Latino intravenous drug users, people with AIDS in mainstream media were overwhelmingly talked about but never spoke themselves. As Juhasz puts it,

> Another nearly definitive convention of alternative AIDS media is that expertise is transferred away from those who have wielded power so criminally for the duration of the epidemic to those who have suffered or fought against the powers-that-be. Alternative tapes give authority about AIDS to people who possess lived experience of the crisis.... Spectators comment upon how empowering it feels to see so many bright, articulate, intense women taking power over the crises of AIDS. (p. 95)

Logistical problems with independent film and video as radical media have been twofold. The first was the collective endeavor and cost of production, especially in film. Even when no one was paid, film stock still had to be bought and its processing paid for; cameras, lights, and sound equipment had to be paid for, too, unless they could be borrowed from a friendly source. Unpaid crews could not work for long periods of time, and furthermore, because crew members were donating their labor, their work attitudes would sometimes fall short of what was needed.

THE PROBLEM OF DISTRIBUTION

If there was a desire to get the work seen nationally, then, a second problem arose, still more acute: distribution and exhibition. Despite all the monumental effort in production, often neither energy nor organizational experience were at hand to cope practically with the absence of a marketing process (Anderson & Goldson, 1993). Movie theater chains were definitively uninterested, as were TV networks and film distribution firms. It remains a serious challenge to broadly disseminate public information (a) that the film/video exists and (b) how to rent it.

Within the United States, some distribution agencies for alternative videos exist, such as the Video Resource Documentation Center in New York City, Facets Video in Chicago, and California Newsreel in San Francisco, but many such videos and films are distributed out of people's living rooms and attics, with perhaps 1 to 10 titles per home distributor. Again, this in no way represents a marketing operation, merely a poorly publicized mail-order service. The vast majority of video stores neither know nor wish to know of such titles. As Juhasz (1995) describes AIDS videos,

> When factoring an AIDS video into the already small network of alternative distribution companies willing to distribute low-budget, progressive, educational video, things become even more difficult. . . . Most alternative AIDS tapes require some complex interweaving of these particularized distribution networks. . . . Furthermore, the people who most need to see AIDS tapes . . . are the disenfranchised members of our society who are not going to be reached by even the methods of progressive distribution . . . which means nothing less than labor-intensive, pro-active strategies that take the tape to the people that need it . . . This means phone calls, follow-up, letter campaigns, follow-up, then long train rides to hard-to-find agencies, a small audience, and then, finally, few of the institutionally accepted markers of success. . . . A *successful* screening finds a tape playing to fifteen mem-

> bers of an HIV support group or women's club, the tape introduced by the makers and then discussed afterward. (pp. 216-217)

Thus, brilliant as a number of these productions are, and large as the dent on public debate might be if they were widely seen, and exciting as is the use of film and video as radical media, there remains a huge shortfall in the United States between manufacture and use. Perhaps equally, U.S. film audiences lack the cultural preparation to engage with their subject matter—becuase they are not presented in the blockbuster style that U.S. audiences have been trained to value. This also militates against their impact. Arguably, the huge creative potential in American film and video culture lies fallow to a considerable degree. The major countervailing factor is constituted by the over 300 public access television facilities across the United States and a number of the projects that feed into these stations, reviewed in Laura Stein's Chapter 20.

However, we need also to step back a little and recognize that many radical film and video projects do not seek a national audience. They are made for local groups in specific conditions, and their audience is easily able to see them. We should beware of gigantism in our analysis of radical media, of dismissing the local as weightless.[5] Examples are many across the world, from India to Canada and from South Africa to Brazil (cf. Thede & Ambrosi, 1992). Leuthold (1998, pp. 124-130) discusses the way some Native American video work particularly emphasizes locality and why that is significant for Native American aesthetics and political concerns. For some of the range of Latin American popular video, in particular, see also Aufderheide (1992) and Rodríguez (in press).

THE PROBLEM OF FUNDING

One such instance is TV Maxabomba, a poorly funded street/community video project that has been in action since 1988 in Rancho Fundo, a neighborhood in Rio de Janeiro (Mayer, 1998; Percq, 1998). Rancho Fundo is one small part of Baixada Fluminense, the huge and desperately poor zone to the north of Rio that does not even figure on tourist maps of the city. TV Maxabomba emerged as an energizer of ongoing local protests about the town hall's total neglect of the neighborhood, meaning, for example, that refuse was never collected, resulting in fires, rat epidemics, and other health-hazards. Photographing confrontations with the mayor and screening local protests and public discussions were a significant part of the video project's success. The project became quite famous in other parts of Brazil and even in international development policy circles and, thus, developed a kind of second existence on that level as a model for what could be done with video at the grass roots. But its primary purpose was precisely local, to get the authorities to return to the neighborhood the taxes they paid in the form of urban services and generally to give the neighborhood a much stronger sense of its social dignity and political capacity (cf. Huesca, 1995).

A different example is the work of Indian zero-budget documentarian Anand Patwardhan, whose documentaries on the politics of religious fundamentalism in India, on the treatment of the poor in Mumbai, on the devastation caused by the construction of the Narmada dam in central India, and on other themes have had both a local and a national resonance—even an international one in the Indian diaspora.[6]

In Britain, in the 1980s, a different dynamic was to be seen (Daniels & Gerson, 1989; Mercer, 1988; Pines, 1988). Partly as a result of the patronage of Channel 4 TV at that time, and partly with funds from some local councils in London and elsewhere with a leftist elected majority, a black film movement quite suddenly emerged with works that at last gave voice to cultures, experiences, aspirations, and questions virtually denied expression hitherto in mainstream British media. This was independent work but work that received patronage from certain established institutions and that was both aired on TV and made available in film format. The programmers did not put it on at prime time, but nonetheless it was there and screened on what was then only a four-channel national TV service.

Summary: Paradoxically, it is in some ways easier to "see" media formats that dominated earlier epochs than it is to evaluate film and video, especially in an era when many parts of the world are awash with them, and the other parts would mostly like to be. The lacuna in research information to date about audiences for radical media somehow looms especially large when considering video and film technologies. Nonetheless, the examples cited show clearly the continuing theme of cofabulation between social movements and media, while at the same time illustrating cases of national minority ethnic communities' and local inner-city communities' self-assertion and empowerment through these media projects. Video and film's recapitulation and condensation of the separate strands of earlier media technologies—sound, print, animation, color, editing, imagery, artwork—give them particularly rich possibilities in assisting the constitution and development of alternative public spheres. Judged as single projects, the point at which they are "finished" is the point at which the interactivity in their reception hangs both on the political context and on the activism of their audiences; yet, if they are judged as individual moments in an ongoing flow of movements and media projects over time, the interactivity index is much higher than it might first appear. One documentary on nuclear perils fed into the next and the next and the next, to the point where in combination with the movements, a partial halt was called to the nuclear arms race between the United States and Soviet Russia and to the construction of new nuclear power stations.

Another significant question, which different types of video project may relate to in quite different ways, is the issue of distribution. A technical solution to this may appear over time through development of higher and higher bandwidth cables for Internet use, but technological fixes for political problems have such a dismal history that great caution is warranted before relaxing into that potential as if it were a sure thing. But here we are moving directly into the subject area of the next chapter.

NOTES

1. For an informative look at interesting examples of independent television broadcasting in a number of Western European nations up to the end of the 1980s, see Jankowski et al. (1992). For a comparative analysis of the first phase of public access television in Canada, the United States, and Britain, see Berrigan (1977), and for a more recent review of public access television in Britain, see Dovey (1993).

2. For a survey of radical video projects in the Third World, see also the chapters by Batty, Kuttab, Fox and Braden in Dowmunt (1993). For further information on Brazil during the 1990s, see Bekes (1996). The active use of video by the Kayapù people of Brazil's interior, in pursuit of their demands for security and autonomy, is discussed in Turner (1992). The problems and prospects for Inuit broadcasting in northern Canada are reviewed by Valaskakis (1992).

3. In the first edition of *Radical Media* (Downing, 1984), I devoted a chapter to this organization and another to its former West Coast counterpart, Califor-

nia Newsreel, which later during the 1990s distinguished itself by bringing a whole raft of African and African American films into public U.S. circulation on relatively low-cost video.

4. There is, however, an argument that the culture of television in Britain, as in other European nations, was originally founded on a public service model and thus that when commercial TV began, its personnel and the public at large shared certain expectations about television that were sharply different from the expectations typical of U.S. audiences, formed in an almost strictly commercial broadcasting tradition (cf. McChesney, 1993).

5. I owe this emphasis to Clemencia Rodríguez's comments on an earlier draft. Her own work on video collectives of poor women in Bogotá, which came to similar conclusions, is cited Chapter 4.

6. His films available in the United States from First Run/Icarus in New York City are *Prisoners of Conscience* (1978), *A Time to Rise* (1981), *Bombay Our City* (1985), *In Memory of Friends* (1990), *In the Name of God* (1991), *Father, Son, and Holy War* (1994), and *Narmada Diary* (1995). When I say zero budget, I mean that when I asked Patwardhan what size his crew was for his documentaries, he pointed at himself; and when one of the students in my department asked him about time code, he explained that the equipment he used was too old to have it.

17

Radical Internet Use

Tamara Villarreal Ford and Genève Gil

This chapter addresses the potential of radical Internet communication for social change. Key to the realization of this radical potential is the formation of new spheres of communicative action by peoples' movements, by which we mean, "autonomous, democratic civil society as it expresses itself in organization independent of the state and its formal corporate structures" (Esteva & Prakash, 1998, p. 11). Such communicative action is illustrated in some detail by analyzing two models of Internet activism, the San Francisco-based Institute for Global Communications and the on-line presence of the Zapatista movement of Chiapas, Mexico.

First, however, we will note certain economic, political, and legislative trends that threaten to convert the Internet into yet another commercial medium, stripped of its unique potential for facilitating progressive political debate and transformation. Driving the discussion is a concept advanced by Boal (1995, p. 5), who has used the term *enclosures* to describe these trends, referring back to the Enclosures Movement in 17th-century Britain, namely, the continual fencing off of land in common use for big landowners' private use, whereby previously free farmers suddenly found themselves forced to be wage laborers for the gentry. He suggests that if today, information is switched for land, the trends point in exactly the same direction.

Thus, although some Internet enthusiasts have hyped its democratic essence, we need to retain caution, thinking of its potential in this regard as partially realized but also as constantly in danger of being foreclosed. And although more traditional mechanisms of corporate hegemony in media and of state censorship are reasonably widely understood, we have thought it useful to detail in this chapter some of the most recent control mechanisms operating on this newer communication technology to set radical Internet use in its full context.

- The Internet's democratic potential
- Access and empowerment
- Information enclosures
- Regulatory legislation
- Privatization
- Intellectual property and copyright
- Infowar
- Sustaining the networks
- Case study 1: the Institute for Global Communications
- Case study 2: the Zapatista movement

The Internet represents a new era for alternative media. As an interconnected infrastructure for multiple forms of communications, it facilitates an era of convergence of media technologies. By providing for the easy transmittal of simple texts as well as the means to combine and recombine a range of media formats and social actors, it allows for an unprecedented distribution of knowledge and resources to virtually anywhere in the globe.

The Internet is potentially our first global public sphere, a medium through which politics could be made truly participatory at both regional and international levels. And the Internet is the first medium through which individuals and independent collectives throughout the globe may hope to communicate, in their own voices, with an international audience of millions. Thus the purely technical possibilities for the Internet as a public sphere are unlimited.[1]

The methods of information exchange made possible in the cyberspace of the Internet are many and diverse, allowing for a great variety of communication styles, strategies, and functions. Popular forms and forums of interaction include personal and collective websites, newsgroups, E-mail, on-line chat sessions, conferencing, mailing lists, bulletin boards, search engines,and databases. These and other means of online communication facilitate extraordinary new possibilities, such as the unlimited, free distribution of software, dissemination of published and unpublished texts, exhibition of multimedia art, documentation of events, and real-time long-distance conversation at low cost. For the first time, a medium accessible to a vast number of individuals and collectives worldwide allows for the global transmission of virtually any information.

Moreover, the audience has a greater degree of control of production in this medium. Testimonials, uncensored freelance journalism, reports by human rights organizations, videos and interactive media, multilingual discussion forums, support group meetings, and political strategy sessions are conducted, uploaded, transmitted, circulated, and posted on-line daily.

These computer networks have augmented not replaced other essential forms of organizing, from face-to-face encounters to radio programs, underground newspaper articles, subversive artwork, music, and alternative television. However, computers have also made possible a more rapid dissemination and exchange of information and analysis than has ever been possible in grassroots movements. With simple software programs, archiving resources is relatively easy, and this enables accessible reservoirs of information unlike anything before.

Despite all this communicative potential, there are considerable and growing problems with its development as a democratic medium. Scholars such as Carey (1989) and McChesney (1996) have documented the trajectories of other technological developments originally introduced with utopian expectations of democratic progress, such as electricity, mail, telegraph, telephone, radio, television, and fax; these have all been turned into industries dominated by business, with further developments in their technologies manipulated for profit. As business has followed a path of increasing monopoly in each of these industries, social actors have been forced to seek new avenues of communication. As McChesney aptly observes,

> The primary function of the nonprofit sector in U.S. communication has been to pioneer the new technologies when they were not yet con-

> sidered profitable . . . once the technologies proved profitable, however, they were turned over to private interests with negligeable compensations. (p. 8)

Given industry's control of communications, alternative media producers have been forced to seek new avenues of communication, and the rapid expansion of computer networks for purposes of alternative communication can be seen, in part, as a response to such forces. Whereas access to radio and television broadcasting has been limited, and the costs of long distance telephone and fax are prohibitive for sustained interaction, computer networks have provided dynamic new means of grassroots organizing and solidarity (Acción Zapatista, 1996a).

Critics have noted that enclosure is all-too-often seen in the increasing commercialization of the Internet, and limited access to electronic resources makes these new communications networks subject to a hierarchy of access.[2] Women, people of color, and other marginalized groups tend to be underrepresented. Alternative media of all kinds tend to remain in the hands of media-literate professionals (Hamelink, 1995). Furthermore, the Internet is only as useful as it is available, and, in 1995, at least 80% of the world's people were estimated to be without even the most rudimentary telecommunications.[3] Even within the United States, where service is most ubiquitous, there are marked disparities. In 1996, Clinton promised that every child would gain access to the Internet during his administration. Yet, a year later, "only 9% of classrooms, labs, and libraries in public schools [were] connected to the Net, and the proportion [was] half that for schools with poorer students" (Shapiro, 1997, p. 2). Universal access to the Internet sounds good, but it is expensive,[4] and questions of how it will be funded are yet to be resolved. Furthermore, access is not just a matter of telecommunications equipment, it is also a question of media literacy, computer networking skills, and funds to pay Internet specialists.

Networks have the further potential, by allowing for new forms of electronic collaboration, to help with radically dissolving the set disciplines of knowledge production and to unite activism and scholarly research. Academic environments have proactively fostered the creation and development of the Internet. Those affiliated with such public or private institutions have had ready access to both the skills and technology necessary for the production of Internet resources. On the other hand, academic environments can also be quite infertile ground for these developments. Although administrators publicly endorse cross-disciplinary or distance collaborative work, the institutional structure of discrete disciplines still tends to fragment knowledge. In addition, the applications of such university work are being ever more scaled toward commercial markets or conservative policies. Educational institutions have become increasingly dependent on corporate or foundation money,[5] and conservative think tanks outspend public interest media by a margin of 13 to 1 (see Massachi & Cowan, 1994, and <http://www.cco.org> Center for Campus Organizing). Academic research in the public interest may still be valid in principle, but it is ever harder to realize in practice.

Critics of the Internet have also claimed that information on the Internet is often unreliable, transient, or biased. There is some truth to these claims. Websites can be subjective, and they do tend to move or disappear due to authors' changing circumstances, organizational instability, and lack of resources. But such criticism is disempowering rather than constructive. First, it assumes that Internet readers do not exercise critical judgment in granting credibility to sources or assessing situations from many points of view. Second, the problem of stability could be offset with funding for the systematic archiving of Internet resources. Last, such criticism ignores the fact that mainstream media also represent particular points of view and often deliver considerably less than the full truth (Herman & Chomsky, 1988).

Thus, a radical media approach to the Internet is essential: It consists of people's participation in creating interactive forms of communication that act as a countervailing force to the one-way flows inherent in commercial media. Despite the problems cited here, significant as they are, the Internet is proving already to be a powerful medium for global civil society. Although access is still limited and unevenly distributed, it is nonetheless growing worldwide, even in rural and impoverished regions. Because many of the world's people depend on traditional forms of communication, the merger of the Internet with other media makes it a valuable resource, even for those without direct access—a possibility amply demonstrated by the Internet presence of the Zapatistas, an impoverished, indigenous resistance movement from the southeastern jungles of Mexico.

Internet use is also having an interesting impact on social and media activism. Traditionally, radical media activists have functioned as reporters or documentarians, mediating news and analysis of current events and social movements. But two things are happening to change this. First, through electronic networks, the articulators of social movements are increasingly able to speak for themselves, through documents posted directly to the Internet. This prompts the question of "whether we can move from strategies of giving voice to the voiceless to strategies by which people speak for themselves" (Hamelink, 1995, p. 141). Second, as a result of current socioeconomic trends, social activists are increasingly on the defensive, struggling to protect civil liberties and human rights, while simultaneously challenging regressive economic policies. In this process, too, the boundaries separating grassroots activists and radical media makers are increasingly blurred.

A great many strategies of enclosure threaten to undermine the existence of the Internet as we know it today, even within the least likely arenas. The promise of computer networks is threatened everywhere by concerted campaigns of disempowerment being waged by state and market forces. In his article, "Streetcorners in Cyberspace," Shapiro (1995) outlines some of the dangers of current trends toward the rapid privatization of the Internet (Shapiro, 1995). Using the imaginary virtual communities of *Cyberkeley* and *Cyburbia* as polar models, Shapiro argues that we need to preserve and protect a space for public discourse on-line, as we do in physical space. In *Cyberkeley,* Internet users must occasionally pass through certain public Internet gateways where anyone is free to speak and gather. These spaces, like actual street corners or parks, afford the public the opportunity to be exposed to a range of contrasting views and even to learn of the existence of alternatives to commercial sites. In *Cyburbia,* the realm being fashioned by corporate and political interests for the maximization of profit and minimization of dissent, users can—and often must—avoid all public discourse and head straight for the cybermall.

We will now proceed to note some U.S. legislative trends at the close of the 1990s, privatization strategies, intellectual property issues, and infowar scares. There are numerous other instances not mentioned here, and comparable struggles will certainly continue to arise. In essence, we are faced with an immensely powerful trend to enclosure, away from the radical inclusivity enabled in principle by the Internet.[6]

In February 1996, drastic changes in the national communication infrastructure were effected when the U.S. Congress passed the Telecommunications Act. Although it promised to increase services, stimulate competition, and lower prices, the new Act did not demonstrate any such effects. Instead, it contributed to an erosion of the public sphere, threatened civil liberties, curbed public access to information, and paved the way for unprecedented levels of media mergers and vertical integration.[7]

The Telecom package included the Communications Decency Act of 1995, which sought to eliminate "indecent" communication on the Internet, ostensibly to protect children from exposure to pornographic media.[8] This piece of legislation, immediately challenged by the American Civil Liberties Union, was ruled unconstitutional by the Supreme Court in 1997. Despite its eventual demise, the fact that it was carried by Congress and President Clinton is cause for concern, for it is likely to return in other forms. Implementation of the Communications Decency Act would have imposed alarming restrictions on the exchange of knowledge, perceptions, and resources in cyberspace. Not only did the Act criminalize, for example, the representation of a nude classical Greek sculpture in any arena accessible to minors, it also prohibited open discussion of crucial issues such as sexual health.

Fortunately, popular opposition to the Act was notably swift and widespread from the outset. The blue ribbon campaign for free speech[9] in response to the Communications Decency Act was arguably the most notable strike to date in the short history of the U.S. Internet public. Ultimately, in this particular case, the Internet has escaped enclosure. However, the Communications Decency Act is only one of a plethora of past and present efforts to limit freedom of access, expression, and production in the Internet world. Unfortunately, other strategies of appropriation and control have largely escaped the public's attention and have encountered slight resistance.

Alternative on-line communication is increasingly subject to campaigns of intentional disempowerment (Hamelink, 1995, pp. 123-127) and information enclosure (Boal, 1995, p. 5), which threaten to undermine its present effectiveness and future potential. Yet, it seems that many Internet participants are largely unaware of these dangers. Like international trade agreements, decisions affecting the rights and interests of the public in the communication arena are made in semi-secrecy, and legislation is often drafted by communication industry lobbyists. The fact is that the U.S. government, which subsidized the Internet from the beginning, was rapidly clearing a path during the 1990s for the wholesale corporatization of cyberspace. Shapiro (1995) summarizes the process:

> The federal government has been gradually transferring the backbone of the U.S. portion of the global computer network to companies such as IBM and MCI as part of a larger plan to privatize cyberspace. But the crucial step was taken on April 30 [1995] when the National Science Foundation shut down its part of the Internet, which began in the 1970s as a Defense Department communication tool. That left the corporate giants in charge. (p. 1)

As McChesney (1996) aptly observes,

> The primary function of the nonprofit sector in U.S. communication has been to pioneer the new technologies when they were not yet considered profitable . . . Once the technologies proved profitable, however, they were turned over to private interests with negligible compensations. (p. 8)

The most profound effect of the 1996 Act—the virtual give-away of the digital spectrum (estimated by *The Washington Post* to be worth as much as $70 billion (cited in McChesney, 1997, p. 254)—received essentially no press coverage outside of the business pages (Hickey, 1997, p. 11). This was rated one of the top 10 underreported stories of 1995 by Project Censored (Jensen, 1997). The telecommunications sectors of most of the world were nonprofit state-owned monopolies through the 1970s. "Today they are being privatized in perhaps the largest liquidation of public property in the history of capitalism" (McChesney, 1996, p. 5). Furthermore, Schiller (1995, p. 24) notes that this came at a time when there was a widening gap in income, despite a period of economic growth, and that this development promised to separate even further the information haves from the have-nots.[10] As McChesney (1997) affirmed, the Internet "has already turned dramatically away from the non-commercial, nonprofit, independent and open public sphere that it promised to be just a few years ago" (p. 93).

In this environment, the term *access* begins to disappear from the discourse, replaced by the notion of a "marketplace of ideas." But markets only give people a range of what is profitable, not what is possible, and they have a strong bias toward rewarding ideas supportive of the status quo.[11] Thus, knowledge as a common good is destroyed. This is inherent in the root meaning of *privatization* (private = to deprive): It deprives communities of access to their common heritage and renders it the entitlement of individual owners (Hamelink, 1995, pp. 128-130).

Furthermore, when information is commodified, the battle is on for consumer attention. With corporate dominance of the Internet, businesses engage marketing and public relations firms to do everything they can to steer users to their sites and away from others.

The issues of intellectual property and copyright constitute key aspects of rendering information and culture into commodities. U.S. intellectual property policy sets the tone internationally and is the subject of intense debate at such international gatherings as the World Intellectual Property Organization (WIPO) conventions. In both domestic and international policy gatherings, participation is usually limited to business and state interests. Like other areas of information infrastructure policy, the subject of copyright is rarely systematically addressed in mainstream media, leaving technical associations, public interest organizations, and business lobbies to provide most of the information that does exist.[12]

However, for specialists following these trends, the writing was already on the wall. The examples that follow are to illustrate the point, for whether actually legislated or modified, they reveal the direction of public policy to which media and Internet activists need to respond.

The 1995 *White Paper on Copyright*, drafted by Bruce Lehman (President Clinton's intellectual property adviser and a former copyright lobbyist), essentially disregarded the public's rights altogether. Samuelson (1996) asserts that the administration wanted "to please the copyright industry, especially members of the Hollywood community . . . vital to the president's re-election bid. And what these copyright industries want in return is more legal control than ever before over the products they distribute."

Samuelson goes on to outline a maximalist agenda framed to secure for copyright holders all imaginable sources of income. These would include (a) controlling every use of copyrighted works in digital form; (b) controlling every transmission of works in digital form; (c) eliminating "fair use" rights whenever a use might be licensed; (d) terminating first sale rights, which the public has long enjoyed in the print world; (e) attaching copyright management information to digital copies to trace where each copy resides and what is being done with it; (f) protecting technologically every digital copy of work; (g) forcing on-line service providers to become copyright police; and (h) teaching the new copyright rules to children.

Another trend-setting case in this direction was the Espionage Act of 1996, which empowered intelligence agencies to investigate the activities of ordinary people worldwide in an effort to protect the intellectual property rights of U.S. corporations, by defining such rights as "vital to national security."

> The Economic Espionage Act takes espionage from military domains to economic domains. It redefines intellectual property infringement as a crime, and justifies the use of intelligence agencies to deal with issues of science and technology exchanges . . . such that the free exchange of knowledge, technologies and ideas . . . is now being defined as espionage. (Shiva, 1996)

Other attempts to constrain freedom of expression threatened to limit the power of the Internet as a vehicle for social change, while simultaneously constraining individuals' freedom to support social movements in more traditional ways. These efforts were woven around a rhetoric of fear and paranoia. A 1993 Rand report entitled *CyberWar is Coming!* popularized the notion of "information warfare," whereby conflicts of the future will not be fought on the ground but through networks and public opinion and by immobilizing pivotal electric power-supply switchpoints. The report also paints social activists—particularly those in the developed world who support Third World struggles against repressive regimes—as part of the new post-Soviet enemy. This was not only a think piece. In the wake of the Oklahoma City bombings, for example, the Clinton Administration proposed the 1995 Omnibus Counter-Terrorism Act, which extended the powers of the FBI, and thereby seriously infringed on civil liberties and individual privacy through new forms of surveillance. The Act also prescribed prison terms and fines for groups or individuals using the Internet to collect or transfer funds to *any* group that a U.S. President might decide to designate as terrorist.[13] Thus, we have seen that the Internet battle is an ongoing process between corporate and state control, on the one hand, and attempts to use a given medium in a critical and liberating direction. However, there is a further component of this battle that now needs to be considered: the sustainability of radical media.

Although the costs of basic access are declining, the public may be seeing less information from radical sources on the Internet.

Much of the funding for radical media projects, especially those using computer networks, has come from foundation support. But funding for such media has always been insufficient, and it is even scarcer for computer networking projects with radical content. The vast majority of the computer projects that will be funded are those that do not significantly challenge the status quo. Unfortunately, foundations, although increasingly wealthy,[14] have no mandate for public accountability and often "do not distribute even the minimum yearly contribution required by law—5% of their assets" (Brugman, Redmond, & Ecklund, 1997, p. 19).[15] Thus, a lack of financial support for projects providing alternative media on-line is increasingly a liability for Internet activists and their audiences. Jim Naureckas of Fairness and Accuracy In Reporting (FAIR) provides this explanation:

> We haven't been able to justify hiring someone to do the web full-time, in part, frankly, because unlike our magazine and even our radio show, it has to be 100 percent subsidized. And while the magazine has at least 18,000 readers who are committed enough at least to pay $19 a year for it, and the radio show presumably reaches several times that many people (it is syndicated on 100 stations), the web still reaches what is by comparison a niche market. That said, we do see the web as a useful way to get information out, and would like to make it more accessible as a means of getting information about FAIR and our work—especially for students. To this end we've found a couple of dedicated volunteers who are now working on a full upgrade of the site—in the not too distant future, we should have filled in the gaps left by the site's languishing since mid-1996. (Personal communication, December 2, 1997)

At the end of the 20th century, diverse groups were enacting various strategies of access and empowerment via independent networks. On a media-access level, Free Speech TV[16] was providing video digitization, storage, and server-streaming access for independent video makers without access to advanced technologies. On a media networking level, the Direct Action Media Network (DAMN) was forming an alternative on-line news distribution service for reports of protests, demonstrations, and countermedia actions.[17] And on a coordinated empowerment level, Peoples Global Action,[18] led by indigenous peoples' networks from all of the five continents, began an ongoing movement intent on using the Internet to coordinate and publicize interventions from the margins in the global debate on information and economic policies.

INSTITUTE FOR GLOBAL COMMUNICATIONS

The Institute for Global Communications illustrates the convergence of such independent networks. One of the first and largest activist sites on the Internet, it has a particularly well-documented history, which allows us to trace the trajectory of its development since the early days of the Internet. Beginning in 1987, the IGC provided computer networking tools for international communication and information exchange.[19] Together with partner networks in the Association for Progressive Communications (APC),[20] the IGC Networks—PeaceNet, EcoNet, ConflictNet, LaborNet, and WomensNet[21]—consituted in those years the world's only computer communication system dedicated solely to environmental preservation, peace, and human rights.

In the decade since IGC cofounded APC, it introduced many nonprofit groups to computer networking and served tens of thousands of individuals, nonprofits, and progressive causes in more than 130 countries. With APC, IGC participated as a communication service provider at major international meetings, including the 1992 United Nations Conference on the Environment and Development (UNCED) in Rio de Janeiro; the 1993 U.N. World Conference on Human Rights (WCHR) in Vienna; the U.N. Conferences and Global Fora at the 1994 World Conference on Population and Development in Cairo, and the 1995 World Conference on Women in Beijing.

As of this writing, over 18,000 international computer users were affiliated with IGC networks, and the organization hosted over 300 websites for leading national and grassroots organizations. In addition, it provided several hundred public conferences that facilitated distribution of information in the form of events calendars, newsletters, legislative alerts, funding sources, press releases, action updates, breaking stories, and calls for support, as well as ongoing discussions. IGC was also an access point for the usenet system of U.S. interuniversity bulletin boards and provided information services, such as links to an on-line news finder that helped locate current news stories and databases of speakers, U.S. Congress and world leaders, media, grant-making foundations, or bibliographies. In addition, its members could send a telex or fax directly from their IGC account, providing affordable communication to those not on the Internet.

Standard with membership were software kits for Windows or Mac, including Eudora Pro and Netscape. Basic E-mail services included Majordomo Internet mailing lists, with digest and autoreply mailers.[22] Standard web service[23] included a domain name service, where clients could register their own unique address on the Internet for use with E-mail and website addresses. Professional web services include a secure commerce server for credit card transactions; Intranet password control for privacy, security, pay-per-view, or members only; and advanced search tools. IGC also provided technical support to its users and information on "netiquette."

IGC has historically provided users with its services through a variety of text-based user interfaces, including E-mail, telnet, FTP, gopher, archie, veronica, and WAIS. In fact, 25% of users still had text-only access, and the majority of content was posted through E-mail and then archived on the Web. High-tech users accessing IGC through its website encountered a clean, graphically designed home page linking to each network and information about IGC services and affiliates.

The IGC website unified the five networks with standardized user interfaces divided into four content areas: Alerts and Announcements, Headlines, Highlights, and Features. Each network had a conference for Alerts and Announcements that required an immediate response. Headlines were messages or news stories that were presented to each user the first time they logged onto IGC on any given day. Each network had a distinct headline to which members could post these notices, and if such messages were relevant to more than one network, they might be sent to more than one. Highlights consisted of articles from *Net News*, IGC's bimonthly newsletter, which was mailed to all users and posted to the conference igc.netnews. Features provided on-line links to those IGC member websites that were particularly timely or relevant to the network's constituencies.

The initial IGC network, Peacenet, was founded in San Francisco in 1986 by a coalition of nonprofit organizations who wanted to create "the world's first complete network dedicated exclusively to peace, human rights and social justice" (Frederick, 1993, p. 222). With initial operating funds of $60,000, the organizational strategy was to empower people with on-line access and enable them to build the network's content (Friedland, 1996).

In 1987, Peacenet joined with EcoNet to incorporate as IGC, a nonprofit project of the Tides Foundation. The organization went on to incorporate other member groups serving a variety of constituencies: ConflictNet (1989), LaborNet (1992), and WomensNet (1995). Anti-Racism.net, a joint effort with ProjectChange, was launched in 1999.[24] Making its first international link with the British network GreenNet in 1988, IGC began to connect with nongovernmental organizations (NGOs) around the world; and in 1990, it joined with six international partners to form the APC, which by 1997 included member organizations from 25 countries.[25]

In the first decade of its growth,[26] IGC grew from a staff of 6 to (at times) as many as 50. In 1987, IGC set up an office in a former warehouse space in San Francisco. Over the next decade, the organization built and maintained an activist base, primarily as an Internet Service Provider (ISP) and secondarily as a content and organizational services provider. By 1996, IGC had 36 employees and had moved into a new space, housed with the Tides Foundation at San Francisco's Presidio. Yet, in 2000, the organization had scaled back to a significantly smaller staff due to strategic changes in operations.

Throughout the first decade of its history, IGC served as a facilitator of access and content provision. It provided valuable access to the Internet in the early years of the technology's diffusion in the United States and during the early 1990s enjoyed a small (3%) but steady rise in ISP income.[27] But as the ISP market began to be more developed by business, the pattern diminished.[28] The mid-1990s marked a period of great change for IGC, characterized by a financial crisis accompanied by a staff crisis. In 1996, the staff voted to become unionized to protect not just their jobs but also the resources that had been achieved through dedication to the organization's mission and early years of action. When IGC employees voted to be represented by the Service Employees International Union, Local 790, they made it the first fully unionized ISP in the United States. Alair MacLean, a member of the union organizing committee and director of IGC's Environmental Justice Networking Project, described the reasons as follows:

> The emergence of the Internet has raised new issues in workplaces that we have sought to address. We were delighted about the result, and hope it will inspire other Internet workers to examine issues about pay, working conditions, diversity and workplace hazards related to keyboard use and repetitive strain injury.[29]

But there were also other reasons for this labor struggle. In the early 1990s, IGC moved away from a consensus model and toward a corporate hierarchical model of organization. This was problematic, given that the staff had not been prepared for this shift. It was also true that few of the staff, who had previously operated as independent coordinators, had the skills or desires to exercise leadership. In addition, IGC's organizational structure left its board without fiscal accountability. Given the problems of private foundations already outlined in this chapter, the Board began to look less to grantwriting in the nonprofit and foundation sphere and more toward pay for service. This meant a greater emphasis on marketing and corporate funding.

In late 1997, the IGC board hired a new executive director. The decision was controversial, given that her prior position had been in management at KPFA and Pacifica News, organizations then under fire by alternative media activists, who perceived the management as being coopted by corporate funding agendas (see Chapter 21). The new executive director outlined her priorities as follows:

> There has been much talk of focusing IGC's attention on serving our members through extended services and consulting on Internet use. I absolutely agree with that direction. Additionally, our conferences and Networks must be improved and expanded. Can we do all that and continue to run the day to day functions of an ISP? Are there ways to outsource some of the more routine functions allowing us to provide more comprehensive customized services for our users? By narrowing our services can we provide better service to more users? These are the types of questions I see IGC asking, and my goal is to facilitate that discussion and set in motion a clear strategic plan that leads us to our goals. (Mallin, 1997)

In addition to its vulnerability to the vicissitudes of foundation funding, IGC faced other external menaces to its operations, revolving around the rhetoric of infowar and terrorism already mentioned. A 1995 Pentagon Report on strategic uses of the Internet (Swett, 1995) devoted a section to IGC because it represented "the largest and most active international political groups using the Internet" and, therefore, "a review of the IGC can provide a good perspective on the breadth of DoD [Department of Defense]-relevant information available on the Internet." The report included 11 points detailing why IGC was relevant, including its hosting of "The Left List . . . a discussion forum dedicated to bringing together activists organizing for fundamental social change and creating a common meeting ground for electronic discussion, debate, and collaboration." The report continued, "There were also 'alternative news sources' emerging overseas, that can play a significant, if slanted, role in filling gaps left by the reports issued by the mainstream news media. The most extensive set of alternative news networks appears to be operated by the IGC."

Furthermore, in the summer of 1997, IGC experienced a first-ever serious denial of service attack originating from Spain. The target was IGC's hosting of the *Euskal Herria Journal* (EHJ), a Basque magazine of culture that also reported on human rights violations and—most controversially—"described the history and ideology of the radical Basque political party, Herri Batasuna, and of Euskadi Ta Askatasuna (ETA), the armed group that since 1968 has committed killings, kidnapings, and bombings in the name of Basque independence" (Mason, 1997). In actions IGC denounced as vigilante censorship, "mail-bomb" campaigns were deployed by unknown actors using various techniques of communication sabotage, such as attacking IGC E-mail servers with thousands of anonymously sent E-mail messages. Fueled by an ETA kidnaping-murder of a town councillor, which aroused unprecedented street protests throughout Spain, including the Basque province, as well as reports in Spain's leading daily newspaper, *El País*, detailing the strikes and including IGC's address, the mailbomb campaign was successful in jamming communication to and from IGC, blocking out even legitimate letters of protest.

The severity of the attack left IGC little choice but to remove the EHJ site from its server.[30] But the organization was able to use the situation constructively to examine its role as a service provider and to develop an expanded policy with a clear set of responsibilities to its members and public constituencies. In the end, IGC clarified that although advocating violence is in direct conflict with its mission statement, reporting on groups who do so was not—and, in fact, was an essential component of peaceful resolution to conflict. They vowed to beef up security and to maintain a consistent website and member policy based on mission statements of potential member organizations. An IGC staff member provided a detailed account of events in IGC *NetNews*:

> As activists, we respected the tactic of a letter-writing campaign to register a political protest but deplored the outright vandalism on our servers. As Internet service providers, we felt strongly that a danger-

> ous precedent could be set by letting a controversial site be "mail bombed" off of the Internet. . . . Above all, we felt the weight of our commitment to the nearly 13,000 other individuals and organizations that depend on IGC for their Internet services. (Mason, 1997)

The EHJ case marked a crucial threat to democratic communication in the alternative sectors of the Internet. Of particular interest, Mason's account demonstrates how IGC organized against the censorship (its external communication): finding mainstream media interested in the story, soliciting and publishing statements of support, and ensuring that EHJ was successfully installed on mirror sites. In relation to internal organization, IGC reformed its website review process, combining management and staff meetings with an ideas conference and other vehicles for member input.

Internal and external factors were changing IGC. The organization had been struggling in the increasingly commercialized Internet environment and shifting from an emphasis on service to an emphasis on product. It had been obtaining significantly less of its operational funding from foundation support and was being increasingly forced to sustain itself through subscriber-based services. At the same time, it had somewhat outlived its initial purpose of providing Internet service connections in the United States. In December 1997, IGC announced plans to cease being an ISP and instead offer independent access to its services at $5 per conference per month via outside service providers. After much discussion internally and with the larger IGC membership, the switch went through in September 1999, with Mindspring Enterprises providing a variety of Internet service plans ranging from $6.95 to $19.95 per month and Topica, Inc., providing the conference services for free.

EZLN

Our second case study, about how the Zapatista movement has used the Internet, begins on New Year's Eve, 1994, as politicians in Mexico City celebrated the enactment of the North American Free Trade Agreement (NAFTA) and the trumpeted entry of Mexico into the First World. An indigenous army emerged from the Lacandón jungle and seized control of the municipal offices and police stations of four towns in Chiapas. The

Ejército Zapatista de Liberación Nacional (EZLN; Zapatista National Liberation Army) declared war on the Mexican government that night, claiming an "inalienable right to alter or modify their form of government."[31] In their first public statement, the Declaration from the Lacandón Jungle,[32] the Zapatistas described their movement as a 500-year struggle for indigenous autonomy, equality, and freedom and demanded that the following basic requirements be made accessible to their communities: employment, land, housing, food, health, education, independence, freedom, democracy, justice, and peace. Within hours, "computer screens around the world sparked with news of the uprising" (Halleck, 1994, p. 1). The declaration of war was picked up by the Mexican weekly newspaper, *La Jornada,* and reproduced on-line in Mexico City. Translated into numerous languages, it made its way via Internet into the hands of academics, journalists, activists, and human rights workers around the globe. With this unprecedented intervention into the dominant national discourse, the indigenous army had irrevocably shattered the silence of centuries.

While Mexico ostensibly functioned at that point as a democratic parliamentary state, the reality was that a single party (the Institutional Revolutionary Party, or PRI) had controlled the venues of economic and political power since 1929. The largest television network was popularly referred to as "the fourth power" or as the PRI "Ministry of Culture," on a par with executive, judicial, and legislative branches of the federal government. "Most Mexicans get their news from TV, particularly the Televisa network . . . which captures 90 per cent of the viewing public . . . a major supporter of the government" (Cockburn, 1994, p. 4). And yet, within weeks of the uprising, the Zapatistas had influenced this media monopoly:

> The uses of the net to present the stance of the Zapatistas during the negotiations [with the government] forced even Televisa, the government-controlled television network, to report the official demands of the guerrillas. Indeed, the EZLN was able to get its side of the story across during a critical moment in the negotiation process when the government prematurely announced a peace agreement. (Halleck, 1994, p. 3)

Given that the Mexican government had long been successful in regulating both the content and distribution of news nationwide, the fact that the EZLN opened a space in which to speak and be heard was an extraordinary achievement.

Thus, the communications strategy of the EZLN from the very outset was to take actions that secured them immediate national and international attention, including reports of their demands in both print and broadcast media. This approach later involved piquing the interest of media editors by inviting famous people to visit communities of resistance in the Lacandón. The Zapatistas hosted a great number of politicians, actors, writers, and intellectuals, including Cuauhtémoc Cárdenas (Mexican presidential candidate in 1988 and 1994 and first-ever Mexico City mayor from 1997), Uruguayan writer Eduardo Galeano, North American movie director Oliver Stone, Mexican actresses Ofelia Medina and Rosario Ibarra, and Danielle Mitterand, the widow of the former French president. By courting the mainstream media in these ways, the Zapatistas periodically established a presence in dominant discursive circles around the globe.

A far more powerful strategy of articulation employed by the EZLN, however, consisted of transmitting their demands without mainstream media filtering. This approach was crucial to their survival. If an international audience had not been actively and consistently following the movements of the Mexican government against the Zapatistas, the EZLN would most likely have been crushed in its early years.[33] The Zapatistas inspired a flourishing, widespread, and varied network of radical media communication that afforded them the opportunity to communicate directly with civil society. As a result, civil society was motivated and able to respond directly to the requests of the EZLN for citizen participation in their project. The very existence of the Zapatistas depended on this web of interlocking, autonomously controlled and operated media. But of these media, the one most crucial to the Zapatista movement was the Internet.

The way in which the Zapatistas conceived of dialogue, on or off the Internet, as a vehicle for political action was integrally related to their conception of the public sphere as an arena for dialogic praxis.[34] Their actions and pronouncements resonated deeply with Fraser's (1993) conception of a truly transformative communication.[35] The EZLN sought since its inception to facilitate the emergence of a public sphere—an "arena of discursive interaction . . . for the production and circulation of discourses that can in principle be critical of the state" (Fraser, 1993, p. 110). Because the EZLN comprised people historically excluded from hegemonic discourse on the basis of gender, social status, economic assets, cultural values, and race, the dialogue they initiated was, by definition, an arena of radical inclusivity. Furthermore, the Zapatistas recognized from the start the existence of myriad other subaltern counterpublics and called for dynamic and ongoing interaction between them. The "subordinated social groups" enumerated by Fraser—"women, workers, peoples of color, and gays and lesbians"—were either represented in the EZLN to begin with or addressed specifically in the EZLN's appeals for collaboration with other social movements, oppressed peoples, and civil alliances.

Meanwhile, the Zapatista movement made every effort to involve members of the intellectual and political elite as well as the upper and middle classes. By doing so, the EZLN attempted to construct what Fraser (1993) describes as "an additional, more comprehensive arena in which members of different, more limited publics talk across lines of cultural diversity" (p. 126). The EZLN explicitly refers to this arena as the dialogical realm of civil society. Their insistence that civil society must have a discursive space separate from the state accords with Fraser's second interpretation of civil society as "the informally mobilized body of nongovernmental discursive opinion that can serve as a counterweight to the state" (p. 134).

This civil discursive space was crucial in Mexico because there was no space within the dominant political arena in which people could participate in the state's decision-making processes. Although the Zapatistas did not seek political power at any level, they insisted on the end of electoral fraud in Mexico and encouraged the involvement of all citizens in national and local political issues. The foremost objective of the Zapatistas, throughout, was to encourage Mexican civil society to discover, through dialogue, an understanding of its collective needs, values, visions, and goals, thus creating a collective voice with which the public would be able to pressure the power structure to respond. They also challenged supporters throughout the globe to carve out spaces within their own countries, regions, and neighborhoods for the constructive analysis of issues affecting their lives. In other words, the Zapatistas were less concerned with garnering a following for their specific cause than with inspiring others to engage in transformative dialogical praxis at local and national levels.

The organizational structure of the Zapatista movement also served as a model of alternative social and political relations. The Zapatista collective had no leader, no second-in-command, and no official mandates. The Zapatista army itself functioned as a hierarchical, military organization, but it did not occupy a position of strategic power within the movement. Instead, it was held accountable to an indigenous decision-making body made up of several committees whose members represented participant communities and whose decisions were made through a process of dialogic consensus building. Thus, "the Zapatistas appear to have achieved a new political synthesis that subordinates [the army's] actions to frameworks of collective and democratic decision-making developed out of local traditions" (Autonomedia, 1994, p. 17). This communitarian process of arriving at decisions involved traveling from village to village and translating each proposal into several indigenous languages for discussion, then returning to the central committee and debating the results in Spanish—a process that might take weeks or even months to conclude. In this way, the Zapatistas functioned as a microcosm of the global communication they had inspired. Internet communications, for example, were routinely translated into any number of languages and disseminated to communities thousands of miles apart, often resulting in coordinated solidarity actions involving the participation of individuals worldwide. The manner in which such support was generated reflected the Zapatistas' communication paradigm to some extent, as well, given that the information circulated via Internet travels circuitously from peer to peer, collective and individual, with no predetermined patterns of access, editorial control, or outcome.

This process of community building through cross-cultural dialogical praxis was the EZLN's most powerful strategy of resistance, unification, and survival. Their greatest strength was their ability to engage in this constant, creative endeavor, not only in their own communities but in another space, a virtual realm constructed through the radical use of communication technologies worldwide. In this way, their movement was, from its inception, an international phenomenon. Information regarding the conditions in which the Zapatistas lived, their objectives and demands, and the events that took place as their movement unfolded were transmitted at local, national, and international levels via fax machine, videotape, audiotape, radio, telephone, newsletters, national and local newspapers, published books and articles, leaflets, graffiti, live performance, and artwork. Yet, the most effective and innovative of any medium employed by Zapatista sympathizers was the Internet.

Two of the most popular public forums on-line were the mailing list (which distributes messages to members via E-mail) and the newsgroup (which functions as a Web-based bulletin board). Soon after the appearance of the EZLN in January 1994, several lists began distributing daily reports on the Zapatistas, including Chiapas95, Chiapas-L, MexPaz, and Mexico94. Numerous newsgroups focused on events in Chiapas, as well, including soc.culture.mexican and soc.culture.latin-america.[36] The objective of these forums was to distribute or discuss information not reported—fully, accurately, or at all—in mainstream media. In the words of one Internet news gatherer, "We try to provide a service that presents a different view on the news from the regular U.S. and Mexican media. We do this by searching many news sources and selecting the news which would otherwise get lost in the noise."[37] Reverend Pablo Romo of the Fray Bartolomé Human Rights Center in San Cristóbal de Las Casas, Chiapas, expressed the same notion in the following words: "Our mission is strictly informative. We use the Internet to inform people abroad of what is happening here, but mainly to counter the government's disinformation" (Robberson, 1995, p. A1).

Another font of electronic information on the EZLN is the web page, which has been used by individuals and institutions alike to post data and interpretive analyses of the Zapatista struggle, as well as video, animation, photography, and audio files. Many universities and nonprofit organizations host websites on Mexican issues, with links to news- and discussion groups, university servers in Mexico, archives of Zapatista commuiqués and publications such as the *NACLA Report on the Americas.* The International Service for Peace (SIPAZ) has a bilingual website that contains periodic reports on human rights violations in Mexico, a chronology of events in Chiapas, and an invitation to join peace delegations in Zapatista territory. By providing "objective and credible . . . information and analysis on the conflict and peace process" to a global audience via Internet, SIPAZ and other such organizations have facilitated the emergence of an international solidarity network attuned to the issues and struggles of the Zapatista movement on a daily basis. Given that "international public opinion has already played a key role in limiting the scope of the violence at the most explosive moments of the conflict," there can be no doubt that the dissemination of reliable information on-line has been essential to the survival of the Zapatista movement (SIPAZ).

Web pages constructed by individuals are as effective as institutional ones, if not more so. ¡Ya Basta!—the EZLN Page, created and maintained by Justin Paulson of Santa Cruz, California, is possibly the most often consulted of all EZLN websites.[38] Conceived in the spring of 1994 as a means of making accurate information on the Zapatista uprising widely available, this site includes selected EZLN communiqués in four languages, news reports, articles, and action alerts from international print and electronic sources, contact information for the President of Mexico and embassies worldwide, and information on how to contribute humanitarian aid to Chiapan villages or become a peace camp volunteer. At times, Paulson has even provided the means of sending electronic letters of support to the Zapatista army or indigenous villagers in Chiapas—missives composed on his page, transmitted via E-mail to Mexican solidarity workers, and conveyed in print form into Zapatista hands. This is but one of many sites that demonstrate the potential of the individual to contribute immeasurably to a movement of international dimensions through the diligent exploitation of the Internet as an informative and interactive medium.[39]

People who participate in posting and debating information on the Internet occupy a discursive realm outside of mainstream media. They may speak freely and still enjoy a wide audience, a remarkable opportunity in a world in which information and its means of distribution are so closely guarded by politicians and corporate interests. Their articles are not cut by politically cautious editors, silenced by government scrutiny, or constrained by a need to maximize profits.[40] In the world of net journalism, anyone with access to the Internet is able to publish. Many Chiapas events were reported nearly live by people who were there, who would otherwise have had no means of providing thousands of readers with their firsthand accounts. Global net-trotters discussed an extraordinary range of issues omitted or misrepresented by the mainstream press, such as Mexican election fraud, state violence, and corruption; U.S. support of the Mexican military; the underlying objectives of neoliberal economic initiatives (such as NAFTA); indigenous feminism and the role of women in the EZLN; and the unequal class, ethnic, and race relations that precipitated the Zapatista conflict.

The two most crucial functions of the Internet in support of the Zapatista struggle were to initiate protests against real or impending military attacks on Zapatista territory and to engender new forms of ongoing, cross-cultural participatory politics. To demonstrate the particular impact of these two different strategies, we will explore a handful of the more remarkable Internet moments in the history of the Zapatista movement.

On January 13, 1995, Riordon Roett, a consultant to the Chase Manhattan Bank, sent a four-page report on Mexico to the bank's top clients.[41] Roett, a Johns Hopkins University professor of Latin American studies and former president of the Latin American Studies Association, also distributed this report to a number of senators, including then presidential candidate, Sen. Bob Dole. In it, he wrote,

> There are three areas in which the current monetary crisis can undermine political stability in Mexico. The first is Chiapas; the second is the upcoming state elections; and the third is the role of the labor unions. . . . The government will need to eliminate the Zapatistas to demonstrate their effective control of the national territory and of security policy. . . . The Zedillo administration will need to consider carefully whether or not to allow opposition victories if fairly won at the ballot box.

This memo was leaked, published in the newsletter *Counterpunch* (see Cockburn & Silverstein, 1995), and then instantly posted on the Internet. Due to the international scandal that ensued, Chase Manhattan fired Roett. This was an example of the kind of publicity that impeded the Mexican military from destroying the Zapatista army and surrounding communities in an all-out military offensive.

Weeks after the Roett report was written, a military solution was, indeed, attempted in Mexico, but the government was unable to achieve its full and final objective. The government issued warrants for the arrest of a spokesman named Marcos and other Zapatistas. Human rights centers such as the CONPAZ (Coordination of NGOs for Peace) office were broken into and vandalized (Benjamin, 1995). And, on February 9, 1995, the federal army invaded the Zapatista community of Aguascalientes and surrounding villages. Suspected Zapatista collaborators were abducted and tortured. Indigenous pueblos were ransacked, fields were burned, water supplies contaminated, personal belongings destroyed, unarmed citizens threatened and forcibly removed from their homes. The Zapatista community center of Aguascalientes, internationally renowned as the site of the 1994 National Democratic Convention, was razed to the ground.[42] Zapatistas, their supporters, and other indigenous groups with no involvement in the Zapatista movement fled the violence. "By mid-February, some 10,000 indigenous people had taken to the jungle to escape the Mexican army" (Benjamin, 1995, p. 3). The Mexican military would later build a military camp over Aguascalientes—ground that had once been the locus of Zapatista dialogue and community building for local indigenous groups, Mexican activists, and international visitors alike.

Zapatistas and their supporters in Mexico responded immediately with international appeals for solidarity. CONPAZ and the Fray Bartolomé de las Casas Human Rights Center released a statement proclaiming "a campaign for the 'Right to Information,' in order to counter the campaign of disinformation and intimidation being carried out against civil society" (Rumsey, 1995). A February 11 communiqué from the Zapatistas stated that "the Mexican army used helicopters to drop five bombs near Altamirano and La Garrucha and machine-gun other communities" and described the climate of terror engendered by forcible evictions, threats, torture, and military occupation in numerous indigenous villages.[43] News from Chiapas made its way with difficulty through military lines, but once information reached Mexico City, it was dispatched via Internet to global news and discussion groups within minutes. The resounding concatenation of solidarity actions worldwide proved enough to interrupt the military offensive, although the damage was never repaired.

> The central squares of Mexico City and other urban centers were jammed with protesters. Embassies were taken over or boycotted in the United States, Spain, France, Germany, and elsewhere. Letters of protest were published daily in *La Jornada* newspaper from Nobel Prize laureates, Italian artists, Australian parliamentarians, U.S. filmmakers—you name it. And a steady stream of observer delegations from around the world relayed the abuses committed by the army to all corners of the globe.
>
> This outcry forced the government to change its tune. On March 13, the Law for Dialogue, Reconciliation, and a Dignified Peace, approved by the President and the Mexican Congress, formally suspended the arrest warrants and called for new talks within thirty days. (Benjamin, 1995, p. 4)

If the Internet was indispensable to the Zapatistas as an urgent action medium in moments of crisis, it was equally useful in facilitating community building through dialogue, a process without which there would be no solidarity. An example of one such dialogical exchange was the *Consulta Nacional e Internacional* (National and International Plebiscite) organized by the EZLN in 1994. The Consulta was elaborated during the National Democratic Convention in Aguascalientes in August 1994, as a way of soliciting direct feedback from Mexican and international civil society regarding its opinion of the Zapatistas' demands and the role of the EZLN as a political entity. The Consulta consisted of six questions, including "Should the EZLN join with other organizations to form a new political organization?" The EZLN produced a video to accompany the questionnaire, in which EZLN spokesman Subcomandante Marcos explains the meaning and purpose of each question. In this video, as in other communication, the Zapatistas make clear that they were prepared to follow the instructions of their respondents, even if that should entail restructuring their organization and reconceptualizing their goals. The Consulta was translated and distributed internationally in print and electronic form. While activists enlisted pedestrians' participation in Mexico City, Mexican delegates to the United Nations Conference on Women distributed the questions to other participants in Beijing. In all, over 1.3 million responses were received by the EZLN from respondents in China, Spain, Italy, France, Germany, Denmark, Switzerland, Sweden, England, the United States, South America, Canada, New Zealand, Greece, and Mexico. Once again, the breadth of this collective action was made possible by the Internet, and yet, it would not have succeeded without the use of more traditional means and media.

Forging links between disparate media, activists, organizations, and social movements has been the focus of much debate in Zapatista communication and events. In July and August 1996, the First Intercontinental Encuentro for Humanity and Against Neoliberalism was hosted by the Zapatistas in Chiapas and attended by 4,000 participants from 42 countries (Acción Zapatista, 1996b; Duncan & Ruggiero, 1997). The convergence there of individuals from five continents, and the recognition of marked similarities in their struggles against economic and political domination, sparked an interest in greater cross-cultural communication and support. This desire was directly addressed by Subcomandante Marcos in his closing statement, the Second Declaration from La Realidad,[44] in which he proposed the formation of an intercontinental network of alternative communication. This network, he suggested, "will be the medium in which distinct resistances may support one another." Furthermore, "this intercontinental network of resistance is not an organizing structure; it doesn't have a central head or decision maker; it has no central command or hierarchies. We are the network, all of us who resist" (Duncan & Ruggiero, 1997, p. 48). Inspired by his proposal, Encuentro participants later elaborated a formal invitation for the creation of the Red Intercontinental de Comunicación Alternativa (International Alternative Communication Network, or RICA). Activists, academics, and humanitarian organizations responded with new international Internet mailing lists and websites devoted specifically to opening new lines of communication between different language groups, political identities, and ideological perspectives. There were also encuentros, conferences, on-line interactive events, and other initiatives that focused on the contributions of independent media projects to political struggle.

One such endeavor was a Freeing the Media Teach-In in New York City, for which Subcomandante Marcos composed a video message:[45]

> "The work of independent media", said Marcos, "is to tell the history of social struggle in the world." Marcos went on to advocate that media activists fight to open spaces within the mass media monopolies (to acknowledge news of social movements), and at the same time, to continue developing a network of independent media and information. (Duncan & Ruggiero, 1997, p. 48)

In July 1997, over 3,000 participants joined the second intercontinental encounter in Spain, from which emerged more concrete proposals for the purposeful development of this network of networks linking related causes and media globally.

The Internet proved to be an invaluable resource to the Zapatistas, despite the fact that Chiapas had not the telecommunications infrastructure to support any significant on-line presence of civil society in the region. The indigenous villages from which the Zapatistas arose scarcely had access to phone lines, let alone computers.[46] Many of the Zapatistas themselves did not speak Spanish, and most were not able to read, let alone manipulate technological advances to their advantage. These villagers lacked access to clean water, basic health care, or elementary education; clearly, they had no independent access to media technology of any kind. Yet, their presence on the Internet became one of the foremost examples of successful on-line activism.

Zapatista media strategies proved to be immensely effective models of transformative action through communication. By capturing the attention of mainstream media, the EZLN intermittently sparked international recognition of their cause, inspiring individuals to spontaneously establish an independent global network of communication on- and off-line. These radical media then became the means for supporters to share information regarding repressive and violent actions of government and economic and military forces. Such actions were virulently denounced in public demonstrations and protests, which were then reported by the press, and the cycle continued.

The most essential aspect of this exemplary international network of resistance was the passionate commitment of participants to the Zapatista cause. The alternative media machine facilitating global awareness of indigenous struggles in the Lacandón jungle was the creation of individuals who spent the greater part of their free time, for years,[47] forging the links one at a time. The emergence and persistence of this global current of solidarity with Zapatismo merits reflection. What inspired such concerted devotion? Certainly, the conditions that caused the Zapatistas to rise up were reprehensible, and their demands were simple and just—but that, in itself, is not the answer. Rather, the Zapatistas articulated a vision for humanity that resonated with individuals across lines of class, race, religion, gender, nationality, and myriad other aspects of social, economic, and political difference.

The Zapatistas themselves demonstrated a remarkable ability to act as a collective of individuals and groups without waging internal power struggles. The women within the movement effected their own revolutionary agenda, demonstrating the ability of the Zapatista movement to grow and change from within. The public forum the EZLN so persistently advocated is the kind of space that people in every nation and locality must struggle to create and protect, if they are to participate in the decisions that most affect their lives. Furthermore, the Zapatistas explicitly sought to initiate constructive discourse between individuals and collectives from radically different backgrounds and worldviews. Finally, and perhaps most important, the EZLN always encouraged its supporters to test the lessons of the Zapatista struggle within their own communities. Thus, the Zapatistas offered both theoretical and empirical models of alternative communication and political participation, which inspired individuals across the globe and in vastly differing circumstances to devote themselves to a complementary struggle in support of and in conjunction with the Zapatista cause.

Summary: The Internet has still to "settle down," although, as this chapter makes clear, it will continue to be a battle ground between the forces in favor of social justice and human rights and the aggressive corporate order for which these are easily dispensable luxuries. Exactly how that battle will be fought and where has still to unfold. However, the aspects of radical Internet use covered here, and similar case studies that there was no space to detail, are proof positive that the drive to democratize the media communication process is a continuing one. From the *Flugschrift* War to the Digital Enclosures battle, the story has a distinct continuity. In Part III, however, we will slow our pace somewhat to examine in much more careful detail than this panoramic overview has made possible a number of significant cases of radical media, including their forms of social organization.

NOTES

1. The Internet's rate of growth in its first few years was staggering. In 1992, the Internet was expanding by 20% every single month (Sterling, 1993). By 1999, 3 billion E-mail messages were being sent every day (Church, 1999). Just 130 websites in June 1993 had grown to an estimated 650,000 websites in January 1997 (Gray, 1997, p. 1). In June 1997, the number of Internet hosts (servers or addresses) had grown to 19,540,000 from a mere 213 in 1981 (Network Wizards, 1997, p. 1). And by 1997, 194 out of 240 countries had joined the Internet (MIDS, 1997, p. 1). Inevitably, in such a fast-moving situation, some of the specific details we cite in this chapter, although accurate as of December 1997, will change.

2. For example, Group 2828 (1997), using worldwide experience with the Zapatista struggle as a point of departure, addresses some of the foremost problems with networks: Net action by individuals all too often is separate from real communities, causing information overload, lack of vision as to what to do with the information, and difficulties with the discourse of networks. They suggest an alternative metaphor of the network as hammock: a structure that supports bodies, as opposed to a structure that may entrap them.

3. Cited in "Panos Media Briefing No. 23/April 1997 Telecommunications, Development and the Market: The promises and the problems" <http://www.oneworld.org/panos/briefing/telecoms.htm>

4. One study "by the consulting firm McKinsey & Company estimated that giving every public classroom access to the Internet by 2005, with a computer for every five students, would require a one-time outlay of $47 billion, plus $14 billion annually for operations and maintenance. Even the most modest plan—putting a computer lab with 25 wired PCs in every school by 2000—would cost about $11 billion plus $4 billion annually, according to the study" (Shapiro, 1997, p. 2).

5. For further elaboration on this, see Soley (1995).

6. For more on the history of the Internet, see Elmer-Dewitt (1993) and Sterling (1993).

7. For further discussion of the effects of the 1996 Act, see Nader, Love, & Saindon (1995). It is also worth noting that in the year following the Act, the Federal Communications Commission increased hostile and forcible actions against pirate radio stations, ransacking offices, keeping media activists under surveillance, and arresting people at gunpoint in the middle of the night. Links between pirate radio and alternative Internet news networks are strong and growing. Significantly, the Act also gave increased authority to the FCC to police the Internet (Cockburn, 1997). Clearly, the climate for radical media stood to be negatively affected by the FCC's increasing activism in this area and even stronger mesh with corporate agendas than historically in evidence previously.

8. Under the Communications Decency Act, individuals or service providers found responsible for making "obscene, lewd, lascivious, filthy, or indecent" material available on-line could be fined up to $100,000 and spend 2 years in jail for each infraction. For more information, see Shapiro, 1995; Abernathy, 1995; and Blumenfeld and Cohen, 1996.

9. Led by the Electronic Frontier Foundation, this campaign called for blue ribbons to be posted on-line in support of free speech (http://www.eff.org/blueribbon.html). As part of this campaign, more than 1,500 websites were temporarily blacked out in response to the signing of the 1996 Telecommunications Act (http://www.eff.org/BlueRibbon/activism.html).

10. There is also fear that rate hikes in basic services will be used to subsidize the development of an advanced telecom infrastructure that will primarily benefit the information "haves".

11. McChesney (1996) provides a detailed critique of the "marketplace of ideas" ideology.

12. At the time of this writing, two significant bills had just passed Congress. The first was the No Electronic Theft (NET) Act, which imposed criminal penalties on copyright infringement even when no money had changed hands. This legislation empowered industry police to go after those who share, not sell, unauthorized copies of valuable software. The second was the Digital Era Copyright Enhancement Act, which has widespread support from libraries, industry associations, and public interest organizations. Supporters said it balanced industry demands with public educational fair use rights. However, not all of these supporters had the public interest in mind, and the notion of "balancing" did nothing to expand the possibilities of digital information sharing, reducing the debate to merely retaining usage rights already guaranteed for traditional media.

13. The term *omnibus* denotes umbrella legislation for a number of similar bills introduced by various members of the House and Senate. Although civil libertarians were able to block the privacy measures included in the Act, such as undue surveillance and restrictions on encryption technology, Senate Bill 735, most commonly known as the Antiterrorism and Effective Death Penalty

Act of 1996, became law. For legislative history and details of this particular bill see: <http://thomas.loc.gov/cgi-bin/bdquery/z?d104:SN00735:@@@L>.

14. Following Reagan Era economic policies, wealth has increasingly been diverted from income tax into private foundations. From 1980-1992, foundation holdings grew from $48 billion to $226 billion, an increase of 372% (Brugman et al., 1997).

15. The *San Francisco Bay Guardian* has estimated that if the largest 15 foundations in the Bay Area each contributed their full 5%, an additional $75 million in funds would be available to nonprofits (Brugman et al., 1997).

16. The Denver-based Free Speech TV site, http://www.freespeech.org, is a Web-based video broadcast hub, housing over 300 on-demand RealMedia files, with new programs posted daily. Billing itself as a "daily source for progressive counter-media", the website is an extension of the Free Speech TV cable network, which broadcasts alternative programming to nearly 7 million homes.

17. <http://damn.tao.ca> This site is hosted by Tao Communications, a Toronto media collective that provides services such as e-mail accounts, majordomo list-serv technologies, archiving and webtools to activists around the globe.

18. Peoples Global Action is an ongoing forum with biennial meetings that seek to stimulate worldwide resistance to neoliberal economic adjustments imposed by the World Trade Organization and trade agreements such as NAFTA and GATT. See: <http://www.agp.org/agp/indexen.html>

19. The IGC mission statement reads "To expand and inspire movements for peace, economic and social justice, human rights and environmental sustainability around the world by providing and developing accessible computer networking tools." IGC online <http://www.igc.org>

20. The APC is a coalition of computer networks providing services to over 30,000 activists and organizations in more than 130 countries.

21. ConflictNet, the only one of these whose mission is not immediately clear from the title, serves groups and individuals working for social justice and conflict resolution. ConflictNet's resources include guidelines for choosing a neutral third party, sample case development in conflict resolution, extensive biblographies, legislative updates, educational materials, and newsletters from around the world.

22. These are E-mail tools to disseminate electronic brochures and fact sheets via an electronic robot that automatically sends out material and provides a monthly log of people who requested the information.

23. Standard Web Site is currently $30 per month. The Pro Web Site is currently $100 per month.

24. <http://www.anti-racism.net> ProjectChange was created by the Levi Strauss Foundation to address racial prejudice and institutional racism.

25."As of May 1997, there are 25 member networks who form the backbone of the APC. Member networks commit time and resources to support the growth and diversity of the APC and exchange information and technical support with over 40 partner networks. Partner networks work closely with APC members and often provide the only source of computer communication for NGOs in their country." From the APC on-line brochure: <http://www.apc.org>.

26. A larger history of the IGC can be found in Frederick, 1996.

27. This pattern, which occurred without any type of marketing, allowed the organization to be complacent in its fund development efforts. With the ISP glut, IGC was suddenly forced to scramble for new sources of income.

28. IGC Internal Conference: Topic 178: Monthly User Growth Reports 1993-1997.

29. IGC NetNews, October 1996 <http://www.igc.org/igc/about/.edit970612/netnews.oct.html>

30. IGC NetNews: October 1997. The expanded policy was approved by the IGC Advisory Board on September 10, 1997. "Since their site was attacked, the publishers of EHJ have reconstituted themselves as the Congress for Peace in Euskal Herria (CPEH), expanding their mission to include working with lawyers and grassroots groups in the Basque Country" (Mason, 1997).

31. From the first Declaration from the Lacandón Jungle. In this line, the EZLN is quoting Article 39 of the Mexican Constitution.

32. Original Spanish versions of all four Declarations from the Lacandón Jungle are on-line at <http://www.ezln.org/communiques.html>. English translations of the first two can be found in *Zapatistas!: Documents of the New Mexican Revolution* (Autonomedia, 1994).

33. See the discussion of the Riordan Roett report below.

34. The Zapatistas routinely invited visitors into their villages to exchange political visions and elaborate alternatives to neoliberal economic policies. The first such gathering was the National Democratic Convention, which occurred in August 1994 in the Chiapan village of Guadalupe Tepeyac (renamed Aguascalientes). This encuentro comprised more than 6,000 delegates from Mexico and abroad, who broke through a federal army encampment to attend. The event was conceived as a venue for civil society to convene before the pending Mexican presidential elections "to organize civil expression and the defense of popular will" (Second Declaration of the Lacandón Jungle, 1994). Among other projects, the EZLN invited delegates to participate in the elaboration of a new Mexican constitution.

35. Fraser (1993) proposes an alternative interpretation of public sphere, based on, yet moving beyond, the discursive arena described in Jürgen Habermas's writings. See discussion of her argument in Part I.

36. Websites containing information on these lists and newsgroups may be consulted at the following locations:

Chiapas95 <http://www.eco.utexas.edu/Homepages/Faculty/Cleaver/chiapas95.html>

Chiapas-L <gopher://profmexis.sar.net:70/11/foros/chiapas-l>

MexPaz <http://www.ibw.com.ni/dlabs/latinoamerica/mexpaz.html>

Mexico94 <http://library.wustl.edu/listmgr/devel-l/Apr1995/0024.html>

soc.culture.mexican <http://www.public.iastate.edu/rjsalvad/scmfaq/charter.html>

soc.culture.latin-america <http://www.phoaks.com/phoaks2/newsgroups/soc/culture/latin-america/index.html >

37. José Briones is referring here to MexNews, a group of volunteers that search for news of Mexico on the Internet and post their findings on the lists Mexico94/2000 and Chiapas-L, after which they get reposted to the newsgroup soc.culture.mexican.

38. In December 1997, the website's automatic counter indicated that the page had been accessed 166,663 times in 14 months. The page is located at <http://www.ezln.org/>.

39. One point of departure for exploring Zapatista-related resources on the Internet is *Zapatistas in Cyberspace: A Guide to Analysis & Information* by Professor Harry Cleaver of the University of Texas at Austin. This site briefly describes some 70 notable electronic sources of information, interaction, and analysis pertaining to Zapatismo, including articles, news and discussion forums, web pages, archives, books, and multimedia projects available on-line. <http://www.eco.utexas.edu/faculty/Cleaver/zapsincyber.html>

40. With commercial and legislative campaigns to control Internet communication already under way, popular political movements in the future may not have the option of benefitting from cyber-democracy as this one has.

41. This memo is available on-line in the January 1995 Chiapas95 archives at <gopher://mundo.eco.utexas.edu:70/11/mailing/chiapas95.archive>

42. Aguascalientes, formerly called Guadalupe Tepeyac, housed a convention center constructed by the Zapatistas for the purpose of facilitating international political and intercultural debate. This public sphere in the middle of the Lacandón jungle consisted of a covered amphitheater with a seating capacity of 8,000, replete with lighting, microphones, and videotaping equipment. In addition to this discursive space, there were sleeping quarters, cooking fires, latrines, and parking areas.

43. This communiqué is available on-line in the February 1995 Chiapas95 archives, at <gopher://mundo.eco.utexas.edu:70/11/mailing/chiapas95.archive>. See the message dated February 12, 1995 and entitled Último Comunicado del EZLNO. See also OEZLN/Ana Maria interv.(English) dated February 19, 1995.

44. The English translation of this document is available on-line at *Chiapas for the World, for Humanity and Against Neoliberalism,* <http://www.physics.mcgill.ca/oscarh/EncuentroIntercontinental/ChiapMunIng/clausura.html#seg>. The original Spanish version is at <http://www.ezln.org/archive/segunda-lacandona.html>.

45. Freeing the Media was organized by The Learning Alliance, Paper Tiger, and FAIR (Duncan & Ruggiero, 1997, p. 48).

46. In a Zapatista village, the nearest phone line may be 50 miles away, and it is a region where indigenous villagers often travel by foot.

47. Cleaver (1995) outlines the interwoven linkages of Zapatista support and traces some of this networking to anti-NAFTA organizing, which created international linkages in the years just prior to the Zapatista rebellion. A version of this is available in Holloway and Peláez (1998, pp. 81-103), a book that offers further reading on the evolution of the Zapatista movement.

Extended Case Studies

18

The Portuguese Explosion: The Collapse of Dictatorship and Colonialism, 1974-1975

Portugal, population 9 million and still one of the less affluent European nations, hardly seems to hold a candle to the United States or the former Soviet empire, or even Italy, the other nations whose radical media we shall examine in this final section. Its affairs may seem, then, a matter of rather recondite curiosity. Not so four centuries ago, when Portugal's dominions stretched from Brazil to Macao, and it held the very doubtful honor of having pioneered European colonialism in Africa, in what is now Morocco. But that was then, and this is now.

Yet, this view is misguided on three counts. One is general: the automatic equation of size with significance. The minimal size of the ship from which the Boston rebels hurled the tea chests had no bearing on the huge repercussions of that defiance.

The second is that when our radical media story begins in 1974,[1] Portugal, even having lost Brazil as a colony some 150 years previously, was still ostensibly master of Angola and Mozambique (along with some much smaller African domains). These two colonies, with discreet U.S. and British support (see Minter, 1972), were part of a bloc of racist white regimes that then still ran the whole of southern Africa with the exception of Zambia and Botswana, the others being Rhodesia, now Zimbabwe; South West Africa, mandated to the Republic of South Africa's control in 1919, now Namibia; and in particular, apartheid-run South Africa itself.

A glance at the map will show the gigantic terrain entailed, although it will show neither the natural riches involved nor the scale of repression imposed by colonial rule. Thus, the reversal of colonial policy in little Portugal, supported 100% by the radical media that flourished in the overthrow of the fascist regime, had long-term implications for the African continent. In the months of this study (April 1974-November 1975), there were two major coup attempts to restore the previous regime, and radical media played an important role in developing a public opinion that effectively resisted these efforts to turn the clock back. At a stroke, the apartheid regime in South Africa and the white minority regime in Rhodesia lost two key supporting neighbor states. The writing was on the wall, and 20 years later, Nelson Mandela took office as South Africa's president in the first free election in the country's history.

Third, the experiments in self-managed media in Lisbon were of immense international interest at the time, with those in favor of media change watching with fascination how they developed, while conservative commentators and policy makers were using precisely these media as litmus tests for the direction of the Portuguese revolution. At one point, U.S. national security adviser Henry Kissinger became convinced that Portugal was lost to the West, a strange concept to say the least, but nonetheless one that gives some sense to the international reverberations of the Portuguese revolt. As mentioned already in the segment on radio in Part II, southern Europe as well as southern Africa had a totally different political complexion on April 25, 1974, the day the old regime was overthrown. Right next door in Spain, dictator Franco was still alive and had been in power since 1939; when he died in 1976, Portugal was no longer available as a reactionary neighbor. In Greece, a fascist military junta that had seized power in 1967 was still in control, collapsing later that year. In Italy, the conservative Christian Democrats were still in power after 26 years, and broadcast media were comprehensively responsive to their bidding: The huge free radio movement was still aborning.

Paradoxically, however, we shall see repeatedly that foreign perceptions and even the perceptions of Portuguese political leaders were way off in their interpretation of what these media activists saw themselves as doing.

We will focus mainly on two cases of self-managed radical media in the hectic months from April 1974 through November 1975, namely the newspaper *República* and the radio station Rádio Renascença.[2] Let us, however, preface our review of these media with some basic information about what happened in Portugal during that period.

BRIEF BACKGROUND

As of April 25, 1974, in what was termed afterward the "revolution of the carnations" because of the flowers members of the public placed in the rifle barrels of the troops who overthrew the government, the fascist and colonialist regime in Portugal, which had been in place since 1926, was finally sent packing—but peacefully, hence the carnations—by the Armed Forces Movement, a coalition of modernizing and revolutionary army officers, many of them captains. The standard of living for most of Portugal's population was not much different then from that in its African colonies, and it was clear to the revolution's leaders not only that the colonies were an international embarrassment, but that paying the military costs of retaining them was a colossal drain on Portugal's meager resources for its own development. Lisbon and the south were mostly ecstatic at the change; Porto and the north were more conservative and much more apprehensive.

The big question was where would this now lead. For some, it was enough to shed the burden of colonialism. For others, integration into capitalist Western Europe was the goal. For others, alliance with the Soviet bloc. For others, the aim was developing a radical democracy, ahead of both Western and Eastern Europe. And naturally for many, day-to-day survival and a somewhat better living standard were high on the agenda.

The survival of the revolution was fragile. In September 1974 and in March 1975, attempted military coups tried but failed to reverse all the leftward movement. In November 1975, there was a much more successful and sharp switch in government policy, rather unambiguous signals of which were the dynamiting of Rádio Renascença and, in January 1976, the forcible closure of *República* (all in the name of democracy, of course).

REPÚBLICA

In April 1974, this newspaper was under Portuguese Socialist Party (PSP) management. In 1975, it made a major transition, examined below, to being a self-managed daily newspaper without party affiliation. Its career was an exceptionally stormy one, and there are bitterly contested accounts of what happened in those years. Its shift to self-management was publicly criticized by an interesting line-up: not only by Portuguese and foreign conservatives, but by the PSP, and also by the French and Italian communist parties. Along with Rádio Renascença, therefore, its internal organization was a long way from being purely an internal affair.

Before April 25, 1974, *República* was the only tolerated daily opposition paper in Portugal. Inevitably, however, its opposition had been a rather muted affair, given the state censor''s office.[3] For example, when *República* sent its journalists to the 1973 conference of the Portuguese Socialist Party, held by necessity outside Portugal in Grenoble, France, the newspaper was forbidden to print any of the proceedings, including even an interview with the PSP leader, Mário Soares. It lost the money spent and the interview. Soares, however, used to write regular articles for the newspaper from Paris, under the pseudonym Clain d'Estaigne, a play on words[4] never picked up by the censors.

Only in the brief 2-week run-up to national elections (so-named), when an official period of grace permitted the press to be a little more candid than it was normally allowed to be, could *República* express any significant opposition to the regime. It was a symbol of resistance rather than resistance itself.

A Change of Owners

In 1971, the PSP acquired a majority holding in the paper and proceeded to put in its own editors, Raúl Rêgo and Vitor Direito. Some PSP members were also among the journalists and the printers. According to Rêgo, the printers were among the best paid in Lisbon because of the PSP's commitment to the working class. In these years, according to one PCP (communist party) member, formerly a *República* journalist, relations inside the paper were very good, with a general sense of unity in opposition to the old regime. Everyone to whom I spoke agreed, however, that hostilities broke out between the management and the staff remarkably soon after April 25.

The view put forcefully—and very simplistically—to me by Rêgo was that Portugal in 1974 was akin to someone bedridden for 48 years (i.e., under fascism) who suddenly had to walk in a democracy. Rêgo argued that this was the only light in which the *República* events made any sense. The evidence, however, shows that *República*'s career was determined by less atmospheric and rather more tangible processes and events than Rêgo claimed.

The struggles inside the paper in the first year of the revolution can only be understood against the background of socialist party and communist party rivalry for leadership of the revolt against fascism, as well as their shared assumption—shared, moreover, by all other major political parties—that control of the media meant control of the revolution itself. This is an important question. Much of what we have studied so far has implicitly identified state or commercial ownership as the primary sources of control over mainstream media, but in the Portuguese case, political party control and religious control (in the case of Rádio Renascença) were the dominant issues.

As the first 12 months proceeded, the PCP became the dominant force in mass information, controlling the Lisbon dailies, one of which was the quality newspaper, *Diario de Noticias* (Daily News). The PSP found itself with only *República,* because it was its majority shareholder. From the PSP point of view, to have one paper in this overall context was not asking too much, especially if it owned it financially.

Rêgo insisted to me that *República* was never simply a party newspaper. There is, despite his insistence, considerable evidence of actions that indicate PSP determination to use the paper that way; and in turn, these actions were at the root of the strife inside the paper. For example, Soares himself used to telephone the paper repeatedly, insisting it cover particular stories. On one occasion, another leading PSP figure was interviewed about a NATO visit to Portugal and then tried to insist on seeing the interview to OK it before publication. Editorial policy at certain points indicated the PSP affiliation with great clarity. An example was the relegation to the inside pages of reporting about a huge Intersindical (the PCP-dominated labor union federation) demonstration, whereas a tiny PSP picket was given front page coverage with a photograph. Another instance was the repeated hiring of new pro-PSP journalists. Those who balked at writing what seemed to be purely PSP communication projects were often refused any assignments at all by the editors. It has to be said that PCP-dominated newspapers were no better, *O Século* entirely disregarding, for instance, a giant PSP demonstration in July 1975 (Mesquita, 1994, p. 362).

The reaction of the PCP journalists on the *República* staff was to leave as a group, albeit accompanied by some others, in April 1975. They gravitated, predictably enough, to the four Lisbon dailies with a strong PCP presence. Many felt, beyond their frustrations, that some kind of explosion was likely within the paper after they left, but at the time, none would have predicted the actual course of events. Indeed, one PCP journalist said that in retrospect, he regretted they had all left because in his view, if the PCP group had stayed, it could have limited the conflict to the issue of editorial interference and so have forced the editors into resigning over censorship. As it was, he concluded, the PSP lost the battle for control of the newspaper but won the international propaganda war against the leftward trend of the Portuguese revolution by drawing to the attention of the NATO powers a supposedly growing encroachment on press freedom in Portugal—with the PSP cast in the role of embattled heroes. Indeed, the PSP actually gave this as their reason for walking out of the government coalition in July 1975. A great deal pivoted at that time on the chain of events in Portugal's radical media.[5]

Thus, the newspaper became a case from which to squeeze political advantage rather than a mass medium valued for itself. For example, the paper's format was shoddy, reflecting the antique machinery on which it was printed. Although the money to install new presses was available—as the later founding of *A Luta* demonstrated—the PSP never bothered to do so. The PSP used the smear of PCP control to its advantage in its own international circles, although in other circles, the smear had no impact: The French daily *Libération,* then self-managed, and the far Left Italian weekly *Lotta Continua,* neither known for sympathy with the communist party, both sent support messages to the *República* workers.

To underscore the point about the fiction of PCP control, when eventually the Council of the Revolution, then the supreme governing body of the country, handed back the keys of the press building to representatives of the management and workers in July, the workers' representative was Luis Porto, a PSP activist. Finally, for all its public talk about media freedom, objectivity, and pluralism, the PSP approved the

November 1975 dynamiting of Rádio Renascença's transmitter and decreed the nationalization of another radical station, Rádio Clube Português. After November 25, 1975, the PSP moved, in conjunction with other parties in government, to begin to rein in dissonant voices in the media at large.

The Printers' Strike

A major turning point came on May 2, 1975 (after the departure of the PCP journalists), when the newspaper's printers went on strike. "It was as though my secretary here in Parliament refused to type my letters!" expostulated Rêgo to me in April 1980, his fury still unabated. His words conveyed the ideology of personal ownership very precisely. What had originally provoked his anger was this strike. He and the PSP consistently interpreted it as a PCP plot among the arrogant *República* printers to wrench control of the paper from the PSP. The PSP leadership insisted that the printers wanted to write the paper themselves, as though that too was inconceivable (although it was not, in fact, the printers' demand): "the madness that took over *República,*" as Rêgo put it.

The strike lasted several days. The printers' initial demand was for an internal reorganization and a ban on hiring new journalists unless this was negotiated and approved by the workers on the paper. This was clearly designed to choke off the packing of *República* with PSP nominees.

The strikers elected a Workers' Co-ordinating Committee (CCT) from the Workers' General Assembly. This committee was elected by occupational sections, with 1 representative per 15 workers in each section. The committee was mandated to negotiate a statute of independence for the paper's political line. On May 6, the committee approved a working document that proposed dialogue with the management on the issues of how the different sections of the paper should be re-organized. It also demanded financial and political party independence—especially the latter—for the paper. It further urged regular reviews of the paper's management structure. The continuing thread, however, was the demand for a nonsectarian paper of the Left: "All the progressive parties must be treated in the same manner," said the May 6 document. It added, finally, that the arbiters of the paper's nonsectarian policy were to be its workers, through their democratic institutions, such as the General Assembly and the CCT.

This demand for an open paper was certainly not a demand for the exclusion of the PSP perspective or for hegemony of the PCP perspective. Yet, it proved to be a demand that was quite impossible for *República*'s management to contemplate. Like all the other major parties, the PSP was trapped in the manipulative—and deterministic—assumption that media control granted control of the revolution's direction. On May 14, Belo Marques, finance director of the newspaper and a close ally of the PCP, submitted his resignation. The CCT asked him to remain but called for the resignation of the rest of the management. In an action that demonstrated the printers' degree of determination, the CCT also organized a picket of the newspaper in case of a management attempt to seize the presses.

On May 19, most of the journalists refused to write for the paper anymore, taking as their pretext the CCT's refusal to print management's account of the paper's internal crisis in a forthcoming issue of the paper. The CCT responded by suspending the management, with the support of 93 out of the 140 present at the assembly meeting (the paper's full strength being about 190). It then brought the paper out for one day with Belo Marques's name on the masthead. That day, the PSP mounted a demonstration outside the newspaper. Soares headed it and, in an exchange with the workers, told them they were "objectively playing the game of reaction." One replied, "This is not the PSP headquarters. You and your colleague Cunhal must recognize the strength of the workers. You have to stop playing games with the people. Both of you, go back to where you used to live!" Lumping Soares together in the same sentence with PCP leader Alvaro Cunhal, and telling both to return to the places they lived while in political exile, is indicative of the true state of feelings on the paper's staff at that time.

COPCON (an elite Army unit) promptly intervened in the situation. A night of fruitless negotiations followed, with the government's information minister in the chair, yet openly supporting the management. (In an interview on May 23 in the weekly *Expresso,* he said he was "convinced" the workers were in the wrong.) At 6 a.m., the *República* offices were evacuated and sealed off. The paper was not on the streets again until July 10, when it was re-opened with an official military director but actually under its workers' control. (A little later, Belo Marques left the paper after his plan for *República* was turned down, despite his almost irreplaceable grip on the paper's administration and finances.)

Thus, the striking printers opposed the newspaper's sectarian adherence to the PSP but never demanded that they should write it themselves. On the contrary, they expressed in the context of *República* the general Portuguese public's growing sense of alienation and impotence at the destruction of the revolution's impulse by vicious feuding between leftist political parties. Their demand was simple, and in one sense negative: that *República* should not be dragged down to that level. The more positive notion of a newspaper "of the mass base" that dominated the period of self-management, was a notion that only surfaced well after the strike, not before it. As the printers put it in their manifesto,

> We the workers of *República* are conscious of being in a society lacking science and education, in which especially there is absent a politics of information which, instead of disabling the poor and exploited working classes, gives them intellectual and economic power.... We declare that in information it is the workers who have the power to decide that the fruit of their labor—the newspaper—should be devoted to activities concerned with the transformation of mankind and of life, and not with the aggressive objectives of political leaders, not with privileges of corrupt minorities, or with political party exhibitionism. ("Breve nota," 1980)

The period of self-management at *República* was thus extremely short, lasting only from July 10 to November 25, when *República,* like all other media, was forcibly closed by government decree. Both Rádio Clube Português and Rádio Renascença enjoyed a much longer experience of self-management. Nonetheless, these 5 months were important for the Portuguese movement and for the accumulated experience of radical media organizations.[6]

A Period of Independence

The first change in *República*'s organization was the influx of new journalists to replace the old PSP members who had left. Most of the latter were rehired on the short-lived daily *A Luta* (The Struggle) published by the PSP. Many of the new people on the paper were students, with no previous journalistic experience of any kind, and they joined the paper purely out of political commitment to its struggle. *República*'s funds were critically low, because the former PSP owners sequestered whatever they could from its finances. Advertising revenue dried up, then resumed, but only at a trickle.

Thus, wages were difficult to pay, as were all of the paper's bills. Its newsprint bill, for instance, was enormous, and the government refused to help it to pay. Eventually, the workers decided in their Assembly to ask for public support, and they held a mass demonstration on the April 25 bridge (formerly the Salazar[7] bridge—a suspension bridge that straddles the wide Tagus estuary to Lisbon harbor). This appeal realized no less than 700,000 escudos, a tangible index of the popular support *República* enjoyed. All the same, it was practically impossible to send journalists anywhere to report on events because of the paper's financial morass. And there was no decision at *República*, unlike the action at Rádio Renascença, that everyone should receive the same wage. Last, the printers were less than enthusiastic about having a large body of volunteer collaborators on the paper, because they felt this could open it to a fresh wave of political party colonization.

This complex of factors quickly dictated the kind of paper that the new *República* could be. Under self-management it rapidly transformed itself into a newspaper of the base, dependent to a large extent on information given to it, rather than ferreted out by its journalists. It was, as a result, a highly combative newspaper, giving almost all its attention to immediate popular struggles. Its coverage of two types of struggle was especially strong: the squatters' movement, led largely by women; and the political conflicts inside the armed forces' barracks, mostly between the politicized soldiers and their reactionary officers. It is hardly surprising that conservative and centrist forces inside Portugal were dismayed and angry at this trend in the paper.

As was predictable from the May printers' strike, the new *República* gave voice to criticisms of the official political parties of the Left and to the desire for people's power over the revolution's direction. In the words of its own new statutes, published in the issue of August 1, 1975,

> The newspaper *República* is oriented on marxist principles and takes it as given that the workers' emancipation and liberation are the activity of the workers themselves. It is involved in an uncompromising defense of a line of National Independence against the superpowers' hegemony, and moreover fights all forms of class collaboration. . . . The working class and other exploited classes must intervene critically in the content of the newspaper *República* through their independent organs of popular will. . . . So that the newspaper *República* may fulfill the

> specific mission of this constitution, it must be controlled by all the workers through their executive organ the CCT. . . . The final organ of decision is the workers' Plenary. . . . We recognize as its legitimate source of information, communications from the commissions of workers, squatters, unemployed, soldiers, sailors, and all the base organs representing the Portuguese workers. (Fernandes, 1980, p. 14)

Like Rádio Renascença workers, *República*'s workers also saw the revolutionary movement in Portugal as their ultimate employer and authority. As anyone might suppose, this was not always a straightforward matter to realize in practice. Relations with the other workers' commissions did not assume a stable form but were only realized in the context of particular struggles and for the duration of those struggles. In that sense, any notion of regular and continuing intervention by the paper's readership proved extremely problematic. One commission might present highly localized and fragmented accounts of the problems it encountered or might itself be divided along party lines. Often, the commissions themselves looked to *República* for guidance, rather then the reverse; and this guidance was rarely forthcoming. Thus, the movement itself was not sufficiently unified or organized to be able to govern the newspaper's output in any consistently meaningful way.

Internally, however, the paper did not move to cancel the division between intellectual and manual labor (as would have been predicted from PSP claims about the printers' arrogance). Admittedly, the official military director played a purely formal role. But the printers themselves were content simply to act as custodians of the paper's political party independence and openness—its conscience, not its censors. The journalists continued to write *República,* with only occasional contributions from its administrative staff or its printers. The other contributors were, as noted, the commissions. There was plenty of discussion between printers and journalists, and a number of ideas certainly originated with the printers, but the paper's overall content remained in the journalists' hands.

Beyond this, there existed the simple fact of diversity among both journalists and printers. Not all the journalists had the same skills or experience, so that invariably there emerged an informal hierarchy among them. Among the printers, there were some still locked into a purely trade union consciousness; others were mainly preoccupied with maintaining their jobs, and yet others, often the younger printers, were evincing a rapid growth toward political activism. Those with the most active say in the paper's operation were those who were politically active, whether journalists or printers.

The printers, however, were resigned to the continuing fact of the division between intellectual and manual labor. They found it easier than some slightly guilt-ridden *República* journalists did to accept the sheer fact of the more seasoned journalists' education, wider perspective, writing experience, and grasp of the emerging political system in Portugal.

It is in the light of these practical realities that we should interpret the election in September 1975 by the workers' plenary of a political commission to review the paper's content each day before it "went to bed." The commission was composed of four people. All four were printers concerned with layout, for the simple reason that when the paper was being written, the layout printers were the only ones with the time to work on its contents with a second group of four, the editorial coordinating committee, composed of journalists. The whole CCT was too large a body to do this, as even more obviously was the workers' Plenary. Thus, in the everyday running of the paper, these eight people with varying political perspectives were effectively in control of the details. The political commission in practice rarely intervened politically, being concerned rather on the level of feasible headlines and such practical matters.

For key political questions, either the CCT was invoked or the Plenary, if the CCT felt unable to resolve the issue itself. Anyone was free to approach any of these bodies at any time. An example of a decision referred to the Plenary was when the CCT considered a series of articles politically slandering Mário Soares. The Plenary refused to publish them. On another occasion, the Plenary was called to approve or reject publication of an interview with Captain Fernandes (one of the original planners of April 25, who had just distributed 1,500 guns to revolutionary activists). It approved this interview.

The Political Gap

In the end, the fundamental problem facing *República* under self-management was not its penniless condition, nor the collective's political or journalistic experience, but the huge gap between the politics of the movement and official party politics. At the grass roots, there were numerous independent creative initiatives, but these had no authentic reflection in official politics. None of the major political parties took up any of these moves.

Consequently, people began to stop bothering about overall political realities. Whereas the parties, even the tiny ones, were talking nonstop about the problem of state power, the public was talking about its immediate struggles—and hoping things would turn out all right overall. People quite often even combined their own local initiatives, with a continuing reliance on one or another of the existing leftist parties at the national level.

There was no apparent resolution of this crushing problem. Jorge Almeida Fernandes cites a foreign revolutionary, actively engaged in the Portuguese events, who proposed through the pages of *República* that the paper should become the directing center of the nonparty political movement. He observes dryly, "The utopia inside the newspaper was always a more realistic one" (Fernandes, 1980, p. 15). The paper backed the popular movement but always hoped for time, for a period of grace in which the movement could coalesce—as though the tensions in Portugal between the forces at odds with each other could continue without some resolution. Fernandes (1980) quotes from *República*'s report of the paratroopers' dynamiting of Rádio Renascença:

> The only alternative to counter-revolution . . . is to reinforce mass mobilization, and organization, in order to reinforce the centralization of popular power and the worker-farmer alliance, and to reinforce the soldiers' and workers' ability to respond and take the political initiative. (p. 15)

The analysis was flawless; but the means were unavailable. November 25 followed swiftly.

When the *República* collective met to discuss its reaction to the events of November 25, there was a prompt split essentially between the older and younger members. The younger ones wanted to bring out *República* as quickly as possible to help to rally popular resistance. The older ones wanted to keep their heads down and save their jobs if they possibly could. But only about 30 people were there, arguing for hours into the night. The paper did come out again, in spite of the older workers' fears, until November 30, but by that time the new government had effective overall control, and in January 1976, it closed *República*.

Lessons From Experience

Despite its short period of self-management, *República*'s experience is instructive. Not only does its history demonstrate the practical viability of media self-management, it demonstrates that this is possible even with limited funds and journalistic experience. The key to its success was its living relationship to the ongoing political movement in Portugal. For example, a former *República* journalist told me how at one stage in late 1975, when the PCP was extremely hostile to all strikes and was expressing this daily through its control of much of the Lisbon press, she was the only newspaper journalist to whom the Lisbon Metro workers would speak while they were on strike. The success of *República*'s public appeal on the April 25 bridge is another instance of this close relation between the paper and the movement at large.

This bond with workers, with squatters, with the barracks, with African liberation movement spokespeople in Lisbon, was the foundation of *República*'s viability. The official attacks by the socialist party and the communist party's disapproval both bounced harmlessly off *República,* given this mass support. (The most effective attack the PSP contrived was to get distributors in the north of Portugal outside Porto to refuse to handle *República* and to distribute *A Luta* instead.)

At the same time, the problems of the movement were also *República*'s problems, as we have seen. In addition, as in the case of Rádio Renascença, the sheer pressure of events each day meant that a number of deeply important issues tended never to surface: the place of imaginative material in the paper's communication, the implications of decolonization for Portugal's self-understanding, the position of women in Portugal. In this last instance, it must be said in fairness that women often intervened in the paper as squatters or as strikers and that the four women journalists on the paper, according to one of them, were treated without any form of discrimination. Finally, another major social problem in Portugal, illiteracy, meant that *República* was essentially a workers' paper, read only in the main industrial towns and cities.

In the final analysis, however, *República*'s strength lay in the dedication of its collective to the movement's right to self-determination, a political position that always echoed the everyday practice of direct democracy inside the paper. The bond between these two aspects of the revolutionary process was never snapped, even though *República* could not single-handedly support the momentum of the revolution against the events of November 25. *República* stands, nonetheless, as a compelling testimony to the extraordinary potential of self-activity by the working class, even in the face of crushing difficulties.

RÁDIO RENASCENÇA

The station's name meant Rebirth Radio. Before the April revolution, it had ostensibly been a Catholic station, and after November 1975, it reverted to its previous ownership. Along with *República,* Rádio Renascença was trumpeted as a scandalous case of left-wing censorship by the PSP in its attempt to bring international pressure to bear against its own opponents inside Portugal. Interference with the freedom of religion was added to interference with press freedom in this instance. But what was the real story of these 19 months of self-managed communication?

The story has to begin with the character of Rádio Renascença before the 1974 revolution. Only in name was it a Catholic station. Its output included a single half-hour on religion each day, usually a broadcast Mass or rosary recitation. Its ownership, as the radio collective discovered later in 1974 when they had taken control, was in the hands, not of the Catholic Church, but of an obscure property company with an address in the Algarve (the southern coast of Portugal), which nonetheless had no known involvement in real estate in that region.

Its financial affairs were handled by an advertising agency called Intervoz, one of whose leading board members had the doubtful distinction of leading the attempted naval invasion of Conakry, Guinea, in 1970 (as an attempt to deter Guinean support for the liberation struggle against Portuguese colonial rule in neighboring Guiné-Bissau). Thus, the station was to all intents and purposes on the far Right, dedicated to maintaining Portugal's colonial possessions, and only in the most superficial sense a Catholic institution.

A clear illustration of what this meant in practice is the way its journalists used to be regularly censored before the April revolution if they were even to refer to the so-called social doctrines of the Second Vatican Council. These doctrines represented rather vaguely defined positions on elementary social justice, but they were obviously considered dangerously close to leftist dynamite by the management.

There was discreet opposition within Renascença to this censorship, although clearly nothing much was possible by way of effectively defying it before April 1974. To some extent, the Cardinal of Lisbon was not only aware of this opposition within the station but quietly tolerated it, seeing it as his role to maintain a balance between the Portuguese bishops' conference, unashamedly reactionary in character, and the emerging liberalized Catholicism increasingly popular among lay intellectuals (cf. Grohs, 1976). His ambivalent position would prove to be important in shaping the station's future during its period of self-management.

Two issues, above and beyond the events of April 25 itself, were turning points in the shift to self-management in Renascença. The first was the censorship that continued in force at the station after that climactic date, and the second was hiring policy. However, self-management developed only in the Lisbon station; the other main station in Porto remained under the old management without a break, which came to have particular significance at one juncture, as we shall see.

The Issue of Censorship

The censorship issue arose in the first days after April 25. Initially, the management took the line that the political crisis would blow over, that nothing of substance was changing, and that the station should continue to operate as usual. But then the exiled leaders of the official Left began to return. A communist party member at Rádio Renascença took the initiative of recording an interview with Cunhal. Its news value was indisputable, because it would have been the first time Cunhal's voice was heard from a radio station inside Portugal.

Given the organization of the station's news division at the time, this journalist would have been able, had he so chosen, to include the interview in the next news bulletin before the senior management could have intervened to stop it. Instead, he decided formally to ask their permission to broadcast the interview, precisely to force the censorship issue. Not surprisingly, they refused him permission outright. The long simmering issue of censorship burst instantly to the surface, and the radio workers went on strike. The strike lasted only a few hours, but by the end of those few hours, the radio workers had added to the demand to end censorship a further demand to have their poor physical working conditions improved. They also elected their own workers' committee.

The management, true to its political colors, refused point-blank to recognize or negotiate with the committee. Undeterred, the committee contacted the Armed Forces Movement (MFA) to acquaint it with the situation that had arisen. The MFA responded by first contacting the administration and then, once it was clear that this would be fruitless as a way of settling the dispute, proceeded to send in its nominee to act as intermediary between the workers' committee and the management. Before April 25, such a concession of legitimacy to the workers' grievances would have been unimaginable. Thus, the radio workers took considerable heart from the MFA's response.

The second confrontation on hiring policy came shortly afterward. The management proposed to require seven trainees to take psychological tests. The station staff smelled a rat and objected. Once again, the MFA was called in and sent a new intermediary. The management, by now throughly enraged by the MFA's alliance with "its" insubordinate workers, simply withdrew from the station. Intersindical (the communist party-dominated trade union federation) took over the payment of the seven trainees' wages, and shortly after this, the management discontinued payment of all wages (except to a number of "trusties," who stayed comfortably at home until after November 1975, on full salary, and then smoothly resumed their duties as though nothing had ever happened). "So," as one of Renascença's former journalists put it, "we simply got on with it ourselves." This simple statement, however, does less than justice to the enormous external hazards they faced during their period of self-management—although unlike *República,* the station enjoyed a remarkably peaceful internal life.

The Catholic Hierarchy

The major issue confronting Rádio Renascença was its relation with the Catholic hierarchy. For a long period, the radio collective bent over backward to be accommodating, letting it be known in public and in private that it was hostile not to the church but only to the former management of the station. It stressed that it wished not to seize the church's property but simply to broadcast the new realities of Portuguese life without the reactionary control of the previous administration. The collective, to underline its position, actually offered the church more airtime than it had ever had before. A number of priests publicly supported the moves to make the station independent, which earned them the fury of the Catholic hierarchy. In 1975, the Bishops' Conference denounced "all who present themselves as priests or religious or simple Christians, and are taking advantage of the irresponsible climate of freedom reigning in certain sectors of the media to publicize ideas contrary to the church's thinking."[8]

The hierarchy's response to these overtures was to tell its clergy to refuse all cooperation with Renascença, so that when broadcasting units turned up at churches to tape or broadcast services live, they would be told they were unwelcome. Negotiations dragged on, meanwhile, for nearly a year, although the Cardinal of Lisbon gradually became more inclined to accept the station's new broadcasting policies. Eventually, Renascença's workers succeeded in hammering out a new constitution for the station, and the Cardinal agreed verbally that it was fully in accordance with the social doctrines of Vatican II. The workers also offered to try to compromise on a management council whose personnel were acceptable to the Cardinal.

Never, however, did the Cardinal ratify his verbal consent in writing. At the formal meeting in which he indicated his consent, the workers' representatives signed the constitution document, and the Cardinal promised to countersign it that night so they could have the agreed text the next day. As one of the workers' representatives put it wryly to me in 1980, "I am still waiting to receive that document." It seems likely that the Cardinal was headed off by one of the most aggressively rightist members of the Portuguese bishops' conference, namely, its president, the archbishop of Aveiro, who probably intimidated him with the threat of isolation from his episcopal brethren if he were to countersign the station's constitution.

Throughout these long negotiations, there were also other skirmishes. The former management, doubtless with the church's connivance, tried to get the essential services cut off, ranging from electricity and water to the Reuters telex machine. They also sabotaged Renascença by removing some crucial crystals from the transmitter.

The supply of electricity and water was never actually interrupted, due to prompt solidarity action by the workers' self-management commissions in those services, who refused to interfere with the new Renascença. The affair of the crystals was much more damaging, because without them, the transmitter was useless. At this point, some effective international solidarity emerged: The French section of the Trotskyist Fourth International managed to get hold of the exact replacements and handed them over to Renascença. Both episodes indicated that Renascença had crucial support, which was particularly important for the workers in their beleaguered situation.

Negotiation With Reuters

The episode of the Reuters telex turned out a little differently. Reuters' position was that it could only deal with the properly constituted legal management and that under the new circumstances, it could not even be sure existing bills would be paid. Thus, its representatives argued, they had no alternative but to cut off their telex to Renascença.

The Renascença workers, however, managed to persuade Reuters' Lisbon representative to come to discuss the matter with them. He arrived, put Reuters' view to them, and was at the point of leaving, when they urged him to listen for a moment to their own position. They began to explain to him the modern history of Portugal, its results in the wretched conditions under which many Portuguese lived, and the consequent significance of the April revolution. The Reuters representative listened, thanked them politely, and began to rise to his feet. One or two restraining hands were placed on his shoulders, and he was urged to sit down and hear more. He sat down for a while, then once more rose with the intention of leaving. Again, restraining hands were placed on his shoulders. He asked, in apprehension mixed with irritation, whether he was being detained against his will. He was assured this was not the case and was then presented with a further detailed exposure of the relation between the old Portugal and the new Renascença. To the workers' astonishment and delight, in the end, he agreed to recommend that Reuters reconnect the telex and to assure his superiors of his own confidence that all the telex bills would be paid. And unlike the Cardinal, he kept his word.

Other media newly under self-management, such as Rádio Clube Português, had been allowing Renascença to use their Reuters machines, but it was obviously a victory for Renascença to get its own machines in operation once more.

Relationships With Other Stations

These were not the only external hazards faced by Renascença. The former management's next card was to pay the workers in the Porto station to travel down to a general assembly of all Renascença workers. This—from a management never previously known for its interest in worker democracy—was in the hope it could engineer an overall majority for itself, with the Lisbon workers outnumbered. The Porto station had been expanded immediately following the Lisbon switch to self-management, with more staff and new equipment that could broadcast to most of the country, including Lisbon itself.

However, the Lisbon workers met the Porto workers as they got off the train and asked them to talk with them first, so they could explain their own point of view in taking over the station. The Porto workers agreed, and the end result was that the assembly adopted a united resolution that deprived the old management of any authority to move against the Lisbon station.

These were the management ploys. Their pressure was experienced in concert with the hostility of the PSP and the Popular Democratic Party (PPD—later to retitle itself the Popular Social Democrats).[9] As soon as the radio station workers organized themselves autonomously, these political parties accused them of being hostile to the Catholic Church, of seizing its property, and of interference with its right to broadcast. They pursued this line with special energy abroad, where the image of Portugal fostered by the foreign media was one of a country rapidly lurching from an archaic fascism to an authoritarian communism. In turn, these accounts in the foreign media were regularly used as a lever inside Portugal to try to dislodge the socialist direction of the revolution.

A standard accusation of these two political parties against Renascença was that it was dominated by the PCP. The charge was absurd, because there was only one PCP member at Renascença. A PPD/PSD member who had played an exceptionally active role in most of the committees before and after the switch to self-management himself dismissed the charge as ridiculous.

Indeed, the true position vis-à-vis the PCP was a good deal different from these claims from the Right. To understand it, we have to recount a major clash between Renascença and the church hierarchy, which Renascença's enemies instantly seized on inside and outside the country. In turn, this clash produced not intimacy between the PCP and Renascença but considerable mutual alienation.

A Critical Demonstration

The event that catalyzed these reactions was a demonstration, mostly by elderly women and schoolgirls, outside the Cardinal's house in June 1975. The demonstration had been called to appeal for the "return" of the Lisbon Renascença studios to the Catholic Church's control, although as we have seen, that had never been the reality. One of the far Left parties, Popular Democratic Unity (UDP), with a particularly strong commitment to revolutionary media democracy as a foundation of socialist development, arrived a couple of hours later at the Cardinal's house and staged a counterdemonstration. Faced with this new contingent of "atheistic communists," the church demonstrators anxiously sought refuge in the Cardinal's mansion.

The Cardinal telephoned the MFA and demanded army protection for them. A military detachment turned up, but instead of placing itself between the rival groups or telling the UDP group it had made its point and should move on, it told the pro-church contingent it had to get into the army trucks and be driven away. The elderly women had a difficult time climbing into the trucks, and some of the soldiers seized the opportunity to fondle the older schoolgirls as they shoved them in.

This behavior gave Renascença's opponents a perfect propaganda victory. For it was the fifth provisional government, headed by General Vasco Gonçalves (well known to have been in close sympathy with the PCP for many years) that had sent the troops. Their apparent partiality was laid at the door of the presumed partiality of Gonçalves himself and of the PCP toward Renascença, and their enmity both to the church and broadcasting freedom. Just a few days later, the Pope sent a public note to the Cardinal expressing his "concern" at conflicts involving the church in Portugal. The hierarchy organized demonstrations in a number of cities—but not Lisbon—with demonstrators shouting slogans such as "Renascença belongs to the people."

The pressure became so intense at that point that the PPD member I interviewed had resigned from the station. Paradoxically, in view of the accusations from the Right, the station's only PCP member had argued, unsuccessfully, that the counterdemonstration should be held at the head office of the old management, rather than outside the Cardinal's residence, to make it fully clear whom Renascença was attacking. On June 20, the PCP issued a statement describing the UDP demonstration as having played into the hands of "the enemies of the revolutionary forces."

Once the PSP and PPD campaigns around this incident were in full swing, however, it became rapidly apparent to both the PCP and to the Gonçalves administration that in the international arena, Renascença was now (with *República*) the major symbol of their alleged authoritarian tendencies. They came to the conclusion that it would be better to deprive their opponents of this symbolic weapon. Thus, on July 1, Gonçalves and his Minister of Social Communication publicly urged the Lisbon Renascença workers to return the station to its former owners. He also called in some of them privately and frankly told them of his own dilemma, of being perfectly agreeable to what they were doing, but of wanting to safeguard the revolution as a whole.

The reaction of quite a large number of Renascença workers to his appeal was to dismiss it as part of a general PCP drive to assert hegemony over the Portuguese revolution. The tone of many Renascença broadcasts on the PCP became hostile as a result, to the point where Intersindical refused to pay the seven trainees' salaries any further and the PCP member resigned his seat on the workers' commission (although he remained at work in the station). Thus, the actual relation of the PCP to Rádio Renascença was far from the one ascribed to it by the PSP, the PPD, and their international media echoes.

The station was closed down on September 29 but re-opened following a major far Left demonstration on October 21. On November 7, paratroopers dynamited the transmitter.

However, the experience of self-management in Rádio Renascença was not only one of constant threats to its existence. This book is centrally concerned with a realistic appraisal of the problems of media self-management, but it should not be thought that the station only experienced hostile criticism from the outside. Renascença enjoyed powerful support from the political movement in Portugal. We have already seen how the electricity and water supply workers came to their aid, and there were plenty of other examples beyond these.

This support was most evident during those periods, especially in 1975, when it looked as though Renascença might be physically attacked. Instantly, masses of people flooded into the streets around the station in central Lisbon to defend "their" station. The atmosphere was electric, with some people playing guitars and other instruments most of the night to keep the defenders' spirits up. Several Renascença workers described these experiences of human warmth and solidarity as unforgettable, the living proof of their work's significance to the mass movement in Portugal. People stayed day after day. Spontaneous support was frequent on every level. Even while relations with the PCP leadership were strained almost to the breaking point, many PCP members told Renascença workers during a tour they made through Alentejo—a PCP stronghold in the rural south—how much they appreciated Renascença's broadcasts. Following Gonçalves' appeal, the station asked Lisbon's Industrial Belt workers and others how they felt. Their answer was a demonstration of many thousands of workers who marched past the station in orderly lines in their work clothes. (Following this, the Council of the Revolution rescinded a directive to return the station to its former owners.)

Assessing the Experience

In assessing Renascença's experience of self-management, therefore, it is absolutely impossible to divorce this experience from its relation with these various outside forces, from the Catholic Church and the PSP through to the mass movement of which it was an integral part. Self-management is not a blissful celebration of socialist nirvana but a way of organizing production, and in this case, of organizing mass communication. The true nature of self-management does not emerge only when social struggles have died away; rather, self-management is a form of involvement with those struggles, inside them.

Let us turn now to examine some main features of the internal organization of Rádio Renascença as it developed during its period of autonomy.

Like a large number of other firms and businesses in Portugal at that time, Rádio Renascença elected a workers' commission of eight people in the first weeks after April 25. One of the key internal decisions taken by the commission was to equalize all salaries, an action that contributed greatly both to the cohesion and unity of the collective and to the avoidance of entrenched new hierarchies inside it. Neither *República* nor Rádio Clube Português ever took this step.

However, the activity of this commission was concerned almost exclusively with external relations: negotiating with the MFA, the Council of the Revolution, the Catholic Church, the political parties, Intersindical, and foreign countries. The heavy external pressures faced by the station render this concentration entirely understandable. The constant threats from outside had a powerful unifying effect on the Renascença workers, who were also fortunate under the circumstances in having had no major group among themselves aligned with existing political parties that might have generated sectarian splits in their ranks. General assemblies of workers could be and regularly were called to work through major issues and problems.

Thus, the daily work of the radio station was largely unsupervised and remarkably conflict-free. The content was utterly different from what it had previously been, but the basic areas of responsibility remained much what they had been before the changeover.

The combination of these hazards with the incredible pace of events in 1974 and 1975 had other effects on the station's internal life. Arguably, it may have led to too facile a unity at certain points. Some individuals working quite happily and unquestioningly in Renascença before April 25 instantly transformed themselves into red-hot revolutionaries once it became clear which way the wind was blowing. Their motivation was never really queried.

Perhaps worse, one worker at the station was almost certainly an ex-member of PIDE (the fascist secret police, with a well-justified reputation for brutal torture), and another was a priest who probably acted as the Cardinal's spy throughout the long negotiations with the church. Practically no one would countenance sending either of them packing from the station. About the alleged ex-PIDE agent, a typical reaction was, "Well, he has a wife and a family, how can we strip him of his job?" This last reaction was particularly surprising, given that even the normally pacific Portuguese came close on many occasions to killing PIDE agents who were recognized after April 25.

The PCP member of Rádio Renascença with whom I spoke was of the view that the station badly lacked a coherent policy line and, therefore, any basis on which to hammer out plans for the future. Without taking the further step of agreeing with him that the appropriate line for the station would have been the PCP line, his criticism seems nonetheless to be grounded. There were never any workers' assemblies on, for example, how to broadcast, or what a revolutionary broadcasting policy would be, or the role of imaginative material in broadcasting, or the role of women in mass communication. And although it might be said that such discussion would have been a luxury in view of the November 1975 bombing of the transmitter by the government, and that events were far too hectic to allow for long-term reflection, such arguments are short-sighted. They discouraged preparation, thus putting people completely at the mercy of events.

Furthermore, a dangerous complacency about existing communication policy was encouraged, as employees rested on the laurels of the obvious support Renascença enjoyed rather than seeking to deepen it. The internal organization of Lisbon Renascença seems to have experienced a possibly temporary honeymoon, which would have been very likely to change over time, had not the Portuguese revolution been abruptly halted.

In retrospect, Renascença's virtual burial in the immediate was recognized by some of its former workers as having led to problems. Early on, the workers decided to broadcast only Portuguese music or foreign revolutionary music and to discard American or American-style popular music, which was dismissed as a manifestation of cultural imperialism, pure and simple. Very early in the morning, they would broadcast traditional rural songs for the peasants getting up to start work in the countryside. This programming was appreciated, but the musical diet soon became extremely thin. The policy was never changed, however.

On another level, Renascença became a political junkies' station. News bulletins were often an hour in length, and although it was easy to find material for them from the rush of events, and people did listen to them all the way through, the output was pitched at one level only, that of immediate political struggles and developments. As one former Renascença worker said dryly, "Imagination was not in power in Renascença."[10]

For another Renascença ex-worker, the key error was not trying to achieve workers' control at the Porto station as well. This failure left the much more conservatively inclined north of the country without a committed revolutionary paper or radio station (illiteracy was high, and *República*'s distribution was often interfered with). Leaving the Porto station under its previous management had also, as we saw, made it much easier for the latter to buy new equipment to extend broadcasting into the south of the country. It is hard to know how feasible it would have been to extend workers' democracy to the Porto station, but it is significant that no concerted attempt to bring it about was ever made.

We must examine again, however, the crucial question of the relation between the Lisbon station and the political movement. "We always saw the people as our employers," said one former Renascença worker, and it is clear that this was the hallmark of the station's relation to the Portuguese people, as well as to representatives of colonized Mozambique, Angola, and Guinea-Bissau. Predictably enough, the station's employees learned fairly quickly that this relation could not be defined in a purely instantaneous way; that if a worker turned up expressing a factory grievance, for instance, it was always sensible to check first with the workers' commission there in case it was just a purely individual complaint. In cases where different groups of workers had opposing positions, Renascença's line was pluralistic, namely, to give each viewpoint access to the airwaves.

The only political organization within the movement that was denied access was the MRPP (Movement for the Reorganization of the Party of the Proletariat, one of the pro-China groups). This refusal was based on two considerations. First, the MRPP always insisted on broadcasting its own bulletins itself, whereas other groups and organizations trusted the Renascença workers to read their statements for them. Second, MRPP bulletins were always saturated with empty and strident slogans, such as "Death to imperialism!" or "Death to Social-fascism!,"[11] which harangued listeners rather than communicating with them.

Aside from this, Renascença believed in allowing open access to all tendencies and currents in the movement. Indeed, it was both striking and moving, according to one of its former workers, how people politically mute for 48 years under fascism transformed themselves at a stroke into eloquent and fully coherent speakers, evincing no microphone nerves or communicative incompetence. Workers, housewives, and farmers alike spoke fluently and effectively without rehearsal, let alone training. Women were extremely active in the squatters' movement and, in that capacity in particular, spoke vividly over the radio on many occasions. Indeed, the opposition Renascença encountered was always from the official parties, Left and Right, and from the Catholic Church, never from Portuguese workers and farmers.

Renascença also had good relations with both Frelimo and the MPLA, the anticolonial guerrilla groups in Mozambique and Angola, respectively, and the station gave their Lisbon representatives full access to the airwaves to communicate their independence demands to the Portuguese public. The implications of decolonization for Portugal itself, however, either in terms of its national self-understanding or in terms of the rapid arrival in Portugal of some hundreds of thousands of returnees from the ex-colonies (the *retornados*), were as little examined by Renascença as by other revolutionary media.

The last point that needs making in relation to Renascença is in some ways a contradiction of the observation about its overemphasis on immediacy. The other side of that coin is that immediacy was also its greatest strength. There is no question but that the voices of the movement were heard and the movement's critical moments communicated vividly as a result of Renascença's "immersion" in the ongoing struggles and developments of the period.

One person to whom I spoke recalled vividly, as if it had been the previous day, the voice of one of Renascença's workers phoning an on-the-spot account of a pitched battle between demonstrators and the police. He himself had been beaten by police with a nightstick, the police were massing for another charge, and he was saying over the phone, "There's blood running over my face, and I can scarcely stand, but this is what's happening now." On another occasion, my respondent phoned in and played a song from his record collection about Sacco and Vanzetti, the Italian revolutionaries executed in the United States on trumped-up charges in the 1920s. This went out over the airwaves, and straightaway, a long discussion on the air followed with people phoning in their views and arguments.

In this sense, Renascença's achievement was a centerpiece of the movement—not seeking to impose its views on the movement, but assisting the movement's self-development. Like *República* and Rádio Clube Português, its early demise robbed the Portuguese movement, and socialists in general, of a valuable development in the experience of revolutionary communication. Indeed, a distinctive feature of the radio collective's operation was that despite its constant shortage of funds and the drying up of advertising revenue following the move to self-management, it consistently refused advertisements with either sexist or political party content. Autonomy was a reality in Renascença.

Summary: The Portuguese story underscores the close connections of radical media with social and political movements, questions of media organization, of relationships between technical specialists and writers or journalists, of political party or religious media control, of the acutely sensitive role of radical media in a period of intense and rapid political change, of the linkages between the wider democratic force of socialist political movements and the internal structure of movement media. It also raises the interesting question of how little form matters in periods of fierce political contestation—compare the form of *samizdat* media—yet how significant the aesthetics of various media are in maintaining the public's interest over the longer term. Imagination and playing within familiar genres have an important part to play in radical media. Radical media cannot be purely rational-cognitive, and last.

NOTES

1. My research for this chapter was based, aside from library research, on a month I spent in Lisbon in 1980 with the aid of a British ESRC (then SSRC) grant and a term's research leave from Greenwich University (then Thames Polytechnic), interviewing radical media activists who had been energetic during the 1974-1975 period, especially in *República* and Rádio Renascença. I have shortened the original treatment in the first edition but have not amended it.

2. In the first edition of this book (Downing, 1984), I also reviewed a second radio station, Rádio Clube Português, which I have omitted here only for reasons of space.

3. For information concerning censorship under the fascist regime, see Commissão do Livro Negro sobre Fascismo (1980). For general information on the media scenario before and during the revolution, see Seaton and Pimlott (1980) and Mesquita (1994). My gratitude to Dr. Helena Souza of the Communication Department of the University of Braga for making a copy of the second reference available to me and to Dr. Jean Seaton, who allowed me to see an advance copy of her essay in time for the first edition of this book. My own reading of the situation diverges from both these accounts at certain points.

4. The French pronunciation of this spuriously French name would approximate *clandestine.*

5. Mesquita (1994) is primarily concerned to divine the PCP's intentions regarding *República,* concluding that the PCP chose to walk away from it in order not to intensify the rift with the PSP, but leaving PCP printers to make the newspaper unmanageable for the PSP. This may well be true, but his analysis consequently pays little attention to the actual state of affairs in the newspaper. And for him, the far Left and its media activism are ciphers never explored.

6. At a Lisbon political rally on April 25, 1980, when I was carrying a special copy of *República* brought out as a commemorative issue by the PSP, some people asked to see the paper in the hope that it might be reappearing. At the time, I was standing on the edge of a large PCP contingent. One PCP worker actually took the PCP's news handout and made as if to hang on to *República* and throw the handout away. *República* had clearly lodged itself in Portuguese workers' minds as a demonstration of what workers had achieved for themselves, and could achieve by themselves.

7. Portugal's dictator from 1926 through his death in 1968.

8. Cited in a manuscript version of an article on media in the Portuguese revolution by Brazilian researcher Fernando Perrone, which Professor Perrone kindly shared with me in the early 1980s.

9. As one of my interlocutors pointed out to me, it was symptomatic of the intensely energized political climate in Portugal at that time that even the conservative parties felt obliged to assume leftist titles. The largest right-wing party named itself Center Social Democrats, and even the small party that sought to restore Portugal's monarchy called itself the People's Monarchy Party.

10. "All power to the imagination!" was one of the most famous slogans, derived from situationism, in the upheavals in Paris in May-June 1968.

11. "Social fascist," the Stalinist insult of choice for social democratic parties until Hitler came to power and repressed social democrats and communists alike, was revived by the Chinese Communist Party in the 1970s and applied to Moscow-line communist parties. All the baby-size pro-China clone parties around the world instantly echoed the Chinese party's searching insight.

19

Italy: Three Decades of Radical Media

Italian political history since Mussolini, and especially since the end of the 1960s, has been tremendously complex. For many casual observers, only the fact that Italian governments have tended to come and go with amazing rapidity has really caught their attention, along perhaps with occasional spectacular stories of the Sicilian Mafia, evoking the *Godfather* movies. And so, Italy remains a sun-drenched tourist trap dripping with ancient and medieval history, *pasta con sugo*, . . . and the Pope.

Let us complicate this picture a little, just enough to set the scene for the daily newspaper (*Il Manifesto*) and the two radio stations (Radio Popolare, Milan, and Controradio, Florence) that we shall be studying.[1] These three radical media are interesting in part because of their sheer longevity, which contrasts with the fairly short-run if epochal story of Portugal's *República* and Rádio Renascença. Longevity was also a fairly important criterion for the case studies I included in the first edition of this book (Downing, 1984), because I wanted to show that media of this type were by no means all just a flash in the pan. In addition, I was anxious to explore how radical media could not only function but actually survive over time with self-managed structures and on low budgets. These considerations, along with their intimate relation with social movements and oppositional cultures, made these Italian examples particularly intriguing.

BRIEF BACKGROUND

The political turbulence in France was more or less confined to 1968 and 1969, and in Portugal to 1974 and 1975. Italy and Poland, in very different ways, continued to evince political unrest over a much more sustained period. The sources of unrest varied in Italy (for an overview, see Smith, 1997, pp. 455-497; McCarthy, 1995): Leftist student and factory worker upsurges and strikes; terror tactics from the ultra Right (see Ferraresi, 1996 (such as bombs in public places); terrorism from the Left (the Red Brigades' murder of premier Aldo Moro[2] in 1978 and of numerous policemen); Mafia terror (the murder of top police investigators, public critics, rivals); secret governments within the government and heavy-duty financial corruption (the P.2 scandal and the Vatican Bank[3]); the seemingly impending electoral victory of Western Europe's largest communist party (the PCI), and its corresponding alienation from the rebellious younger generation of Italians; the emergence of a wildly implausible government coalition for a short period in the 1990s, composed of three entirely new political agencies (a somewhat reformed neo-fascist party, a northern separatist party, and a new party headed by Berlusconi, Italy's media mega-entrepreneur, a man barely known until 10 years earlier).

Yet, despite the turmoil, Italy also enjoyed a remarkable core of social and economic stability, to the point where sometimes these dramatic events, screaming from banner headlines and endlessly chewed over on TV and in the press, could seem almost epiphenomenal. Italy's average living standards—which meant the rich north was really remarkably affluent—surpassed Britain's in the early 1980s. Perhaps the most striking change, at least in terms of Italians' frequent national self-understanding, was the switch during the second half of the century from being a nation that always exported its people to the United States and elsewhere in the Americas and Europe to being a nation that began by importing labor from its own poverty-stricken south to northern factories and then finally began to import workers from various African countries, south Asia, the Philippines, and elsewhere.[4] Within this complex mixture of change and stability, the three radical alternative media originated on which we will now focus. All three, however, were born at particularly intense points in political time and against a background of seemingly unending Christian Democratic Party rule, combined with the PCI's move to the Right—toward common sense for some, toward collaboration with a reactionary and archaic system for others.

IL MANIFESTO, ROME

On April 28, 1971, a new daily newspaper was launched, *Il Manifesto*,[5] selling for the absurdly low price of 50 lire. The first issue had only four pages, no advertisements, and uncompromising political analysis. In its first year, the newspaper sold 30,000 to 40,000 copies a day. Even given the weak national presence of the Italian daily press, this 1% share was still quite creditable. Moreover, *Il Manifesto*'s readers were activists.

The newspaper was founded by a group expelled from the communist party in 1969 for critiquing what they saw as the PCI's steady rightward drift. They were also pro-China rather than pro-Moscow in the split within the world communist movement at the time, albeit based on a false international image then current of China, where Mao's supposed encouragement of vigorous popular participation contrasted with the dour Soviet commitment to hierarchy. Some, but not all of its first staff members had journalistic experience. Their primary affiliation was with the splinter party they had formed when they were expelled from the PCI, the Party of Proletarian Unity, whose acronym was PdUP. This affiliation would lead to problems for the newspaper, as we shall shortly see.

Il Manifesto's internal organization set out to be democratic. Both the chief editor and a switchboard operator received the same miserably low salary, as did everyone else. Internal open meetings were held daily to review policy, so that specialists could hear alternative views before writing their columns. The printers, three floors down, were not part of the collective, for their communist party affiliations would have made this impractical in view of *Il Manifesto*'s split from the PCI. Predictably, however, despite good intentions, technical staff often felt less a part of the paper than the journalists, and from time to time women journalists, too, found themselves subtly excluded, sometimes by attitudes, but more often by structural factors. A key instance of the latter was the daily 7:30 p.m. production meeting: Women with children typically felt they had to be home before that hour—or were pressured by their husbands to be—and so they could not participate.

Over the 1970s, the newspaper's fortunes rose and fell with different political tides. However, with the explosion of the student movements of 1977 and 1978, and with the Red Brigades' kidnaping of Premier Moro, *Il Manifesto* found itself suddenly squeezed from numerous directions. For student revolutionaries, the paper was simply a minor variation on the PCI theme and part of an antirevolutionary edifice. For the PCI, it was unacceptable that the newspaper argued for negotiating Moro's release (on the ground that the terrorism problem was being used by the then government to frighten the public into sticking with a conservative law-and-order politics). Four national dailies mounted a campaign against *Il Manifesto,* claiming its stance was tantamount to a concealed argument in favor of terrorist tactics. PdUP's women members were deserting it in droves to join the feminist movement, which suddenly mushroomed at that time. And because the paper defined itself as PdUP's mouthpiece, on the Leninist transmission-belt model of party-controlled radical media, its journalists found they were permitted to critique any political stance in Italy *except* this small splinter party's.

Something had to give, and the chain binding the paper to PdUP was finally broken in 1979. This helped considerably, because it enabled *Il Manifesto* to become what its journalists mostly wanted it to be: a forum for the Left. The newspaper opened itself to a wide range of contributors, from an unknown caller reporting on a demonstration in a town in Sicily that no other media were covering through informed commentary on U.S. politics from a professor up north in Turin. In major cities, *Il Manifesto* organized members' groups whose activities were similarly ecumenical, and open national conferences were held on hot political topics. The newspaper was trying to develop a different and closer relation with its readers than was conventional with the press.

Il Manifesto's language and intellectual level, however, were very demanding. Although in 1981, it finally admitted photos, cartoons, and sports reports, it was still a tough read for anyone without a university degree. One whole page of an issue of the paper (in July 1980) was devoted to the French neo-Freudian Jacques Lacan and his relation to feminist theory. In early 1982, after heated debate, two pages were set aside daily for everyday issues and popular arts, but much of the paper continued to be rather hard going.

The years from 1983 through 1997 saw a series of shifts in *Il Manifesto*'s contribution to Italian life. The earlier years, during which conservative government policies seemed to be carrying all before them, were inevitably a rather dispiriting era for the newspaper. Its one major campaigning moment in those years came in response to the Craxi government's attack during 1984 and 1985 on *la scala mobile*. Literally meaning "the escalator," the term was used in Italy as political shorthand for the automatic indexing of wages and pensions, a major achievement of the 1970s that had been negotiated by the unions to offset consumer vulnerability to price inflation. In the end, Craxi won,[6] and the public's protections were indeed slashed, but *Il Manifesto* staffers who had been active in the campaign felt they had fought with intense energy and resolve. "It was a good fight, the right fight," said one.

However, the momentous chain of events that would eventually see the entire Soviet system dismantled in 1991 was also emerging at the same time. Gorbachev was installed as Soviet leader in 1985 and by 1986 was beginning to call a halt to the war in Afghanistan and to negotiate nuclear disarmament with the West. By 1988, there were pronounced signals of a growing openness in certain Moscow-based print media. This openness, in turn, gave space to increasingly insistent demands for national independence, both in the Soviet republics and in some of the Eastern European nations within the Soviet bloc.

These developments would have very disturbing effects on the newspaper's self-definition, not least as a result of the PCI's decision—following the Soviet bloc's collapse—to retitle itself the Party of the Democratic Left. Even then *Il Manifesto*'s general line was as follows: Gorbachev was the urgently needed reformer who would purify the Soviet system and bestow on it—or unleash within it, it was not clear—a new energy and moral force that would change the global political equation to the pronounced disadvantage of much of capitalism's fundamental dynamic. In other words, their view and Gorbachev's own perceptions of his role were very much in sync.[7] This meant, however, that the reports coming from their own correspondent in Moscow were often most unwelcome, to the point of leading to many queries about his information. Sometimes, a dual definition of Soviet realities appeared in the newspaper, one in the stories he filed, the other in the political commentary columns. The correspondent's stories indicated with ever-increasing clarity that Gorbachev was losing his ability to lead a more and more disgruntled Soviet public, which was angered and frustrated by the decline in living standards and the economic disruption generated by *perestroika* policies. This messy situation did not fit with the leading editorial staff's preferred view of things. It was a disquieting omen of the difficulty the newspaper might have in coming to terms with some admittedly seismic political changes.[8]

During the middle and later 1980s, the newspaper chugged along with about 30,000 to 35,000 daily circulation. Two events in the first half of the 1990s, however, lifted its fortunes briefly, and it found itself selling 65,000 to 70,000 copies daily for certain periods of time. *Il Manifesto* took on a considerable number of extra staff, totaling about 160 at the peak, and to its surprise switched from being what one staffer called an "artisanal" newspaper to becoming a moderately substantial—and therefore much more complex and necessarily businesslike—operation. At this time, *Il Manifesto* was among the first daily newspapers in Italy to computerize its operations. (This expansion and its problematic implications will be reviewed below.)

The events that stimulated these changes in fortune were the 1990-1991 war against Iraq by the United States and its allies[9] and the 1994 ascent to power of the new coalition between the separatist Northern League, media magnate Berlusconi's Forza Italia, and Alleanza Nazionale (heir to a neo-fascist party). *Il Manifesto* was the single Italian newspaper that denounced the second Gulf war in unequivocal terms, whereas the rest of the major media were offering a Hallelujah chorus in support. This meant that its information and critiques of the war were the only national source of genuinely dissonant information.

The government coalition only lasted about 6 months, but during that time, its most insistent media opponent was *Il Manifesto.* The heart of its opposition was directed at the participation in government of Alleanza Nazionale, which it defined as effectively a resurrection of Mussolini (symbolically, even the dictator's granddaughter ran for office in Naples). The newspaper organized a huge antifascist demonstration in Milan on April 25, the 50th anniversary of Mussolini's execution by the Partisans and their public display of his body in Milan's Piazzale Loreto.

Thereafter, however, the newspaper's fortunes began to subside again, with a 2-year period from 1995 through 1997 during which the newspaper was being subsidized by *cassa integrazione* funds.[10] This culminated in a deep crisis in the summer of 1997, when the Banca di Roma refused to extend further credit without either a major new infusion of cash or substantial firings. Because the former option was unfeasible, the firings were the only recourse. For a newspaper that had organized itself as a collective for 26 years, this was an extremely bitter prospect. Long-time staffers found the situation intensely depressing and very alarming, too: Few of their numbers could automatically assume they would be exempt from whatever cuts would have to be made.

The newspaper's procedure in handling this crisis is important to note, because the quality of a collectively run media enterprise is not only determined by what it does at the outset or in periods of success but also—and perhaps especially—by how it copes over time with crisis and the threat of collapse.

Two general assembly meetings were called, held in the morning so as not to interfere with the production of the newspaper, to discuss how to proceed. These were composed of journalists and technical workers, following *Il Manifesto*'s traditions. Each meeting stretched over 2 days, and both were more heavily attended by technicians than by journalists, probably because the former felt more vulnerable to cost-cutting measures. The second meeting was held to ratify the decisions taken by the first. Few attended second time around, probably because the first meeting had already approved two motions with 72% approval from those present. In general, discussion at these meetings was far less energetic than had been the case in earlier years.

The two motions were to institute a specific program of cuts in positions, totaling up to 40, and to set up a union committee to oversee the needs and situations faced by those cut. The union committee (*comitato di redazione*) was standard in other newspapers, but the *Il Manifesto* collective had always hoped that the management-labor divide could be avoided within its own ranks. Equally, the fact that the new management board would be composed of two journalists and two technical workers, elected in each case only by their peers, represented another retreat from the collective's steady attempt to elide, where possible, those professional differences.

There was considerable agreement among those with whom I spoke about a number of the causes of *Il Manifesto*'s decline and critical situation. In particular, two were singled out as major factors, one the general crisis of the Italian daily press and the other the protracted confusion of the Italian political system in transition. Some staffers, however, pointed further to internal organizational issues within the newspaper,[11] others to what they felt were issues of the newspaper's problematic identity and inadequate attempts to resolve it.

It was certainly true that the situation of the Italian daily press had gotten considerably worse in the 1980s and 1990s. By 1997, to try to persuade a reluctant public[12] to read its products, the mainstream newspaper industry was offering a whole series of "gadgets," as the Italians themselves named them, from cheap videos to special glossy fashion supplements, and from CDs to pocket-size short stories by famous authors (Maupassant, Dostoevsky). These came with the newspaper, sometimes costing as much or more than the actual paper itself. The fact that the industry had opted for this approach and was busily competing to see which gadgets would offer the greatest inducement to readers already proved that daily newspapers were uninteresting to the Italian public. This situation, however, made it all the harder for *Il Manifesto,* which did not have the corporate backing to issue all these incentives. *Il Manifesto* was typically the second newspaper that people bought, and the extra gadget cost of the first paper would often soak up the lire otherwise available for that purchase.

As regards the transition in Italian politics from the relative postwar stability of permanent Christian Democrat dominance and PCI challenge, it was unclear how the Italian government would be organized in the future, but it seemed certain that it would not revert to the old system just as it had been.[13] For *Il Manifesto,* the difficulty was acute. It had always been a sympathetic critic of the PCI, it had argued during the debate over renaming the PCI that it should hold on to its original name, and the paper still enshrined the word *communist* on its own masthead. With whom could it align itself, in an era when the PDS seemed to be competing with the British Labor Party ("New Labor") for the title of which, among traditional European parties of the Left, could be named the most dedicated convert to free-market policies?

The newspaper's traditional political space had simply closed up. The original parties of the Left had moved to the Center Right, whereas their effective alternative was represented in one way or another by the parties of the Berlusconi coalition. Only *Communist Refoundation,* offering the comforting reassurances of the pre-1989 scenario and a classical transmission-belt newspaper[14] to the surviving faithful, was to be seen on the Left. What is more, from having been a newspaper principally identified in the public mind with campaigns as a mobilizing newspaper, *Il Manifesto* was now being forced to re-evaluate that role, along with its inherited internal culture.

I was told that the roots of the political problem lay very deep, buried, indeed, in the perspective of the senior staff on the significance of the Gorbachev phenomenon, which was discussed previously. If the future politics of the planet indeed had lain with a reformed Soviet system and the flourishing of relatively independent Marxist parties committed to democracy, such as the old PCI, then the long-term heretical role of *Il Manifesto* would have been sealed with history's approval.

Such was not to be the case. Nor was it, perhaps, to be the case that a visceral appeal to antifascist sentiment (represented by the April 25 Milan march), to admittedly well-founded fears and memories, would be sufficient to respond effectively to the new political trends represented by a largely converted party of the traditional ultra Right (Alleanza Nazionale), a party fusing tremendous media power with political power (Berlusconi), or a separatist party led by frothing racist demagogues but drawing its support from within sectors infuriated by the effects of overcentralized government (the Northern League).

How was the newspaper to respond? How was it to secure a committed readership among the younger intelligentsia? How was it to carve out a role for itself, in the midst of downsizing and within the general collapse of enthusiasm for the daily press in Italy? Some respondents felt that attempts had been made, although they disagreed about their effectiveness, to address this: the launch of the tabloid format of the paper in 1994; the failed attempt to launch a weekly special for younger readers, *Extra,* which was put out in extravagantly postmodernist computer screen format; or the intermittent graphics and layout changes in the main newspaper.

A critic of these attempts described them as obsessive but superficial, failing to grapple either with the actual interests of a younger readership or with the deep implications of the collapse of Sovietism and its ramifications within the Italian political spectrum or with the new realities represented by Berlusconi or the Northern League. In this view, *Il Manifesto* had never acted as a forum for readers and correspondents to debate the significance of these tumultuous and perplexing developments. Instead, it had sought to give its readers wise political guidance, not far removed, perhaps, from the traditional desire to provide them with the correct line. Was the problem, as other staffers suggested, that their "bishops"—the nucleus of former PCI heretics who had founded the newspaper—were still overly dominant in its policies and direction.

In some ways, a poster and T-shirt published at the time of the 1994 switch to tabloid format, with the aim of publicizing it, may suggest a part of the problem that was still to be addressed at the core of the *Il Manifesto* project. It showed a smiling baby's face and by its side the words, *La rivoluzione non russa,* a wordplay that signified both "The non-Russian revolution" and "The revolution is not snoring." The question left in abeyance by this major attempt at self-redefinition—a large version of the poster was still hanging at the main entrance to the offices in summer 1997—was how far the discourse of revolution, any discourse of revolution, Russian or not, snoring or not, still had any purchase on the Italian public's deepest aspirations, hopes, or fears. Was *Il Manifesto* in danger of having to supply to the public the key questions as well as the answers? Would a tabloid format, as such, have a profound impact? (Journalists always attribute far more significance to layout changes than do their readers.) Would not a baby be, unfortunately, a rather witless and naive, even cheap expression of the rising generation?

Bringing together (a) a sustained attack on neoliberal dogma and its destructive policy impact with (b) a nuanced, exploratory probing of new modes of political life and cultural expression would probably fill a rather large niche in Italian media production. It would certainly be of interest to the youthful intelligentsia who were the key to *Il Manifesto*'s future. A final comment on a further aspect of *Il Manifesto* is in order. Over its lifespan, the newspaper had also acted as a training school for numerous future journalists who could have gotten their professional seasoning in no other way. In the process, seeing not only the downside of internal democracy but also its many pluses, their eyes were permanently opened to alternative possibilities for organizing media.

RADIO POPOLARE (PEOPLE'S RADIO)

This station was started in 1976 by a group of five people then working at one of Milan's first socialist stations, Radio Milano Centrale. Characteristically for Radio Popolare, called Radiopop, they worked carefully to prepare the project for practically a year before setting it in motion. The five had grown increasingly restive at the continual encroachment of PCI domination over Radio Milano Centrale. They were committed from the start to enabling everyone on the Left to communicate with each other—hence the station's name.

Their preparation had involved discussions with both the PCI and the socialist party as the two major parties in Milan's city council. Each of the parties had representatives on the station's board. This early determination to have a satisfactory relationship with the immediate realities of official politics in Milan undoubtedly contributed to the station's initial positive image in the city. The mainstream parties were not attacking it as a juvenile ultra-leftist project and, indeed, were among its political sponsors. Very fortunately, too, for Radio Popolare, the parties never made any attempt to colonize it, as they had consistently done with state broadcasting.

There was also a degree of stability of personnel at the station. Although the five original organizers had all left by 1980, 9 out of the 11 full-timers in summer 1980 had been involved from the moment the station had actually gone on the air. Possibly, the regular payment of salaries had something to do with this: In summer 1980, every full-timer, including the technician, received 350,000 lire a month. This was hardly a princely sum—especially if its quite frequent nonarrival 2 months out of 12 is taken into account—but all the same, such compensation was quite uncharacteristic of the other independent leftist stations. Also, the collective's method of handling wages during financial difficulties was to pay those most in need first, the degree of need being established as best as could be by collective discussion.

Milan, sometimes called the capital of the north in Italy, is a city with the wide range of economic activities that characterize the average metropolis. It is neither a cultural center like Venice and Florence nor a city dominated by a single industry like Turin. Factory and office labor, professionals and businesses, the university, fashionable and spacious neighborhoods, grayer and tougher quarters, air pollution during the winter months leading to heavy fogs—all these combine to make Milan a city similar in its ambience to a large number of northern European cities. Its political culture is and was definitely to the Left, however.

Radiopop was and is situated not far from the famous Piazzale Loreto where Mussolini's body was displayed after his execution. In 1980, the station was on a side-street in a row house that it occupied entirely. Inside, furnishings were functional at best. Soundproofing in the studios was homemade, consisting of cheap curtain material draped around the walls and ceilings. The premises were distinctly crowded, with members of the collective having to edge past each other in the tiny studios as one program drew to a close and the next program's producers came to take up their places at the microphones. By 1997, Radiopop had moved to larger premises in the same neighborhood, and its technical fittings had been considerably upgraded.

The unique feature of Radiopop from the very outset was its members' determination to enable the socialist public to communicate with itself. Their first elected director, Biagio Longo, had expressed this goal in an article in the journal *aut aut* in 1978:

> [For us, what is crucial is] the recognition that the class, the proletarian masses, are never the same thing as the organizations and even the movements in which they express themselves from time to time. We refuse to reduce the multiplicity, the richness, the diversity of people's perspectives . . . (not) flattening them into a mono-language, and without dispersing them into ghettoized or colonized spaces. (pp. 24-25)

This shows clearly the distinctive character of Radiopop as a project: its attempt to encourage and develop a lateral communication outside the existing channels of communication that regularly separate people into social categories of sex, age, party membership, political activism, educational background, and the rest. To develop people's capacity to communicate on a mass level across these barriers, neither accepting the barriers as inevitable nor denying their existence, is indeed fundamental.

The usual criticisms leveled by the far Left against Radiopop were twofold. The first was that it had lost its ability to attack the city government, because of its desire not to alienate members of the parties that ran the city. The second objection was that Radiopop was gradually becoming a little institution, developing its own professional journalists who could then claim the right to interpret reality for the rest of us: "to choose what slice of reality to put first, to decide which protagonists to consider," as Longo put it in summarizing this accusation.

Radiopop's reaction to these charges was that they were preconceived and schematic. The station pointed to its involvement in numerous Milan campaigns involving abortion rights, compulsory military service, and factory issues. The clarity critics professed to enjoy about the key struggles and who was leading them, or what was the next phase of the revolutionary movement, was bogus. Who could claim unerring insight into these matters? Yet, if Radiopop were to become simply the voice of one or more groups, it would effectively be claiming this bogus clarity for itself.

The Radiopop *compagni* insisted, however, that to accuse them of that kind of negative "professionalism" blurred certain vital issues. Their argument was as follows: It is a hollow pretense to claim that radio workers should or can be exactly the same people as those involved in struggles in the community or at work—in the terms used on the Left in Italy then, the "subjects of information" and the "subjects of struggle" must become the same individuals. The only way to approach the real distinction between people who operate a radio station and those who are active in particular campaigns, they argued, is to be honest about it: "to make this contradiction clear as a means of controlling it," as Longo (1978, p. 20) put it in his article.

Second, constant instant access to the airwaves for those involved in particular struggles means the station becomes identified as only concerned with those particular sections of the public. The station ceases to be a forum for the widest possible spectrum. Furthermore, not to recognize that unpaid people at the core of a radio station are always those with the time, energy, and interest to be involved—and perhaps, financial support from their families—presupposes that radio activists automatically represent "the people." Yet, again and again in its early days, Radiopop found it was recruiting its activists from the same pool: young people and students. In no way did immediacy guarantee representativeness.

Third, the practical results of immediacy, spontaneity, and lack of professionalism were a habit of muddling through the day's programming, confusion and ignorance about how to program, and an ever tighter circle of mutually reinforcing station activists, despite an avowed commitment to open access.

The use of language was an important dimension of this issue for Radiopop, distinguishing it from *Il Manifesto*. Fofi (1978) wrote on the station's policy in its early days, contrasting it with the briefly famous Radio Alice in Bologna. His basic point was that the Radio Alice collective could easily identify the subject of struggle with the subject of information exactly because, in their case, the contributors and the listeners came from precisely the same narrow social band. As he put it, the strength of Alice's language was that it could be

> richer and fresher, because it is the language of a particular cultural and social stratum, which is created and invented every day . . . [though] the risk is of creating a ghetto communication that is not concerned to speak with "the others," but [with] only its peers. (p. 48)

His comments on Radiopop are lengthy but informative:

> [Radiopop's] network of "informers," contacts, listening points, while not perfect, has guaranteed an interchange between informers and informed, between transmitters and receivers, which has no equivalent in any communication initiative in postwar Italy. . . . It is clear that Radio Popolare's language is less innovative, given its problems of mediating, that it does not require liberated invention and creativity, but the discovery of a median language, because the ordinary person and the worker do not, or do not yet, speak the same language as the kids in the clubs, or the student, or the feminist. . . . What is taking place is the fruit of a process of cultural exchange, following on the class redefinitions of which we are part, an exchange constructed inside the class, where the stably employed and the unstably employed have the possibility of speaking and listening to each other in turn. (Fofi, 1978, p. 48)

Equally significant is the use of imaginative material in programming. Any discussion of communication democracy that omits this dimension omits the fact that the democratic subjects themselves are flesh and blood, not concrete and steel; that they have feelings, fantasies and fears, humor and pain. The discussions in the first two parts of this book about art, performance art, situationism, street theater, satire, song, and dance all serve to underscore the significance of this issue. Straight political news always risks becoming simply a hobby, elevated to be sure, but still a hobby, not a mission.

As of the mid-1990s, the imaginative dimension—described by one activist as *radiofonica* rather than journalism—was alive and well in Radiopop, although still struggling for space with the hard news types. Satire was a quite popular program feature. One instance was a Sunday program called "Bar Sport," first begun in 1984, which poked fun at typical conversations between sports fans. Another took on TV programs: For example, in one case, a song contest was held regarding a program with material that was notoriously full of schlock; viewers were invited to turn the sound down on their TV sets and listen to parodies of the songs broadcast simultaneously from Radiopop (the station's everyday name). In 1994, 100,000 people attended a maxi-screen Bar Sport event centered on the soccer World Cup. This *Mystery Science Theater 3000* style was used to considerable effect over the years in a variety of programs.

Music programming was another area of importance, although it took rather different paths at Radiopop than at commercial radio stations. As of 1997, the station was a sufficiently strong presence on the music scene to be able to get musicians and bands passing through Milan to give live studio performances. The plan for 1998 was to try to devote a half hour every day to a live performance, from improvised acoustic guitar to African groups to rock, or to a live interview with a musician. The programming by then was very diverse: "World music" was certainly very strong, but there was also a lively European classical music program, and the station had steered a path into rock music without—as some of its staff initially deeply feared—becoming a prisoner of the record companies.

Marina Petrillo, one of the two coproducers of the weekday show, "Patchanka,"[15] which ran from 2 to 3:30 p.m. daily, explained her programming strategy as an attempt to "widen the landscape" for younger listeners in particular. Political issues delivered straight from the shoulder constituted pretty "heavy luggage" for the contemporary audience. Introducing them via music was much more likely, in her view, to develop a questioning attitude. It was pointless complaining that younger audiences were not articulating themselves within the discourse adhered to by the 1968 generation. The issue was to start from where they were.

In Petrillo's strategy, this meant devoting special programs to the music in films such as *Dead Man Walking* to provoke discussion of issues such as capital punishment. It also meant analyzing all the current trends of rock music and including in this a discussion of cartoons, books, video games, fashion, comics, the cinema, the whole gamut of rock culture. "An easy song can lead to a heavy issue," said Petrillo, both summarizing her approach and simultaneously chiding the sector of Radiopop's audience that wanted the station simply to reaffirm its own long-honed political instincts. "Let's just help people develop their own critical skills for a commercial world," she concluded, underlining that too much talk on the airwaves alienated young people.

Radiopop's journalistic function and its more generic cultural function did have a mildly competitive relationship with each other. In the view of the news staff, the journalistic function represented the station's most heavy-duty contribution.[16] From this section, a significant proportion of the staff had been able to move into mainstream media, using the station in part—not necessarily instrumentally—as their training ground. Those who used radio rather as a popular art form, who were entranced by its technical possibilities rather than seeing it as a convenient tool for journalism, were sometimes regarded by news staffers as contributing but not as the station's backbone. The technical and creative staff tended to have less career mobility, with more of a commitment over the long haul to the Radiopop project.

Too much should not be made of this division in analyzing the station. It is simply an honest reflection of the way in which cultural divisions will emerge in political projects of this and other types. The division is considerably less damaging than the contemptuous tendency visible in a number of these media, around the time of my 1980 research, to write off the administrative and financial staff's work as tedious stuff fit only for drones with no balls. Or for women.

Three further dimensions of Radiopop will be addressed now: its finances, women's roles in the station, and the station's relation to the city's public.

Radiopop's Finances

The question of finances will be subdivided for the present purpose into financial structure and advertising/programming software policies. As of 1990, Radiopop had adopted a new corporate status. From 1983 through 1990, it had been an unusual type of limited liability company, owned 50% by political parties and labor unions and 50% by the staff and registered members of the station cooperative. The change took place to put party and union influence at a greater remove, and so, all political bodies were limited to a collective maximum of 15% share ownership, the station cooperative to 35%, and individual listeners invited to buy into the remaining 50%. As of 1997, these latter totaled 13,000 people, some of them owning just a single share, some larger numbers. (Annual donations were also provided by 12,000 listeners, many of them also shareholders.) Besides raising needed money, the purpose was to give the listeners a tangible sense of a stake in the station and its community of listeners.[17]

Radiopop's adaptation of advertising and program management software makes for a particularly interesting story.[18] At standard commercial radio stations, it was normal by the mid-1990s to have software programs installed to ensure that commercial breaks took place on a set schedule; disk jockeys or producers were compelled to conform strictly. Radiopop sought and managed to achieve a modified package, warning that ads would interrupt the programming automatically in 5 minutes' time unless a moment for the "commercial break" was selected before then. The difference in philosophy is clear: For the commercial stations, ads took absolute priority; for Radiopop, the contents and the pacing of the programs took priority. Suggesting the iron laws of commercialized communication priorities, the company technicians selling the software had considerable difficulty in coming to terms with Radiopop's request to adapt it in this way. Not that the operation was particularly complex. It simply did not seem to make sense.

The station met with similar bafflement in regard to the musical program management software it wanted. Again, at a standard commercial station, the software package gives the executive music programmer total control over which tracks are played and which are replayed. This enables a tight relationship to be realized between the record companies and the station, to the probable commercial advantage of both, but to the disadvantage of fresh (as opposed to merely new) music, especially if produced by small labels. Radiopop, by contrast, wanted each of its program producers to retain autonomy in this sphere. The software company's technicians simply could not believe their ears, and seriously supposed they had misunderstood the request.

Women at Radiopop

The story of women at Radiopop is illuminating. At the beginning of the 1980s, although women were involved full-time and part-time, they did not constitute a power bloc but participated as individuals. Many more had been involved in 1977 and 1978, with numerous programs on women and work, women and culture, women and health, and other themes, most of which had been organized by a separate women's collective within the station. Then, the number of women involved had shrunk, for a range of reasons including practical personal problems, switching to better paid media work, or simply experiencing exhaustion. Also, separatism had disappeared as a major feature of the

Italian women's movement by the early 1980s. One part-timer said the men had had time by 1980 to adjust to feminist perspectives and that the real difference within the *compagni* was between those committed to personal politics and those more committed to external politics, rather than between men and women as such. In the collective's discussions on personal politics, there was often much more tension in the air than on the external realm.

As regards other forms of women's participation, the mid-morning "open microphone" program each day attracted many telephone contributions from women, most of them young, often housewives or teachers and much more rarely women factory workers. The other point at which basic feminist politics tended to surface was during the nighttime music and phone-ins, when the station was at its most spontaneous. Feminist politics was not a burning issue inside the collective in 1980. There were no policy discussions on women, although those on youth were frequent. In 1981, however, with two national referenda being organized on the question of abortion, one by Catholic activists and the other by the radical party representing only a moderately pro-abortion position, the issue constituted a prominent topic in phone-ins and in programming. Radiopop declared itself against both positions, although especially vigorously against the Catholic "Movement for Life."

As of the mid-1990s, the situation seemed rather similar. A younger staff member with whom I spoke felt that it would be mistaken to devote too much attention to the persistence of gender issues within the station. This was, she said, because the station had been through the mill of many of the passions and contradictions of feminist movements in the 1970s and early 1980s. By the early 1990s, women staffers had come to feel that some of the positions staked out in those fights had become self-caricatures, and the women had begun to distance themselves somewhat from the sharper positions taken earlier. Men staffers had also felt "in their own skin" the onslaught of the feminists within the station and had matured in some cases in the process.

By 1997, the program staff composition was more or less evenly balanced overall between men and women. The evening show from 5 to 9 p.m. was produced by a team of six, three of each gender. About a third of the directors were women. However, some of these more optimistic signs concealed what were, we might hope, transitional problems. For example, women were much less evident in the news section. Furthermore, a number had been at the station from its early days, when its professionalism was less in evidence, and thus had much less technical training. This meant their ability to carry out certain functions was limited, and they often found themselves more or less confined within the station, not getting out to do the interviews or other assignments.[19]

One particular episode had demonstrated the complexities of the station's transition on gender issues. National elections had been approaching, and three men staffers were chosen to run the live coverage. A huge debate broke out in the station around the question of why it was that women staffers were not thought worthy of contributing to this high-profile, high-status special program. Conceivably, the issue had mixed causes: the less developed professional profile of some women staffers, the enduring gender assumptions of some men staffers, and maybe in particular, an unexamined, rather smug assumption that politically correct attitudes somehow "must" obtain within a highly politicized station such as Radiopop; as a result, there was no call for people to question themselves.

In the end, one woman who had substantial technical training was placed on the election coverage team. She felt that she was being selected more to take the sting out of an internal row than to acknowledge her technical skills, which were perfectly well known at the time of the original selection. Being singled out this way, she also felt some concerns for the other women, although they all talked it through with each other, and the women staffers supported her taking part. It was a contested, although not an epochal event, which demonstrated the ongoing dilemmas of working out gender equity, even within a radical collective that on many levels was committed to taking these matters very seriously.

Radiopop and Milan's Publics

From its original mission of trying to provide a forum for the city's leftist publics, *Radiopop* further evolved to a goal of trying to provide what its director as of 1997, Marcello Lorrai, termed a "radio community." In the Milan of 1976, with a quite strongly interconnected public on the Left, that community already existed, even if it was often divided by varying visions of the path to socialism. Twenty years later, Milan had much less of that texture and felt much more atomized to those of its inhabitants who remembered earlier decades. In the new context, providing a community linked, in the first instance, by its members' habit of listening to the station, represented an interesting second phase of the station's contribution to the city's life. As of early 1994, Popolare Network's weekly listening audience stood at over 1.25 million.

This radio community was more than simply a metaphor for a radio-listening habit. Several different examples illustrate how.

For instance, the station organized a number of events in the city every year to which its listeners came in considerable numbers. One was Border Trophy (the English words were used), which consisted of a city-wide treasure hunt in which players formed small groups to take part.

Another, in place since 1986, was Extrafesta, a play on the words *festa* (festival), *extra* (extraordinary, special), and *extracomunitari* community outsiders), the official terminology to denote immigrants.[20] Extrafesta was a 2-day celebration of immigrants and their cultures, including popular music concerts, cosmopolitan foods, and other aspects of the international presence in Milan. The festival's slogan, coined in conscious opposition to the waves of racist hostility that emerged in Italy during the 1980s, was, "No one in my country is a foreigner."[21] Community, in other words, did not stop with Italian-origin *milanesi.*

Indeed, beginning in 1980, the station ran a weekly Arabic-language program, Radio Shabi, the only station in Milan to offer such an opportunity to North African and Middle Eastern migrants. Sergio Ferrentino, long active in the station, said that Radiopop was the closest thing Milan had to an immigrants' radio station, offering them a voice in several different ways.

Like Controradio, Radiopop was also particularly active in the youth music scene. More than any other agency in the city, it was responsible for bringing world music artists to public attention, first in Milan and, on occasion, in all of Italy. The internationally acclaimed Senegalese singer Youssou N'dor was only one example of the station's record in this regard. The station also cosponsored the production of world music CDs. But, the concerts it helped organize were also places in which community was built, and a community built on a wider sense of cultural connectivity than a purely traditional, local community.[22] Other interesting dimensions of the station's development through the 1980s and into the 1990s included the development of the Popolare Network, which initially included some seven other stations, and its use of satellites.

The network began in 1992. Its founding members were Radiopop and the alternative stations in Brescia, Verona, Conegliano, Venice, Bologna, Florence (Controradio, which is discussed below) and Rome. By

1996, stations had been added in Turin, Mestre (replacing Venice), Bolzano (two stations), Arezzo, Vicenza, Genova, Taranto, Trento, Pescara, Piacenza, Savignano, and Crema. Some of these stations were very active and even did repeater-broadcasts on a variety of local frequencies in different communities nearby. Others were much simpler operations.

Also in 1994, to improve the signal from and to these stations, Radiopop switched out of traditional land-line communication and leased some transponder time on Eutelsat II. From time to time, this was used for a quasi-national open-microphone program, especially in conjunction with the Bologna and the Rome stations. Every weekday, the programs from 6 to 8:40 a.m. were always broadcast by satellite, as were news bulletins varying between 10 and 20 minutes in length at six other points in the day. On weekends, only news bulletins were aired using the satellite.[23] As of 1996, a couple of stations in Monaco and Innsbruck began pulling down some programs.

To close out on Radiopop, it should be said that there was a very clear split between the station's reputation, which according to Ferrentino became stronger and stronger the further away from Milan people were, and the quite often ruthless self-criticism that was common inside the station itself. "The trouble is," he observed with a touch of humor, "that often our brutally honest self-criticism does not seem to get to solving our problems."

CONTRORADIO, FLORENCE

Until the end of 1980, Controradio (Counter-radio) was located in a narrow street quite a distance away from the tourist centers and expensive shops that make up the visitor's image of Florence. Entrance to the radio station was through a bare hallway and up some well-used stairs. The station occupied three rooms, none of them large. Decor and furnishings were at a minimum, and the studio itself was soundproofed with sheets of black plastic and egg boxes nailed into the wall. By 1997, the station had moved to a rather large house, also well away from the city center. At that time, Controradio was probably the most securely established of the three radical media in this study.

Controradio began its life in 1975. Initially, the station was directly tied to the organization, Lotta Continua,[24] seeing itself as a local radio equivalent of the newspaper. The Florence Lotta Continua group continued, even after the national organization dissolved itself in 1976, to use the newspaper *Lotta Continua* as its central reference point, reading news bulletins directly from it, as though it was the most authoritative source of news and political commentary in Italy. However, it became increasingly difficult to maintain this relationship with the newspaper alone, particularly given the paper's relative weakness as a news source on issues outside youth movements, women's movements, and student movements in Italy. But perhaps the final push toward independent development for Controradio was the weekly newspaper *Lotta Continua*'s own move toward a pluralism of the Left after the organization's collapse in 1976.

In 1977, the station hit the national news in Italy, accused by the right-wing daily, *La Nazione*, of being the headquarters of urban guerrilla warfare in Florence. The accusation was made during a period of media paranoia about student upsurges in Rome and Bologna. Police swooped into the station and made off with some supposedly incriminating tapes, but nothing ever came of the whole affair. The incident was dramatic but not at all revealing of the station's actual political role then or since. By 1980, the station no longer saw itself as one link in a national revolutionary strategy coordinated from any central point. Its politics were still to the Left, but it had redefined its place in the revolutionary process—and, indeed, had redefined that process itself. One of its members defined three established routes for former movement activists in Italy: joining the left wing of the PCI, joining a terrorist group, and surrendering to political apathy. Controradio, he said, was struggling to create a fourth path—a path without existing models, except the negative models of American "free" radio stations, and perhaps the positive models of northern Europe's social democratic politics.

The Controradio collective at that time did not see itself as a party or a group but defined its task as being a facilitator, putting the radio at the disposal of Florence's public to express itself, as Radiopop did in Milan. The station also adopted the same shift toward a new professionalism. Back at the height of the 1977-1978 movements, Controradio policy had been to open the microphone to anyone on the Left who wanted to say anything. This had led to a serious degree of disorganization on the radio, particularly when the decline of those movements and the end of the novelty of democratic radio stations meant that fewer people were anxious to communicate by radio. The result had been that music had come to dominate the station's output, simply because it was the easiest way to run the station on an ad hoc basis. If a yawning gap opened up, they could always put on a record. And then another, and then another.

This drift began to provoke intense discussion within the Controradio collective on the practical implications of their policy. The eventual outcome of these discussions was that they rejected once and for all the notion that the radio was simply an empty box to be filled with anything or everything. It also meant that once having defined themselves as information activists, they were bound to make decisions about whether they agreed with the political perspectives and practical abilities of the people who came to them with a project for broadcast communication. The project might be excellent, but the necessary experience to realize it successfully might well be lacking.

The collective was not establishing itself as a little clique. Although it had a core of 10 full-timers and 15 part-timers, a considerable number of other people also worked with Controradio on a variety of short-term and long-term projects. Each morning was given over to the open-microphone phone-in program, where listeners could and did express their views spontaneously. The station also took considerable time and trouble to help people use the medium effectively.

Financial Issues

In 1980, however, Controradio had put itself in a position of overwhelming financial dependence on the Florence Socialist Party. This relationship, entailing considerable political dependence, did not lead to the station's prospering. It was still very much a "politics-in-command" station. By the latter part of 1982, the station was teetering toward collapse, and indeed, it closed down, bankrupt, for 2 weeks in November of that year. Some members paid off the debts, and the station was reestablished as a limited liability company. It then re-opened, with a different mandate, remaining open 24 hours a day through the end of the 1990s.

This is not to say that nirvana has reigned ever since. There was a particularly traumatic, quite protracted battle within the station in 1986. Three staffers, active within the station, attempted over an extended period of time to agitate to have the station taken over by a Florence businessman (whose paychecks they already were covertly accepting in addition to their Controradio salaries). In immediate financial terms, the proposition was not unattractive, potentially offering stability and higher salaries for those retained under the projected new management. The conflict raged on, but eventually, the offer was rejected, and the three left the station.

This was a battle for the station's soul. Controradio had made a definitive decision as of the crisis of its closing in 1982 that it would run itself on advertising income or not at all.[25] Its commercial direction, then, was not at issue. At the heart of the struggle was whether that was to be all. Controradio's distinctive mix was to maintain financial stability based on commercial realities and a clearly defined organizational hierarchy, but to combine that structure with socially conscious programming. Mario Bufono, the director, described it as "generically progressive, but completely un-ideological." Controradio had always had an especially strong track record with young people, and it was not prepared to risk that role in the life of the city by signing itself over to an individual entrepreneur.

Perhaps the most interesting issue to address about the remodeled Controradio is how these dual imperatives of commercial success and social commitment were handled. Organizationally, the advertising staff and the programming staff, although on perfectly good terms individually, maintained an arm's length relationship. This meant that if a program was being prepared that would in some way be likely to annoy a given advertiser, it was the program makers' responsibility to inform the advertising department in a timely fashion—but not to negotiate program contents in any way. This gave the advertising department a chance, if it chose, to initiate contact with the advertiser to maintain a good working relationship with them. But that was all. Some advertisers were lost as a result.

The advertising staff's comment on this situation is interesting. On balance, argued Marco Imponente, these intermittent confrontations actually helped the station. They extended its credibility with its listeners and even generated a measure of public trust among more casual listeners. In turn, that contributed to listener loyalty and served the station well over the longer term. During the 1986 conflict, the station's advertising profile became much less clearly defined for a while as a result of the tight relationship pursued by the three "fifth column"[26] staffers with the would-be owner. In Imponente's view, Controradio had suffered a temporary decline in listener confidence as a result. After that experience, said Sara Maggi, a long-time station activist, it was resolved never again to become dependent on any one advertiser.

Controradio served a particular niche in the market, namely, young people, most of them 14 to 30 years old. Often, those who advertised most were discos or record companies whose products had a special youth appeal.[27] Yet, even the larger record companies, which often pursue aggressive tactics to promote their wares in both radio stations and record stores, were well aware that for their purposes, Controradio was a pivotal outlet to young people in Florence—not excluding the many young tourists and temporary students from abroad who populate the city virtually 12 months of the year. For this reason, the station found itself less at the mercy of these firms than is often the case. Indeed, Controradio's advertising rates were actually higher than those of a number of its competitors in the city. Even the Chamber of Commerce was keen to advertise with the station.

At the beginning of the 1990s, the station canceled its contract with an advertising broker on the ground that its specific market needs were being insufficiently targeted. Along with similar stations such as Radiopop, Controradio set out to develop its own advertising chain contract, based on the needs of the stations in the Popolare Network. By mid 1997, this process was largely computerized, and by then, the network could offer advertisers up to 20 stations, nearly all in the affluent center and north of the country.

Controradio's technical base had also been upgraded with these funds, with the result that its programs could now be heard as far away as Pisa and Livorno, and—importantly during the summer months—on the coast as well, where the station held the No. 2 spot in that period of the year. Only two counties in Tuscany province were out of of its range.[28]

Examples of Controradio's social responsibility would include its coverage of issues of racism and of police violence against young people. At intervals in the later 1980s, sudden outbursts of racist violence in Florence targeted small communities of migrants from Africa, who were often concentrated in street selling. These attacks were not encouraged by the power structure, except by one particularly virulent Florence city councilman. At the same time, the violence did reflect one current of Tuscan opinion. Controradio decided to report directly from Piazza Fiorentina, the site of one particular outbreak, and to set up interviews and discussions in the square among those affected by the violence and their supporters. The station even invited the councilman to air his views, with the intention of letting the public know clearly what it was for which he stood.

Influence With Listeners

The general public response was positive to the station's role during these events. Massimo Smuraglia estimated that a network of antiracist activist groups in Tuscany had considerably more clout than the racist current in the province and that within that network, Controradio was a very important force.

Another aspect of Controradio's programming relevant to this issue was its foreign language slots. Programs were regularly broadcast in Arabic, Chinese, Eritrean, and Wolof (the principal language of Senegal), with the aid of some funds from both the Tuscan provincial government and the European Union.

On a different occasion, when the state police (the *carabinieri,* noted for their very aggressive tactics) invaded a local *centro sociale*[29] known as *La Baracca di Scandice,* Controradio broadcast phone calls from its young residents from the spot. These immediately served to dispute the justifications offered by the police for their attack on the centro. The station then followed up with a major counterinformation exposé on the episode, demonstrating overwhelmingly that the behavior of the carabinieri had been unprovoked.

This latter episode is typical of the type of relationship forged between young people and the station. Consistently over the years, the station reported on the real undertow of life, in Florence in particular and Tuscany more generally. Controradio was alone in its alertness to social movements and to changing currents of opinion among young people. The rock concerts and disco live performances that it organized were not simply a means of attracting and retaining listeners, although they fulfilled that function as well. They were also means of keeping the station's finger on the pulse of the young. As one staffer put it, when people think of Florence and Tuscany, even in Italy, they think primarily of vacations and leisure, but they are often unaware that the region possesses its own dynamic and energy quite unconnected with tourism.

In turn, along with the reputation Controradio enjoyed for accurate reporting and from time to time scooping the other media in Florence, especially in relation to youth issues, this ongoing rapport made the station a source. The Florence media would quite often cite an event in terms of its having been reported by Controradio, and thus being news. Furthermore, the station's reporters were more energetic than the average Florence journalists. One of them, Osvaldo Sabato, described to me how he would not ask questions at press conferences during the official session but would stop afterward for specific interviews, thus often giving the Controradio news reports a freshness compared to those prepared by its more lackadaisical competitors.

It was central to Controradio's news policy to cover multiple dimensions of issues to enable listeners to reflect on them and not simply to relay micro-scatters of aseptic factoids, like the on-the-hour news flash at many commercial stations that represents a token gesture toward informing the public. An example would be the station's steady concentration on environmental impact issues related to the supervelocity rail network projected for Milan, Bologna, Florence, and Rome, rather than simply recording the signing of construction contracts. Another example would be the station's constant attention to the housing problem in Florence, which is acute despite the fact that 7,000 apartments often stand empty. At the far end of this concern with information are the occasional multihour public affairs specials the station puts on without commercial interruptions.

Reviewing the Past

Looking back over the 20 years he had spent with the station, Smuraglia felt there had been gains and losses. In the early years, Controradio had known exactly the audience to whom it was broadcasting, namely, the insurgent students and other young people in the city. The station's programming could be extremely spontaneous and flexible (perhaps it had a tendency to be random). Even the ads Controradio took were principally personal classified ads. The energy in the station came from its being composed of enthusiastic volunteers, afire with the excitement of the new media project.

Twenty years later, the news the station provided was broader and more accurate. The station's organization was stable, and people were paid (albeit very poorly). The listening audience now, like the ads, is much more generic, less clearly identifiable. Programming is predictable but perhaps overly routinized. Smuraglia made it clear that this was his sense of the passage of events, not everyone's.

At the same time, he saw some definite progress in the external political context. Until the end of the 1980s, Italy had been dominated by party politics. Now, Smuraglia sensed, a civic society was in the process of active formation, a society that had shaken off the yoke of dependency on political parties. The *mani pulite* scandals and revelations,[30] the virtual collapse of the Christian Democrats, the shrinkage of the communists, had all contributed to a growing movement of political activism in many parts of Italy. The forms this activism took were not conventional ones. They might center around building a car park or a public trash-incinerator, but often, they would generate much more momentum than would be expected from a seemingly single-issue matter. And within that kind of context, Controradio would be exceptionally well-placed.

One final feature of Controradio is its basic organizational structure. In terms of hierarchy, although there was often a cheerful, friendly atmosphere in the station among the 20- and 30-somethings who worked there, authority was clearly defined. The director was the director, and the buck, indeed, stopped with him. A further important feature of the station is that people worked for minimum wages and often interchanged jobs. Margherita Calvalli, for example, worked as news reader, editor, phone interviewer, and general overseer of details for press conferences. Some Italian commentators have suggested that Italian community radio works because it functions at what are called "Japanese levels" of pay and flexibility. Whatever the truth in this, Controradio did seem to be able to combine energy, commitment, and a good working atmosphere with a productive organization of tasks. The station represented a very interesting working model for future radical alternative radio.

Summary: Liperi (1997) has noted the extraordinary mushrooming of energy in the 1970s, especially in popular music but also in "audiovisual production centers, alternative graphics laboratories, sound recording studios, poetry and literature workshops. . . . The rock concerts were also the occasion to discuss, debate, not just political issues but also music" (pp. 107, 109). Something of the same pent-up energy was visible in Italy, as it was in Portugal, not quite as intense, but longer-lasting. It seems hard to imagine today that the free radio movement talk shows with live phone calls from ordinary citizens would be a vivid irruption of the real world into broadcasting, but the kind of broadcasting the Christian Democrats in power reproduced and monopolized was completely stifling and one-way.

One other major outflow from the free radio movement in Italy was the so-called *Centri Sociali.*[31] The literal translation, social centers, gives no sense at all of what they were. A whole group of them, independently organized, were spread out across the nation, and they operated as multipurpose, largely self-managed centers where young people could find basic living information, develop autonomous cultural projects of all kinds, talk politics, and play or listen to music. Sometimes, funds were forthcoming from city councils for certain cultural programs. Conservative media opinion loved to dwell on the centri as centers for drug sales and dependency, "illicit" sexual escapades, crime, and the rest. These places typically had an uneasy and conflictual relation with the police. They represented, however, the continuation of oppositional culture, relatively autonomous zones where young people could work out their own tactics for living and develop their own cultural forms. Together with sections of the Italian ecology movement of the 1980s, these centers for 20 years were the keeper of the flame of resistance and independence.

NOTES

1. My research for this chapter was based on a 3-month period I spent in Italy in 1980, continuous with my time in Portugal and conducting the same type of interviews. With the help of a University of Texas travel grant in 1997, I returned to re-interview staff at the three continuing radical media I had researched and written about in the first edition. Some helpful sources on the Italian background have included Forgacs and Lumley (1996), Passerini (1996), Putnam (1993), Tarrow (1989), Bobbio (1979), and Red Notes (1978, 1979, 1981).

2. Moro stood for a reconciliation between the conservative Christian Democrat party, which had run Italy since the war but was riddled with corruption and steadily losing support, and the increasingly center-leftist communist party, which had no record of corruption at that time but a strong track record in city government. The Red Brigades dumped his body, after negotiations for his release did not pan out, midway between the head offices of the two parties in Rome.

3. P.2 was a top-secret Masonic lodge that wielded quite extraordinary power in government and in mainstream media for over two decades. The Vatican Bank was only one of the Italian banks deeply implicated in illegal activities, far from the biggest, but its involvement is an index of how extensive was the network of corruption and the abuse of power.

4. The excellent feature film *Lamerica* (1994, director Gianni Amelio, U.S. distributor New Yorker Films, New York City) beautifully summarizes this transition in the story of some white-collar criminals, making quick money off Italian foreign aid schemes, who think they can do the same with Italian aid to post-communist Albania. The scene at the end is unforgettable, when the lead protagonist finds himself, after a series of mishaps, in shabby clothes looking as destitute as his fellow passengers on an Albanian ship full of illegal immi-

grants headed for Italy. Obviously, he is likely to have great difficulty persuading the Italian authorities he is not himself an undocumented immigrant; he may not even be let off the boat to make his case. He and the immigrants look exactly like a boatful of Italians headed for Ellis Island at the beginning of the 20th century.

5. In Italian, the word means both manifesto and poster.

6. He won that fight. Former premier Bettino Craxi went into self-imposed exile in Tunisia to avoid going to jail on corruption charges involving his years in office. He died there in 2000 and was denied a state burial.

7. Unlike most Western media, however, their interpretation of the collapse was not that it meant a giddy ascent into the wonders of parliamentary democracy and the glories of the free market, but rather that it heralded disorder and misery, a prediction that many, from Bosnian Muslims to Russian pensioners to the 100,000 Chechen and Russian victims of the 1994-1995 Chechnya war, discovered to be only too true.

8. At the same time, there was unity within the newspaper on the question of Yeltsin, Gorbachev's nemesis and eventual successor as leader of post-Soviet Russia, who was seen as power-obsessed and program-free.

9. Often referred to later as "the" Gulf War. Because there had been, from 1980 to 1988, a savage war in the Gulf between Iraq and Iran, in which large numbers of people were killed or maimed on both sides, it seems odd to refer to the second tragic episode as though it had been the only one. The U.S. government, along with some other Western governments, supplied weapons to both sides in the earlier conflict. Is the defining element of a war the on-the-ground involvement of human beings from the United States? Is that how "a" war becomes "the" war?

10. *Cassa integrazione* was the official term for state subsidy to ailing enterprises. At that point, the subsidy was worth 5 billion lire a year, one sixth of turnover.

11. These were of considerable interest in terms of developing a bank of experience in organizing radical media. With the newspaper's sudden expansion earlier in the 1990s, large numbers of new staff had been brought on board all at once. There had been no probationary period during which they could be dismissed if unsuitable, nor any systematic attempt to inculcate them with the ethos of *Il Manifesto*'s project. This was a time when, in certain sectors of society, it was quite chic to read the newspaper and thus perhaps even more chic to work for it. Also, many of them, as usual at *Il Manifesto,* had a background in political activism, not in journalism. Thus, with the exception of a few interns brought in on the basis of special scholarships, whose employment was not immediately guaranteed, effectively something akin to instant tenure was extended to a very large new intake of staff who arrived almost simultaneously. The vectors at work in that situation were numerous. The informality characteristic of the newspaper's earlier period, the absence of any explicit set of rules, the often indeterminate nature of the hierarchy, and not least the fact that with no official career structure at the paper, staffers with perhaps a couple of decades behind them preferred to bring on board new people to undertake the boring editing chores, reserving for themselves the more interesting corre-

spondents' tasks, in some staffers' view all combined to make the transition to a more professional project uncoordinated and thus difficult to achieve.

12. It should be said that the problem was squarely with the daily press, not with the public, who read the rather better weekly press in large numbers. The quality of the daily press in Italy would be the subject of another study, but suffice it to say that its coverage of the theatrical antics and arcane mysteries of Italy's governing class "at work" was typically wordy, uninformative, uninviting speculation.

13. Not to say that the old system was finished: The *camorra,* the *'ndrangheta* and the *mafia* were still very powerful forces in Campania, Calabria, and Sicily, and significant money was undoubtedly still changing hands for favors at the top.

14. Although this newspaper, too, had reduced readership because it had siphoned off some thousands of *Il Manifesto* readers, who had stuck until then with *Il Manifesto* because it was the newspaper furthest to the Left. Whether this was a readership the newspaper really needed for its longer term future was unclear.

15. The title was a fusion of different words associated with world music styles, with *Patch* derived from the Latin American *pachugo,* the *ka* redolent of Slavic cultures, and so on.

16. The station did have a number of major scoops to its credit, which got it national attention. Among them was the first announcement of the attack on Baghdad in the second Gulf War in January 1991 and the use of information on the war from Arab nations' radio stations via their Arabic program producers. Later the same year, the station achieved another exclusive, via a direct telephone link set up as a result of a personal friendship network of coworkers, to an apartment in Moscow overlooking the Russian White House parliament building at the time of the attempted coup d'état in August 1991. An Italian-speaking Russian, observing the scene and using reports from Radio Ekho Moskvy from within the White House, was able to give an account of the sequence of events unparalleled elsewhere in Italian media. A further instance was the announcement, diffused over the Popolare Network on December 15, 1992, that a court had set Craxi's bail on extensive charges of corruption. This was not exactly a scoop, in that the major media got the story at the same time as Radiopop. But Radiopop was the only media institution with the courage to publicize it. The other media protected themselves by citing Radiopop as the source of the news item.

17. Some commented that this structure of authority had a built-in contradiction, in the classic mode of self-managed firms, in that the same people were forced to choose between raising their salaries and investing in the firm's future, specifically in new technology in Radiopop's case. It is true. Yet, in the longer term, it is to be hoped that dilemmas of this kind will not have to be left to "wise-daddy" managements but that the general public can learn to handle them for itself—potentially more wisely over time than unaccountable top executives.

18. Information on these points, and some others on the technical front, is drawn from an article by Barbara Fenati (1996).

19. It seemed as though a well-structured part-time training and mentoring program might take care of some of these issues, but at the time of my interviews, this did not appear to be on the agenda.

20. The community in question was somewhat blurred, designating either the European Union, formerly known as the European Community, or simply Italy itself.

21. The word for foreigner is *straniero* and for stranger *estraneo* (and for strange, *strano*). Underlying the use of the term for immigrants, although technically correct on one level, is a second undercurrent of meaning, implicitly distrustful and defensive, a sense not too distant from the use of the term *alien* for immigrants in the United States. Within this fuller spread of meaning, the slogan was particularly apposite.

22. The view was expressed by some other community radio activists that the station was always at risk of being held prisoner by its listener members and thus was unable to experiment independently and adapt to changing conditions. A different version of the same comment came from those who saw the station as overly politicized by the *sessantottini*, the generation of 1968. In this view, the leadership of the 1968 generation had largely emerged from extremely well-placed families and had dedicated itself with almost monklike self-discipline to the pursuit of political activism, forsaking in the process the usual involvements in raising children and pursuing a job or a career, while also sacrificing permanently any links with the wealth of the families from which they came. A kind of secular church of the political martyrs, Jesuits for socialism. Now that the political culture had altered, went the argument, leaving that whole era behind amid a welter of recriminations concerning Red terrorism and the descent into drug dependency, and now that the new young generation found most political discourse or activism less appealing than the prospect of living on Mars, Radiopop was in danger of ending up like a beached whale. Even those younger people who were regular listeners were all too often the children, not so much of the hyperactivists of 1968, but of individuals who had been fairly solidly active in the penumbra of those movements. Was it then a community or a steadily aging club?

23. There had been inconclusive discussions about switching again to ISDN-line communication, but the costs, of course, were high whereas the costs for satellites had been plummeting.

24. For an insider's account of Lotta Continua (Permanent Struggle), but one that is reasonably self-critical, see Bobbio (1979). The group was at the center of the student tumults from 1969 to 1976, when it dissolved itself in a famous congress at Rimini. It sought active links with labor militants and was perhaps best remembered for its relentless public campaign against a Milan police superintendent, Luigi Calabresi, whom it accused of dropping a political detainee to his death from a high floor of the police building in 1969. Giuseppe Pinelli, the anarchist who died in the fall, had been detained on suspicion of planting a bomb in a Milan bank that killed a number of people; in

reality, the bomb was one of about 100 planted that year by neofascists to create a climate of tension and anxiety that would lead to public readiness for a dictatorial regime to create order again. Calabresi was shot dead in front of his house in 1972. The saga continued for years, for in 1988, a former Lotta Continua member named, in return for amnesty, two leaders of the organization as having, with him, planned and executed the murder. The trials, Italy-fashion, dragged on for more years, and in 1997, both men were jailed for life, consistently denying having done it (although one, the former Lotta Continua leader, admitted the campaign had set up a climate in which someone would be likely to make an attempt on Calabresi's life). A leftist judge—there are such people in Italy—had concluded during the trials that Calabresi had not murdered Pinelli, although he did not conclude who had. Nobel Literature prize winner Dario Fò wrote a play satirizing the police account of Pinelli's death in custody, which was performed internationally (*The Accidental Death of an Anarchist*), but for a number of Italians, this 25-year saga to some degree served as a sad and dispiriting requiem to the passions and energy of the extraparliamentary Left of a previous generation.

25. In its early years, it had a much more suspicious policy toward taking advertising, although nonetheless recognizing that it could not survive without it.

26. A term used by one of my respondents.

27. Despite being asked to do so, Controradio did not accept advertising from supermarket chains. The station also refused advertising from any source with connections to hunting, such as leather stores.

28. At Controradio as at Radiopop, Internet radio was an option that had not been carefully entertained as of 1997.

29. The direct translation of the term as "social centers" gives no sense at all of their cultural and political significance. Emerging first as the student movements waned around 1980, these centers gave space in many different ways to young people's autonomous cultural activities. They were organized in different ways and had varying histories and degrees of impact, but they represented an important element in urban youth culture over the 1980s and 1990s.

30. *Mani pulite* meant "clean hands"; it was shorthand for a series of revelations of official corruption on a scale that surprised even cynical Italians.

31. See Consorzio Aaster (1996) for a good account, organized in cooperation with the young people, of two major *centri sociali* in Milan.

20

Access Television and Grassroots Political Communication in the United States

Laura Stein

Public access television began in North America in the late 1960s and early 1970s as a radical experiment in democratic communication. Access television supporters hoped to break the lock that commercial interests held on the television medium by bringing nonprofit, grassroots political and cultural programming directly to people's living rooms. By securing inexpensive access to production resources and facilities such as cameras, microphones, studios, and editing equipment, ordinary citizens would be able to construct their own televisual messages and to bypass the framing devices of professional corporate media. Distribution would be accomplished by cable-casting programs on a first-come, first-served basis over local cable systems. Supporters envisioned access television as a public space where, liberated from the economic and editorial constraints of commercial television production, citizens could air their views over the most powerful and pervasive communications medium of the era.

With 25 years of access television practice behind us and calls for access to yet another new technology—the computer network—before us, the question should be asked: Is access television an effective tool for democratic communication? One way to gauge the democratic potential of access television is to examine the strategic use of this resource by radical media projects. Following Downing's (1984, p. 2) definition, the term radical media here applies to media that pose challenges to existing power structures, empower diverse communities and classes, and enable communities of interest to speak to each other. These kinds of media are seldom distributed by American commercial or public television, and their experiences are indicative of the possibilities and limits of access television as a democratic medium. This study profiles three projects currently using access television as a tool for progressive political communication. Drawing on theories of democracy and democratic communication, the study analyzes both the political achievements of these projects and the structural limitations of access television as a forum for democratic communication. The study concludes that although public access has opened up a space for grassroots political communication on television, a restructuring of access television resources would further strengthen the democratic potential of the medium.

To begin, I will review briefly the set of circumstances in which access television came into being and its current structure. The same political and economic factors that precipitated the development of access television also have limited the nature of the services it provides. Access television represents a unique moment in the history of technology in the United States, when progressive groups have managed to secure a genuine public space in the electronic media. Yet, this space has been underused by these groups, subject to inadequate funding, and devoid of government and industry support.

A BRIEF HISTORY OF PUBLIC ACCESS TELEVISION

In the early 1970s, broadcast television consisted of three network channels and a fledgling public broadcasting system. Cable technology seemed to offer a genuine alternative to this highly centralized broadcast market. Although cable had been developed in the 1940s, it was only in the 1970s that it metamorphosed from a technology for extending broadcast reception into a technology able to originate programming over its systems. With its newfound ability to originate programming, its 12-channel carrying capacity, and its image as a local provider of services to discrete communities, cable inspired visions of a more diverse, decentralized, and competitive television market. As one early commentator enthused, "Television can become far more flexible, far more democratic, far more diversified in content, and far more responsive to the full range of pressing needs in today's cities, neighborhoods, towns, and communities" (Smith, 1970, p. 8). The democratic promise of cable was espoused by cable operators, economists of regulation, liberals, policy makers, and progressive groups (Streeter, 1987, p. 181).

Access television came about in large part through a temporary confluence of interests among cable operators, federal regulators, and access activists. Access activism in the 1970s was an outgrowth of 1960s social activism, which advocated participatory democracy as a means to create social and cultural change. The alternative print media of the 1960s sought to create an alternative consciousness in their readers and, ultimately, an alternative culture (Armstrong, 1981, pp. 20-24). Access activism extended the goals of the 1960s radical press to the medium of television. Access activists hoped community members would be able to use cable systems, along with consumer video equipment, to engage in unmediated expression, to increase communication between and among themselves, and to discover and define a grassroots political agenda.[1] Michael Shamberg and the Raindance Corporation (1971), authors of *Guerrilla Media*, which became known as the bible of alternative media, praised cable's potential to create an alternative information infrastructure, or a "grassroots network of indigenous media activity" (p. 9). Although inspired by technological developments, access activists also saw the need to realize their goals in concrete communications policy. The Alternate Media Center in New York, founded by documentary filmmakers George Stoney and Red Burns, served as the organizational center for the political instigation and popularization of access television in the United States (Engelman, 1990, pp. 18-20; Hénaut, 1991, p. 96).

Federal regulators and cable operators were also instrumental in establishing access television. The Federal Communication Commission (FCC) saw an opportunity to promote local programming policies in cable where they had failed with broadcast television. In 1972, the FCC mandated that larger cable operators provide public, educational, and governmental (PEG) access channels, equipment, and facilities (Cable Television Report and Order, 1972) to the communities they served. Cable operators had their own reasons to support the local and community programming potential of cable. Volunteering to provide PEG channels was one way to curry favor with the FCC, which had halted cable expansion from 1968 to 1972 while it deliberated over rules for the medium, and perhaps to preempt federally mandated access television requirements. The offer of PEG channels and services to local communities was also good public relations for cable companies competing among themselves to secure a municipal cable franchise. Early government and industry support led many communities to believe they could rely on the goodwill of cable operators to supply access television resources and facilities, to adequately fund access television operations, and, in some cases, to manage public access channels and facilities.

Not surprisingly, this alliance of interests was short-lived. Once the FCC freeze was lifted and their municipal contracts were secured, many cable operators saw little reason to support public access channels. In addition, whereas cable had been touted as a locally oriented business and technology, the industry saw localism as an economic liability to be overcome. Cable television looked for ways to organize itself around the economies of program distribution rather than the capabilities of its technology. In this respect, cable proved similar to broadcast television, which also derives its socioeconomic power not from its technology or production activities but from control over a distributive activity whose profitability is linked to large economies of scale (Garnham, 1990, p. 65). Cable's extra channel space was to be filled not by local productions but by television reruns and Hollywood films, which could be easily and inexpensively distributed to individual cable systems via satellite. The late 1970s saw the advent and diffusion of satellite program services such as Home Box Office (HBO), Showtime, the Movie Channel, and Nickelodeon. At the same time, the Midwest Video Corporation mounted a legal challenge against federally mandated access television. The Supreme Court struck down FCC public access rules, charging that the FCC had overstepped its jurisdiction by requiring cable operators to act as common carriers (*Federal Communications Commission v. Midwest Video Corp.*, 1979). Public access systems around the country, which had relied on these rules and failed to mention access television specifically in their franchise agreements with cable operators, were shut down (Brenner & Price, 1993, pp. 6-34; Rice, 1980-1981, p. 101). In the future, access television would survive only in communities that lobbied their municipal governments to include public access provisions in the local cable contract.

In the absence of strong governmental or industry support, the continued existence of access television has been precarious and has depended on grassroots politicking within individual communities. This has meant that public access resources and facilities vary from place to place. Some communities offer studio facilities, production equipment, training, and outreach, whereas others provide little more than channel space. What remains constant from city to city are the customary conditions under which access television operates. First, with its nondiscriminatory, first-come, first-served policies, access television establishes an open forum for public communication that is free from editorial control by cable operators. Second, funding for access television must be obtained either from cable operators or city governments. There is no federally mandated funding for access television, and the majority of access television centers are poorly funded (Aufderheide, 1992, p. 62; Rice, 1980-1981, p. 106). Last, access television is conceived of as an exclusively local resource. The facilities and equipment enabling production and distribution are made available only to those living within the immediate community, local citizens are required to sponsor all programming using cable on access television, and there is no structural or administrative support for networking between public access channels.

RADICAL TELEVISION PROJECTS: THREE CASE STUDIES

Since its inception, access television has provided radical media makers with a nonprofit, open forum for the expression of their views. Although the existence of access television has not led to revolutionary social change, as some of its founders had hoped, radical public access programs and distribution ventures constitute ongoing experiments in the development of an alternative information structure and program base. Radical access television projects have been concerned with the political empowerment of producers and viewers and the representation of excluded or underrepresented political and cultural communities. The democratic aspirations of many of these projects are manifest both in the way they are internally organized and managed and in their political strategies and goals. Space limitations will not permit a comprehensive examination of all radical access television projects.[2] Therefore, I have selected three projects for case study: the Committee for Labor Access, Paper Tiger Television, and Deep Dish Television. These projects are distinguished by their conformity to Downing's criteria for radical media, their democratic internal organization, their longevity as access television producers, and their national recognition within the access television community.

Committee for Labor Access (CLA)

Began: 1983

Location: Chicago, Illinois

Activities: produces *Labor Beat,* a bi-weekly news and public affairs program covering labor issues, and *Labor Express,* a weekly, hour-long radio show

Personnel: about seven core producers, 10 volunteers

Screened: access television in Chicago, St. Louis, CUNY-TV in New York, public screenings, *Free Speech TV*

Finance: donations, program sales

Numerous independent producers and producer groups use access television to produce video on labor issues.[3] *Labor Beat* is one of the longest running of these shows and is produced and distributed by the CLA, a coalition of independent video producers, labor activists, and artists. *Labor Beat* engages in "small-format, nano-budget, fast-turnaround, labor video journalism" (L. Duncan, personal communication, May 17, 1996), using consumer grade cameras to produce cheap and timely shows on labor issues. Although CLA demonstrates its solidarity with organized labor through its affiliation with the International Brotherhood of Electrical Workers (IBEW) Local 1220 (a TV production union in Chicago), the group is an independent organization that does not receive financial or administrative support from the IBEW or other unions.

Labor Beat programs focus on local, national, and international labor issues. The show covers topics of interest not only to organized labor but to the labor movement more broadly defined: incorporating all working people regardless of whether they are union members. In recent years, *Labor Beat* has included shows on the effects and implications of the North American Free Trade Agreement, on the leadership change of the AFL-CIO, and on the wave of labor struggles occurring in Illinois. Show producers use documentary techniques, and many of the programs favor a style in which the camera is clearly an active and interested participant in the events and issues it portrays. *Labor Beat* strives to act as a forum for rank-and-file perspectives and interests. Programs document strikes, demonstrations, and other labor conflicts; report on news of specific interest to the labor movement; convey key speeches given by political and labor leaders; carry the highlights of labor conferences; and present interviews with labor leaders. Programs also preserve the history and culture of working people by profiling the daily lives and problems of workers, recording the oral histories of longtime labor activists, and documenting significant events in labor history.

CLA's producer-members compose a board that meets once a month to discuss collective business. These meetings are open forums for planning upcoming shows, devising fund-raising strategies, orchestrating program publicity, debating how best to further the goals of labor television, and dividing collective tasks, such as answering correspondence and overseeing the distribution of shows. Collective work is accomplished on a purely volunteer basis. A few committee members take responsibility for keeping track of finances, distributing tapes, writing grant proposals, and editing programs. Board decisions, formally subject to a majority vote, are generally the product of consensus. The group, which is small and cohesive, seldom disagrees on goals and strategies (P. Donahue, personal communication, May 21, 1996; L. Duncan, personal communication, May 17, 1996).

The collection of program material is largely decentralized. CLA producers generate their own ideas for programs and accept suggestions from rank-and-file workers. In addition to material shot by *Labor Beat's* core producers, CLA receives raw footage from workers and activists around the country, which is then edited for cablecast. Because Chicago's public access center requires producers to submit two new shows a month to retain a series slot, *Labor Beat* faces a rigorous production schedule. The task of editing, which must be done quickly, tends to fall repeatedly to one committee member, giving that member a large say in the final form the shows take (L. Duncan, personal communication, May 17, 1996).

CLA's overarching goal is to empower workers by providing a forum that gives voice to "the lives, experiences, and struggles of working people" (The Committee for Labor Access, 1996). This goal is carried out in part through the inclusion of worker-produced tapes in the series, the training of labor activists in television and radio production, and the creation and maintenance of a distribution network for labor programming. CLA also furthers this goal by creating programming with a point of view different from that of both union bureaucracies and commercial television.

CLA seeks to reflect and represent the interests of rank-and-file workers rather than union bureaucracies. *Labor Beat* provides a forum in which these interests can express themselves more directly:

> Our ten-year stint in covering stories . . . convinces us that, as the labor battle lines pop up, talented and dependable videographers will emerge from the ranks who will provide footage closest to the issues and action. And they will get those interviews from folks who very often understand what's going on better than their representatives hundreds of miles away. (Duncan, 1996, p. 24)

There has been a recurrent tension between the AFL-CIO's idea of labor television and what the rank-and-file produce ("Labor and Access," 1995, p. 26). CLA's programs are not a venue for the views of union bureaucracies. Rather, many of the programs criticize sectors of bureaucratized labor. In "Our Class of People," for example, strikers from Decatur, Illinois, demand access to the AFL-CIO executive council meeting to express displeasure with both the council's weak support for the "war zone" struggles and their reliance on labor-management circles.[4] As the program documented, access to the meeting was refused. Other *Labor Beat* programs continued to support these Midwestern labor struggles.

CLA also produces and distributes images of labor that seldom find their way onto mainstream television. Believing that the interests of corporate media are intrinsically at odds with those of labor, former *Labor Beat* coproducer Bob Hercules (1987) asserts the importance of using access television to increase workers' awareness of excluded perspectives (p. 12). CLA creates opportunities to sensitize workers and others to the antilabor biases of commercial television by addressing this issue in their shows, by facilitating discussions at public screenings, and by involving rank-and-file workers in the production process. Through the production of an ongoing, radical series on labor issues, CLA hopes to contribute to the articulation and development of workers' perspectives on the world.

CLA sees access television as an invaluable resource for the labor movement because it enables people to assert alternative perspectives on labor issues with a relatively small budget (L. Duncan, personal communication, May 17, 1996). Rank-and-file workers are able to disseminate information and analysis on access television that would never pass the gatekeepers of commercial electronic media. That union bureaucracies have failed to recognize the potential of access television as an organizing tool or to provide resources for its use by workers is, in the eyes of CLA, symptomatic of the distance that currently exists between union leadership and working people.

Although access television in Chicago provides CLA with channel space and editing equipment, the group has had to find its own means of publicizing programs, obtaining access to production equipment, and funding the project. Because the local cable company has little interest in publicizing access television programs, CLA has developed its own promotional strategies, including the publication of a newsletter, the public screening of tapes, and special mailings and faxes of brochures and flyers to union locals. CLA also produces a program catalog for labor historians, activists, educators, unionists, and others with a potential interest in buying shows. *Labor Beat* sometimes requires shooting with little notice or taking cameras to distant locations for extended periods of time. CLA has invested in its own camera, microphones, and lighting equipment because the requirements for borrowing these production tools from Chicago's public access center have proven too restrictive. Funding has been a continual problem for *Labor Beat,* which does not receive funds from unions and has been largely unsuccessful at obtaining grants from foundations or arts councils. CLA's budget, including in-kind support, is less than $10,000 per year, and funds are raised through tape sales and donations.

Distribution is important both to the show's potential effectiveness and to its economic survival. CLA has searched for ways to expand program distribution to a wider geographical audience than local access television allows. CLA mails programs to New York and St. Louis for cablecast and currently distributes shows through Free Speech TV (FSTV), a national program service targeting access television centers. Through FSTV, *Labor Beat* can be seen on about 60 public access channels in over 44 cities. CLA is also part of the Union Producers and Programmers Network (UPPNET), a coalition formed in 1989 to support the production, distribution, and preservation of electronic media that address labor issues and the problem of media access. At present, UPPNET and FSTV are collaborating on the development of a national labor television series.

Paper Tiger Television

Began: 1981

Location: New York, New York, and several other locations[5]

Activities: produces weekly show on media criticism, conducts educational workshops on low-budget television production

Personnel: about 10 core members, 15 occasional members, 1 paid part-time distribution coordinator

Screened: access television in Manhattan, Brooklyn, and the Bronx, CUNY-TV in New York, universities, museums

Finance: program sales and rentals, grants

Paper Tiger shows are produced by the Paper Tiger Television collective, a volunteer group of artists, media professionals, and activists. The show began as a special series on *Communications Update,* in which communication theorist and scholar Herb Schiller analyzed the political economy and agenda-setting function of the *New York Times.* From these beginnings, the program evolved into weekly readings of different media publications, programs, and trends by a variety of hosts, many of whom are professional writers, scholars, or media critics. *Readings,* in this case, refers to the critical analysis of a media text, which aims to explore the ideologies and symbolic forms that give the text its meaning and to examine the institutional, political, and economic factors conditioning its production.

Although early shows tended to focus on print publications, such as Teresa Costa Reads *Biker Lifestyle,* Muriel Dimen Reads *Cosmopolitan,* and Natalie Didn't Drown: Joan Braderman Reads the *National Enquirer,* later shows have taken on a broader range of media texts and phenomena. The series has included Mark Crispin Miller on the history of American advertising, Elayne Rapping on soap operas, and Renee Tajima on Asian images in U.S. cinema. Recently, Paper Tiger has begun producing more activist-oriented tapes. As one collective member has stated, "More tapes deal with immediate political controversies and feature direct participants in social struggles, such as labor strikes and abortion rights battles, while maintaining a focus on how media representations do not reflect the realities of life for most people today" (Marcus, 1991, p. 32). This later focus has produced shows on the 1989 United Mine Workers' strike against Pittston Coal Company, New York

City's plans to build an incinerator in a low-income neighborhood, and the Zapatista uprising in Chiapas, Mexico.

Paper Tiger membership consists of a floating core of 10 or more regular members and a diaspora of peripheral members who maintain occasional involvement. The Paper Tiger Television collective allows all members to participate in all aspects of the organization. The collective has two primary activities: the production of shows and program distribution. The group believes that the collective structure allows members equal autonomy and agency within the group, ongoing flexibility in the amount of work they assume, and the chance to exercise and develop a variety of work-related skills. As Stein and Marcus (1990) assert, "A collective may not always function as efficiently as an organization with strict hierarchical structures, but what it lacks in efficiency it makes up for by valuing the opinions and ideas of all of its members." These egalitarian characteristics are a great advantage to a group that relies on volunteer labor.

Members meet once a week at the Paper Tiger office in downtown Manhattan. Meetings are held in the evening to allow those with full-time jobs to attend. These weekly meetings are central to the organization's internal exchange of ideas and maintenance of collective identity.

> The ritual of convergence of opposing powers, fiery debate and collective stewing. Everything is discussed Wednesdays, from upcoming conferences and festivals, demonstrations and lectures, to potential show proposals, aesthetics, goals, and available sublets. Plus screenings of shows new and old for critique. Once every couple of months it's a mailing party where we all get together and stuff envelopes over beers. Live shows are on Wednesdays. Mostly Wednesday night is what makes us a collective. It is the time we all get together to exchange information and get a look at ourselves. (Marcus, 1991, p. 32)

The meetings are the forum for collective decision making regarding the group's activities and goals. Any member of the group may suggest new projects and initiatives or voice opinions on proposed shows. Final decisions are made by group consensus. Group business is discussed and delegated to committees that oversee different aspects of Paper Tiger's operations, such as distribution, fund raising, and office support, and that serve to familiarize collective members with the inner workings of the organization. Committee activities are reported during the weekly meetings.

Show production also is organized collectively. New shows may be suggested either by collective members or by people outside the collective. If the entire collective agrees that the show idea is consistent with Paper Tiger's interests, individual collective members volunteer to work on the show. As with other collective projects or business, a member's role in production varies widely from show to show. A producer of one show may act as preproduction researcher on another or as a camera operator on yet another. The collective often works on several shows at once. With varying production schedules, shows may take anywhere from 2 weeks to 2 years to complete. The credits of each show reflect Paper Tiger's commitment to its identity as a collective, listing the names of those who worked on the show without reference to the specific jobs performed.

The introduction to the series in its second year proclaims,

> [Paper Tiger Television] looks at the communications industry via the media in all of their forms. The power of mass culture rests on the trust of the public. This legitimacy is a paper tiger. Investigation into the corporate structures of the media and critical analysis of their content is one way to demystify the information industry. Developing a critical consciousness about the communications industry is a necessary first step towards democratic control of information resources.

Paper Tiger shows use political economy and critical cultural theory to critique media content and to call attention to the disjuncture between people's lived experiences and media representations. The goal is to create critical viewers with a sophisticated understanding of how and why artifacts of the culture industry adopt particular forms and functions.

Although the content focuses on critical readings of media representations, the aesthetic aims to offer viewers an alternative experience of television. Paper Tiger's style and pace are self-consciously different from that of commercial television. The pacing is uneven. Backdrops and graphics cards are brightly colored and often handmade. Shots sometimes reveal equipment and crew. Mistakes made during production deliberately may be left in the finished tape. This aesthetic, which strives for a "homey" or "friendly" look, has several stated functions. First, it differentiates the show visually from other television in the hopes of catching the attention of potential viewers. Second, Paper Tiger visually highlights the constructed nature of television through its refusal to look slick. Third, it conveys to viewers that flawless production values are not a precondition for having something to say in the televisual medium (Halleck, 1984, pp. 315-316; Halleck, 1993, pp. 416-417). Furthermore, the aesthetic makes a virtue of necessity. Because Paper Tiger's budget will not allow it to mimic the production values of corporate media, its eschews these values from the start and seeks to invent an alternative, but nonetheless engaging, aesthetic.

Paper Tiger TV hopes to demonstrate the larger potential of TV as a political communication resource by offering an alternative vision of the medium. Access television provides Paper Tiger with a space for the creative reworking of the television form. It also provides access to consumers of electronic media. From the collective's perspective, the written word cannot perform the same critical functions as Paper Tiger shows, which rely on contrast with and subversion of the tropes of mainstream television. The collective believes that access television is the only forum capable of hosting the alternative content and style of radical programming. As collective members Stein and Marcus (1990) state,

> Paper Tiger TV believes that by producing shows on public access, it can provide a model of quality, low-budget television and engage in critical discussions and aesthetic experimentation which would never be acceptable to commercial or, in most cases, even public television.

For most of the collective's existence, public access resources in Manhattan consisted of channel space only. Whereas raw materials and incidental expenses, such as tape stock, transportation, and props, are costs that access television producers usually cover themselves, Paper Tiger also was obliged to obtain its own access to cameras, studios, and editing equipment. Funding for these resources comes from grants and from program sales and rentals. Paper Tiger is fortunate to be located in New York, where the state's arts council has been committed to funding video projects. Because New York City access television programs are not listed in *TV Guide,* local newspapers, or cable schedules, the group also must publicize its programs. To this end, Paper Tiger cablecasts shows during a regular series slot so that viewers know when to tune in, and it maintains a mailing list of interested viewers to which it routinely mails program schedules.

Distribution is an integral part of the collective's activities, as well as a primary source of funding. Paper Tiger believes its critiques of the culture industry have both local and national appeal, and it has searched for ways to distribute the show beyond the local Manhattan cable system. In its earlier years, wider distribution was limited by the fact that the group lacked the resources for postage and tape duplication (Halleck, 1984, p. 317). Today, a part-time, paid distribution coordinator fills orders and tracks tape distribution. The group's efforts to develop distribution have included increasing its visibility by screening tapes at festivals and on access television in other communities and by instituting targeted mailings of program catalogs to universities, museums, arts centers, and community groups.

The Deep Dish Television Network

Began: 1986

Location: New York, New York

Activities: maintains a satellite network for the production and distribution of progressive television, coordinates production of national series, programs shows produced by other nonprofit groups

Personnel: three paid employees, hundreds of volunteer producers and series coordinators

Screened: about 250 public access channels throughout the United States, some public television channels

Finance: grants, program sales

In the mid-1980s, members of the Paper Tiger Television collective began organizing a public access satellite network in an effort to build a national infrastructure and audience for progressive television programming. Collective members believed that satellite distribution, long used by commercial program services, would be considerably more efficient, manageable, and cost-effective than mailing tapes to individual access television centers. Testing the feasibility of such a project, Paper Tiger produced a 10-part series of "magazine-style" shows on a variety of topics, rented time on a satellite channel, and transmitted the first Deep Dish TV (DDTV) programming. The series was offered to public access stations and anyone with a receiving dish, free of charge. Over 250 stations around the country telecast the series. This trial run of the public access satellite network seemed to augur new possibilities for the distribution of grassroots programming on a national scale. DDTV emerged from Paper Tiger to become its own organization, with the goal of producing and distributing programming that would challenge the conservative orientation of mainstream TV and allow people to present viewpoints on political and social issues ("Deep Dish Television Directory," 1988, p. 3).

DDTV has pioneered a program format in which independently produced work is assembled into multipart series organized around a central theme. The series examines social issues from regionally and culturally diverse perspectives generally absent from broadcast news. Programs draw on production genres ranging from documentary and public affairs to drama and experimental video and juxtapose highly produced material with the more rough-edged fare typically associated with access television. Programs may consist of works in their entirety or excerpts from a variety of sources. DDTV series have treated a diverse range of subjects, including citizen uses of public access television, social and political change in Asia, grassroots views on environmental issues, the U.S. war in the Persian Gulf, censorship and contemporary threats to civil liberties, the Columbus quincentennary and the struggles of indigenous people around the globe, health care reform, and the growth of the prison industry. DDTV seeks to present perspectives that generally are ignored or marginalized in mainstream debate. The recent health care series, for instance, sought to present progressive perspectives on health reform in a public debate otherwise dominated by policy makers, insurance companies, drug manufacturers, and corporate health care providers. The series included programs on proposals for reform, holistic medicine, reproductive rights and services, health care practices in black communities, prison health policies, community mental health programs, environmental racism, and Native Americans and alcohol abuse.

Three staff members maintain an office in New York City that facilitates network operations and coordinates series production. The staff performs the centralized work of fund raising for each series, initiating program development, assembling press kits, arranging satellite transmission, and publicizing the series. DDTV's board of directors, drawn from the ranks of political and media activists around the country, sets policy for the project. The board deliberates over the final selection of series topics, programming formats, staff hiring and supervision, and strategies for reaching potential audiences.

Individual program production and local scheduling are largely decentralized. DDTV selects series coordinators from varying ethnic, cultural, and gender backgrounds and from different geographical regions of the country. For magazine-style shows, the series coordinator views material submitted by contributing producers from around the country and edits a number of these segments into a finished program. Alternately, DDTV may commission individuals or groups to produce an entire show if a paucity of preproduced material exists. Local coordinating and contributing producers are responsible for generating local publicity, arranging to downlink the programming from the satellite feed, and ensuring that the Deep Dish series is scheduled on their local public access channels. This last step is especially critical because many public access channels will only schedule programming submitted by local community members. When the budget permits, DDTV pays series producers and coordinators a fee for their work.

Recent funding and staff difficulties, as well as a break in series production, have precipitated a restructuring of the office staff and board.[6] For many years, staff positions had been organized hierarchically, with an executive director, a program director, and an operations manager. Currently, staff work is being reorganized into a less hierarchical structure, and a New York-based support group is being established to provide volunteer labor and other resources for the staff. DDTV also is reorganizing the structure of its board, as it found that maintaining a diffuse national board was impractical for an organization that lacked the financial resources and skills necessary for board development, training, communication, and cooperation. To paraphrase one board member, a diverse, broad-based, and representative policy-making group requires laying the necessary groundwork to foster understanding and the ability to work together (L. Davitian, personal communication, May 28, 1996). Although DDTV is still committed to building a diverse organization at all levels, the new board will be made up primarily of members from the New York area.

DDTV aims to distribute programming that allows progressive individuals and groups to represent themselves and their concerns to each other and to larger forums for public debate. DDTV also seeks to demonstrate the potential political uses of access television, satellite transmission, and activist programming to independent producers and activists. Series transmission often is accompanied by a concerted effort to distribute information to activist constituencies on how to use access television resources, how to receive DDTV programming via satellite, and how programming might be used to augment their organizing activities. Through such efforts, DDTV hopes to strengthen a sense of community among activists across wide geographic regions (Halleck, 1993, p. 420). A key assumption of the project is that progressive voices lack a significant outlet in mainstream media. DDTV seeks to provide this outlet and, according to board member Lauren-Glenn Davitian (personal communication, May 28, 1996), to act not just as a TV network but as an organizing force.

For many years, DDTV's prime strategy for making the programs representative of progressive opinion involved openly soliciting ideas from independent producers for series themes and subtopics and compiling material submitted by these producers. "Sick & Tired of Being Sick & Tired," a Deep Dish series on health care reform, signaled a new strategy for the network. Rather than surveying independent video producers, DDTV staff spoke with 98 progressive health care organizations and activist groups to define the series' topics. Devising shows around the local and national agendas of these groups, DDTV developed programs specifically tailored to reflect the needs and concerns of health care activists. DDTV hoped this strategy would familiarize new audiences with the idea of alternative television, to heighten the use-value of programming for activist audiences, and to link progressive groups with access television producers. In addition, this series aimed to strengthen the relationship between access television and national forums of political debate. The series was timed to coincide with the 1994 congressional debates on health care in the hope of adding new voices to the debate and influencing policy outcomes (C. López, personal communication, August 7, 1995).

DDTV's inclusive production style actively searches out and amplifies marginalized voices. This method of production is both time-consuming and administratively complex. As former program director Cynthia López (personal communication, August 7, 1995) notes, a for-profit organization would be unlikely to engage in this process. Indeed, DDTV's activities are conditioned by the fact that its goals are primarily political:

> We are constantly asking what are the most democratic, most empowering models for media production and distribution? Under what circumstances will local activists start using their access stations more? How can we make the programs more interactive with viewers? How can Deep Dish collaborate with other media outlets? . . . How can we facilitate media access for constituencies that are underrepresented and misrepresented in the mainstream media? (Wallner, 1991, p. 34)

As this quote suggests, DDTV is engaged in the project of extending activist activities and struggles into the realm of media and culture. Because there are no models for this type of project, strategies are constantly being tested, evaluated, and reformulated.

DDTV aims to provide a national network for progressive programming through geographically dispersed and locally oriented access television facilities. Access television centers contribute to this project by training amateur producers, supplying production and postproduction equipment to these producers, and offering channel space on which to cablecast the finished series. However, because access television resources have been structured to serve local rather than national communities, DDTV faces a number of problems in trying to build a national infrastructure based on access television. First, many public access centers do not own satellite dishes. Individuals wishing to program DDTV in these areas must obtain access to a satellite dish independently or arrange for nearby public access centers with dishes to send them copies of the programming. Second, DDTV must handle all administrative aspects of networking to hundreds of local stations, placing tremendous demands on the organization's small staff and budget. Administrative tasks include identifying and contacting interested producers and programmers; aggressively promoting its program schedule through mailings, phone calls, and postcards; and contacting programmers afterward to determine the extent of broadcast. These tasks are made more difficult by DDTV's project-by-project orientation, its distribution of only 2 hours of programming per week, and its consequent intermittent presence on local cable schedules. Finally, and perhaps most important, DDTV has had to operate under significant financial constraints. Public access channels are not permitted to carry advertising or to pay for the programming they receive, eliminating them as a potential source of revenue.

Since its inception, DDTV has relied on grants from private foundations, individuals, and government agencies to fund the project. Recent national cutbacks in arts funding have taken a severe toll on the network, which went for 2 years without producing a series and only recently resumed its activities with the production of a 1997 series on criminal justice titled, *Bars and Stripes: Doing Time Inside the Prison Complex.* Current efforts to expand funding sources include direct mail campaigns to people on the DDTV mailing list, establishing a Donor's Club of people willing to pledge sustaining financial support, distributing information via a World Wide Web site, and increasing the marketing of programs to schools and universities, video outlets, bookstores, global TV outlets, and home viewers.

ACCESS TELEVISION AND DEMOCRATIC COMMUNICATION

In assessing the contributions of access television to democratic communication, I will call on two major strands of democratic theory. Laclau and Mouffe's post-structuralist hegemony theory and Benjamin Barber's participatory democratic theory hold considerable explanatory power for the type of activities in which radical media projects are engaged. The CLA, Paper Tiger Television, and DDTV represent overt attempts on the part of radical media makers to engage in political communication. This communication is political in the sense that Laclau and Mouffe (1985) invoke when they define political action.

> When we speak here of the "political" character of these struggles, we do not do so in the restricted sense of demands which are situated at the level of parties and of the State. What we are referring to is a type of action whose objective is the transformation of a social relation which constructs a subject in a relationship of subordination. (p. 153)

Although these radical television projects would like to influence government policies, their more immediate concerns are posed in terms of contesting the frameworks and biases of commercial media and constructing alternative representations of social experience and reality.

If we define democracy, along with Dahl (1989), as a process or system "in which the members regard one another as political equals, are collectively sovereign, and possess all the capacities, resources, and institutions they need in order to govern themselves" (p. 311), then access television may be understood as an institution that provides citizens with some of the necessary communicative tools for self-governance. The radical television projects described here use access television to engage in democratic communication in three ways. First, access television enables its users to reinterpret, reframe, and refute the artifacts, messages, and ideologies of commercial culture from within a dominant forum for political communication. Second, access television allows users a space in which to represent themselves and their interests to the larger community. Finally, access television permits the exercise of democratic functions of speech that are largely absent from commercial media. An examination of each of these points will elaborate further their contribution to democratic processes.

Central to Laclau and Mouffe's (1985) democratic theory are the ideas that social meaning is derived from among a plurality of possible ways of understanding social organization and activity and that this meaning is subject to unending contestation. Radical media projects view television as a site in which to contest such social meaning. For these groups, access television is a feasible and appropriate forum in which to respond to the hegemonic position of the larger medium. Like Habermas's (1962/1989, p. 27) ideal public sphere, which lies between the realm of the economy and the state, access television provides a speech forum that is relatively free from economic and editorial constraints and that permits the discursive reinterpretation and refutation of media forms and symbols. Laclau and Mouffe argue political change must be preceded by "discursive conditions" that alert people to oppressive relationships and thereby make it possible to expose various types of inequality and to transform social and political understanding:

> Our central problem is to identify the discursive conditions for the emergence of a collective action, directed towards struggling against inequalities and challenging relations of subordination. We might also say that our task is to identify the conditions in which a relation of subordination becomes a relation of oppression, and thereby constitutes itself into the site of an antagonism. (p. 153)

Radical television projects take it as axiomatic that television is an important sphere of political communication and that commercial television systematically distorts, biases, and represses the potential diversity of debate and representation. These projects pursue the task of discursively identifying media hegemony in two ways. By critiquing and reworking the televisual form itself, these projects reposition what might otherwise be experienced as transparent meaning into a site of antagonism. By challenging the content of the mainstream media and introducing alternative perspectives on social reality, radical television invites viewers to re-examine and perhaps reformulate their existing viewpoints.

Radical television projects also assert the right of ordinary people to represent their own interests and perspectives in the television medium. Representation is a relatively new and problematic concept in democratic theory. Although the ancient city-states of Greece and Rome theorized a more participatory and direct form of democracy, liberal democratic societies have relied on representative government to solve the modern problem of scale that occurs in applying democratic processes to nation-states. Rule by elected representatives, rather than rule by the people, however, creates a schism between the theory and practice of democracy. Barber (1984, p. 145) argues that a system allowing a few chosen people to govern in all matters all of the time harms participation and citizenship by delegating and alienating the citizens' political will, drastically reducing the scope and exercise of self-government, and destroying political autonomy. Likewise, Dahl (1989, p. 225) notes that representation reduces participation to the relatively passive acts of listening, thinking, and voting. Nonetheless, representative institutions and processes are a fact of life in modern democracies. According to Barber, if democratic societies are to strive toward fuller self-governance, they must increase citizens' abilities to represent themselves and their interests in some public matters at least some of the time. Radical media programs, such as *Labor Beat*, Paper Tiger Television, and DDTV, are motivated largely by the sense that their interests and viewpoints are not represented adequately in public debate. By encouraging workers to describe what is at stake in labor conflicts or allowing health care activists to present alternative plans for health care reform, access television promotes a more participatory concept of democratic representation. Barber (1984, p. 117) sees this participatory process as essential to the formation of legitimate public opinion, which depends on civic education and civic interaction to unite individuals in common purpose and action.

Finally, access television offers radical media projects the opportunity to use speech for a broader range of democratic purposes than mainstream media allow. Barber (1984, pp. 173-178) notes that if political speech is to support reasonable political judgment, it must be affective as well as cognitive and must serve as an impetus to action through its construction of alternative futures, purposes, and visions of community. He further notes that liberal market societies tend to view politics as an adversarial process in which the role of speech is to exchange words "among competing individuals who seek to maximize their self-interests through market interaction" (Barber, 1984, p. 179). As a more participatory forum, access television broadens the possibilities for political communication to incorporate functions of speech considered more democratic by Barber. These include grassroots formulation of issues and problems; the exploration of mutuality in thoughts, feelings, and experiences; affiliation and affection through the development of feelings, concerns, and empathy for others; maintaining autonomy by consistently re-examining and repossessing one's convictions; expression of one's convictions, as well as dissent, frustration, and opposition; the reshaping of political terms and values through reformulation and reconceptualization; and community building through the creation of citizens capable of making informed political judgments. Radical media projects are overtly concerned with many of these speech functions. The projects examined here contribute to the definitions of problems and issues within local, national, and international communities; unite geographically dispersed communities of interest; voice dissent against prevailing political opinion and policy; allow diverse groups to represent themselves and their interests; expose larger communities to a plurality of viewpoints and experiences; offer competing visions of the common good; entreat viewers to re-examine and reformulate their existing convictions; and challenge predominant political and cultural representations.

RETHINKING PUBLIC ACCESS TELEVISION

Access television's legal and regulatory status remain precarious. Although access television traditionally has operated as a public forum, the 1992 Cable Act called the public forum status of access television into question. The Act made cable operators, rather than the public, liable for programs containing indecency (Cable Television Consumer Protection and Competition Act of 1992). In 1996, the U.S. Supreme Court repealed this legislation in *Denver Area Educational Telecommunications Consortium, Inc. v. Federal Communications Commission.* However, the Court refused to decide whether access television should be treated as a public forum in which programmers have free speech rights. Instead, the Court stated that the indecency rules were not applicable to public access channels because indecency had not been a problem on public access and because cable operators traditionally had not exercised editorial control over these channels. The Court also maintained that public access was adequately supervised and that the new law impermissibly altered the relationships established by municipal law, regulation, and contract (*Denver Area Educational Telecommunications*

Consortium, Inc. v. Federal Communications Commission, 1996). Nevertheless, "obscene" or "indecent" programming, as well as hate speech, have tarnished access television's image, alienating potential public access supporters and prompting several communities to question the desirability of maintaining an access television station. The presence of this type of programming has been made possible by the policy of open access. Although many radical media producers feel that without this policy, their work might be censored or suppressed, there is no doubt that open access has been detrimental to both the substance and image of access television.

Besides the perennial problems of legal and regulatory status and public relations, access television harbors a number of structural limitations that prevent it from serving as a more effective resource for democratic communication. Political communication on access television is attenuated by an inadequate governmental provision of the resources necessary to produce and distribute programming, by the bias of localism, and by a lack of ties to larger spheres of discussion and debate.

Many public access centers provide channel space, training, and a moderate level of equipment and facilities. These centers do not provide administrative support for program publicity or for the distribution of programs beyond their local cable system. Publicizing programs is particularly important if shows are to find their intended audiences, and all of the projects examined here devote considerable resources toward developing and maintaining their audience. Distribution beyond the local cable system is necessary both for the financial survival of serious access television projects and for their political reach and effectiveness. Yet, most public access centers facilitate only show production, placing the burden of reaching the audience on the individual access television producer.

Perhaps the most critical and immediate problem for public access projects is funding. These projects rely on combinations of grants, donations, special fund-raising events, and program sales and rentals for financial support. Although the costs of these series are minuscule compared to their commercial media counterparts, the cost of access to the public sphere encompasses more than access to technology itself. The price of communication includes not only the cost of production and exhibition technology but also the financing of labor, administration, distribution, and publicity. Garnham (1990) points out that access to technology does not constitute "access to a mode of communication" (p. 65). The radical media case studies suggest that access television must be viewed holistically as a set of resources that promote access to an audience and not simply to channel space or production equipment. In addition, some type of national program support is necessary if access television is to be effective and affordable. Such support might be funded through the extension of franchise fees or rents to all commercial communication industries that use public goods.

Another limitation of public access is that it is designed primarily to serve local communities. Radical media projects exhibit a range of strategies for overcoming the localism of access television. CLA, Paper Tiger TV, and DDTV address topics and issues of national significance, incorporate work produced and edited by regionally diverse individuals and groups, and aggressively promote widespread program distribution. Although localism may further political participation within small communities, it cannot address the problem of scale that modern nation-states present to any democratic system. Representative democracy has consigned a large part of the political decision-making process to national rather than local representatives. Buying into the longstanding myth of the political effectiveness of the small community and the town meeting (Rowland, 1982, p. 6), early access television activists in the United States ignored the fact that much of the American political process operates through institutions organized at the level of the nation-state. Media produced in small communities may influence agenda setting or foster community building at a local level, but these media currently have no institutionalized means of reaching national audiences. Structuring access television to serve only the local community greatly underuses the medium.

The democratic potential of access television also suffers from its lack of supporting structural links to larger political communities and institutions, which are themselves forums for opinion formation and which command social resources. DDTV's attempts to influence government policy debates and CLA's efforts to confront union bureaucracies with rank-and-file perspectives attempt to rectify this deficiency. Without concrete links to larger institutions, public access lacks a bridging mechanism for the translation of public criticism into political action in the policy realm. The development of stable mechanisms of support for the national distribution of grassroots media and the linking of access television to larger political and cultural forums will determine the ultimate effectiveness of access television as a tool for democratic social change.

Summary: The public access television movement in the United States sought to create a democratic forum that would allow citizens to contribute more directly to the political and cultural lineaments of American society. The experience of radical media projects suggests that access television provides a genuine, if imperfect public space for democratic communication. Groups such as the CLA, Paper Tiger TV, and the Deep Dish Satellite Network use access television to critique and comment on commercial culture, to represent themselves and their viewpoints, and to employ political speech in ways that are both affective and cognitive. Yet, the greater democratic potential of access television is stymied by its insecure legal and regulatory status, its partial provision of the resources necessary to produce and distribute programming, its predominantly local orientation, and its marginalization as a sphere of public debate. Radical media projects have sought to overcome these limitations by obtaining outside funding and resources, instigating national networking activities, and positioning themselves in the sight of larger public forums. Advocates wishing to restructure access television resources must try to foment change by building public awareness of the democratic potential and achievements of access television and by lobbying for a policy environment more conducive to democratic communication.

NOTES

1. In 1968, the first consumer video camera, the Sony Portapak, went on the market. Barnouw (1993, pp. 287-289) notes that consumer video equipment, with its relatively low cost and ease of operation, inspired production activity among a new and diverse range of people.

2. Some notable projects not discussed in this study include Dyke TV in New York City, a lesbian video collective whose programs are shown in over 60 cities across the country; Black Planet Productions (BPP) in New York City, a collective that produces *Not Channel Zero: The Revolution, Televised,* a news and cultural affairs program focusing on African American and Latino concerns; The Mirror Project in Sommerville, Massachusetts, which encourages teenagers from diverse ethnic backgrounds to document their everyday life experiences; *Alternative Views* from Austin, Texas, a news and public affairs program that provides a radical information alternative to mainstream media; and Free Speech TV in Boulder, Colorado, a distribution network that sends progressive programming to more than 60 access channels nationwide.

3. About 40 labor shows appear regularly on local public access stations around the country (Alvarez, 1996, p. 7). Some other prominent labor shows on access include: *LaborVision* in St. Louis, Missouri; the *Labor Video Project* in San Francisco, California; *Labor at the Crossroads* in New York, New York; *Minnesota at Work* in Minneapolis, Minnesota; *This Working Life* in Southern California; *Arkansas Works* in Little Rock, Arkansas; and *Labor Link TV* in San Diego, California.

4. Struggles that occurred in what the labor movement referred to as "the war zone" included the United Auto Workers (UAW) strike against Caterpillar, the United Rubber Workers strike against Bridgestone-Firestone, and the Staley Company's lockout of the United Paperworkers International Union (UPIU) in Decatur, Illinois; the UAW strike against Caterpillar in Peoria, Illinois; and United Mine Workers of America strike against Peabody Coal in southern Illinois.

5. Over the years, satellite groups have formed in San Francisco and San Diego, California, and in other locations. This study, however, refers only to the New York group. The satellite groups are not presumed to share the same organizational structure or even, necessarily, the same goals.

6. This discussion of the current organizational changes at Deep Dish is based on interviews with Deep Dish personnel and on a report written by DeeDee Halleck for the John D. & Catherine T. MacArthur Foundation.

21

KPFA, Berkeley, and Free Radio Berkeley

KPFA was the first listener-supported independent[1] station in the United States. Except for two breaks, the first from August 1950 to May 1951 and the second from July 14-21, 1999, it has broadcast every day since April 15, 1949.

Continuity, however, is only one of the features that distinguishes it from other local radio stations in the United States. In its early days, when the first Cold War and its ultimate expression, McCarthyism, were placing a rigid clamp on political criticism and independent thought, KPFA struck out in the opposite direction. It was, in a sense, an echo from the Roosevelt era and the hopes and optimism that period inspired in many politically committed and internationally minded U.S. intellectuals. The little cluster of half a dozen people who founded the station did so with a philosophy of broadcasting and communication strongly marked with commitment to the First Amendment and a Quaker variety of pacifism. Some had been conscientious objectors during World War II, like the principal founder, Lewis Hill. Some, like Hill, had been imprisoned for their beliefs.[2]

In general, their broadcasting philosophy could be interpreted at first glance as not especially adventurous or radical; indeed, to be rather reminiscent of the British Broadcasting Corporation: Lewis Hill "believed radio and press should not be run by entrepreneurs motivated by profits, but by journalists and artists whose motive would be the most objective and enlightening programming possible" (Stebbins, 1969, p. 41).[3] In fact, he and his cofounders were prepared to take advertisements for an initial period, simply to gather the necessary financial support to bridge the period between what they realized would be minimal listener support and what they trusted would be adequate listener support. As it happened, they never broadcast ads at all, but their view of advertising in U.S. broadcasting was nonetheless hardly equivocal: "Sale of time on KPFA will be . . . governed strictly by an advertising code which eliminates the intrusive, repetitious and in other ways offensive commercialism common in American radio" (Stebbins, 1969, p. 61). This critical broadcasting philosophy and practice do not of themselves seem much more than high-minded. But the context is everything. In 1949, that context was the continued dominance of rampant commercialism on the U.S. airwaves, with the exception of military and police channels, combined with the deadening fear associated with Sen. Joe McCarthy's ascendancy. It should be realized, too, that KPFA's internal structure was highly radical: Everyone was paid the same wage, and decisions were made collectively on all major matters. In addition, KPFA's stated aims were to develop "peace, social justice, promotion of the labor movement, and support of the arts" (Stebbins, 1969, p. 38).

Interestingly, its definition of how to promote the labor movement was not tied to any particular political line on the Left. Hill (cited in Stebbins, 1969) observed, "Unfortunately, the only press and radio sources of consistent and comprehensive labor reporting are either controlled by the Communist party or Stalinist in orientation" (p. 40). However, this did not prevent the station from allowing members of the Communist Party USA (CPUSA) from joining their voices to the numerous other perspectives given airtime. KPFA's position was determinedly liberal, in the classical sense of the term.

Such a view, however, in those years, was officially interpreted as active sympathy for communism. The paradox of KPFA's origins is that in another place and time, it might have been unusual to refuse advertising sponsorship but not radical. At the time, however, the station was a small beacon of political sanity in a national climate of rightist hysteria.

Not surprisingly, therefore, KPFA soon attracted to itself the organized reaction of the far Right in the manner so characteristic of the official exponents of liberal freedoms when taken at their word. Repeatedly, the sledgehammer was heaved on high by official Federal Communications Commission inquiries in response to "listener" complaints, and once, the hammer was wielded by the Senate Internal Security Subcommittee, hoping to pulverize this small challenge to the American way of political communication. Nor were these threats confined to the McCarthy period. In June 1982, the chair of the American Legal Foundation, a body whose conservatism was renowned, petitioned to deny FCC license renewal to a sister station of KPFA in Washington, D.C. That station spent $10,000 to $15,000 to defend itself, a fact assuredly not lost on the wealthy complainant. The Foundation promised, if successful, to go after the licenses of the other four stations in the Pacifica chain, including KPFA. With such valiant seekers-after-truth is the U.S. political establishment adorned.

The fact of these attacks figures at the outset of this account of KPFA. Rather like the legal and police attacks on the underground press of the 1960s and 1970s (cf. Rips, 1981), the extraordinary concentration of effort to uproot these media in the name of freedom is one of the crucial paradoxes of their history. Why were they—are they—deemed so important and threatening when they form such a tiny, fragile element in national media? The paradoxes do not end here, however; equally amazing is their tenacity and survival despite these assaults, despite their minority role in national life, despite their usually acute financial constraints, and despite the organizational crises that have intermittently wracked their internal life.

Having set out this overall view, let me now proceed to a more orderly account of how KPFA has organized itself. I shall present first a greatly abbreviated history of the station and then focus on a number of issues central to its organization up to the early 1980s: the question of power and the division of labor inside the station, its relation to popular political forces and movements outside its walls, and the problem of finances.

This sounds rather dry, almost like an exercise in the sociology of organizations. The flesh on these dry bones, however, consists of key political problems. Is it feasible to organize media democratically? What are the practical hazards in doing so? Are they surmountable? Furthermore, democracy itself is not just an abstract virtue in this case. What are the practical possibilities for women and people of color not simply to broadcast but to broadcast what they want to communicate, both within their own ranks and to a wider audience? Can advertising sponsorship be avoided without financial chaos? Is a chain of such radio stations a viable enterprise? Can such small media stand up to organized onslaughts from the far Right? What are the costs, on all levels? These problems are among those to be examined.

A MINI-HISTORY

KPFA's founders had originally intended to broadcast on AM from the town of Richmond, California. When this proved impossible, they switched to broadcasting on FM in the nearby university town of Berkeley. They began with a revamped 250-watt transmitter that could function at 550 watts, with their antenna on the roof of the building that housed their studio. When KPFA Interim, as it was first called, went off the air in August 1950, it owed $2,000 in bills and nearly $7,000 more in back salaries, a considerable sum of money for the time. In its 16 months of operation, however, it had involved over 2,000 local individuals in making programs, often on topics or in areas not addressed by other media, spanning the range from news to music, drama, and other cultural programming. This involvement of the public was to pay off handsomely in restarting the station. When KPFA came back on the air 9 months later, its supporters had helped to get it a new transmitter and frequency and a solid financial reserve, the latter supplied in part by the Adult Education division of the Ford Foundation.

Unfortunately, no sooner had these financial problems been put in some order than another trend began to interfere with KPFA's efficacy. The national production of FM radios declined from over a million a year in 1947 to 131,000 a year in 1954. By 1954, the only station broadcasting solely on FM in the area was KPFA. In desperation, two volunteers put together 500 FM sets, priced at $30 rather than the usual $50 at that time and got them sold in the district. After these had gone, KPFA sold inexpensive models to subscribers. But with the decline in FM, newspapers and weeklies began to cease printing FM program details. KPFA was destined for a lengthy period of arrested growth.

Hill worked feverishly on other related projects for expansion (a literary magazine, for example), none of which were ever to be properly realized during his lifetime. He appears to have been an anxious, intense, but physically frail man, whose energy and vision were vital to realizing the radio project. His perspective is perhaps best summed up by his own summary of it, from the KPFA Folio of August 1952: "If KPFA is 'with' anything, it is clearly on the side of those who believe in the mind and who endeavor to make responsible mentality more socially effective" (Stebbins, 1969, p. 130).

A whole series of internal wrangles and upsets, combined with the intellectually and politically hostile times in which he was living and the acute difficulty, therefore, of realizing a whole range of fine projects, bore in on him and were among the forces that, tragically, pushed him to take his own life in 1957. His death was the heaviest blow of all to the station; and it is a tribute to Hill himself as well as the others that despite staffers' acute differences at times, the station was sufficiently stable to survive.

Indeed, in 1959, just 2 years after Hill's death, KPFA was joined by its first sister station, KPFK in Los Angeles; in 1960, WBAI in New York was added to the network. In March 1970, KPFT Houston went on the air, only to have its transmitter bombed by the Ku Klux Klan in March and October of that year. The station continued, nonetheless. In 1977, another station opened in Washington, D.C., after a license battle that had ground on since 1968. The Pacifica National News Bureau also began to function on a small scale in Washington, D.C., during the 1970s. Expansion took place, despite the apparently insurmountable blockages of 1957.

During this period, the FCC responded many times to complaints against the station, supposedly from regular citizens but often from an ideological agenda aimed at denying licenses to the Pacifica stations. At one point, too, the Senate Internal Security Subcommittee dragged KPFA over the coals. The attacks were usually concerned with obscenity or with lack of political balance. Obscenity charges usually centered on the use of particular four-letter words in poetry or drama programs, because such terms were not liberally interspersed in public affairs programming. Mores change, and what was once considered abhorrent is less likely to be so viewed now. A single four-letter word as part of a half-hour of poetry is hardly likely to stir much controversy. In the 1950s, it could and did.

The political charges against KPFA revolved around its willingness to allow CPUSA members to broadcast. (As is not widely known, the FCC interpretation of the fairness doctrine then in force in U.S. broadcasting always explicitly excluded the "communist viewpoint" from those perspectives that need to be given adequate time on the air.) The accusations were accurate, as KPFA regularly allowed CPUSA spokespeople to broadcast. It was a politically warped accusation, however, as the overwhelming majority of people broadcasting did not take the CPUSA view, and at least 98% of programs were given over to that majority (Stebbins, 1969, p. 218). Indeed, when the Senate Subcommittee asked why three CPUSA members had been allowed to broadcast, the station manager pointed out that in the same month, KPFA had also given the microphone to a Los Angeles broker, an academic from the Center for the Study of Democratic Institutions, a Unitarian minister, the former chair of a Democratic Party club, a public relations specialist, the president of the Los Angeles chapter of the American Federation of Scientists, and, not least, Caspar Weinberger, then chair of the Central California Republican Party committee (later to be Secretary of Defense in the Reagan administration). They might have added that other conservatives, such as William F. Buckley, had been regular contributors at an earlier time.

These details are recorded to emphasize the committed First Amendment liberalism of the station. It did not define itself as a revolutionary radio station in the sense espoused by the Portuguese and Italian stations examined in Chapters 18 and 19. However, in certain ways, the station did begin to move in a more radical direction in response to the upheavals in the United States, beginning with the civil rights and antiwar movements, the black rebellions in Harlem in 1964 and Watts in 1965, the Free Speech movement at Berkeley, and the emergence of the women's and gay movements. In 1949, inside KPFA, the term *minorities* had meant minority opinions. By 1969, it had come to refer to the explosion in political, ethnic, and gender consciousness that had taken place in the younger generation. And the very notion of taking a loyalty oath, about which the FCC had formally required information from KPFA in October 1963, would already have been patently ludicrous by 1969.

Let us turn now to KPFA's recent organization, and then to the impact of political movements on its functioning.

POWER AND THE DIVISION OF LABOR

The experimental policy of paying all members equally and of having majority votes on programming policy after open discussion was the most nearly revolutionary feature of the early KPFA. It was a policy framed in conscious rejection of the undemocratic structures of national media in the United States, and it is of special concern to this book. How did it work?

It was not that long in the development of the station before a number of people began to observe, if not complain, that the project was effectively being run by a triumvirate of Hill and two close associates. This situation led gradually to a maze of resignations and counterresignations at intervals between 1951 and 1953. Hill wrote in exasperation on July 15, 1953,

> The rejection and choice of leadership by part of the group had, in my own mind, grievously demonstrated that the organizational theory of the Pacifica Foundation is unsound.... Knowing that most of the individuals concerned are intensely sincere, I am forced to the conclusion others have reached before me: that an impossible task confronts these individuals; that the organizational theory is false which requires that engineer, announcer, stenographer, producer, must also be reponsible for the decisions of leadership. (cited in Stebbins, 1969, p. 167)

This is quoted to underline the difficulty, not the impossibility, of making any change in traditional authority patterns or the division of labor in the media. As we shall see, one of the most persistent problems in such attempts has arisen precisely from the view that these structures can simply be wished out of existence by politically determined and dedicated people. At one point, both sides in the wrangle were writing to the Ford Foundation to ask it, respectively, to cancel or to continue its support: This is a measure of the passions involved.

From 1954 to 1957, the disputes seemed and probably were largely resolved. However, in April 1957, Hill, prompted by a budget crisis, chose to fire three staff members, two of them belonging to the California Federation of Teachers, which soon threatened a strike. Hill rejected any possibility of internal inquiry into his decision, as he had authority, being Pacifica's president, to hire and fire. He was, however, overruled by the Committee of Directors, whose reasoning was that whatever the formal realities, KPFA's commitment to the labor movement could not justify such a dismissive response.[4]

Some of what had happened in the station over these first years of its life was perhaps predictable. It had, after all, shifted from a tight-knit group of cofounders to a larger structure of more disparate individuals.

The kind of group culture and history that enables spontaneous, participatory debate on policy and programming is not something that can instantly be grafted onto a large group of people who have not all worked together and grown together over a period of time. This is a real dimension of democratic functioning, and it is ignored at peril, as the case of *Il Manifesto* also demonstrates.

Legally, the Pacifica Foundation had control over all its stations, from Los Angeles to Houston to New York. In practice, until the 1990s, they ran themselves. They had to do so. KPFA, as of the early 1980s, had a manager responsible for the overall running of the station. There were three assistant managers, namely, the chief engineer, the program director, and the assistant to the station manager. They were defined as management and did not belong to UE, the union first established there in the course of a dispute that dragged on through 1964 and 1965. Below the management were department heads (Engineering, Production, Music, Drama and Literature, News, Public Affairs, Women's, Third World). Each head was paid and mostly full-time; each department had two votes in major decision making. There were another eight or so full-timers in addition to the people mentioned.

Below them was a large body of part-timers, defined as people working unpaid for 20 hours a month for a few consecutive months. A further corps of volunteers worked on a more occasional basis, for example on fund-raising drives. The part-timers, but not the volunteers, were unusually and perhaps uniquely covered by the UE contract in certain respects. For example, they had the right to first preference for any paid position that opened up for 60 days or less, and they had the right to participate in the selection of a manager, enjoying collectively 50% of that vote. Departments also had an important say in the selection of all department heads. There was, however, no formal right of recall of department heads or management.

It can readily be seen that the station retained a strong dose of democracy, even given its formal hierarchical structure. How did this work in practice? To answer, we must look at the role of the unpaid workers at the station, the technical division of labor, the union, and the role of people of color and women's groups.[5]

Despite the unusual concessions made to unpaid part-time workers, there was still a great potential for strife inherent in their position in the station. For one thing, their understanding of what went on in other departments of KPFA, let alone in the Pacifica chain, was slight. Their slot was their slot, to which they were often passionately attached and which frequently was central to their personal identity. Collectivist consciousness was often weaker than American individualism.[6] As David Salniker, station manager in 1982, ruefully remarked about the station in general:

> I have yet to have the experience of someone coming to me and urging that their program should be taken off the air. And rarely, of someone coming to me and saying they want to cede their time to give space to a key issue.

He described the prevailing mood at the station during his tenure as "bureaucratically regulated individualism."

By this, he meant that virtually everyone in the station, paid or unpaid, had powerful commitments to his or her particular contributions. General priorities could always be agreed on; their specific implementation was another matter, especially if it came to a reduction of time for any given program. The people in the music program and cultural programs, for instance, although generally progressive, were usually wrapped up in their particular projects and had little detailed sense of contemporary political developments. When push came to shove in this situation, there is no doubt that the unpaid, despite their larger numbers, were able to exert far less influence than the paid. This was so, despite their protracted struggle in the past to get themselves a voice in decision making.

For example, Wednesday evening meetings were open to all workers at the station and were chaired by the program director. This person could either make decisions, in the absence of anything approaching consensus, or defer them for further consideration and debate. This meeting, clearly, could have acted as a forum for debate over programming policy and expression of political differences. In practice, the meetings were usually concerned solely with practicalities or the most general issues. Controversial issues were generally avoided.

Similarly, department heads were supposed to confer at regular meetings with their unpaid staff, although this was more honored in principle than practice in some departments. In the week I was interviewing KPFA staff, the unpaid staff members had called a special meeting to protest the loss of some early evening weekday hours for a new program instituted by the program director. They perceived this as symptomatic of their lack of voice in decision making; the decision also had the effect of cancelling their own programs in some cases. Some part-timers were calling, apparently for the fourth time, for a programmers' bill of rights.

Clearly, the structure did not lead to perfect harmony, even though this was partly due to the individualistic way many staff, paid and unpaid, used the facility of the station. The structure did, however, offer mechanisms for working democratically on a number of problems. It was not a straitjacket.

Some full-timers felt that the major dissatisfactions of the unpaid staff revolved around two issues, although these were not always recognized as such. One was the lack of overall resources to do everything that was desirable; the other was the prevalent individualism, which meant that formal procedures often seemed to be bypassed. Certainly, a number of practices familiar to conventional broadcasting institutions were not in force, such as minutes and agendas for departmental or programming meetings or house rules on terms to avoid in broadcasting. This had not always been true of KPFA, nor was it fated to continue forever. It is, however, one more indication of the confusion that can emerge from impatient neglect of routine procedures, a confusion that may not be any more liberating than pedantically observing them.

The technical division of labor was also part of the station's structure, although in a somewhat muted form. There was no formal rotation of work, for instance, between members of the engineering department and the programmers. On the other hand, because it was small and the kind of station it is, people got "hands-on" experience in a way that would have been impossible at a larger or more formal operation. Similarly, engineers and technicians were not precluded from involvement in program design. The result was that almost all the technicians at KPFA were capable producers, and many programmers were well informed technically. Training classes were organized from time to time on how to operate the board and how to engage in a variety of types of production. For reasons as much practical as political, therefore, the technical division of labor was less heavily entrenched at KPFA than is customary.

Unionization was a very hot potato throughout KPFA's history. We have already mentioned the role of the California Federation of Teachers in one dispute. The reasons for not having a union structure at the very outset are probably obvious, but it was a 1964 management decision to fire—or as it later turned out, to attempt to fire—one of the founding KPFA members, Elsa Knight Thompson, that crystallized the issue. Previous sporadic efforts to organize a union in the station were interpreted by the National Association of Broadcast Engineers and Technicians (now a part of UE) as attempts that had been systematically thwarted by management, and the firing was viewed as victimization. UE called a strike, and half the station (including over half its full-timers) came out. The strike lasted 7 weeks, although the station was only off the air for 3 hours the first day. It was eventually settled, although not to the taste of the principals on either side of the dispute. There were highly personal investments in the attempt to form the union, which went beyond the obvious case for having them. Despite this personal dimension, the time was clearly coming to have such an alternative center of power and redress in the station.

After that episode, the union was a regular part of KPFA until the crisis of the late 1990s. We have already noted its unusual mode of incorporating unpaid staff into the contract, although not without an extensive struggle by them to this end. The formal opportunities for the unpaid staff, the largest single category of station workers, were quite extensive, far more so than would be imaginable in a conventional station. The union functioned well, and particularly so when its elected officers were effective individuals. It had one chief steward and four stewards in the early 1980s, its grievance procedures dated from 1978, and it organized a twice-yearly raise for its paid members, although everyone was paid at more or less the same rate.

KPFA AND EXTERNAL POLITICAL FORCES

Any examination of democratic media structures must go beyond the organization of the medium and survey the interrelation between internal democracy and the access rights of varying interests and groups in the active public. To take an obvious example, it is one thing to have a democratic internal structure, but quite another to have one that is resistant to access demands by women or Third World minorities or that has no members of those sectors of society in power positions in its structure. An issue that directly arises out of this is how to handle political fissures within these or other groups, because no social group is a homogeneous political entity. How are decisions made to broadcast one position on gay rights, say, as against another? KPFA, as contrasted to conventional radio stations, has always been singularly subjected to external political forces of this nature.

Lasar (1999, pp. 207-210) suggests that a significant policy shift took place in the station during the 1960s, away from the emphasis on dialogue that Hill had seen as central to the politics of pacifism and toward the definition of Pacifica as the voice of unvoiced opinion. What commercial media typically failed to address, not least including leftist perspectives, Pacifica stations should seek out and emphasize. This new stance was itself a response to the changing political climate, one in which the knee-jerk reactions of the McCarthy era were beginning to soften. As U.S. involvement in the Vietnam war began to escalate, so did the station's role as a voice of the opposition to the war and as a forum for the Left.[7]

I propose to review two examples from the 1970s and early 1980s that illustrate many of these issues. They are the creation of a Third World Department and the creation of a Women's Department.

The question of Third World minority participation and the significance of the creation of a Third World Department require a little prior clarification, which will also serve in understanding the later emergence of a Women's Department. First, out of all the departments in KPFA, News dominated: It had the most paid staff, the largest budget, the most listeners, and it was the best known and organized department. Second, the cultural programmers, especially in music, had their own highly specialized but dedicated audiences. Some, like its jazz programmer, had been at KPFA virtually since the station started. Many were crucial to fund-raising drives because of this. Yet, as noted above, they were typically wedded to their own paths. News and the cultural sections, therefore, identified the station for many listeners. Yet, within the station, to be a major interest and not to have a department was to be condemned to marginality. Hence, the significance of the Third World and Women's Departments. To be a department gave two votes in major decisions; other departments and interests were forced to negotiate.

The Third World Department

In the early 1970s, there were still only two or three regular workers of color at KPFA. The station had no clearly defined policy regarding them, except that slots were made available to them on an ad hoc basis.

When one full-timer retired in 1972, her position was split into two half-time positions to develop the station's programming on women. One woman appointed was white; the other was a Latina. The Latina drew the conclusion as time went on that there was insufficient real interest in the station in Third World issues, so she left to work in a Latina collective. Before leaving, however, she argued strongly in favor of her half-post being allocated to a specialist in Third World issues. That half-position was left vacant for a long time.

In 1973, and stretching into 1974, there was a strike at the station, arising from a generalized dissatisfaction with the then station manager. The various Third World collectives working in and around KPFA considered the moment opportune to press for a Third World Department and allocation of the half-time position as payment for its head. This demand was met with the argument that people of color should integrate into all departments, which in turn was countered with the position that integration would mean their power would be dispersed and dissipated, because there were fairly few of them at that time. In the course of this struggle, one group marched into the main studio, locked it, and broadcast their demands for a department and a paid position over the air.

Eventually, the concession was made, and a Latino brother and sister team became cofounders of the Third World Department in 1975. Before the strike, she had been program director and he production director. He quickly organized a very good corps, mostly of white males in the first instance, to join in programming on Third World issues. The department also began political work within the station, challenging, for instance, the appropriateness of white reporters covering black events and typical white assumptions about news priorities.

The storms were only beginning, however. The brother and sister were later fired, a major stated reason being their failure to organize volunteers for the department. The firing sparked a hot response from quite a number of people. A new manager failed to resolve the issue and left after losing a confidence vote 2 months later. The Pacifica Foundation became closely embroiled in the dispute. It identified two Third World members as major troublemakers (not the brother and sister) and tried to impose a more intensively hierarchical power structure on its then four stations, declaring pompously that "we anoint" the station managers. (This move came to nothing, not surprisingly, given the many feisty individuals involved in the Pacifica stations.)

Another storm developed over the opening of a news bureau in east Oakland, the largely black industrial city (but also with Asian American and Native American communities) next to Berkeley. The Third World Department was closely involved in this project and helped to raise $5,000 to start it. The senior members of KPFA interpreted this as an attempt by the Third World Department to cut loose from the station, and they voted to freeze spending the money. The Third World Department promptly wrote to the foundation concerned and urged them not to send the grant. The management then proclaimed that anyone working for the Oakland bureau could no longer be considered a KPFA member and consequently voted seven or eight of the most experienced Third World members out of the station. Of those remaining, a number also began to leave, including individuals who had direct involvement in political struggles in Nicaragua and Argentina.

Meanwhile, the News Department decided to try to open a news bureau in the Mission district of San Francisco, in the heart of a Chicano barrio. Local residents quickly asked the station representatives what they thought they were doing there. The News Department instantly assumed, incorrectly, that the Third World Department had put the residents up to it. The Third World Department, however, was incensed that the east Oakland project was treated so poorly at the same time that the News Department was allowed to establish a second bureau in a Third World neighborhood.

The situation eventually resolved itself in favor of the east Oakland bureau, which proceeded to broadcast a daily 15-minute slot (*Talking Drum*) on news and issues, which continued for some years. This episode demonstrates once more how a progressive medium is much more prone to political upheavals and cleavages in the world at large than is a conventional one. Democracy is different, and preferable, but it is not an instant chemical solution to complex social and political issues. For instance, within the Third World Department itself, African Americans, black Hispanics, and Native Americans often expressed the view that white Latin Americans were settlers' offspring and not "really" Third World people. These debates are also part of the real world, especially with the rise of assertiveness by Native Americans throughout the Americas in the latter part of the 20th century. But unlike mainstream media, neither the department nor the station was immune from these disputes.

A part of the history of Bari Scott, the head of the Third World Department in the early 1980s, is an appropriate note on which to conclude this presentation of the role of Third World people inside the station. Scott had experienced her full share of the department's tumults, having been fired twice in the past—each time on New Year's Eve. The first time, the union successfully defended her; the second time, there was no need for this, because she was instantly supported by a majority of her colleagues at the station. Her own history at KPFA is a tribute to the merits of staying inside to fight issues within an institution at least partially open to change. Unromantic, no doubt; but once again, a very different story from the big media. In the long-running and exceptionally deep crisis of the late 1990s, however, the dynamics would change yet again.

The Women's Department

The Women's Department was started in 1981. Women's programs had been a regular feature of KPFA, and programs conveying the rebirth of the women's movement had been in continual evidence for 10 years before the formal announcement of plans for a Women's Department in 1978. The declaration remained a formality, however, until mid-1981, when the first department head was appointed, half-paid out of a Third World department post. In 1982, the department was responsible for only 6 hours of programming a week, 3 of them during midnight hours, as contrasted with the 30 hours assigned to the Third World department (although there was some prospect of expanding on this allocation). Nonetheless, the Women's Department was there, one of the very few in any branch of U.S. broadcasting. The long delay between its announcement and the appointment of its head, which had angered many women to the point of leaving KPFA, eventually receded in significance, and many women activists returned with considerable energy for new projects.

Women's Department members considered its quality of life to be much more supportive and caring than was customary in other departments. The department, however, had not moved to differentiate itself from the other departments by becoming a formal collective. Its first head, Ginny Berson, was committed to seeking out and listening to her members' feelings, but in the final analysis, she had the power to act as she thought fit. We see here once more not the dissolution of power, but its softening in a progressive direction. For example, controversial issues in the women's movement would be talked through before programs were put together, and the programs were then discussed before being aired.

The purpose of the Women's Department, according to Ginny Berson, was exactly the same as that of the women's movement at large. Within KPFA, the Women's Department constituted, first, a place to which women in the station, or new to it, could go. Second, as already noted, it constituted a power base. From this base, it was possible to begin to have an effect on the rest of the station; to encourage feminist programming in general, from sensitivity to masculinist "love" lyrics through to awareness of women's presence, issues, and perspectives in news, public affairs, and cultural programming. Their other major activity was to do programs on standard women's issues, such as domestic violence, abortion, and rape, and on feminist readings of a whole range of topics.

Not every woman in the station was involved with the Women's Department; some men, moreover, according to Ginny Berson, began genuinely trying to change their programming in more feminist directions. But without the base and without the departmental vote, this would have been more difficult. Even though the tendency was still well in evidence at KPFA to say "Oh, that's a women's issue: pass it on to the Women's Department," the department was still there to counterattack and insist issues be dealt with systemically, not ghettoized. Without this base, the whole debate would have been one step further back, with feminist perspectives addressed or rejected quite haphazardly.

Furthermore, having a half-time paid person meant that someone had the time to get an overview of how women's issues were presented in general and of the spectrum needed in women's programming. Ginny Berson found that going through Public Service Announcements (up to 100 a week) had given her a valuable checklist of events and issues to assign the women in her department by their area of interest. The result was a large number of women involved in their programs.

Attitudes toward women within KPFA were not, of course, magically different from those in society in general, with the single exception of gross, unrepentant male chauvinism. The overall culture was one of condemnation of sexism. Expressions of sexism within the station tended to be evidenced largely, by all accounts, in interpersonal one-on-one encounters, not in formal rules or gatherings. Able, experienced women would find their comments not taken as seriously as men's, would find themselves not considered for particular assignments on grounds of their gender, and would encounter a patronizing attitude when proposing new directions. The view that feminism was reducible to lesbianism plus the Equal Rights Amendment was not too hard to find at KPFA. A comparison with Radio Popolare, Milan, discussed in Chapter 19, is not too difficult to make.

Beyond these issues, there had been something of a history of women and people of color finding themselves pitted against each other as groups, all the more easily because there were relatively few women of color at the station. Indeed, the Third World Department had been opposed for some time to the formation of a Women's Department, because it argued that women and women's perspectives were already well-represented inside KPFA (in 1982, for example, two of the four managers and one department head were women). However, the first person to be appointed head of the Women's Department was alert to Third World issues, and relations between the two departments got off to a positive start. As with other problems, so, too, this one is mentioned in the interests of realism: it is hardly unusual in the contemporary United States for white women and Third World people to find themselves asked to divide the crumbs harmoniously between each other.

As noted above in connection with the public meetings at KPFA, these and other strains and stresses tended to be addressed for the most part in private conversation rather than in public. The station contained within it lesbians, homophobes, liberals, anarchists, Marxists, Zionists, and anti-Zionists. Public debates around these subjects, although unlikely to resolve aything, could have split the whole project into multiple factions and destroyed the broadly based coalition it represented. Feminists were not alone in thinking that at least at KPFA you could talk to people individually about these things and that in this respect, it was much better than many other media settings.

Training is the other main point to touch upon in connection with the Women's Department. It is a key topic, because for women, a crippling dimension of technology is that it is defined in many, many ways as a male domain. Women have often found themselves awed by it, even overwhelmed with a false sense of their own inability to confront it. Their tiny numbers in math, science, and engineering careers are partly attributable to the inculcation of this belief into their own thinking from their earliest years. Learning to use media technology successfully can, thus, be a problematic process for women, at least at the outset. Training was, therefore, a particularly important political commitment of the Women's Department.

The amount of time consumed in training was, however, considerable. At one point, the Women's Department was discouraging inexperienced applicants because of this. In the early 1980s, a period of declining employment and welfare payments, the pressures were strong on people to drop everything at KPFA if they could just get a regular wage. This might well have been one reason why so few women of color worked at KPFA, given labor market trends. In practice, KPFA trained people partly by formal instruction and partly by resigning itself to some technical blunders on the air. There was no other way.

In 1982, however, the California Arts Council gave KPFA a grant to do outreach work to women and minority ethnic communities to begin to train them in radio. Two summer concerts were planned to draw attention to the program. As one person observed, however, while KPFA work remained largely unpaid, training would be a particular problem for these groups. Even though the union contract provided for some money for day care, and even though no mother actually told the Women's Department she needed help with programs, it was still highly probable that class factors were invisibly at work, manifest in the low number of women of color working at KPFA.

Openness to the Commuity

Reviewing the station's relations with the outside world, which are after all the acid test of its effective functioning, it is safe to conclude that there was a startling degree of openness in KPFA through nearly all of its history. This is true in contrast with both conventional media and the tiny presses of many left-wing sects. The possibility of dialogue within a broad spectrum on the Left, the potential of alternative media to open up a whole variety of progressive views for debate and consideration, is strikingly demonstrated by KPFA, even taking account of its many problems past and present. One staff-member said to me, in terms that once again evinced the powerful individualism of the station's activists, "We chose to work in KPFA, but not with each other."

Nevertheless, the working experience of coalition and cooperation within a Left so often paralyzed by its own entrenched positions and intrigues is highly positive and constructive. The ruling class, after all, has no idealism (except in the mouths of its professorial and media ideologues), no future vision except its own entrenchment. It can afford to buy off many of its own human traumas. Its passions and commitments exist but are far more easily realizable than the often searing visions, with their fumbling practical approximations, within progressive movements. If we do not learn to work together within those movements, we leave the field amazingly clear to the powers that be. KPFA is a living reminder that, despite huge difficulties inside and out, past and present, such cooperation is viable and creative.

THE 1990s CRISIS

After so many challenges, it might seem impossible to imagine any more—or to believe that another trauma would really threaten extinction. However, by July 14, 1999, when the station was shut down for only the second time in its history, and even then only restarted a week later without any local programming, the most apocalyptic scenario of 50 years had been working itself out. The high—or low—points were as follows.

In the spring of 1995, the Pacifica Board secretly contracted with the American Consulting Group, a union-busting organization. On July 12, 1995, almost 4 years to the day before the 1999 shutdown, the Pacifica Board issued a major policy statement to the five Advisory Boards to KPFA and its sister stations.[8] It began by speaking of "vast changes that [were] to occur at all stations" and promptly went on to underscore with exemplary bluntness that each local Advisory Board "serves at the will and direction of the National Board . . . [its] main responsibility [being] to carry-out [sic] the directives of the National Board and abide by its decisions." In case there was any lingering doubt, the document hammered home the point: "Members of any local Board who do not feel that they can assist Pacifica in its present mission are advised to resign." And the document threatened "appropriate steps" in response to collective or individual actions to "countermand" the National Board's "policies, directives and mandates."

The document's highly confrontational tone set the stage both at KPFA and within the network. A management policy trend to greater secrecy and control over free expression became rapidly evident. One month before the directive was sent, the National Board had announced, in violation of federal communication regulations, that all future finance committee meetings would be closed to the public. In February 1996, a ruling was issued saying that staff would be terminated if they allowed callers to criticize Pacifica policy over the air.[9] In May 1996, the contract with the American Consulting Group was revealed. In August 1997, the affiliate stations in 36 states were given a new clause in their contracts that banned them from running disclaimers concerning the National Board's use of a union-busting firm (American Consulting Group) (Bacon, 1997; Zeltzer, 1999) to expel part-time workers from the union.

Personnel decisions began to become increasingly harsh and contested. In December 1998, Larry Bensky, a long-time KPFA activist, was fired and then reinstated after considerable adverse reaction from listeners. The new KPFA general manager, Nicole Sawaya, permitted him to defend himself on the air. Her contract was not renewed at the close of March 1999, despite—or because—of her having been the most locally respected general manager for quite a number of years. On April 9, Bensky was fired again after promising to discuss Sawaya's nonrenewal on his program. The first of a series of demonstrations against Pacifica National Board policies took place outside KPFA's offices in Berkeley on April 15. On May 9, a major rally was held in support of KPFA in Berkeley, with June Jordan, Holly Near, Barbara Lubin, and others speaking. On June 18, another KPFA veteran, Robbie Osman, was fired for denying that equilibrium had returned to the station (a public claim by Lynne Chadwick, the Pacifica Board's executive director). Another rally took place on June 20 protesting this action, and 14 protesters were arrested the next day for blocking Pacifica's doorway. The day after that, some hundreds turned up at a press conference to denounce these actions in front of the station. Parts of the press conference were played live on the KPFA program, *Flashpoints*.

On June 27, 1999, armed IPSA security guards appeared at the station.[10] On July 12, a leaked memorandum[11] from a Pacifica National Board member to the board's chair was made public. It stated,

> Seriously, I was under the impression there was support in the proper quarters, and a definite majority, for shutting down that unit and reprogramming immediately. Has that changed? Is there consensus among the national staff that anything other than that is acceptable/bearable?

The memo went on to propose that WBAI New York would be a better financial proposition for sale, "as there is a smaller subscriber base without the long and emotional history as the Bay Area . . . a similarly dysfunctional staff though far less effective."

The climax came on the next day, July 13, when long-term KPFA talk-show host Dennis Bernstein broadcast a press conference in which this memorandum was discussed. He was pursued by the IPSA guards into the newsroom, and his confrontation with them went out live, breaking into the evening news. A manager then switched off the station's signal. In the ensuing turmoil, Bernstein and 51 others were arrested.

On July 14, the station was boarded up, and its staff were told they were on paid administrative leave. Daily protests began, including "Camp KPFA," a permanent watch outside the station. Despite large-scale arrests, the protest continued. On July 19, a large benefit concert, put together at high speed in support of the station, was sold out. On July 21, the Pacifica Board had a new line installed to the transmitter to enable KPFA to broadcast from a remote site (Campbell, 1999). Broadcasts of a sister station in Houston were sent out over the air. Two protesters were roughed up by IPSA guards. On July 27, the Berkeley City Council instructed its police force to facilitate peaceful protests and called for the station to be returned to community control.

On August 2, the staff was told to return to work and promised there would be no further gag rule imposed for a test period of 6 to 12 months. However, they were not allowed to inspect the transmitter or transmit local programming until the programming was first produced. And they were under strict instructions that the size and diversity of the local audience must be increased (Selna, 1999).

Many of the changes brought about in the years leading up to my first research into KPFA had been undone in the period since then. Clearly, the inclusion of unpaid staff among union members was a key target in the hiring of American Consulting Group.[12] And along the way in this long battle, both the KPFA Women's Department and the Third World Department had been closed.

What was behind this extraordinary chain of events? They could seem all the more extraordinary on a reading of the Pacifica Board's Strategic Five-Year Plan of April 1997 (*A Vision*, 1997). Because of the secrecy with which the Pacifica National Board conducted its meetings, and its members' united refusal to communicate the nature of their deliberations to members of the public, this document is one of the few sources about their thinking. It was intended for public consumption and must be read in that light, but the first pages offer a bleak analysis of broadcasting in the contemporary United States. With subheadings such as *The Crisis of Democratic Communications, Marginalizing Political Journalism,* and *The Assault on the Public Sphere,* the condition of radio is lambasted as a virtually complete colony of giant media "trusts" such as Time Warner, News Corporation, Sony, and others. The expansion of commercial radio stations with rightist Christian programming is also targeted as a dangerous new phenomenon. And, not least, the board committed itself to a board membership that was at least 50% composed of people of color.

So what differentiated this strongly leftist analysis from the perspectives of most Pacifica broadcasters since the 1960s on the central importance of the Pacifica channel within the "dreary cacophony of crime, mayhem, and sundry disaster stories mingled with pointless celebrity worship and undisguised hawking of products ranging from sneakers to congressional candidates"? Those words are from the 1997 Plan document but could have been written by almost any Pacifica activist over the previous 50 years. The paradox seems acute.

The Left has always suffered from the same self-devouring virus as the ultra Right, and perhaps, some of the rage and venom visible in the struggle between the board and the local programmers at KPFA and the other Pacifica stations could be attributed to that sense of betrayal; the closer people initially consider themselves to be, the greater the explosive passion at times of disagreement. But in this instance, arguably, that passion was more consequence than cause. The cause is important to determine, because of the particular place of Pacifica stations in the American political and media firmament and because of the similar splits quite often arising within radical media in general. These urgently demand analysis and understanding. Ferocious interpersonal and policy quarrels are also well-known at the summit of corporate media, but they are not of interest for present purposes, and their impact is often muffled by money. Not so with radical media, normally scraping along financially.

In a nutshell, the most plausible explanation of the 1999 crisis is that the Pacifica Board considered itself possessed of a progressive yet practical vision for the future of the network, one for which the corporate media dominance their 1997 document excoriated could generate a growing demand. This demand would arise from among the ranks of those wishing to be citizens, not just consumers. Thus, Pacifica—presto!—would become the answer to broadcasting's hypercommercialized crisis, and it is well positioned to do so, because its five stations can be heard by 22% of the U.S. public and in "five of the top ten media markets" (5-Year Plan document). This much is stated explicitly in the document.

Realization of this vision, however, was perceived to be threatened on three fronts: hostile congressional and industry attacks, internal problems, and the lack of time in which to solve the first two issues at leisure before being overwhelmed by them.

The external attacks were real enough. Pacifica, like so many radical media in history, has attracted to itself a seemingly disproportionate share of attention from conservative forces—although only disproportionate if we buy into the view that small-scale radical media are irrelevant. However, from 1994 onward, not only were repeated attacks launched by the Republican congressional majority on federal tax support for the Public Broadcasting System (PBS) and National Public Radio (NPR), but Pacifica was specifically attacked by a series of Republican activists, not least by Senate majority leader and 1996 presidential candidate Robert Dole. Indeed, as early as February 1993, the then KPFA manager was sent to lobby Congress, which was already threatening to cut off Pacifica's funding.

Internally, there were also problems. The 1997 five-year planning document was fairly discreet about what it saw them to be, and it has to be read rather carefully to decode the real nub of the matter. In Part Two, the report makes reference to "real impediments to Pacifica's growth that derive from the limitations of anarchic or bureaucratic systems that are simply dysfunctional in today's fierce competition" and to the Pacifica Board's "inability to fix ineffective and change unsustainable aspects of [our] programming, financing, and basic operations." Later, the document refers to "unpleasant experiences" the board has encountered in the attempt to reform Pacifica—"from character assassination, slander, and misrepresentation to physical threats"—without indicating their source. Under the subsequent heading of *Organizational Culture and Communications*, the planning document announces that the objectives are "(1) to articulate and maintain at all levels of Pacifica clearly defined roles of mutual respect and authority in our working relationships; and (2) to establish and maintain a physically, mentally, and emotionally healthy work culture."

The internal problems, effectively, are seen here as the stranglehold of dyed-in-the-wool, stick-in-the-mud local programmers over the Pacifica channels' output. If this interpretation seems to roam way beyond the fairly guarded language cited, then perhaps reading that language, together with the unguarded language of the leaked memorandum of July 12, 1999, cited earlier, will serve to support it. There is little question that the Pacifica stations, at some periods more than others, have suffered from being colonized by individuals with colossal egos whose identity is irrevocably bound up with their being on the air once a week. At one point at WBAI in New York City during the 1980s, as I know directly, one programmer took up permanent residence in a closet. The station was, in every sense of the word, his world. Indeed, the conditions at WBAI at that time were frankly so often deplorable that I chose to travel to the West Coast from New York, where I then lived, and research KPFA instead, because I wanted to have something positive as well as critical to report. In my experience with Austin Community Access Television in the early 1990s, the same ferocious messianic fervor and colonization of the facility were also much in evidence.[13]

This is absolutely not intended to paint all KPFA programmers with the same brush. It is to acknowledge that in many radical media, problems of this kind persist and weaken those media projects precisely because they are never addressed honestly or systematically. The democratic organization of media is not a panacea that mystically solves organizational problems and failings.

In the 1997 five-year planning document, the Pacifica Board disclaimed that it had "reached the lofty heights of perfection." Nonetheless, its members did lay claim to "an element of the prophetic, so that history will judge that we had the vision to see and the courage to act responsibly." That, in my interpretation, meant their readiness to take the Pacifica stations by the scruff of the neck and wrest control away from the local activists, leaving the latter with "input" but not governance.[14] Only then would the priorities be realized of "economies of scale," putting "resources where there is optimal potential (in terms of audience and finance) for return," allowing them "to bring equipment, technology, staff, and facilities at every operating unit up to at least a minimum broadcast and administrative standard." The 1992 strategic plan had already set in motion a stronger central programming drive, taking space away from local programming, and in early 1999, the Pacifica Board effectively made itself a self-selecting body, canceling representation from the local station boards in its membership.[15] Later in 1999, Pacifica Chair Mary Frances Berry indicated in a semi-impromptu discussion with WBAI staff in New York that selling off that station and KPFA and buying a number of lower-power stations in Atlanta and across the South might well be the option chosen by the Pacifica Board.[16]

It may not be too harsh a judgment to conclude that KPFA and the Pacifica stations, and the Pacifica National Board, were locked into position by rival messianic drives, fed by a shared conviction that Pacifica was the single beacon of light in a broadcasting wilderness.[17] Each side saw itself as a savior and its opposite as the most infuriating and illegitimate of obstacles to survival and success. The Pacifica Board clearly saw its own untrammeled power as required for a solution, and the staff and their supporters not unnaturally—and frankly, reasonably—dug in their heels. It was in part a Beltway-Bay Area fight with no true winners in sight at the time of this writing.

FREE RADIO BERKELEY

Opening up over the airwaves on April 11, 1993, this station was an important and interesting development for at least two reasons. One had to do with the downhill slide at KPFA, for Free Radio Berkeley seemed to have inherited the mantle of the original KPFA. Free Radio Berkeley stood for many of the same principles avowed by Lewis Hill and the Pacifica founders, although their commitment to a diversity of voices and freedom of speech outstripped their traditional-BBC-style vision of quality educative programming. Stephen Dunifer, Free Radio Berkeley's principal founder, built the station's policies around socialist anarchist principles (Sakolsky & Dunifer, 1998, pp. 83-93, 157-180).

The other facet was Free Radio Berkeley's pioneering role in developing the micropower radio movement in the United States and beyond. Important antecedents inspired the Berkeley station: Black Liberation Radio in Springfield, Illinois, in the mid-1980s and the Japanese micropower radio wave, which flourished in the early 1980s (Kogawa, 1985; Sakolsky & Dunifer, 1998, pp. 68-80). But Dunifer's determination to force the FCC to take him to court—FCC rules prohibited stations operating on less than 100 watts—and quite possibly the fact that his project was located in the politicized university town of Berkeley in the equally politicized and generally affluent San Francisco Bay Area, rather than in an African American and poor community, all arguably combined to make his work high profile and thereby to bring it to the attention and interest of other media activists elsewhere in the United States who were developing their own micropower radio projects. Dunifer's missionary energy, bringing his technical engineering skills to bear on advising others about how to handle the practicalities of operating cheap transmitters, fused with other media activists' energy and led to micropower stations opening up in Mexico City and in Chiapas in the later 1990s, and in Haiti, Guatemala, Canada, and other parts of the United States.

For the micropower movement, the principal raison d'être was the dizzying speed of national and global mega-mergers among media, computer, and telecommunications firms during the 1990s. The only location where public speech, rather than speech filtered through the corporate mesh, could be broadcast, so it seemed, was on these tiny, very local stations, each able to broadcast only within a few miles' radius. Of course, in urbanized areas, a considerable number of people could tune in if they wished to and address their fellow citizens as well as listen to them. Compared to setting up an FM or AM radio station, the minimal costs entailed, about $1,000 to $1,500 in the later 1990s, made such projects feasible even within low-income communities.

Such projects faced stiff opposition from the National Association of Broadcasters (NAB), the trade association representing corporate broadcast interests. Its history has consistently been one of encouraging the hounding and marginalization of all noncommercial radio and TV within the United States (Godfried, 1997; McChesney, 1993). The NAB vigorously lobbied both Congress and the FCC to penalize Free Radio Berkeley for breaking the 100-watt rule, and it offered an array of highly specious arguments in support of its contention. These included interference with air traffic control communication and with established radio channels, neither of which claims stood up to technical scrutiny; nevertheless, they sounded plausible to the uninformed.

In late 1999, the FCC announced it would accept micropower broadcasting, after all. This apparent change of heart hid the fact that it proposed to refuse licenses to existing challengers, such as Free Radio Berkeley, that it would permit advertising on these stations, and that it would permit single-agenda owners, rather than opening back up the spectrum for a variety of views. The micropower movement rightly denounced this as a cynical restriction of public access.

It would be an error to assume that the micropower movement was simply a shining David, however. Carol Denney, in her interview in the Sakolsky and Dunifer (1998, pp. 157-164) book, pays tribute to Dunifer's antisexist role within Free Radio Berkeley, but she also underscores the subtle and not-so-subtle exclusionary atmosphere for women generated by a number of the Free Radio Berkeley activists. Black Liberation Radio in Springfield, Illinois, was quite capable of voicing anti-Semitic statements. Some of those most interested in micropower radio were from the ultra Right. Technology, easily accessible or not, does not drive politics or the democratic process.

Summary: A guiding theme of this book is that although the corporate order and the centralized state pose extremely tough obstacles to the realization of a peaceful and democratic process, it is a grave mistake to assume that no serious problems are to be encountered among "the people." There is a kind of triangular relationship here. Neither capitalism nor state power is simply an excrescence that should be surgically removed, leaving the honest and the good untrammeled so they can just get on with bringing about an equitable, productive, and pleasant social order. Each point of the triangle[18] is related to the others in numerous ways. The history of the Left, in the famous ironic epigraph of how the Left forms a firing squad—"Right, now, everyone form a circle!"—is such that the naiveté of only identifying problems that come from above ill befits sensible media activists.

The importance of the KPFA and the Free Radio Berkeley stories is, then, not reduced by their failures. Those failures, as well as their conspicuous successes, are there to provide lessons. A saints-versus-oppressors scenario is only a recipe for disillusionment and fatalism. And in its moralism, it carelessly jettisons the often amazing achievements, constructed with low-to-zero financing, that all-too-human media activists have still managed to generate. Slavitsky and Gleason (1994), for instance, have noted how unusual was Pacifica Radio news in giving voice to activists and in providing broad coverage of international affairs, even when compared with National Public Radio's news, let alone with the corporate news services.

NOTES

1. WCFL Chicago was listener-supported, but up until its sale to Amway in 1978, it was owned by the Chicago Federation of Labor (Godfried, 1997). As we shall see, during the 1990s, it became distressingly clear that KPFA was owned not by its listener supporters but by the Pacifica Foundation, which ultimately had a legal responsibility only to itself. The meaning of the term *independent* refers to the lack of commercialism in the first 50 years of KPFA's existence, not its public ownership. In a revealing episode during the 1999 crisis, nearly 90% of KPFA's listener supporters sent in their annual subscriptions with a rider saying their support was conditional on the station not losing its character. All of those subscriptions were returned. In the meantime, the management was spending large sums of money to hire security guards, a public relations firm, and a firm that specialized in union busting.

2. Lasar (1999, pp. 3-73) provides excellent detail on the experiential and philosophical roots of Hill's and his colleagues' philosophy.

3. See also Lasar (1999) and Land (1999), who focus mostly on KPFA's history through the mid 1960s, but also—more particularly, Land—give some attention to WBAI, New York, KPFA's sister station in the Pacifica Network.

4. This proved, most sadly, to be the final blow for Hill, and the next day he took his own life.

5. The description that follows applies to the early 1980s when I first studied the station.

6. Not only American individualism, it must be said: See the comments on the same phenomenon among the urban intellectual component in the staff of the FMLN guerrilla Radio Venceremos in El Salvador in the 1980s (López Vigil, 1994, pp. 154-160).

7. Land (1999, pp. 113-132) shows how WBAI in New York suffered a huge fall in subscriptions with the end of the Vietnam war in 1975. The links between external movements and radical media are always intimate, if complex.

8. Text is available at http://www.pacfolio.org/document.html.

9. These policies were not only pursued at KPFA. KPFK Los Angeles closed its only Spanish-language public affairs program, *Enfoque Latino,* for having invited discussion of the Pacifica crisis, and it banned one of its award-winning staffers, Robin Urevich, for having published a critical article on the crisis in a small-circulation publication ("Where was/is KPFK? A look at the Pacifica crisis," *Random Lengths,* 8/19/99). See http://www.savepacifica.net.

10. In a document released in early September 1999, Lynn Chadwick, KPFA general manager, admitted to having spent nearly $400,000 on these security guards, and she complained bitterly that the Berkeley police had forced her to do so by failing to do their proper job [www.savepacifica.net].

11. Text available at http://www.savepacifica.net/0713_palmer_letter.html.

12. And in the National Board's attempts to have the National Labor Relations Board declare unpaid staff ineligible to be union members.

13. Former KPFA programmer and supporter Peter Franck similarly refers to the tendency to "ossification" in a talk he gave at the time of the 1999 crisis, reproduced in *Z Magazine* (http://www.zmag.org/CrisesCurEvents/Pacifica/franckint.htm).

14. The term used under the Governance paragraphs in the 1997 Plan: "the right balance between local community input, clear national vision, and governance leadership in order to follow through on the broader goals of the strategic plan. Effective governance is key." It is clear that although community input is named first, the national agenda and management authority outweigh this.

15. They did so on the basis of a ruling from the new Corporation for Public Broadcasting head that local representation was banned under the Public Broadcasting Act. The fact that this individual had previously been a career official with the Voice of America and Radio Martí, the station broadcasting U.S. programming to Cuba, and that the Pacifica Board had requested him to rule on the matter, led many to assume that the request had been orchestrated informally to ensure the desired response. There was nothing in the Act that made this stipulation, but nonetheless the Corporation for Public Broadcasting waved the stick of a withdrawal of $1.4 million to Pacifica if it did not comply.

16. See the report on Berry's remarks by WBAI activist Mimi Rosenberg at http://www.savepacifica.net, transcript dated 8/25/99.

17. The 1997 five-year plan document is quite forceful in its attack on the trend in PBS and NPR to get into bed with corporate interests, using terms such as "collaborate" and "cut deals with," and citing Bill Moyers on "the slippery road to serfdom."

18. Even this triangle does not include the possibility of political party or religious media control, as the Portuguese case studies in Chapter 18 made clear.

22

Samizdat in the Former Soviet Bloc

- The gradually mounting role of radical media in the Soviet bloc from the 1960s through 1991
- Radical media in the Prague Spring
- Polish *Solidarnosc* (Solidarity) and *samizdat*
- The newspaper *Robotnik*
- The *NOWA* underground publishing operation
- From martial law in 1981 to the Communist collapse of 1989

Although many factors came together in the collapse of the former Soviet bloc, radical media were a formidable element in the brew. The Soviet system, launched originally in the midst of the bloodbath of World War I in the name of peace, bread, and justice, was an undertaking that marked the 20th century in many ways; tragically, many of its achievements were for ill in the revolution's homeland and neighboring nations. For some, the history of the Soviet system is 100% negative, and there is no question not only that it never achieved the successes its propaganda claimed, but also that mass slaughter and repression during the Stalin era poisoned its claims on a scale only outdistanced by the Nazis' wars and repression. By the period in which radical media played a critical role, namely, from the mid-1960s through to 1991, when the Soviet Union was officially dissolved, the scale of repression had lessened immeasurably, but a rigid and ruthless system was nonetheless still in place to squelch free public expression and to pound out the party's line.

This history and its meaning for the 20th century would take us too far to pursue here,[1] and so we will focus only on the extraordinary story of radical media in helping to undermine the Soviet dictatorship and, in the process, its direct control over much of central Asia, the Trans-Caucasus, and Eastern Europe from Estonia to Bulgaria. In the annals of such media, their action as solvents gradually contributing to the Soviet Union's collapse represents a particularly remarkable chapter, for not much earlier, the Soviet bloc had appeared virtually impregnable to most observers.[2]

Before getting into the specifics of the story, we need to make one important conceptual and political observation. The leading reason for the significance of radical media in this case is that the Soviet system particularly relied on its channeling and strict control of communication and media, its use of them as a transmission belt for the party's view of reality. Antonín Liehm (1977), a leading radical media activist in the build-up to the Prague Spring, summarized Soviet media culture and the depth of the challenge radical media posed to it in the following terms:

> It is also thanks to the press, radio and television that the Czechoslovak spring was able to mark up another major success to its credit: the re-establishment of horizontal linkages. The Stalinist pyramid does not know, does not admit, does not support, any form of horizontal organization. Every direct contact between the various parts of the pyramid is immediately considered suspect and, dangerous, and thus is expressly forbidden. (p. 92)[3]

OVERVIEW, 1964-1991: THE SPIRALING OF SUBVERSION

Thaw is the term generally applied to certain small and hesitant shifts toward communicative freedom that took place under Soviet Premier Nikita Khrushchev, soon after Stalin's death. By many standards, this had been a cautious and rationed opening up of public expression, but it was nonetheless the first easing in nearly 30 years.[4] In 1964, Soviet leader Khrushchev's ouster heralded a new phase of repression. In 1965, a year later, authors Andrei Sinyavsky and Yuli Daniel were put on trial for publishing outside the Soviet Union and sentenced to severe prison terms. Their punishment sent, and was meant to send, a chilling message to Soviet oppositionists, some of whom nonetheless mounted the very first human rights protest in the Soviet Union on Moscow's Pushkin Square in December 1965.

The further response of a number of oppositionists was to start underground production and circulation of self-published (*samizdat*) poems, novels, and essays, because there was now no hope of their being published any other way. Samizdat publications at that point in time in Soviet Russia (cf. Hopkins, 1983) consisted of typed sheets of paper, most often blurred carbon copies, using all the space on the page, without margins or blank space at the top and bottom. The price of access to one of these documents was to promise to retype it with multiple carbon copies for further readers. This was hardly a dazzling art form, but it was gobbled up greedily, despite the acute risks of imprisonment for those found to be writing samizdat or in possession of such works.[5]

Although our story begins in 1964, resistance to Soviet rule in the rest of the bloc began before then. Milestones were the 1953 Berlin workers' uprising, the 1956 workers' riots in Poznan, Poland, and the attempted revolution in Hungary in 1956.[6] But in 1968, the Soviet suppression of the Prague Spring in the former Czechoslovakia[7] had a much different impact in much of the rest of the bloc outside of Czechoslovakia itself, generating a dogged, slow-burning resistance rather than the Czechs' mostly fatalistic submission.[8] And the roles of radical media in this resistance were considerable.

Briefly, the Czechs and Slovaks had been attempting to create a loyalist reform of the communist system. "Socialism with a human face" was their watchword, partly to signal to the Soviet regime that unlike the Hungarian revolutionaries in 1956, they were not trying to leave the Soviet bloc. The Soviet authorities, unimpressed, soon stamped out their experiment with tanks and an invasion force from most of the Soviet bloc nations.

Reaction elsewhere[9] to this repression of the Czech and Slovak experiment both paralleled and intensified Russian resistance to the new crackdown on public expression that had been taking place in the Soviet Union.

In the meantime, the Polish cauldron had also begun to bubble again, with severe student unrest in spring 1968 that was crushed not only by police billy clubs but also by a vicious anti-Semitic campaign that frightened many members of the small remaining Jewish intelligentsia into emigrating. In 1970, an even bloodier confrontation took place, when demonstrating Polish workers were machine-gunned in Gdansk. These were two further defeats—but not ones that spelled the end of the story. By the mid-1970s, a level of organized opposition was developing in parts of Poland that outpaced anything that had come before it, and radical media were at its core.

Thus, the rollback of minimal communication freedoms in the Soviet Union after Khrushchev, the events in Poland, and the repression of the Czechs' and Slovaks' loyalist reform signaled to all thinking denizens of the Soviet bloc who could be reached by the information that the Soviet bloc's leadership was irrevocably hostile to negotiating real reform. These events made some Russians, and then Poles, Hungarians, and others, all the more determined to generate their own media freedom anyway, whether for literature, political comment, or news of human rights abuse.[10] Thus, samizdat was born and began to spread.

Some other Russian currents were flowing in this direction, too. Guitar poetry, a musical format not unique to Russian culture but anchored in it, had a number of 1960s exponents whose lyrics had in one way or another dealt with issues and themes outside the approved boundaries of official Soviet culture (Smith, 1984). Jazz was another cultural expression rather heavily disapproved by Soviet cultural apparatchiks, in part because it attracted to itself circles of dissident and oppositional thinkers (Starr, 1983). These musical trends were important for the intelligentsia, in particular.

At a later stage, however, as jazz began to lose its dangerous patina, so among the younger generation, and much more widely, Western rock music became frequently symbolic of disgust with the Soviet system—especially when the Soviet authorities confirmed that they themselves indeed interpreted its popularity this way (Ryback, 1989). Audiocassettes of guitar poetry and later of rock music, copied many times, were circulated widely and were known as *magnitizdat*. These embedded an opposition to the regimes that was all the harder to control because of its nonideological diffuseness and the ease of concealing audiocassettes. In young people's eyes, the authorities made themselves look ever more ridiculous and out of touch by trying to suppress the music.

And once the Soviet regimes had lost their youth in large numbers, they had lost their future—not only in fact but also in terms of official political ideology, which pronounced Soviet communism to be the wave of the future of all humanity. Unless the wave were magically to skip a generation or two, this prediction began to look particularly hollow.

Religiously persecuted Soviet citizens almost certainly formed the social base of the majority of samizdat publications. Indeed, samizdat was produced by politically diverse, sometimes mutually hostile groups. Involved were not only the religious and the secular dissidents, with very different goals, but anti-Semitic Russian nationalists along with Jewish dissidents of any stripe, and Ukrainian and other Soviet republic nationalists along with loyalist reformers. (Quite noticeable divergences were also to be found in east-central European dissident circles.) Nonetheless, because of their links with Western journalists and writers and their residence in the two leading cities of Moscow and Leningrad, the secular intelligentsia were those who illegally produced and distributed writings that had the greatest international impact and most unsettled the Soviet bloc elite.

For the Polish intelligentsia, Russian samizdat production acted as a major inspiration. In the course of acting on that influence, Polish samizdat production overtook its model and became far and away the most widespread and impressive within the whole Soviet bloc from the mid-1970s onward.[11] And in turn, it was precisely the *Solidarnosc* movement in Poland that, along with armed resistance in Afghanistan, caused the Soviet system the greatest political problems for the last 15 years of its existence and that did the most to disrupt Soviet hegemony.

There was, then, a remarkable chain of increasingly effective initiatives. The Soviet authorities, keen to put the lid back on their own opposition circles after the ouster of Premier Khrushchev, were particularly concerned to get the Czechs and Slovaks back in line and to squelch their offensive and outrageous experiments, knowing that a number of Russians were observing them with great interest.[12] The Soviet elite was well aware there was student unrest in Poland and that slowly moving forces were in favor of easing up controls in Hungary. Trickles could become a flood. So the Soviets sent in the tanks, thus succeeding in *both* proving their own political bankruptcy *and* systematically sealing off any notion that a political dialogue with them was imaginable.

Thus, the situation offered, for a number of determined Russians and other Soviet citizens, as well as a much larger number of determined

Poles some years later, a single option: to create autonomous public spheres, or as some Polish and Hungarian writers put it, to become engaged in antipolitics.[13] Their vision was realized beyond their wildest imaginings by the massive Polish Solidarnosc movement, at one point numbering 11 million members in a nation of 38 million at the time, and by far the largest alternative public sphere that had ever emerged within the Soviet bloc. Despite its repression under martial law from 1981 to 1985, Solidarnosc shook the Soviet system to its foundations.

Here, I can only underscore the intimate links between this phase and the emergence of *glasnost* policies in the Soviet Union in the mid-1980s (for a detailed presentation, see Downing, 1996). But the pivotal connecting moment was when the new Soviet premier, Mikhail Gorbachev, announced in his first Communist Party Congress speech in March 1986 that the Soviet Union's future depended in large part on canceling out the extreme contradiction eroding Soviet daily life from top to bottom. He was explicit: What had to go was the glaring difference between the official, triumphalist discourse of the system's media and the utterly cynical quality of everyday private conversation.

The logic of his statement was clear. Official media had to become much more like samizdat. Not in appearance, for sure, but in their honesty and diversity. But exciting as this was to some, the horrified reactionaries who heard his speech saw instantaneously what he did not appear to see, namely, that no one knew where, ultimately, to draw the line on how far to go in that direction. However, the brakes were eased, and the truck slowly began to inch downhill.

It picked up speed first with open discussion of ecological problems, already in the fore of the Soviet Union's samizdat (Helsinki Watch, 1987; Komarov, 1978). Concern about the pollution of Lake Baikal had already surfaced in the 1960s, and other issues began to percolate through into specialized bulletins, some of them with carefully restricted circulation. Intermittent plans to divert the giant river Ob's waters to remedy water shortages in central Asia had aroused particular fury among Russian nationalists, who saw Russia's territory being threatened with pillage for the sake of the Asian republics they despised.

And then as glasnost media began to open up the pages on the terrifying history of Stalinist repression, the truck began moving faster and faster (Davies, 1989; Helsinki Watch, 1990; Nove, 1989). Within a little over 2 years, the foundational silences and horrors of Soviet history and the very prospect of a Soviet future were under fierce and widespread public attack.[14] Much of this information had already been circulating in samizdat form, but now it filtered into large circulation media. Historians were subversives: This recovery of collective memory almost instantaneously corroded the legitimacy of Stalin's heirs. In the final 2 years of the Soviet Union (1990-1991), especially in 1991, the use of newer electronic technologies such as fax, E-mail, satellite, and cable also played a major role in allowing activists to force open the public realm (see Ganley, 1996).[15]

Having sketched out the broad lines of the story through to glasnost in the Soviet Union in the late 1980s, I will devote the rest of this chapter to a brief summary of radical media in the blossoming of the Prague Spring and then, in more detail, to radical media and the Solidarnosc movement in Poland. These are stories of tremendous import for an accurate appreciation of the significance of such media in 20th-century history.

Two observations need to be made before we move on, one historical, the other relating generally to this book's argument.

First, this is an appropriate moment to acknowledge that a key part of this alternative media story also belongs to the Western radio stations: the BBC, Deutsche Welle, Voice of America, Radio Liberty, and Radio Free Europe (Shanor, 1985; Semelin, 1997). Their entire history is far too extensive to include here, and it also has its shadow side (cf. Alexeyeva, 1986), but their crucial role—when they were not being jammed—was often to take samizdat publications and broadcast their texts to a wider audience than could possibly have accessed them directly. Yes, of course, they were funded and designed to further the global interests of U.S. and Western corporate powers, but to recognize only that dimension of their operation is to be singularly myopic.

Second, the sequence of events in both Russia and Czechoslovakia was a classic case, paralleled in many other instances cited in this book, of the state's frank acknowledgment—signaled by its repressive practice—of the subversive potency of radical media. It was also, even more significantly, an index of the indelible impact of a period of communicative freedom: The Prague Spring was a much more extensive case than the Soviet thaw, and the 1980-1981 years of Solidarnosc were stronger still. These events demonstrated how a collective experience shaped the persistence of radical media activists' vision of an alternative mode of organizing the public realm. To have known day to day that degree of openness, and then to have it seized and ground into powder, meant only that its possibility no longer felt imaginary, abstract, utopian. On the contrary, its remembered vividness shone all the more brightly in the new, gray setting of "normalization."[16]

This is why such moments of explosion—the Paris Commune, May-June 1968 in Paris; the Prague Spring; the first phase of the Solidarnosc movement through 1981; the many other moments large and small touched on in this book—are often infinitely more potent than their relatively brief existence would suggest. This explains why the ephemeral character of many radical media is no guide to their long-term impact.

MEDIA AND THE PRAGUE SPRING

This story separates fairly naturally into three parts: the antecedents to the Prague spring, the concentrated events of 1968 up to the Soviet invasion of August 21, and the extraordinary week that followed.

What happened in Czechoslovakia in 1968 has often been defined as simply the culmination of long-suppressed intellectual outrage at censorship, combined with national outrage at Soviet domination. The truth encompasses both these dimensions but is much richer and more complex. For example, on the question of censorship: Meetings of farmers and workers provided support for the abolition of censorship in 1968. Regarding Soviet domination, Czechoslovak attitudes to the Soviet Union up to August 1968 were generally positive. No Soviet armies had been on their soil since 1948, and until the early 60s, due to its prewar industrial base, the country had been something of an economic showcase within the Soviet bloc. Overwhelmingly, too, change was desired by people at all levels in the Communist Party itself (Mlynar, 1980).

Czechs and Slovaks saw themselves as simply taking a series of pragmatic steps to redistribute power away from the apex: "the readaptation of socialism to the specific conditions of Czechoslovakia" (Liehm, 1977, p. 86) and "a renaissance of socialism" (Hamsik, 1971, p. 161). Western commentators saw these steps as reinstating parliamentary democracy; Western leftists subjected them to suspicious scrutiny, in case they really were restoring capitalism; and the Soviet bloc's oligarchs regarded them with genuine panic, hearing the tocsin of their own demise. Reformist Czechs and Slovaks found it incomprehensible and frustrating that their perfectly reasonable discussions should be given such loaded interpretations, particularly when their own consensus was for organizing a self-managed socialist order.

The historical character of Czech culture was a factor here. From the 15th-century revolt of Jan Hus and his followers against established religious and political authority, Bohemia and Moravia had represented an island of commitment to religious tolerance and, to some degree, even of democracy in a Europe of sectarian strife and absolutist kingdoms. Setting it totally apart from the other east-central European countries is the fact that in the open election of 1946, the Czechoslovak Communist Party had gained over 35% of the votes and together with the Social Democratic Party, won an absolute majority in parliament. These powerful democratic and pluralistic traditions, although repressed under the Nazis from 1938 to 1945 and under Stalinism beginning in 1948, were very far from dead.

The country's emergence from Stalinist repression was slow and painful, pioneered in the main by filmmakers, economists, sociologists, writers, and certain magazine journalists. Film, especially animated film, was organized in small workshops that made it hard to supervise closely: Cartoons, as we have underscored, can concentrate political critique very effectively. When the economy stagnated, economists' views had to be taken seriously. Sociologists, studying actual life, became willy-nilly spokespeople for what Liehm (1977, p. 50) has called the "parallel reality," that is, everyday experience, as contrasted to government definitions of reality. In particular, the Writers' Union played a significant part. It had its own publishing house, not—by a historical quirk—owned directly by the state, and it also administered the Literary Fund. The latter drew its revenue from receipts on its published books and magazines and especially from its editions of classical texts. In turn, this enabled the Fund to give writers stipends or advances and allowed the Writers' Union an autonomy that, although limited, gave it considerable political weight.

The Writers' Union's first signal victory was one that from a distance seems tragicomic. It was their 1963 conference decision to rehabilitate Kafka as an eminent national writer. Given his enduring mark on world literature and political vision, this seems comic. But given his meticulous dissection of the procedures of unaccountable state power in *The Trial* and *The Castle*, the vote was politically vital in the Czech context.

The two key magazines were the Czech weekly *Literárni noviny* (Literary News) and the Slovak weekly *Kulturny zivot* (Cultural Life). Although subject to censorship, writers enjoyed more freedom than journalists. Indeed, *Literárni noviny* came to be under virtual self-management during 1967, as a result of disputes between the party and the Writers' Union about who should fill its leading posts. This left a formal vacuum of power at its head and so eased its writers' situation still further. Relations between the authorities and the magazine had been strained for a considerable period.[17] In any given week, up to a third of the material in *Literárni noviny* would be confiscated, an index of its writers' continually bucking against censorship rather than the censors' activism.

Matters came to a head in the fourth Writers' Union Congress of June 1967. Without any prior planning (because of the danger of being defined as part of an anti-party group), speaker after speaker, using independently prepared materials, rose to attack the censorship system and the state's muzzling of writers and communicators. The powers-that-be were enraged, banned *Literárni noviny*, threatened to abolish the Writers' Union and seize the Literary Fund, and put an army colonel in charge of a new safe weekly, also entitled *Literárni noviny*. But no one was deceived: All the familiar names had disappeared from the magazine, which was very dull. And the Slovak Writers' Congress publicly denounced the changeover.

This was the most dramatic confrontation to date between communicators and the power center. The power center was obsessed with newspapers, much more than broadcasting or film. It was terrified that the writers' plague might pass to the daily press. For, indeed, there were stirrings inside all the mass media. A particularly significant practice had gathered momentum in the period leading up to 1968 of having journalists tour the country and engage in question-and-answer sessions. Such lateral communication was unprecedented, and in these informal verbal encounters, the journalists were often a great deal more forthcoming about the true situation and their feelings concerning it than they ever felt free to be on the air or on the printed page.

The appetite for change was, therefore, being whetted, but at that point its stimulation consisted of largely separate and mutually insulated endeavors, with no one circle usually being aware of the similar perspectives or even the existence of the others. Havlicek (1973) commented, "In conditions of strictly secret reports flowing from below to the central bureaucratic apparat, which then released selected and manipulated information in little doses, a horizontal understanding . . . had been impossible" (p. 251). The confrontation over *Literární noviny* became a major factor in the January 1968 Communist Party Central Committee decision actually to depose the party leader Antonín Novotny, who had run the country since 1953. With his imminent removal, the efforts of minority media such as *Literární noviny*—which had grown to a circulation of 120,000 in a country of only 14 million—began to be taken up by the major media.

The impact was astonishing. At once, many isolated groups and individuals started to discover their commonality of feelings, frustrations, and aspirations. Perhaps, the media productions with the most impact in the early months were live TV broadcasts of a several-hours-long youth meeting and of a similar type of open discussion at a farm cooperative. In March, a large meeting of 17,000 people was held in Fucik Park Congress Palace in Prague and broadcast live by radio to the whole country. It went on for 6 hours and contained many moving pleas for justice for those wrongly imprisoned and executed in the 1940s and 1950s and for a democratized socialism; the meeting ended by voting overwhelmingly for Novotny's resignation from all posts in the party and the government.

These were major media occurrences but not isolated ones. Journalists began for the first time to be allowed behind the scenes at district and regional party conferences, and the were given immediate reports of debates within the Presidium (even White House arguments are leaked rather than presented). Rapidly, broadcasting switched to searching out the general public and asking people live what they thought about the issues of the day. The readers' columns of the press expanded to handle the flood of correspondence that arrived from masses of people hitherto mute. None of the Novotny regime's idols was sacred: his own son, appointed director of Artia, the foreign languages publishing house, was publicly interviewed because of widespread disbelief in his qualifications for the post. He claimed, in his defense, to have completed his graduate economics course at the Prague School of Economics. The station was immediately telephoned by the school's rector, who set the record right on the air by pointing out that Novotny's son had dropped out of school after 2 years.

This instance mirrored many others. Leading regime figures were telephoned on the air and asked questions about public policy; after they had finished speaking, the lines were opened for critical comment from listeners. One semiweekly radio program, *Songs With a Telephone,* became especially well known for its work in this realm. The impact of the media on the power structure was formidable in certain cases. The then-defense minister gave a particularly low-level performance on TV. Soon afterward, he resigned, embarrassed out of office. The trade union newspaper *Pract* wrote an editorial on the art of knowing when to resign. Not many days later, this was followed by the resignation of the head of the trade union federation.

Perhaps the tensest broadcasting encounters were radio interviews with people whom the regime had tortured in the 1940s and 1950s or with former prison guards in such institutions. One TV program actually brought together some of those who had been tortured with their former tormentors. Of all issues, this was the most sensitive, and it had been the most absolutely censored, for it laid bare the real character of the post-1948 regime. Justice for those deeply or irrevocably wronged in that period was a major preoccupation of political debate in the Prague Spring.

The public's reaction was extraordinary. People were buying six or seven newspapers a day, and some were listening to the radio till 3 a.m. In some homes, both radio and TV would be on in the same room, with the listeners attending first to one and then to the other, depending on what was being said.[18]

Regime figures rarely shared this enthusiasm. We have already seen the acute embarrassment experienced by some. Many were exceedingly nervous with the media, being totally unaccustomed to any form of accountability or public contact. Even such major reformers as Josef Smrkovsky took the view that the media had run ahead of themselves. In a press interview in Moscow, possibly tailored for Soviet Politburo consumption, he nonetheless bluntly affirmed that once the journalists had talked themselves out, it would be necessary to clip their wings (cited by Jezdinsky, 1973, p. 265). The view was common at the top that journalists now thought themselves to be the natural organizers of the country, although this arrogance was actually to be found only among a minuscule number. Thus, even reform-minded politicians were still strongly stamped by the secretive traditions of the past, and they found media openness unnerving rather than exhilarating. Their reaction was not shared by most people, who for the first time found they were being empowered to act as citizens rather than as cogs.

It should be said, however, that there were far-reaching changes in the official definition of the media between April and August 1968. The April manifesto of the new Communist Party direction, the Action Program, described the media as "state institutions." The media policy document prepared for the Communist Party's 14th Congress, scheduled for September and held in secret during the first days of the Soviet occupation, had revised *state* to *social* and asserted that "it is only natural that their activity should be kept under review by the representative organs of the people" (cited by Havlicek, 1973, p. 250)—that is, parliament, not permanent state officials.

Journalists themselves changed rapidly during 1968. Some were encouraged to vacate their posts by financial inducements to early retirement. A number of older, even fairly conservative journalists welcomed the change in media direction, not so much because they had a deep desire for change but because they felt less anxious about getting into trouble for what they wrote. Others became suddenly and quite unpredictably radicalized. In *Rude Právo,* the party newspaper, its reactionary editor was simply outvoted at editorial meetings.

Most important, many media executives stepped down. This meant that new appointments had to be made with party approval; and because no one on the side of reform wished them to be made until the personnel in power in the party had been changed at the forthcoming 14th Party Congress, no one was in a hurry to urge that the vacancies be filled. Thus, in the absence of the former controllers, media workers simply got on with their jobs. In this fashion, the media really became self-managed.

In some cases, journalists wrote contrary to their editors' instructions. In most of these cases, Jezdinsky (1973) reported, "there was no punishment or even reprimand, since any tampering with an author's text would be considered a violation of the proclaimed freedom of the press" (p. 267). In other cases, when journalists were forbidden by a superior to write about certain issues, they proceeded to write stories about how and why they were being censored. The journalists also reformed their own organization, the Journalists' Association, which previously had been packed with hacks and nonentities. In April 1968, they formed the Prague City Organization of the Journalists' Association (more journalists worked in Prague than anywhere else), which would be responsive to their needs and wishes.

In general, once journalists began managing their own production, they became active in demystifying the past and in preparing people to take an active role in public decision making. This also meant debunking the political codewords prevalent in the previous official discourse.

Phrases were held up for scrutiny, such as "the readjustment of prices" (= price increases), "love of truth" (= readiness to denounce one's neighbor), and "love of humanity" (= relentless repression of dissent). Preparing people to act responsibly in the present was widely defined by journalists as developing "critical distrust of the government" in the period when it was unclear whether the reformers would go as far and as fast as the mass of the public wished.[19]

One final but crucial dimension of the Prague Spring must be underlined. It is quite clear that the activists in the cause of reform were initially students and intellectuals. Workers, long accustomed to being refused their own rights to organize autonomously and perpetually bearing the brunt of mistaken policy changes from above, were initially suspicious and slow to be closely involved. As the weeks went by, however, the long-dormant political and union consciousness still present within the Czech working class began to revive and to impinge ever more forcefully on the situation. As a result, self-management structures in industry outlasted the Soviet invasion for well over a year before the new pro-Soviet regime could reassert control. Not the slowness, but the tenacity with which this change of involvement took place within the Czech working class is deeply encouraging, given that it had been deprived of political engagement for a full 30 years of the Nazi occupation, with just a brief lull from 1945 to 1948.

The story of these media in resisting the Soviet occupation is extraordinary. Jezdinsky (1973, p. 275) writes that they helped to destroy the original Soviet plans quickly to form a pro-occupation government and to liquidate reformist leaders.

How did they do this? First, there was massive cooperation by people in official quarters with media workers—in the post office and the army, as well as nonjournalistic staff of the media themselves. Second, a whole network of radio transmitters had originally been installed in the country to act as an alternative communication network in the event of a NATO attack. In August 1968, this network was mobilized to defend the country against the Warsaw Pact forces.

Stations broadcast 24 hours a day during that week, giving news of the Soviet occupation, urging people to stay calm, challenging the credibility of Soviet claims, announcing the license plate numbers of secret police cars, and even giving weather reports to farmers. A number of large enterprises had their own transmitters, which were used both to broadcast and to jam Soviet broadcasts. There were frequent reassertions of unity between the Czech and Slovak peoples. Programs were also broadcast in minority languages: Czechoslovakia's quarter of a million gypsies were addressed in Romany, and other broadcasts were made in Polish, Hungarian, Ruthenian, and Russian. After 5 days, four different TV channels were operating secretly, compared to the normal two.

Wechsburg (1969) has described the situation graphically:

> Old ladies brought the (media) workers flowers and cookies, telling a Soviet patrol to look for them in the opposite direction. There were stations that stayed in one place, and also mobile ones, many, it seemed, under control of the Czechoslovak army. (p. 32)

He also cites the final announcement of the last independent radio: "We want to assure you that we will never betray you. We've become a living part of the nation and of the Communist Party.[20] You gave us a mandate and we fulfilled it, day and night" (p. 110).

SOLIDARNOSC

There was a decisive difference between the Prague Spring and Polish media experience from 1976 to 1989. In Poland, with a few notable exceptions, the media that expressed mass consciousness and debate were organized independently and survived despite sustained efforts to crush them. Rather than a reform sponsored by many leading elements within the regime, the Polish experiment consisted of an endeavor to solve the nation's chronic problems in economy, politics, culture, public ethics, and social morale by developing a carefully bounded opposition movement, deeply conscious of the limits set on its freedom to maneuver by the Soviet invasions of Hungary and Czechoslovakia. Solidarnosc, despite its internal divisions, was agreed on this; so, overwhelmingly, were the organizers of underground media.

The story of these years has been told in so many books and articles[21] that it would be pointless to recount it in detail here. Basically, it began within working class circles in the Baltic seaports of Gdansk, Gdynia, and Szczecin from the 1950s through the early 1970s (Goodwyn, 1991; Laba, 1991). Beginning in 1976, the first attempts were made at joint action between those circles and the radical Warsaw intelligentsia. By 1980, a huge insurgent nonviolent labor movement had developed in

Poland, which called itself Solidarnosc. Increasingly tense relations characterized its relations with the Polish Communist Party elite (and behind them, the Soviet elite), until in December 1981, the Polish government instituted martial law and interned nearly 5,000 Solidarnosc activists. Solidarnosc was suspended, then banned in 1982, and martial law continued through 1985. There followed an increasingly restive period culminating in the peaceful transition to a non-Communist government in 1989.

Censorship under the Sovietized regime was systematic (although not as harshly enforced as in Romania or post-1968 Czechoslovakia). For instance, the state archives of the 1956 Poznan workers' uprising did not contain the court records but instead a note from the political police in the file stating "materials with no historical value" (cited in Starski, 1982, p. 131). The 1940 Soviet army massacre of thousands of unarmed Polish officers at Katyn was systematically dated by the authorities in 1941, when the Nazis held the territory ("it is necessary," wrote the censor in 1975, "to stress the undesirability of an exhaustive treatment of the Katyn affair in either historical or, more particularly, in journalistic works"; cited in Swianewicz, 1979, p. 195). When such deformations are common and condoned, then a whole people's culture, historical awareness, and sense of public ethics are seriously undermined. Media language, too, as noted in the Czech case above, was wooden, dreary, jargonized.

These factors go a long way toward explaining the widespread skepticism of media in Poland, the fierce hunger for reliable information. Skepticism of official media has been perfectly summed up for a Western readership by Adam Szcypiorski:[22]

> Foreigners thus sometimes find Poland to be a country of bizarre reactionaries who refuse to believe the crimes of the Chilean junta, are sceptical about the problems of terrorism in Italy, reject as untrue reports of racial segregation in South Africa, approve of the *Berufsverbot* in West Germany, and so on. A mind fed on garbage becomes poisoned. (cited in Steven, 1982, p. 261, note 2)

The corresponding yearning for reliable information was the motor that drove the unofficial media that began to blossom from 1976 onward, to an extent that took even their organizers by surprise. *Puls* (Pulse), a literary magazine, cost 10 times the price of the official literary periodicals, but only the problems in producing it held its run at 2,000. *Gazeta Krakowska,* a remarkably independent Krakow paper even though it was officially produced, had a cover price of 1 zlota but an unofficial Warsaw price of 300 zloty. It printed half a million copies, but its editor estimated that without the endemic paper shortages,[23] it could have sold 3 million.

Information Bulletin 8 (February 1977) set out the case for such media unambiguously:

> The information [this] contains serves the cause of openness in public life and constitutes a chronicle of reprisals both against its culture and its heritage. By disseminating this bulletin you are acting within your rights, and playing a part in their defense. Read it, copy it, and pass it on. Expose cases of violation of civil rights. Remember—by destroying this bulletin you are sealing your own lips, and those of others. (cited in Raina, 1981, p. 55, note 15)

The key element in the Polish situation that has been left out until now is the place of the Catholic Church, the most confusing element in the situation for outsiders. Newsreels of hard-bitten shipyard workers confessing to priests, kneeling to receive communion, and singing to the Virgin Mary while in the midst of a militant occupation of shipyard and docks unprecedented in postwar Poland, undoubtedly mystified many outside observers at the time, including myself. The especially conservative stance of the Polish Catholic hierarchy on doctrine and personal ethics, compared to say the Dutch or even the American Catholic hierarchy, served to make the problem even more intractable.

However, the Catholic Church had always been identified with Polish national aspirations, throughout the 123 years since the nation was chopped up and divided between Russia, Germany, and the Hapsburg Empire. Despite dismaying concessions to anti-Semitism in the interwar years, the clergy played a significant role during the Nazi era in the 1944 Warsaw Uprising, and during the sovietized period after the war, the church provided the only alternative public space in Polish life. Its grip on postwar Polish life was intensified by the demographics of postwar Poland: The large prewar Jewish population were the victims of genocide; the national frontiers had shifted westward, with the inadvertent effect of reducing the Orthodox Christian population; and the

German minority had been expelled after the war. Thus, Poland was more Catholic and monolingual than it had been for many centuries.

It is true, indeed, that the Catholic hierarchy was extremely traditionalist. Yet, only by hierarchical organization was the institution at that time protected from the State, as theologian Stanislawa Grabska explained:

> Take the situation of a parish. If the parish priest tries to democratize the parish, by involving lay people, or organizing a commission to oversee economic matters, then, very soon, a proportion of those lay people will turn out to be members of the political police. And how is he to detect them? How is he to involve people without immediately coming under the influence of the government? (cited in Potel, 1982, p. 101)

We see, then, a society void of opportunities for public communication except within the strict confines of a traditionalist Catholic Church, a different illustration of the *mestizaje* of which Martín-Barbero (1993) writes. Our task in the remainder of this chapter is to record how the explosion of secular underground media took place from 1976 and continued under martial law.

The Explosion of Underground Media

The struggle over media formed a major strand throughout the conflicts of those years. In 1976, after many striking workers at Radom and the Ursus plant had been arrested, some badly beaten up, jailed, and blacklisted from work, a group of Warsaw intelligentsia decided to set up KOR (Committee for Workers' Self-Defense). Its members included heterodox Marxists, a distinguished abbot, and unaffiliated humanitarians. The first of the new wave of underground media were the signed KOR communiqués and *U Pragu* (On the Verge).

There were two noteworthy features of KOR, in particular. First, its members actually put their names on the communiqués, a courageous action that challenged the official culture of intimidation. Second, KOR publicized the details of individual workers and their families victimized by the police and collected funds to support them financially, legally, and medically. The communiqués, rather like the Russian *Chronicle of Current Events*, concerned themselves almost exclusively with these cases. Whereas in 1968 the student intellectuals had protested alone, and in 1970 the Baltic workers had stood alone, for the first time, an attempt was under way to join forces. The people involved had about as much idea as the proverbial flower cracking through concrete of the dramatic impact these sometimes barely legible typed sheets were about to have.

The power structure reacted sharply, although not instantly, and jailed a number of KOR's members. However, they and the 1976 strikers were all freed in an amnesty on July 22, 1977. The stage was now set for the next confrontation. KOR changed its name to KOS, short for Social Self-Defense Committee. Several new publications emerged, such as the *Information Bulletin* (after the paper by the same name from the 1944 Warsaw Uprising), *Glos* (Voice), *Robotnik* (Worker), *Spotkania* (Meetings), *Opinia,* and others. KOR and ROPCIO (Movement in Support of Human Rights) generally supported this activity. The only official expression of KOR remained the communiqués. ROPCIO was closely tied to the monthly *Opinia.*

From 1977 through 1980, a stream, then a torrent, and finally a flood of underground publications[24] emerged, representing a wide range of viewpoints on how to deal with the Polish crisis. Initially reproduced by the most primitive methods (the classical Soviet samizdat method of typing with carbon paper), the technology gradually became more and more sophisticated—and correspondingly subject to stiffer and stiffer fines and sentences if people were caught. The central node in this publishing system, although not its only outlet, was the publishing house NOWA (Niezalezna Oficyna Wydawnicza, independent publishing house). At its peak, NOWA was using no less than 5 tons of paper a month and had printed more than 200 pamphlets, journals, and books: an incredible achievement for a venture defined as illegal by the authorities and repressed whenever the opportunity arose.

The underground press became more and more visible over time, in the sense that people would begin to display its titles and those of the émigré press openly on their bookshelves. Then, people started to read this material openly on the buses and trains and in other public spaces. Finally, it became extremely chic to have read a wide range of underground publications. Distribution points for this literature came to be well known and intensively patronized.

In addition, there were important symbolic forms of radical communications analyzed by Laba (1991, pp. 140-153) and by Kubik (1994). Laba examines cartoons of Solidarnosc leader Lech Walesa, portraying him as Everyman, as trickster, and as antihero, as well as the sharply different message of the grandiose and aggressive depictions of official Communist leaders. Kubik examines various other cases, but especially the mnemonic significance of the wooden cross first set up where the Gdansk workers had been gunned down in 1970 and then the tall triple steel cross erected later in its place.

Thus, by the time Solidarnosc emerged in August 1980 out of the worker occupation of the Gdansk shipyard, there was already an amazing volume of independently produced print media, ranging from national and foreign literary classics to modern novels and poetry, from heavyweight political journals to single-issue flyers and posters. The third demand of the Inter-Factory Strike Committee (the embryo of Solidarnosc) in the unprecedented public negotiations with the Polish prime minister, broadcast by loudspeaker throughout the shipyards,[25] concerned media. The Strike Committee demanded an end to censorship except for state and economic secrets and pornography, and protection of the rights of atheists and believers alike (Ascherson, 1982, pp. 174-175).

The tempestuous months between then and December 1981 were to see repeated struggles over the right to independent media communication. The state, having almost no journalists of talent to defend itself and with most of its broadcasting crews and printers belonging or sympathetic to Solidarnosc, was reduced to pathetically crude attempts at disinformation that nobody believed, to news blackouts on key events, and to sporadic repression of independent communication projects. By the late summer of 1981, with the economy in deeper and deeper crisis, the authorities opted to try to place the blame on Solidarnosc, and this became the main thrust of their media strategy in the short term. In August 1981, five leading members of the Polish Journalists' Association, journalists on state papers, issued the following press response:

> We feel it our duty to draw attention to the fact that the most recent propaganda campaign is helping create the mood of confrontation. . . . [The media] are condemning a partner who is not allowed to speak for himself. . . . A whole series of interventions by the censorship have served to promote a version of events that is out of keeping with the truth. (cited in Ruane, 1982, p. 223)

Only the Solidarnosc newspaper published this statement; its publication, however, was bitterly denounced by government spokespeople.

Solidarnosc, faced with persistent refusal to grant it the access to the airwaves it had been promised in 1980, decided to fight. It called a newspaper strike for August 19 to 20, 1981, which it promised to call off if allowed to explain its case on radio or TV. The government refused, saying that Solidarnosc already published a weekly paper of over half a million copies and "an avalanche of leaflets and posters." The strike itself was successful. Even *Trybuna Ludu*, the party newspaper, had to be printed on the small presses of the party's Central Committee. Most newspaper stands refused to accept the few papers that did get printed. Then, because the government had refused to send a crew consisting only of Solidarnosc members to the Second Solidarnosc Congress in September, the union refused access to any official Polish TV crews. At the Congress itself, there was an overwhelming vote in favor of public control of the media.

Meanwhile, the state was moving into action. The political police began arresting increasing numbers of independent media vendors, usually in major public places at the busiest time of the day, as though trying to spark a clash. Secretly, even at the end of 1980, the police collected the names of all Solidarnosc members with important communications jobs. All regional broadcasting was declared subject to strict central control from Warsaw, and nothing could be broadcast from Gdansk. Technical breakdowns in communication were arranged to block undesirable broadcasts. Only technical staff specially vetted by the police were to work in an emergency, and all broadcasting stations were carefully guarded to prevent any intrusion by "undesirable" people.[26]

Once martial law was instituted, the tenuous control General Jaruzelski's junta[27] enjoyed over the minds of media personnel was illustrated by the fact that just one radio channel, one TV channel, two national dailies (belonging to the party and the Army), and a few minor provincial papers were allowed to continue until the new authorities felt their grip was sufficiently secure.

However, even a year after martial law was imposed, the deputy chief of the political police said his squads had seized over a million leaflets, silenced 11 radio transmitters, found 380 printing shops, and confiscated nearly 500 typewriters (Nowak, 1983). One of the first major messages from these sources after martial law was a detailed set of instructions on how to make your own copy machine.

We will pause now for a moment to examine two major examples of Polish samizdat dating from that period, noting some others in passing, and then will return to the story of radical samizdat under martial law. The two cases I will present are short case histories of how alternative public spheres were constructed in Polish society. I will focus on *Robotnik* (Worker) and on NOWA itself, the central node in Poland's underground media. This list is far from exhaustive. A full treatment would have to deal with the Solidarnosc weekly paper, even though it submitted itself to censorship; with *Jednosc* (Unity), a weekly paper published in Szczecin without censorship; with underground political and literary magazines such as *Puls, Glos* and *Zapis*; with regional papers such as *Solidarnosc z Gdanskiem* (Solidarity With Gdansk) published in Lodz and the remarkably independent *Gazeta Krakowska* (Steven, 1982, Chapter 12); with the processes that enabled Andrej Wajda to make and exhibit two extraordinary feature films deeply critical of the regime, *Man of Marble* and *Man of Iron*, and other filmmakers to produce sometimes equally critical films; with the making and impact of the documentary *Workers 1980*; and with the diffusion of numerous audiocassettes of those negotiations through Polish factories. A book would also have to address the impact of broadcasting material from all these sources via Radio Free Europe.

What follows, however, is by way of giving a preliminary view of radical media at that time in Poland. It is based on the testimony of some of those deeply involved, living at the time of interviews in the early 1980s in exile in the United States.

Robotnik ("Worker")

Of all the mass publications,[28] this one played the crucial role in forging an alliance between the intellectual opposition in Warsaw and the workers' opposition outside in the Ursus factory, Gdansk, Szczecin, Katowice, Nowa Huta, and elsewhere. The process was not a magic one. Indeed, given the almost universal problems in such a coalition, added to repression by the political police, it is surprising to see how successful it was. Furthermore, few people would have been more surprised than the *Robotnik* staff themselves, despite their hopes.

After the initial phase of practical assistance to the Radom and Ursus workers had passed in 1976, the future *Robotnik* group started to organize workers' study groups. A number of workers came up to Warsaw and took part in the discussion. However, this project was not fruitful. The workers knew that association with Warsaw radicals could easily lead to further repression, and the study groups were not producing enough practical results to appeal to the workers involved. As one staff member put it, "Not every victim from the crowd is able to become a conscious activist."

Back to the drawing board. A member of the group, Wojtek Onyskiewicz—"who is known to have visions," as one of his colleagues pleasantly put it—argued for starting a newspaper to act as the instrument and connecting link for the formation of workers' commissions. These latter were explicitly conceived following the model of the illegal labor unions formed in Franco's Spain.

Typed on sheets of 8 by 11-inch paper, single-spaced, without margins, and folded in four for discreet distribution, the first issue of 400 copies hardly looked like a conventional newspaper. Nonetheless, its very specific, down-to-earth contents and the fact that it was not official created enormous demand. From hectographic reproduction, its publishers moved to silk-screen printing, the logic at the time being that if the police were to seize their printing technology, they would not be financially prevented from starting over. In silk-screen printing, three people were needed initially to produce in large quantities: one to pull down the press, a second to lift it up again, and a third to remove the printed sheet and replace it with a blank one. "A technical revolution," as one of them cheerfully put it, took place between Issues 8 and 9, consisting of using the elastic from a pair of briefs instead of crew member No. 2. Production of Issue 9 rose to 3,000 copies. By Issue 16, the newspaper had three columns; by about the 20th, its publishers were paying to have it printed, by the 40th, they were paying several printers' teams. Issue 60, a chronicle of the August 1980 strikes, hit 70,000 copies.

Mushrooming growth, indeed. Distribution was organized by sending packets of the paper to 50 different locations, where they would be individually distributed. Distribution carried less severe penalties than printing, and in certain localities, it was done fairly openly. Lech Walesa, leader of Solidarnosc, was better known to most shipyard workers in Gdansk as a *Robotnik* distributor at the gates than as a former electrician in the yards.

This is not to say the paper was left in peace by the police. People were arrested, beaten up, and continually harassed. One woman activist faced an attempt to have her small daughter thrown out of preschool. A miner lost his bonuses and was put on the lowest pay scale; his windows were painted over, and cow dung was put under his front door;

his wife, who had distant relatives in West Germany, was told that there was no future for her in Poland and that she should leave for the Federal Republic.

Regarding reader feedback, for a long while, there was nothing for the editorial board to go on beyond the rapidly mounting demand for the paper. Readers' letters were few and far between. Thus, the editors had to produce *Robotnik* according to their own lights. However, after a time, they began to add some articles with wider focus to their usual copy on strikes, labor conditions, industrial mismanagement and corruption, and agricultural conditions. They had begun to sense that their readers were now ready to consider larger questions. Thus, it was that historical articles on Poland, biographical sketches of leaders of the Polish Social Democratic Party (extremely influential between the two world wars and still a source of inspiration to many Polish activists at that time), articles on the Pope's 1979 visit and on the 60th anniversary of Polish independence, became important parts of the paper. This shift in emphasis coincided with the switch to three columns: The first was used for issues of the moment, the other two for more analytical pieces.

The paper's political thrust was an antidogmatic egalitarianism, derived in equal part from certain fundamental tenets of the socialist and Christian traditions. Not that its editorial group decided on a "line"; it was simply the character of their project. The choice of the title was born out of the specific experiences of Polish workers in 1956, 1970, and 1976, rather than a theoretical Marxist tradition. "Our concept," said Henryk Wujec, "was based on help in the creation of a workers' movement. We sought to aid in the rebirth of workers' self-awareness." It should be added here that the *Robotnik* group was totally isolated within Warsaw's oppositional circles during its first years of activity. Most people they knew in those circles thought there were very different priorities in opposing the regime.

At the same time, it should not be thought that *Robotnik* had easy communication with workers. To begin with, terms such as *trade union* and *working class* had to be systematically shunned because they had been debased by the regime's official Marxist discourse. But the editorial problems went deeper than this. "To supply financial and legal aid," said Irena Wojcicka, "was relatively easy. Whereas to understand one another, to extract information, was extremely difficult." None of the *Robotnik* group considered themselves writers. They found that "with each sentence, it was necessary to ask ten questions in order that it be understood (by the readers)." Witold Luczywo added that in this kind of journalistic work, "it is not so important whether you are able to converse well, but rather if you are able to listen well and whether you are sensitive to language."

The editorial group divided labor according to particular abilities. One person, for instance, was excellent at interviewing but not at writing. Another specialized in programmatic and historical texts. Another was a gifted writer. Yet another concerned himself with distribution and technical matters. Editing, at least to begin with, was the specific function of three women members. People were paid travel expenses but otherwise did work in their spare time. KOR helped financially, as did some union activists in the West, but not with large sums. Only in 1980 did they begin to charge for the paper.

Robotnik's initial relation to the Gdansk workers' movement was somewhat conflictual. The editorial group argued that the official unions' election procedures should be used to put up some reform candidates. Independent unions alarmed them, because they saw these as likely to be without practical clout. As they began to discuss the issues further with Gdansk leaders such as Walesa, Anna Walentinowicz, and Alina Pienkowska, and as they saw the growing level of organized militancy in the shipyards, the *Robotnik* group came to sense that an explosive movement was in gestation.[29] The communication problems of the editorial group scarcely existed between the workers and engineers who composed most of the Gdansk leadership. They spoke an easy common language and had successfully studied together issues in Polish history and existing labor legislation. Conditions in Warsaw, dominated as they were in so many capital cities by a heavy concentration of intellectuals, were not nearly as conducive to the bridges the *Robotnik* group was trying to build.

Their Charter of Workers' Rights, published in the summer of 1979, proved to be the real turning point in attracting worker activists to engage with them—rather than simply be "dissident workers," as Witold Luczywo put it. The Charter put forward a highly concrete program, with many elements that resurfaced in the 1980 Gdansk Agreement. It included demands for improvements in cost-of-living allowances, a minimum wage, the reduction of pay differentials, and the abolition of secret privileges. It called for open allocation of bonuses, holidays, and accommodation; a steady curtailment of the working week to 40 hours; and stricter oversight by workers of their health and safety at work. The right to strike and the cessation of pressure on individuals to inform on their fellow workers were also important elements in the Charter, as was the call for independent trade unions.

It was at this point, then, that *Robotnik*'s contribution to the development of the Solidarnosc movement finally emerged. Its trajectory had not been a straightforward or an easy one, but it is most instructive. During 1981, the paper voluntarily went into liquidation, considering that it had now served its purpose and that its members could best address themselves to new projects.

NOWA

This underground publishing operation was the heart of autonomous radical media in Poland from 1976 to 1981. There were a number of other publishing ventures as well, and as time went on, state publishing houses came to be used for illicit printing after hours (to start with by bribing printers, and then later, as Solidarnosc grew, as an act of political commitment by many printers). NOWA marked the first step beyond the normal Polish and Soviet samizdat method of typing 10 copies in exchange for the right to read the manuscript. This is how KOR's communiqués and the *Information Bulletin* were produced initially, but their success was so huge, the enthusiasm of people for getting involved in this work so great, that underground media consumers began to transform themselves into media producers.

NOWA began with the simplest techniques. They used wooden frames and silk screens, providing hundreds of pages per matrix. Gradually, they moved to spirit duplicators, then to mimeo, and finally to photocopiers and offset lithograph. Although a few of these machines were brought in from abroad, a considerable number were models thrown out by factories and offices and then reconditioned by NOWA activists. NOWA circles became extremely expert at making their own reproductive devices.

At its height, the NOWA operation came to involve a considerable division of labor. There were not only machinery experts but people with cars who would help with transport (and who quickly became expert at knowing whether the police were on their tail), other people who would buy paper,[30] still others who would buy powerful light bulbs for drying the ink quickly, and others who would organize the printing. Some people made their apartments or cellars or garages available for printing, for storage, for distribution. Some would volunteer to clean up after a printing run. Others would cut and staple. Those who needed money urgently would be paid; others would work for nothing. Yet, no one knew the whole operation, as the greater the decentralization, the greater the security. Each operation would usually be set at a different place and time.

The editorial committee consisted of four people, led by a redoubtable former nuclear chemist, Miroslav Chojecki, who had been sacked from the Institute for Nuclear Research in 1976 for publicly supporting the striking workers at Radom and Ursus. In the 4 years between 1977 and 1980, his home was searched 17 times, and he spent nearly 200 days in detention, of which just 5 were explicitly stated as having to do with NOWA. Other pretexts for jailing him included counterfeiting money and printing season tickets for bus travel, as well as poisoning, murder, and theft charges. No evidence, needless to say, was ever brought forward to substantiate these allegations, but the police would walk off, nonetheless, with books, manuscripts, and a typewriter. As Chojecki said to the judge on one occasion,

> Why has this repression come down on me, on my colleagues in the Independent Publishing-Workshop NOWA? Really, the authorities should simply ignore it, since they can put up against it highly efficient printing presses, newspapers with a circulation of millions, radio and television. (quoted in Raina, 1981, p. 60)

One wonders whether the fact that these mass media were of far less significance than NOWA's products was lost on the judge.

Printing was the riskiest and most arduous of all the tasks. It meant in practice that two people lived together for a week in a cellar or a bedroom, eating, sleeping, working, and—when they could—relaxing together. All their food went in with them, and they never left the room where they were working except to go to the bathroom. By the end of the week, they were usually exhausted, ink-stained, and claustrophobic—but with an extraordinary sense of achievement.

Avoiding police interference became a major art. One leading NOWA activist recalled how the police would follow him to a certain point and then just wait, perhaps in relays for weeks on end, for him to pass that way again so they could follow him for the next leg of his journey. Once, he took a taxi over a bridge in Warsaw, with anywhere between two and seven police cars tailing the taxi. Halfway over he jumped out, ran down some steps leading off the bridge, leapt into a friend's waiting car, and sped away. NOWA workers never discussed anything on the phone or in their own apartments. Police plants, called plugs, also had to be avoided. Usually, newcomers were accepted with references from friends and then awarded a gradually escalating level of trust. In all, NOWA only lost a ton of paper and a couple of machines, and this as a result of carelessness, not infiltration.

Editorially, NOWA strongly adhered to the refusal to insist on any one political line for its publications. It saw itself as enabling a forum, a new public sphere for debate, through which a lost 30 or 40 years of Polish culture could be re-created. Initially, NOWA looked at just three major factors when considering a proposal for publication, although these criteria became more complex over time. One was intellectual quality, the second topicality and likely demand for the text, and third, but by no means last, was its size, because of the logistics of production. Editorial meetings sometimes went on throughout the night and involved major battles. Decisions to reject for publication were sometimes reviewed later and reversed. NOWA operated with majority decisions after due debate.

When Solidarnosc was born, NOWA was largely taken up by that organization and practically became its publishing wing. The staff were eventually paid, the editorial board expanded its number considerably, permanent premises were found, and more trade union publishing was used. Until martial law, NOWA functioned as a highly professional publishing house.

Martial Law and Beyond

As noted above, in 1982, the clandestine press was already up and running (Helsinki Watch 1986). Blumsztajn (1988, pp. 18-20), on the basis of the best figures then available to him, found 662 different publications, about a quarter of them based in Warsaw, and another quarter based in Gdansk, Krakow, and Wroclaw, with the rest spread over another 30 to 40 towns across Poland. Many were extremely rudimentary in format. Their contents included denouncements and exposures of the martial law regime, news on political prisoners and their treatment, and poems (this last category representing also about 25% of the books published in that year).

As the 1980s went by, Solidarnosc's role as a labor union declined, almost inevitably given its clandestine operation, and its coverage of labor issues fell off accordingly. It began to devote itself more and more to political and especially to historical analysis. The latter, given the acute distortions of 20th-century Polish history in officially approved textbooks, represented the effort to recover the real past and debates about the past from doctrinaire party sources. During the period from 1982 to 1985, no less than 3,200 books and pamphlets were published, mostly in Warsaw, Krakow, and Wroclaw, typically in a run of 1,000 to 2,000 copies. During this period, too, a conservative nationalist underground press began to make a stronger appearance than previously. The principal publication, however, was the Solidarnosc weekly, *Tygodnik Mazowsze,* which had a run of about 40,000 copies, often passed many times from hand to hand, from 1982 onward.

Publications of these kinds were not the only radical alternative media (Helsinki Watch, 1986). Mock postage stamps (Kobylnski, 1989) were printed and attached to envelopes with pictures of Walesa, murdered Solidarnosc activist Father Popieluszko, or interwar Polish President Jozef Pilsudski. Legal postage stamps were also sometimes written over with political messages. Initially, these were actually produced inside the internment camps. NOWA, reconstituted, circulated a number of videos, including a banned feature film, Ryszard Bugajski's *The Interrogation* (1981), which uncompromisingly portrayed torture in a Stalinist Polish jail of the late 1940s. There was even a series of guerrilla radio broadcasts around the country by Radio Solidarnosc.

Not that Poland was simply bifurcated into pro- and anti-Solidarnosc camps. Some of the official labor unions became quite militant and, indeed, waged a series of crippling strikes in mining areas in 1988 that took Solidarnosc leaders totally by surprise. There was also a situationist-style group, the Orange Alternative (Goban-Klas, 1994, pp. 197-198; Misztal, 1992), that staged ironic street theater events, especially in Wroclaw, such as International Secret Policemen's Day or Who's Afraid Of Toilet Paper? (mocking the endemic shortage of this indelicate but much-needed item in Poland's supposedly advanced socialist economy). The Orange Alternative was popular neither with the authorities nor with Solidarnosc leaders.

In an acute analysis of the later 1980s, Jakubowicz (1990) has proposed that by then, there had grown up three public spheres in Poland: the official media, underground media, and Catholic media. Whereas during the martial law period, the church's media had reverted to being the only alternative legal public sphere, and some talented journalists had dramatically raised the quality of church publications by writing for them, by 1989, these writers had mostly found secular outlets, sometimes alternating between alternative media and official media then in the process of testing the political waters.

Summary: Of the case studies in Part III, Czech and Polish radical alternative media in the periods studied certainly faced far and away the greatest repression of their activities. They are important, therefore, on that ground alone, for they illustrate how such relatively severe obstacles have been tackled. But these case studies are also important for two further reasons. One is that collectively, over time, these media were instrumental in helping to bring about significant political change in one of the most entrenched empires of the 20th century. The other is that they operated in favor of justice and cultural enhancement in the teeth of a lying rhetoric of socialist progress.

But what about the miseries of post-Soviet Russia in the 1990s? Is the story of radical media quite so positive, once a longer view is taken? The answer, I would suggest, is threefold. First, the most basic purpose of this book is to demonstrate that small-scale radical media have often had a major social impact. Feeling good about the impact does not alter it one way or the other. Second, although life did become extremely tough for many Russians, Ukrainians, and others, the Sovietized economies were also slowing to a crawl. Stasis would not have improved the public's lot, and even though aspects of nostalgia were entirely understandable, turning the clock back to the oil revenue-rich 1970s was simply not feasible. Finally, it is not part of this book's argument that the switch to a capitalist market economy solves all or most major problems, all the more if it is run by a kleptocracy. The need for active radical media is just as strong as it ever was.

NOTES

1. For an absorbing attempt to do so, see Hobsbawm (1994). It perhaps needs saying, given the seemingly widespread joys of ethnic stereotyping, that over 20 million Soviet citizens gave their lives in World War II to rid the world of the Nazi state. My commentary here on the Soviet system is not about Russians, Ukrainians, Uzbeks, and the other Soviet nationalities who sacrificed

many times over the tally of the Western allies. For the image of the Soviet Union as a liberated zone in the otherwise inexorable rise of fascism, see the Preface and Conclusions to this book.

2. Naturally, media were not sole agents. Lewin (1988), for example, has argued that long-term processes of mass education and urbanization in the Soviet Union played a very significant role in developing a resistant, skeptical political culture. I have pursued the interconnected factors in the Soviet Union's demise at more length elsewhere (Downing, 1996).

3. Compare the rather similar citation from Rudolf Bahro (1978), dissident writer in the former East Germany, on the "power of disposal over the social nervous system, the hierarchy of information-processing. . . . At the bottom, the various particular interests find themselves systematically isolated, so that they have no prospect of being directly taken into account in the synthesis" (pp. 300-303). For a descriptive account of the Soviet media system in its heyday, see Remington (1988) and Downing (1996, pp. 36-105).

4. The most famous symbol of this dissent at the time was the first account of Stalin's forced-labor camps published in the Soviet Union, Aleksandr Solzhenitsyn's *One Day in the Life of Ivan Denisovich.* Chapters 19 through 38 of Michael Scammell's (1984) biography of Solzhenitsyn offer a fascinating account of its publication and the context. Priscilla Johnson McMillan (1965) and Dina Spechler (1982) provide helpful accounts of the cultural politics of the Khrushchev era.

5. Legally, up to nine copies could be typed with the aid of interleaved sheets of carbon paper. There were, of course, many other laws in the Soviet penal code that were invoked against those who availed themselves of this law to communicate their thoughts freely. Every typewriter was registered, with a paper copy of its keys' peculiarities on file so that the source of offending typescripts could be identified. (When photocopier machines came into use, access to them was also meticulously controlled.)

6. It is worth noting that at a number of these events, there was a radical media dimension. Journalists were prominent among those active in the Hungarian revolution, with Budapest's radio headquarters a key site in the battles that ensued; in the Prague Spring; in Polish Solidarnosc; and in the movement against the Soviet dictatorship in the 1980s. The rebellious Poznan workers destroyed a jamming station that blocked broadcasts from Radio Free Europe and other Western radio stations.

7. The Czechs and the Slovaks, two peoples speaking very similar languages, had been shoved together in one country following the First World War and had never taken to the merger with tremendous enthusiasm; following the collapse of the Soviet system, they separated peacefully into two separate states.

8. H. Gordon Skilling (1989) has surveyed those forms of oppositional media that did operate over the next 20-year period in Czechoslovakia, including Charter 77 and the Jazz Section of the Musicians' Union, but he is forced to conclude that neither the level of activity nor the character of the reprisals matched those under a number of other repressive regimes at the time (p. 43).

9. Seeing the newspaper headlines announcing the Soviet invasion, I exclaimed to my companion, "These bastards are just the same fucking imperialists as the Americans in Vietnam!"; meanwhile Karpati Zoltan, a distinguished Hungarian oral history researcher, was tearing up his Communist Party card in rage. Our separate reactions—we did not know of each other's existence until 10 years later—exemplified a far wider expression of outrage that never simmered down. At the same time, without in any way mitigating the Soviet action, it did not compare with the deaths of 1 million to 2 million Vietnamese and nearly 60,000 Americans, to say nothing of the maiming of numerous survivors.

10. The best single source on Soviet dissent at that phase is Alexeyeva (1987), but see also the essays in Tökés (1975). The single most famous Soviet samizdat publication was the journal, *Chronicle of Current Events* (Hopkins, 1983), begun in 1968, which appeared steadily if irregularly and simply listed without comment all the details known concerning dissidents' arrests, sentences, prison location, and similar factual matters. Loyalist Marxist critiques of Soviet society at that time can be found in *Samizdat Register I and II* (Medvedev, 1978, 1982). Leonid Plyushch (1979), Andrei Amalrik (1982), Petro Grigorenko (1982), Lev Kopelev (1969), and, of course, especially Andrei Sakharov (1974) were major dissident voices in that period.

11. The Poles, at the height of their samizdat operation, were producing whole books, nicely bound, and quarterly journals, as well as much simpler documents. It should not be thought, however, that only the Soviets and the Poles generated samizdat; such publications were also important in Hungary, not least in the ecological realm (Downing, 1996, pp. 101-102).

12. Offensive and outrageous more widely than might be supposed: I cannot resist quoting a distinguished British judge (they all are, naturally), who huffed to a barrister acquaintance of mine in 1968 that he was glad the Soviets had sent the tanks into Czechoslovakia because "someone's got to do something about all these damned students making trouble everywhere!"

13. Cf. Konrád 1984. The empirical implications of the term will become clearer below, but its rhetorical message was a total rejection of any dialogue with an illegitimate, corrupt, and repressive regime that consistently flouted international laws to which it was signatory, especially the 1975 Helsinki Convention on human rights. Instead, activists should behave as they would in a free and democratic society, engaging in peaceful political opposition as and how they saw fit (Ost, 1990).

14. In Part II, many alternative media were reviewed but not dolls. At this point in time, even dolls became radical symbols. The Russian *matrioshki*, a series of hollow wooden dolls nesting one inside the other, began to be sold on the weekend trestle tables in Ismailovo Park in Moscow and then later on Arbat in the center, but with a difference. Now, the dolls portrayed Soviet rulers. First, they safely lampooned Brezhnev, who was already condemned by his successor Gorbachev as corrupt and ineffective, but then the dollmakers began to go both backward and forward in history, portraying Khrushchev (until then a nonperson since his ouster), then a cruel Stalin, and then Brezh-

nev's two sickly successors, Andropov and Chernenko, whose brief tenures in office before dying symbolized the regime's inertia. Finally, Lenin, until then sacrosanct, was added and Yeltsin, initially respected as Gorbachev's pugnacious challenger. A whole critical history lesson. See Condee and Padunov (1991).

15. The dating is important: Some commentators have sweepingly asserted that telecommunications brought down the Soviet Union. This technological fetishism is both historically inaccurate and conceptually inept.

16. The term used by the Soviet-installed regime for its policies, which sought to undo all the gains of the Prague Spring.

17. The magazine was even denied permission to reprint an excerpt from a technical magazine that had run an article on the astronomical costs incurred through mistakes in planning Prague's new underground railroad, a sum equivalent to building 6,000 new apartments (Hamsik, 1971, p. 126).

18. The comparison with Portugal and Algeria is irresistable; see Chapter 18.

19. When it later became clear that a Soviet invasion was on the list of possibilities, this definition changed to one of "critical cooperation" with the government.

20. The inclusion of the Communist Party here is yet another index of how loyalist this reform movement was; it also proves the extent to which the party was seen as a Czech and Slovak institution, not simply an alien political entity foisted on them by the Soviets. Perhaps, the charge of naiveté can be thrown at them—but then the totally rational and cynical will never intentionally set any movement for change in motion anyway.

21. For example, *Survey* (Volume 24, No. 4, 1979 and Volume 25, Number 1, 1980); Ascherson (1982); Ruane (1982); Potel (1982); Starski (1982); Brumberg (1983); Garton Ash (1983, 1990); Helsinki Watch (1986); Blumsztajn (1988); Jakubowicz (1990). I discuss the Polish media scenario during these years at some length in Downing (1996).

22. The *Berufsverbot* was the West German law barring members of the Communist Party from civil service positions, including teachers and railroad workers.

23. A standard method of censorship in the former Soviet bloc (Kowalski, 1988).

24. Historically, it is important to note that Basket 3 of the Helsinki Agreements, signed by the United States and the Soviet Union in 1975, along with Poland and other East European governments, guaranteed certain civic and communication rights. Oppositionists in Eastern Europe seized on these as giving them constitutional rights of dissent and free expression; the sovietized regimes, of course, had no intention of permitting this.

25. The events were filmed live in an extraordinary documentary, *Workers 1980*.

26. These preparations were listed in *Uncensored Poland News Bulletin* (2/19/82: 31-32), published by the Information Centre for Polish Affairs in the United Kingdom.

27. Historically, again, a debate continues to the time of writing, and may never end, as to whether Jaruzelski was right in thinking it best to intervene to avoid the Soviet military doing so. See Rosenberg (1995, pp. 125-258) for an absorbing discussion of the issue. Certainly, one of those he put in jail, KOR and Solidarnosc activist Adam Michnik, later to be editor of one of Poland's leading dailies, *Gazeta Wyborcza*, subsequently developed a warm personal rapport with him.

28. Some information here is also drawn from *Robotnik, Tygodnik Solidarnosc* (April 10, 1981), p. 14. I am indebted to Ana Mayer for translating this article for me. Quotations from *Robotnik* activists below are all drawn from this source.

29. Goodwyn (1991) and Laba (1991) fiercely dispute Staniszkis (1984) and, in turn, are fiercely disputed by Bernhard (1993) and Kubik (1994) concerning the genesis of Solidarnosc. For Staniszkis, its concepts arose from the Warsaw intelligentsia, the Pope's 1979 visit to Poland, and foreign radio stations. For Goodwyn and Laba, those factors were epiphenomenal compared to the autonomous growth over decades of political consciousness and organization among workers in the Baltic seaports. For Bernhard and Kubik, this position is only partially accurate and tends to make heroes of the working class. The account I have given here is based on the most careful reading I could muster from a variety of sources and gives full weight to the possibility and reality of working-class self-organization, without denying agency to middle-class intellectual activists.

30. Blumsztajn (1988, pp. 55-61) points out that buying paper sounds straightforward, until the quota of a 500-sheet package per person per month is recalled—and even then, the purchaser was required to show an identity card and give a name and address. The martial law period underground weekly *Tygodnik Mazowsze*, with a run of 40,000 copies, needed 650 of these for each issue. A car carrying a substantial volume of paper at night would give itself away to the police simply by the fact its headlights would be pointing upward at a steeper angle than normal. During martial law, the price of gasoline and of paper was sharply increased, and gasoline was tightly rationed. Far more people carrying finished publications were arrested than were printers, and if the charges included stealing paper or other materials, intermittent political amnesties would not apply. In 1986, 154 political prisoners out of 278 had been arrested or sentenced for transporting independent publications. These problems were already present in the period from 1976 to 1981, but they became even more acute under martial law. However, the picture was not unrelievedly gloomy: Corrupt public officials frequently helped out with supplies for a bribe, and as the book publishing aspect of samizdat became more established, it was possible to pay authors and set up a much more genuinely independent operation, where authors did not depend for their income entirely on the state.

23

A Hexagon by Way of a Conclusion

Squashing all the media experience and energy reviewed up to this point into a tight scientific format of proven conclusions would do great and unjust violence to the open-ended and often coruscating scenarios we have witnessed. Closing down open spaces and putting clamps on the imagination is precisely what these radical media have fought.

What I propose to do instead is to draw out a few recurring themes and chew on the succulent things gently for a moment more.

They form a hexagon of sorts: artistic flair and punch, memory levels, pragmatic realities, social movements, time frame, the power structure. Let us look at them one by one while trying to hold onto the five other points to which they are intimately related in a variety of ways.

ARTISTIC FLAIR

Artistic flair and punch are the oppositional sparks in popular and even mass culture, in resistant religious practice, in political and social satire. Bakhtin's Rabelaisian marketplace, Berlin dada, Scott's weapons of the weak, the situationists, all resonate with this flair, which need not necessarily be noisy or obscene or cutting or outrageous. Sojourner Truth's little *cartes de visite* have a place here, just as much as ACT-UP performance art, Paper Tiger Television or, in its heyday, the vernacular Bible. Early Russian samizdat, for all its blurry, carbon copy, marginless, beyond-the-margins existence, had it too. At the heart of the sparks is that close interactivity that Brecht called cofabulation, that Benjamin saw as the valid aura of an artwork, that I have addressed by calling radical media audiences the joint architects of the text, that Freire and Bakhtin in their different ways described as dialogic. This interactivity, this dialogue, does not by itself create the precise aesthetic charge, but it is within its arc that the charge builds up and is explosive.

MEMORY LEVELS

Memory levels we have spoken of before in connection with the division between ephemeral radical media and longer term ones. I suggested that the former are like mind bombs—short, sharp, skewing, skewering, easily memorable—and that the latter build gradually and imperceptibly like coral reefs from myriads of iterations (in fact, this second process is most characteristic of mainstream media). The two are bound together, not separate. At the same time, the long-term overall memory of periods of intense social movement activity in which all kinds of media play key roles can be immensely influential. When we get to the question of time frame, we will revisit this.

PRAGMATIC REALITIES

Pragmatic realities are those on which we particularly concentrated in the longer case studies in Part III—the organizational dynamic of radical media over time (Chapter 19's Italian examples), the problem in sustaining intense levels of energy and direct democracy in such media (Chapter 18's Portuguese examples), survival under repressive regimes, the relation between the wider democracy of a social movement and the internal democracy of a radical media project. Socialist anarchist and feminist models of radical media organization and the practice of self-management are pivotal issues under this heading. So, in the case of media projects that seek a national audience, is the question of distribution. How far, too, can radical media maintain creative imagination, the sparks of which we wrote a moment ago, over the long haul? I do not intend the presence of a question mark as an implicit indication that this is not feasible, but neither is it plain sailing.

Some writers on radical media have zeroed in on their organizational mechanics rather than dynamics (cf. Fountain, 1988; Landry, 1985). These, too, are important pragmatic dimensions. In the first edition of this book (Downing, 1984) and in this book's Chapter 19 on the Italian case studies and Chapter 21's KPFA case study, I have done some of the same. Chapter 6 underscores how important this is. But there is a tendency to mount a festival of righteous cynical amusement at the marketing ignorance and accountancy follies of these radical media projects and sagely to pronounce them doomed to death and inanition because of these flaws. Atton (1999) brings a sensibly cautious perspective to discussion of this issue, underscoring that many of these media never set themselves the goals for success that their critics seem instinctively to presume are universal: longevity, profitability, stability, news chain sales. Indeed, Dickinson (1997, p. 239) suggests that mainstream media, so obsessed with these goals as absolutes and quite often squeezing out creativity and imagination in the process, could do well to learn from the venturesomeness of radical media.

SOCIAL MOVEMENTS

Social movements, local and global—among Mexican-U.S. border communities fighting corporate pollution, trans-Atlantic African communities struggling to end slavery, women demanding good, affordable, and nearby child care, international human rights campaigns—are the life blood of these media, and they are the movements' oxygen. This reframes the notion of interactivity in another way. Not that this imagery implies the two must live and die simultaneously, for radical media overall are longer lasting than any given social movement's trajectory—unless we use *social movement* in a generic sense, such as anticolonialism, feminism, labor. However, the relationship is evident sociologically, not ethically or politically, not only in the case of radical media that seek to increase developmental power and enable liberation but also in the instance of repressive radical media, the media of authoritarian populism and fascist movements. It is evident in the interaction between social communication networks and radical media and in community (where that may be said to exist in some defined and meaningful sense). We return inevitably to notions both of dialogue and of conversation, the former more generic, the latter more specifically concerned with the pragmatics of everyday talking, including its media forms.

TIME FRAME

Time frame is often the unexamined root of pointless disputes concerning radical media. There are genuinely absorbing and informative studies of radical media that see them nonetheless as bounded by the 1960s counterculture and its aftermath (e.g., Dickinson, 1997; Fountain, 1988; Peck, 1985; Roszak 1995; and a flood of more general books on that period).[1] It is to be hoped that Part II of this book will help to dispel that unnecessarily period-bound assumption and will restore radical media to their place as historical constants, albeit ever in flux. But beyond this, there is the question of long-term consequences, of kinds unimagined by and quite possibly inconceivable to empiricist audience researchers.

At least three types of consequence suggest themselves.

One is that the energy poured into and drawn from radical media projects continues on in many other projects over decades, in a way that could not possibly be ascertained by audience questionnaires (On a scale of one to five, where five is *very much* and one is *not at all*, how did you like that radio program, Madam?). Popular music, the ecology movement, the *centri sociali* in Italy in the 1980s and 1990s; glasnost activists from the thaw era in the latter years of the Soviet bloc; the San Francisco Bay Area as a hive of oppositional culture and the long-term role of KPFA; radical theater's contestation of the Thatcher government's harsh social policies: These are just some illustrations.

Another is the prefigurative politics on which we cited Sheila Rowbotham earlier in the book and on which so much of her history writing has focused.[2] Repeatedly, she shows how women's contestations of the given order have foreshadowed later movements and demands, as well as concessions won (although never securely). This is an important insight for radical media projects, as well, both in what they set out to achieve and also at times in their very process, as Huesca (1995) and Rodríguez (in press) underscore in their studies. Here, we return to the question of memory and radical media, not in the sense of radical media as recovering memory that had been banished, as per the role of history in the last years of the Soviet Union or in Argentina subsequent to the Dirty War of 1976 to 1982, but in the sense of media activism that may fail in its most immediate objectives for many reasons, including internal ones, but that nonetheless lights a flame that, like some trick birthday cake candles, obstinately refuses to be doused. These radical media in practice often offer a vision, either from their contents or their making or their interaction with social movements, or all three, that bends like the willow in a gale but does not uproot.

And furthermore, we need to relate radical media projects to notions such as those of Bey (1991), who has written about Temporary Autonomous Zones, and the historical studies of Sakolsky and Koehnline (1993) and Wilson (1995), who have explored what is known of temporary places of refuge with relatively egalitarian economic and political forms of organization. Hakim Bey argues that notions of a revolution against state power to achieve a permanent condition of social progress have led and will lead to pointless martyrdom and/or betrayal of the revolutionaries' principles, so that the best and most realistic option is to try to develop autonomous zones of freedom. In the contemporary era, these will not necessarily be in specific spaces, as with the *cimarrones*/ maroons and their *palenques/quilombos* of the slavery era (see Price, 1973). But, they still are "built" in the realistic knowledge that they are sure to be temporary, sure to be torn down sooner or later, but while they exist, they work and offer some of the most intense experiences of living that life may offer.

We may instance the days of March 1977 in Bologna, of the Paris of May and June 1968, of the workers' occupation of the Seattle shipyards in 1919 and the Gdansk shipyards in 1980, of the 1974 Portuguese revolution of the carnations, of the underground press in 1960s and 1970s Britain, of which Nelson (1989) writes,

> If "success" is regarded in terms distinct from "winning," and the counter-culture is regarded as contributing to the development of an already rich corpus of ideas and experiences within the anarchist tradition, then the movement can certainly be accounted a success . . . in so doing it could be of critical historical importance in the long run. (p. 143)

There are many other such historical moments—only some have been described in this book—that suggest a permanent validity to the temporary. Such memories, yes, may degenerate into a nostalgia that goes nowhere, but they often spur further activity in the same and allied directions. Of course, there is also burnout, there is middle-aged disavowal of youthful excess, and there are deeply negative experiences, whether of psychic gangsterism by would-be leaders or actual terrorism as per the Italian Red Brigades, which may indeed permanently sour those who have been scarred by them. Perfectly understandably. But there is a whole lot else to be learned and gained beside the shadow side, and this must not to be forgotten, either.

THE POWER STRUCTURE

The sixth and final point of the hexagon, which I have very consciously left until last precisely not to wallow in it, is established power—of the state, of official religion, of political parties, of patriarchy, of global capitalism and its transnational nodes. These are the obstacles and the targets of radical media. However, in some brilliant passages in an otherwise sometimes labored book, Michel de Certeau (1984) warns against the danger of obsessing with and thereby making a fetish of the power structure, against

> the fundamental but often exclusive and obsessive analysis that seeks to describe institutions and the mechanisms of *repression*. . . . But this elucidation of the apparatus by itself has the disadvantage of *not seeing* practices which are heterogeneous to it and which it represses or thinks it represses. . . . When one examines this fleeting and permanent reality carefully, one has the impression of exploring the night-side of societies, a night longer than their day . . . a maritime immensity on which socioeconomic and political structures appear as ephemeral islands. . . . [This] restores what was earlier called "popular culture," but it does so in order to transform what was represented as a matrix-force of history into a mobile infinity of tactics. (p. 41)

He argues for the corresponding urgency of focusing on the immense force of everyday "clever tricks of the weak within the order established by the strong, an art of putting one over on the adversary on his own turf . . . maneuverable, polymorph mobilities, jubilant, poetic, and warlike discoveries" (p. 40). The argument here is reminiscent of Scott's (1985, 1990) analysis of the "weapons of the weak" and his description of the vast continent between overt rebellion and passivity. It is equally reminiscent of the situationists' concept of *détournement*, of which dada's use of everyday objects to dethrone "art," Heartfield's photomontage, "re-decorating" commercial billboards, and culture-jamming are just some instances. How far de Certeau's perspective is able to deal with a regime as repressive as a brutal military dictatorship is obviously open to question, but for less absolute power situations, it opens up important vistas for radical media.

Yet, I have to confess that as an Italian friend of many years, once a journalist on *Il Manifesto,* says of himself, I, too, find myself in the strange position personally of being politically on the extreme Right... of the extreme Left. On some levels, I resonate with, in their varying emphases, de Certeau and Scott and Gramsci and the situationists and am most at ease in straightforward opposition and in the search of temporary autonomous zones and prefigurative politics. On others, I find it hard to discount the importance of trying to make a dent in media and communication policies that otherwise are the happy hunting ground of corporate leaders who draft legislation for our supposed political representatives.

On this level, I resonate with arguments such as those of McLaughlin (1995), Sholle (1995), and Trend (1993), from feminist and socialist perspectives, in favor of activists' interventions into the state's communication policy process and against thinking we can safely get by through inhabiting separate counter public realms. I also think that Charlotte Ryan's (1991) advocacy of a mainstream media news strategy for the Left is tremendously important.

This book has dwelt exclusively on another plane, and it would take a different book to engage at the same level with policy-making strategies, but in the end, it seems to me that the communication issues posed by the global corporate scenario are such that only dual activity by radical media makers and radical policy activists has the prospect of letting the public construct for themselves any kind of zone worth inhabiting. The most recent phase of the KPFA story at the time of writing might suggest that this is implausible, but I view that as defensive and ultimately self-destructive cynicism. The whole lesson to be learned from the KPFA debacle at the end of the 1990s is just how critical such collaboration will be in future, how much we lose by defending our 100% rectitude.

And finally, just to turn this dilemma into a triangle, I equally find myself impressed and invigorated by the accounts of women in grassroots communication, such as in Riaño (1994) and Rodríguez (in press). Sheila Rowbotham's (1975, 1989, 1991) work has the same exciting quality. There is something about the ferocious appetite for splitting and denunciating in the history of the situationists and some other socialist anarchists, something overdramatized, something on the edge of narcissistic and masculinist, something amazingly arrogant in their conviction they have their finger on the international pulse. Their analyses, their refusal to compromise, their flaming insights, their challenges, are magnificently yeasty; but the small victories of women in everyday life are equally so. For the ongoing realities of the majority, *their* news, and their *type* of news, underpin the importance of radical media in a key dimension that much else in this book has sought to underscore. Many examples through this book have concerned women's media, but the point at issue is even more than that. It is the significance of all the rebellious communication media of the officially unheard.

NOTES

1. Armstrong (1981) and Nelson (1989), despite their primary focus on the 1960s, maintain a somewhat longer perspective but not a markedly international one.

2. See her early *Hidden From History* (Rowbotham, 1975) and her more recent essays collected in *The Past Is Before Us* (1989) and *Women in Movement* (1992).

References

Abernathy, J. (1995, May 13). Feds target the internet. *PC World, 13,* 68.

Abrahams, R. D. (1992) *Singing the master: The emergence of African American culture in the plantation South.* New York: Pantheon.

Acción Zapatista. (1996a). *Zapatistas in cyberspace: Against neoliberalism* (Pamphlets for the First Intercontinental Encuentro) [On-line]. Available: http://www.utexas.edu/students/nave/neolib.html

Acción Zapatista. (1996a). *Zapatistas in cyberspace: A guide to analysis and information* [On-line]. Available: http://www.eco.utexas.edu/Homepages/Faculty/Cleaver/zapsincyber.html

Adams Sitney, P. (1979). *Visionary film: The American avantgarde 1943-1978.* New York: Oxford University Press.

Adamson, W. (1987). Gramsci and the politics of civil society. *Praxis Internatiional, 7*(3-4), 320-339.

Adkins, H. (1995). Schafft neue ausdrucksformen! In I. Antonowa & J. Merkert (Eds.), *Berlin Moskau 1900-1950* (pp. 233-237). München: Prestel-Verlag.

Adorno, T. W. (1975). Culture industry reconsidered. *New German Critique, 6,* 12-19.

Agosín, M. (1987). *Scraps of life: Chilean arpilleras.* Trenton, NJ: Red Sea Press.

Aldridge, R. C. (1983). *First strike! The Pentagon's strategy for nuclear war.* Boston: South End Press.

Alexander, W. (1981). *Film on the left: American documentary film from 1931 to 1942.* Princeton, NJ: Princeton University Press.

Alexeyeva, L. (1986). *U.S. broadcasting to the Soviet Union.* New York: Helsinki Watch (now Human Rights Watch).

Alexeyeva, L. (1987). *Soviet dissent: Contemporary movements for national, religious, and human rights.* Middletown, CT: Wesleyan University Press.
Allen, A. T. (1984). *Satire and society in Wilhelmine Germany: Kladderadatsch and Simplicissimus 1890-1914.* Lexington: University of Kentucky Press.
Alter, N. (1996). *Vietnam protest theatre: The television war on stage.* Bloomington: Indiana University Press.
Althusser, L. (1971). Ideology and ideological state apparatuses (Notes toward an investigation). In L. Althusser, *Lenin and philosophy* (pp. 121-173). London: New Left Books.
Alvarez, S. (1996). Do you have a labor program on your community channel? *Community Media Review, 19*(2), 7, 27-28.
Álvarez, S. (1990). *Engendering democracy in Brazil: Women's movements in transition politics.* Princeton, NJ: Princeton University Press.
Amalrik, A. (1982). *Notes of a revolutionary.* New York: Knopf.
Anderson, K., & Goldson, A. (1993). Alternating currents: Alternative television inside and outside of the academy. *Social Text, 35,* 56-71.
Anderson, P. (1977). The antinomies of Antonio Gramsci. *New Left Review, 100,* 5-78.
Anderson, P. (1991). *The printed image and the transformation of popular culture 1790-1860.* Oxford, UK: Clarendon.
Andreotti, L. (1996). Introduction: The urban politics of the Internationale Situationniste (1957-1972). In L. Andreotti & X. Costa (Eds.), *Situacionistes: Art, política, urbanisme/Situationists: Art, politics, urbanism* (pp. 11-35). Barcelona, Spain: Musei d'Art Contemporani.
Andreotti, L., & Costa, X. (Eds.). (1996) *Situacionistes: Art, política, urbanisme/Situationists: Art, politics, urbanism.* Barcelona, Spain: Musei d'Art Contemporani.
Antonowa, I., & Merkert, J. (Eds.). (1995). *Berlin Moskau 1900-1950.* München: Prestel-Verlag.
Appadurai, A. (1996). *Modernity at large: Cultural dimensions of globalization.* Minneapolis: University of Minnesota Press.
Arato, A., & Cohen, J. (1992). *Civil society and political theory.* Cambridge: MIT Press.
Armstrong, D. (1981). *A trumpet to arms: Alternative media in America.* Los Angeles: J. P. Tarcher.
Armstrong, N. (1987). *Desire and domestic fiction: A political history of the novel.* New York: Oxford University Press.
Aronson, J. (1972). *Deadline for the media: Today's challenges to press, TV, and radio.* New York: Bobbs-Merrill.
Ascherson, N. (1982). *The Polish August* (2nd ed.). New York: Viking.
Atton, C. (1999). A reassessment of the alternative press. *Media, Culture, & Society, 21*(1), 51-76.
Aufderheide, P. (1992). Cable television and the public interest. *Journal of Communication, 42*(1), 52-65.
Autonomedia. (1994). *¡Zapatistas! Documents of the new Mexican revolution.* Brooklyn, NY: Author.

autori molti compagni. (1977). *Bologna marzo 1977 . . . fatti nostri.* Verona: Bertani Editore.

Baca, J., Neumaier, D., & Angelo, N. (1985). Our people are the internal exiles. In D. Kahn & D. Neumaier (Eds.), *Cultures in contention* (pp. 62-75). Seattle. WA: The Real Comet Press.

Bacon, D. (1997, April 1). *Pacifica and the unions* [On-line]. Available: http://www.radio4all.org/fp/bacon.htm.

Bagdikian, B. (1999). *The media monopoly* (6th ed.). Boston: Beacon.

Bahro, R. (1978). *The alternative.* London: New Left Books.

Bakhtin, M. M. (1981). *The dialogic imagination.* Austin: The University of Texas Press.

Bakhtin, M. M. (1984). *Rabelais and his world.* Bloomington: Indiana University Press.

Baldelli, P. (1977). *Informazione e controinformazione.* Milan, Italy: Mazzotta.

Barber, B. (1984). *Strong democracy: Participatory politics for a new age.* Berkeley: University of California Press.

Barlow, W. (1999). *Voice over: The making of black radio.* Philadelphia: Temple University Press.

Barmé, G., & Minford, J. (1989) *Seeds of fire: Chinese voices of conscience.* New York: Noonday Press.

Barnouw, E. (1990). *Tube of plenty: The evolution of American television* (2nd ed.). New York: Oxford University Press.

Barnouw, E. (1993). *Documentary: A history of the non-fiction film* (2nd ed.). New York: Oxford University Press.

Bascetta, M., Dominijanni, I., & Gagliardo, R. (1997). *Millenovecento settanta sette.* Rome: Manifestolibri, La Talpa di Biblioteca 20.

Bekes, J. P. (1996). *Public spheres and private empires: and politics in Brazil.* Master's thesis, University of Texas at Austin.

Belchem, J. (1996) *Popular radicalism in nineteenth-century Britain.* Basingstoke: Macmillan.

Benjamin, M. (1995, May). On the road with the Zapatistas: Mexican crackdown in Chiapas. *The Progressive, 59*(5), 28.

Benjamin, W. (1973). The work of art in the age of mechanical reproduction. In H. Arendt (Ed.), *Illuminations* (pp. 219-253). London: Fontana.

Benn, D. W. (1989). *Persuasion and Soviet politics.* Cambridge, UK: Basil Blackwell.

Bennett, T. (1992). Putting policy into cultural studies. In L. Grossberg, C. Nelson, & P. Treichler (Eds.), *Cultural studies* (pp. 23-34). New York: Routledge.

Bernhard, M. H. (1993). *The origins of democratization in Poland: Workers, intellectuals, and oppositional politics, 1976-1980.* New York: Columbia University Press.

Berrigan, F. (Ed.). (1977). *Access: Some western models of community media.* Paris: UNESCO.

Berry, V., & Manning-Miller, C. L. (Eds.). (1996). *Mediated messages and African American culture: Contemporary issues.* Thousand Oaks, CA: Sage.

Betz, H.-G., & Immerfall, S. (Eds.). (1998). *The new politics of the right: Neo-populist parties and movements in established democracies.* New York: St Martin's.

Bey, H. (1991). The temporary autonomous zone. In *T.A.Z.: The temporary autonomous zone, ontological anarchy, poetic terrorism* (pp. 95-141). New York: Autonomedia.

Bietenholz, P. G. (1990). Édition et réforme à Bâle, 1517-1565. In J.-F. Gilmont (Ed.), *La réforme et le livre: L'Europe de l'imprimé (1517-1570)* (pp. 239-268). Paris: Les Éditions du Cerf.

Bischoff, S. (1978). Radio Verte Fessenheim. *Ikon, 1*(2), 192-200.

Blee, K. M. (1993). *Women of the klan: Racism and gender in the 1920s.* Berkeley: University of California Press.

Blumenfeld & Cohen, Technology Law Group. (1996). *Overview of the Telecommunications Act of 1996* [On-line]. Available: http://www.technologylaw.com/techlaw/act_summary.html

Blumsztajn, S. (1988). *Une pologne hors censure.* Paris: Solidarité France-Pologne.

Boal, A. (1997). *Jeux pour acteurs et non-acteurs: Pratique du théâtre de l'opprimé.* Paris: La Découverte.

Boal, I. A. (1995). A flow of monsters: Luddism and virtual technologies. In J. Brook & I. A. Boal (Eds.), *Resisting the virtual life: The culture and politics of information* (pp. 3-16). San Francisco: City Lights.

Bobbio, L. (1979). *Lotta continua: Storia di una organizzazione rivoluzionaria.* Rome: Savelli Editore.

Bodek, R. (1997). *Proletarian performance in Weimar Berlin: Agitprop, chorus, and Brecht.* Columbus, SC: Camden House.

Bold, A. (Ed.). (1970). *The Penguin book of socialist verse.* Harmondsworth, UK: Penguin.

Bolster, W. J. (1997). *Black Jacks: African American seamen in the age of sail.* Cambridge, MA: Harvard University Press.

Bonfil Batalla, G. (1996). *México profundo: Reclaiming a civilization.* Austin: University of Texas Press.

Boyle, D. (1997). *Subject to change: Guerrilla television revisited.* New York: Oxford University Press.

Brecht, B. (1983). Radio as a means of communication. In A. Mattelart & S. Siegelaub (Eds.), *Communication and class struggle 2: Liberation, socialism* (pp. 169-171). Bagnolet, France: International Mass Media Research Center.

Brenner, D. L., & Price, M. E. (1993). *Cable television and other nonbroadcast video.* New York: Clark Boardman Callaghan.

Brentlinger, J. (1995). *The best of what we are: Reflections on the Nicaraguan revolution.* Amherst: University of Massachusetts Press.

Breve nota sobre "O Caso." (1980, May). *Gazeta do Mês, 1,* 14.

Brook, J., & Boal, I. A. (Eds.). (1995). *Resisting the virtual life: The culture and politics of information.* San Francisco: City Lights.

Broonzy, B. B., Slim, M., & Williamson, D. B. (1946/1990). *Blues in the Mississippi night* [CD]. New York: Rykodisc, USA. (Originally recorded in 1946; first released on record in 1957; re-released on CD with a booklet written by Alan Lomax in 1990.)

Broude, N., & Garrard, M. D. (1994). Introduction: Feminism and art in the twentieth century. In N. Broude & M. D. Garrard (Eds.), *The power of feminist art: The American movement of the 1970s, history and impact* (pp. 10-29). New York: Harry Abrams.

Broyles-González, Y. (1994). *El teatro campesino: Theater in the Chicano movement.* Austin: University of Texas Press.

Brugman, B., Redmond, T., & Ecklund, E. (1997, October 8). Pulling the strings: 31st anniversary issue investigative report. *San Francisco Bay Guardian.*

Brumberg, A. (Ed.). (1983). *Poland: Genesis of a revolution.* New York: Vintage.

Burke, P. (1986). Revolution in popular culture. In R. Porter & M. Teich (Eds.), *Revolution in history* (pp. 206-225). New York: Cambridge University Press.

Busch, C. (1981). *Was sie immer schon über freie radios wissen wollten, aber nie zu fragen wagten.* Münster, Germany: Author.

Bushnell, J. (1989). *Moscow graffiti.* Evanston, IL: Northwestern University Press.

Cable Television Consumer Protection and Competition Act of 1992, Pub. L. No. 102-385, 106 Stat. 1460 (1992).

Cable Television Report and Order, 36 FCC 2d 143 (1972).

Calhoun, C. (Ed.). (1993). *Habermas and the public sphere.* Cambridge: MIT Press.

Campbell, S. (1999, July 15). Scab radio? On the scene as Pacific Bell rewires KPFA's transmitter. *San Francisco Bay Guardian.* Available: http://www.superlists.com/kpfa/first.html.

Canning, C. (1996). *Feminist theaters in the U.S.A.: Staging women's experience.* New York: Routledge.

Carey, J. (1989). *Communication as culture: Essays on media and society.* Boston: Unwin Hyman.

Carey, J. (1995). The press, public opinion, and public discourse. In T. Glasser & C. T. Salmon (Eds.), *Public opinion and the communication of consent* (pp. 373-402). New York: Guilford.

Carlin, J. (1997, May). A farewell to arms. *Wired.*

Chaffee, L. (1989). Political graffiti and wall painting in greater Buenos Aires: An alternative communication system. *Studies in Latin American Popular Culture, 8,* 37-60.

Chaffee, L. (1990). The popular culture [of] political persuasion in Paraguay: Communication and public art. *Studies in Latin American Popular Culture, 9,* 127-148.

Chen, R. (1982). *Democracy wall and the unofficial journals. In Studies in Chinese terminology* (Vol. 20). Berkeley: University of California, Berkeley, Center for Chinese Studies.

Chochlowa, J. (1995). Meschrabpom. In I. Antonowa & J. Merkert (Eds.), *Berlin Moskau 1900-1950* (pp. 193-197). München: Prestel-Verlag.

Chrisman, M. U. (1990). L'édition protestante à Strasbourg, 1519-1560. In J.-F. Gilmont (Ed.), *La réforme et le livre: L'Europe de l'imprimé (1517-1570)* (pp. 217-238). Paris: Les Éditions du Cerf.

Church, G. J. (1999, October 4). The economy of the future? *Time,* p. 14. <http://www.time.com/time/magazine/articles/0,3266,31522-1,00.html>

Cleaver, H. (1995). *The electronic fabric of struggle* [On-line]. Available: http://www.eco.utexas.edu/faculty/Cleaver/zaps.html

Cochran, F., & Ross, L. (1993), *Procreating white supremacy: Women and the far right*. Atlanta, GA: Center for Democratic Renewal.
Cockburn, A. (1994). A fistful of promises. *New Statesman and Society, 7,* 294.
Cockburn, A. (1997, December 15). Free radio, crazy cops, and broken windows. *The Nation*, p. 9.
Cockburn, A., & Silverstein, K. (1995). Major U.S. bank urges Zapatista wipe-out: A litmus test for Mexico's stability. *Counterpunch,* 2(3).
Cojean, A., & Eskenazi, F. (1986). *FM: La folle histoire des radios libres.* Paris: Bernard Grasset.
Collectif A/Traverso. (1977). *Radio Alice, Radio libre.* Paris: J.-P. Delarge.
Colletti, L. (1972). *From Rousseau to Lenin.* London: New Left Books.
Collovald, A., & Neveu, E. (1999). Political satire on French television. *Modern & Contemporary France,* 7(3), 339-349.
Commissão do Livro Negro sobre o Fascismo. (1980). *A política do informaçao no regime fascista.* Sintra: Grafica-Europa.
Committee for Labor Access. (1996). Grant proposal. Chicago: Author.
Condee, N., & Padunov, V. (1991). *Makulakul'tura*: Reprocessing culture. *October, 57,* 79-103.
Consorzio Aaster, Centro sociale Cox 18, Centro sociale Leoncavallo, Primo Moroni. (1996). *Centri sociali: Geografie del desiderio.* Milan: Shake Edizioni Underground.
Cooper, S. (1996). Walter Benjamin and technology: Social form and the recovery of aura. *Arena Journal, 6,* 145-170.
Crimp, D., with Rolston, A. (1990). *AIDS demographics.* Seattle, WA: Bay Press.
Cronyn, H., McKane, R., & Watts, S. (Eds.). (1995). *Voices of conscience: Poetry from oppression.* North Shields, UK: Iron Press.
Curran, J., & Seaton, J. (1991). *Power without responsibility: The press and broadcasting in Britain* (4th ed.). London: Routledge.
Dahl, R. A. (1989). *Democracy and its critics.* New Haven, CT: Yale University Press.
Dale, S. (1996). *McLuhan's children: The Greenpeace message and the media.* Toronto: Between The Lines.
Daniels, T., & Gerson, J. (Eds.). (1989). *The colour black: Black images in British television.* London: British Film Institute.
Darnton, R. (1995). *The forbidden best-sellers of pre-revolutionary France.* New York: Norton.
Dates, J., & Barlow, W. (Eds.). (1993). *Split image: African Americans and the mass media* (2nd ed.). Washington, DC: Howard University Press.
Dauncey, H., & Hare, G. (1999). French youth talk radio: The free market and free speech. *Media, Culture, & Society,* 21(1), 93-108.
Davies, R. W. (1989). *Soviet history in the Gorbachev revolution.* Bloomington: Indiana University Press.
Davis, D. B. (1970). *The problem of slavery in Western culture.* Harmondsworth, UK: Penguin.
De Certeau, M. (1984) *The practice of everyday life.* Berkeley: University of California Press.

Deep dish TV network directory: A networking tool and resource guide for producers, programmers, and activists. (1988). New York: Deep Dish Television Network.

De Lima, V. A. (1979). *The ideas of Paulo Freire on communication and culture.* PhD dissertation, University of Illinois at Urbana, Institute for Communication Research.

De Micheli, M. (1978). *Mostra John Heartfield: il fotomontaggio politico.* Milan: Mazzotta Editore.

De Tarlé, A. (1979). France: The monopoly that won't divide. In A. Smith (Ed.), *Television and political life: Studies in six European countries* (pp. 41-75). London: Macmillan.

Denver Area Educational Telecommunications Consortium, Inc. et al. v. Federal Communications Commission et al., 135 L Ed 2d 888 (1996).

Dickinson, R. (1997). *Imprinting the sticks: The alternative press beyond London* (Popular Cultural Studies, Vol. 12). Aldershot, UK: Arena.

Donald, D. (1996). *The age of caricature: Satirical prints in the reign of George III.* New Haven, CT: Yale University Press.

Dovey, J. (1993). Access television in the UK. In T. Dowmunt (Ed.), *Channels of resistance: Global television and local empowerment* (pp. 163-175). London: British Film Institute.

Dowmunt, T. (Ed.). (1993). *Channels of resistance: Global television and local empowerment.* London: British Film Institute.

Downing, J. (1980). *The media machine.* London: Pluto Press.

Downing, J. (1984). *Radical media: The political organization of alternative communication.* Boston: South End Press.

Downing, J. (Ed.). (1987). *Film and politics in the third world.* New York: Autonomedia.

Downing, J. (1988a). The alternative public realm: The organization of the 1980s anti-nuclear press in West Germany and Britain. *Media, Culture, and Society, 10,* 163-181.

Downing, J. (1988b). *The Cosby Show* and American racial discourse. In T. A. van Dijk & G. Smitherman-Donaldson (Eds.), *Discourse and discrimination* (pp. 46-73). Detroit: Wayne State University Press.

Downing, J. (1989). Computers for political change: PeaceNet and public data access. *Journal of Communication, 39*(3), 154-162.

Downing, J. (1990a). Ethnic minority radio in the United States. *Howard Journal of Communication, 2*(2), 135-148.

Downing, J. (1990b). Political video in the United States: A statement for the 1990s. In B. Osborn (Ed.), *At arm's length: (Taking a good hard look at) artists' video* (pp. 101-131). New York: The Kitchen.

Downing, J. (1992). Spanish-language media in the greater New York region during the 1980s. In S. Riggins (Ed.), *Ethnic minority media: An international perspective* (pp. 256-275). Thousand Oaks, CA: Sage.

Downing, J. (1996). *Internationalizing media theory: Transition, power, culture: Reflections on media in Russia, Poland, and Hungary, 1980-1995.* London: Sage.

Downing, J. (1999a). Global networks toward new communities. In *The promise of global networks* (Annual review of the Institute for Information Studies, pp. 137-159). Queenstown, MD: The Aspen Institute.

Downing, J. (1999b). "Hate speech" and "First Amendment absolutism" discourses in the U.S. *Discourse and Society, 10*(2), 175-189.

Drew, J. (1995). Media activism and radical democracy. In J. Brook & I. A. Boal (Eds.), *Resisting the virtual life: The culture and politics of information* (pp. 71-83). San Francisco: City Lights.

Dubin, S. C. (1992). *Arresting images: Impolitic art and uncivil actions.* London: Routledge.

Dunaway, D. (1998). Community radio at the beginning of the 21st century. *The Public/Javnost, 5*(2), 87-103.

Duncan, K., & Ruggiero, G. (1997, October 10). On the growing free media movement: Recent trends in radical media organizing. *Z Magazine, 10*(10), 47-50.

Duncan, L. (1996). Labor television beyond the beltway. *Community Media Review, 19*(2), 13, 22-24.

Dunn, T. (1996). *The militarization of the U.S.-Mexico border, 1978-1992: Low-intensity conflict doctrine comes home.* Austin, TX: University of Texas Press.

Elmer-Dewitt, P. (1993). First nation in cyberspace (the internet), *Time, 142*(24), 62.

Engelman, R. (1990). The origins of public access cable television, 1966-1972. *Journalism Monographs* (Serial No. 123).

Entman, R. M. (1989). *Democracy without citizens: Media and the decay of American politics.* New York: Oxford University Press.

Enzensberger, H.-M. (1974). Constituents of a theory of the media. In H. M. Enzensberger (Ed.), *The consciousness industry* (pp. 95-128). New York: Seabury.

Esteva, G., & Prakash, M. S. (1998). *Grassroots postmodernism: Remaking the soil of cultures.* London: Zed.

Evans, D. (1992). *John Heartfield AIZ: Arbeiter-Illustrierte Zeitung and Volks Illustrierte 1930-38.* New York: Kent Fine Art.

Evans, S. M. (1979). *Personal politics: The roots of women's liberation in the civil rights movement and the new left.* New York: Knopf.

Fabré, Geneviève (1994). African American commemorative celebrations in the nineteenth century. In G. Fabré & R. O'Meally (Eds.), *History and memory in African American culture* (pp. 72-91). New York: Oxford University Press.

Fanon, F. (1968). *Sociologie d'une révolution (L'an cinq de la révolution algérienne).* Paris: Maspéro.

Favre, P. (1999). Les manifestations de rue entre espace privé et espace publique. In B. François & E. Neveu (Eds.), *Espaces publiques mosaïques: Acteurs, arènes et rhètoriques des débats publics contemporains* (pp. 135-152). Rennes: Presses Universitaires de Rennes.

Federal Communications Commission v. Midwest Video Corporation, 440 U.S. 689 (1979).

Felshin, N. (Ed.). (1995). *But is it art? The spirit of art as activism.* Seattle, WA: Bay Press.

Femia, J. V. (1981). *Gramsci's political thought: Hegemony, consciousness, and the revolutionary process.* Oxford, UK: Clarendon.

Fenati, B. (1996, December). Dal salto della puntina al satellite digitale: I venti anni de Radio Popolare. *ERREPI*, pp. 10-13.

Fernandes, J. A. (1980, May). Duas ou tres coisas que eu sei do *República. Gazeta do Mês,* pp. 14-15.

Ferraresi, F. (1996). *Threats to democracy: The radical right in Italy after the war.* Princeton, NJ: Princeton University Press.

Findlen, P. (1993). Humanism, politics, and pornography in Renaissance Italy. In L. Hunt (Ed.), *The invention of pornography: Obscenity and the origins of modernity, 1500-1800* (pp. 49-108). New York: Zone Books.

Findley, P. (1994). Conscientization and social movements in Canada: The relevance of Paulo Freire's ideas in contemporary politics. In P. L. McLaren & C. Lankshear (Eds.), *Politics of liberation: Paths from Freire* (pp. 108-122). New York: Routledge.

Fiske, J. (1988). *Television culture.* New York: Methuen.

Fiske, J. (1995). *Media matters.* Minneapolis: University of Minnesota Press.

Fitzpatrick, S. (Ed.). (1978). *Cultural revolution in Russia, 1928-1931.* Bloomington: Indiana University Press.

Flood, J. L. (1990). Le livre dans le monde germanique à l'époque de la Réforme. In J.-F. Gilmont (Ed.), *La réforme et le livre: L'Europe de l'imprimé (1517-1570)* (pp. 29-104). Paris: Les Éditions du Cerf.

Fofi, G. (1978). Lottare su due fronti. *aut aut, 163,* 46-52.

Forgacs, D. (1988). *An Antonio Gramsci reader: Selected writings 1916-1935.* New York: Schocken.

Forgacs, D., & Lumley, R. (Eds.). (1996). *Italian cultural studies: An introduction.* New York: Oxford University Press.

Foucault, M. (1977). *Discipline and punish: The birth of the prison.* New York: Pantheon.

Fountain, N. (1988). *Underground: The London alternative press 1966-74.* London: Routledge.

Fox, C. F. (1999). *The fence and the river: Culture and politics at the U.S.-Mexican border.* Minneapolis: University of Minnesota Press.

François, B., & Neveu, E. (Eds.). (1999). *Espaces publiques mosaïques: Acteurs, arènes et rhètoriques des débats publics contemporains.* Rennes: Presses Universitaires de Rennes.

Fraser, N. (1993). Rethinking the public sphere: A contribution to the critique of actually existing democracy. In C. Calhoun (Ed.), *Habermas and the public sphere* (pp. 109-142). Cambridge: MIT Press.

Frederick, H. (1993). Computer communication in cross-border coalition-building: North American NGO networking against NAFTA. *Gazette: The International Journal of Mass Communication Studies, 50*(2/3), 217-241.

Frederick, H. (1996). Computer networks and the emergence of global civil society: The case of the association for progressive communication (APC). In L. M. Harasim (Ed.), *Globalizing networks: Computers and international communication.* Cambridge: MIT Press.

Freeman, J. (1975). *The politics of women's liberation.* New York: David McKay.

Freire, P. (1970). *Pedagogy of the oppressed.* New York: Herder & Herder.

Freire, P. (1972). *Cultural action for freedom.* Harmondsworth, UK: Penguin.

Freire, P. (1974). *Education for critical consciousness.* London: Sheed & Ward.

Friedland, L. A. (1996). Electronic democracy and the new citizenship. *Media, Culture, & Society, 18*(2), 185-212.

Gabriel, T. (1982). *Third cinema in the third world.* Ann Arbor, MI: UMI Research Press.

Gallo, M. (Ed.). (1974). *The poster in history.* New York: New American Library.

Gamaleri, G. (Ed.). *Un posto nell'etere: Le radio locali in Italia.* Rome: Edizioni Paoline.

Ganley, G. (1996). *The unglued empire: The Soviet experience with communications technologies.* Norwood, NJ: Ablex.

García Espinosa, J. (1983). For an imperfect cinema. In A. Mattelart & S. Siegelaub (Eds.), *Communication and class struggle 2: Liberation, socialism* (pp. 295-300). Bagnolet, France: International Mass Media Research Center.

Garitaonandia, C. (1988). *La radio en España 1923-1939: De altavoz musical a arma de propaganda.* Madrid: Siglo XXI de España Editores.

Garnham, N. (1990). *Capitalism and communication: Global culture and the economics of information.* Newbury Park, CA: Sage.

Garofalo, T. M. (1994). *To rescue and conserve our culture: Community radio on Colombia's Pacific littoral.* Master's thesis, University of Texas at Austin, Institute for Latin American Studies.

Garton Ash, T. (1983). *The Polish revolution: Solidarity.* New York: Scribner.

Garton Ash, T. (1990). *We the people: The revolutions of '89* Harmondsworth, UK: Penguin.

Genovese, E. D. (1975) *Roll, Jordan, roll: The world the slaves made.* London: André Deutsch.

Gettleman, M. E., Lacefield, P., Menashe, L., Mermelstein, D., & Radosh, R. (Eds.). (1981). *El Salvador: Central America in the new Cold War.* New York: Grove.

Gever, M. (1985). Video politics: Early feminist projects. In D. Kahn & D. Neumaier (Eds.), *Cultures in contention* (pp. 92-101). Seattle, WA: The Real Comet Press.

Gillespie, M. (1995). *Television, ethnicity, and cultural change.* London: Routledge.

Gilmont, J.-F. (1990a). Introduction. In J.-F. Gilmont (Ed.), *La réforme et le livre: L'Europe de l'imprimé (1517-1570)* (pp. 9-17). Paris: Les Éditions du Cerf.

Gilmont, J.-F. (Ed.). (1990b) *La réforme et le livre: l'Europe de l'imprimé (1517-1570).* Paris: Les Éditions du Cerf.

Ginzburg, E. S. (1967). *Journey into the whirlwind.* New York: Harcourt Brace Jovanovich.

Girard, B. (Ed.). (1992). *A passion for radio: Radio waves and community.* Montréal: Black Rose Books.

Gitlin, T. (1980). *The whole world is watching: Mass media in the making and unmaking of the new left.* Berkeley: University of California Press.

Gitlin, T. (1983). *Inside prime time.* New York: Pantheon.

Gleason, A., Kenez, P., & Stites, R. (Eds.). (1985). *Bolshevik culture: Experiment and order in the Russian revolution.* Bloomington: Indiana University Press.

Goban-Klas, T. (1994). *The orchestration of the media: The politics of mass communications in Communist Poland and the aftermath.* Boulder, CO: Westview.

Godfried, N. (1997). *WCFL: Chicago's voice of labor, 1926-78.* Urbana: University of Illinois Press.

Goldman, E. (1970). *Living my life* (2 vols.). New York: Dover.

Goldman, E. (1974). *Anarchism and other essays.* New York: Dover.

Goldstein, R. J. (1989). *Censorship of political caricature in nineteenth century France.* Kent, OH: Kent State University Press.

Goodwyn, L. (1991). *Breaking the barrier: The rise of Solidarity in Poland.* New York: Oxford University Press.

Graeve, I. (1995). Klassenauge versus neues sehen. In I. Antonowa & J. Merkert (Eds.), *Berlin Moskau 1900-1950* (pp. 221-225). München: Prestel-Verlag.

Gramsci, A. (1971) *Prison Notebooks,* (Quintin Hoare & Geoffrey-Nowell Smith, Eds.). London: Lawrence & Wishart.

Gray, H. (1995). *Watching race: Television and the struggle for "Blackness."* Minneapolis: University of Minnesota Press.

Gray, M. (1997). *Web growth summary* [On-line]. Available: http://www.mit.edu/people/mkgray/net/web-growth-summary.html

Greek-Oriental Rebetica, 1911-1937 (1991). El Cerrito, CA: Arhoolie Productions.

Gregor, U., & Klejman, N. (1995). Deutscher und sowjetischer film. In I. Antonowa & J. Merkert (Eds.), *Berlin Moskau 1900-1950* (pp. 199-203). München: Prestel-Verlag.

Grigorenko, P. (1982). *Memoirs.* New York: Norton.

Grispigni, M. (1997). *Il settantasette.* Milan: Il Saggiatore.

Grohs, G. (1976). The church in Portugal after the coup of 1974. *Iberian Studies, 1,* 34-40.

Group 2828. (1997). *Net—Which Net?* Paper delivered to the Second Intercontinental Encuentro, Madrid Spain. Available: http://www.pangea.org/encuentro and http://www.eco.utexas.edu/homepages/faculty/Cleaver/wk1net.html

Guérin, D. (1965). *La peste brune.* Paris: Maspéro.

Gumucio Dagron, A., & Cajías, L. (Eds.). (1989). *Las radios mineras de Bolivia.* La Paz: CIMCA-UNESCO.

Habermas, J. (1987). *The theory of communicative action.* Boston, MA: Beacon. (Original work published 1984)

Habermas, J. (1989) *Strukturwandel der Öffentlichkeit* (The Structural Transformation of the Public Sphere). Cambridge: MIT Press. (Original work published 1962)

Hackett, R. A. (1991). *News and dissent: The press and the politics of peace in Canada.* Norwood, NJ: Ablex.

Hackett, R. A. (1993). *Engulfed: Peace protest and America's press during the Gulf War* (Occasional Paper). New York: New York University, Center for War, Peace and the News Media.

Hall, S. (1986). Gramsci's relevance for the study of race and ethnicity. In D. Morley & K.-H. Chen (Eds.), *Stuart Hall: Critical dialogues in cultural studies* (pp. 411-440). New York: Routledge.

Halleck, D. (1984). Paper tiger television: Smashing the myths of the information industry every week on public access cable. *Media, Culture, and Society, 6,* 313-318.

Halleck, D. (1993). Deep dish TV: Community video from geostationary orbit. *Leonardo, 26*(5), 415-420.
Halleck, D. (1994, September/October). Zapatistas on-line. *NACLA Report on the Americas, 28,* 30.
Hallett, M. (1999). *The spectacle of difference: Graphic satire in the age of Hogarth.* New Haven, CT: Yale University Press.
Hallin, D. C. (1986). *The "uncensored" war: The media and Vietnam.* New York: Oxford University Press.
Halloran, J., Elliott, P., & Murdock, G. (1970). *Demonstrations and communication.* Harmondsworth, UK: Penguin.
Hamelink, C. (1995). *World communication: Disempowerment and self-empowerment.* New York: Zed Books.
Hamsik, D. (1971). *Writers against rulers.* London: Hutchinson.
Hanchard, M. (1995). Black Cinderalla? Race and the public sphere in Brazil. *Public Culture, 15,* 165-185.
Hardt, H. (1993). Alternative views of democracy: Theories of culture and communication in the United States. In S. Splichal & J. Wasko (Eds.), *Communication and democracy* (pp. 87-102). Norwood, NJ: Ablex Publishing Corporation.
Harris, M. W. (1992). *The rise of the gospel blues: The music of Thomas Andrew Dorsey in the urban church.* New York: Oxford University Press.
Havlicek, D. (1973). Mass media and their impact on Czechoslovak politics in 1968. In V. V. Kusin (Ed.), *The Czechoslovak reform movement 1968.* Santa Barbara, CA: ABC Clio Press.
Held, D. (1987). *Models of democracy.* Stanford, CA: Stanford University Press.
Heller, S., & Anderson, G. (1992). *The savage mirror: The art of contemporary caricature.* New York: Watson-Guptill.
Helsinki Watch. (1986). *Reinventing civil society: Poland's quiet revolution 1981-1986.* New York: Author.
Helsinki Watch. (1987). *From below: Independent peace and environmental movements in Eastern Europe and the USSR.* New York: Author.
Helsinki Watch. (1990). *Nyeformaly: Civil society in the USSR.* New York: Author.
Hénaut, D. T. (1991). Video stories from the dawn of time. *Visual Anthropology Review, 7*(2), 85-101.
Hercules, B. (1987). Labor beat. *Community Television Review, 10*(2), 12-13.
Herman, E. S. (1992). *Beyond hypocrisy: Decoding the news in an age of propaganda.* Boston: South End Press.
Herman, E. S. (1999). *The myth of the liberal media: An Edward Herman reader.* New York: Peter Lang.
Herman, E. S., & Chomsky, N. (1988). *Manufacturing consent.* New York: Pantheon.
Herman, E. S., & McChesney, R. W. (1997). *The global media: The new missionaries of corporate capitalism.* Washington, DC: Cassell.
Hersh, S. (1983). *The price of power: Kissinger in the Nixon White House.* New York: Summit.
Hertsgaard, M. (1988). *On bended knee: The press and the Reagan presidency.* New York: Farrar Straus Giroux.
Hickey, N. (1997, June/July). Jurassic pork. *Cybernautics Digest,* pp. 10-17.

Hill, C. (1975). *The world turned upside down: Radical ideas during the English Revolution*. Harmondsworth, UK: Penguin.

Hilliard, R. L., & Keith, M. C. (1999). *Waves of rancor: Tuning in the radical right.* Armonk, NY: M. E. Sharpe.

Hinks, P. B. (1997). *To awaken my afflicted brethren: David Walker and the problem of antebellum slave resistance.* University Park: The Pennsylvania State University Press.

Hinz, R. (1981). *Käthe Kollwitz: Graphics, posters, drawings.* New York: Pantheon.

Hobsbawm, E. J. (1994). *The age of extremes: A history of the world, 1914-1991.* New York: Pantheon.

Hoernle, E. (1983). The worker's eye. In A. Mattelart & S. Siegelaub (Eds.), *Communication and class struggle 2: Liberation, socialism.* Bagnolet, France: International Mass Media Research Center.

Hoffmann, L. (1995). Die proletarische theater Berlins und der impuls proletkult. In I. Antonowa & J. Merkert (Eds.), *Berlin Moskau 1900-1950* (pp. 227-231). München: Prestel-Verlag.

Höllering, F. (1983). The conquest of machines that can observe things. In A. Mattelart & S. Siegelaub (Eds.), *Communication and class struggle 2: Liberation, socialism.* Bagnolet, France: International Mass Media Research Center.

Hollis, P. (1970). *The pauper press: A study in working class radicalism of the 1830s.* Oxford, UK: Oxford University Press.

Holloway, J., & Peláez, E. (Eds.). (1998). *Zapatista! Reinventing revolution from the ground up.* London: Pluto.

Hopkins, M. (1983). *Russia's underground press.* New York: Praeger.

Horkheimer, M., & Adorno, T. (1987). The culture industry: Enlightenment as mass deception. In M. Horkheimer & T. Adorno (Eds.), *Dialectic of enlightenment* (pp. 120-167). New York: Continuum.

Huesca, R. (1995). A procedural view of participatory communication: Lessons from Bolivian tin miners' radio. *Media, Culture, & Society, 17,* 101-119.

Huesca, R., & Dervin, B. (1994). Theory and practice in Latin American alternative communication research. *Journal of Communication, 44*(4), 53-73.

Hunt, L. (Ed.). (1993). *The invention of pornography: Obscenity and the origins of modernity, 1500-1800.* New York: Zone Books.

Hunter, T. (1997). *To joy my freedom: Southern Black women's lives and labors after the Civil War.* Cambridge, MA: Harvard University Press.

Husband, C. (1988). Racist humour and racist ideology in British television, or I laughed till you cried. In C. Powell & G. E. C. Paton (Eds.), *Humour in society: Resistance and control* (pp. 149-178). London: Macmillan.

Husband, C. (1996). The right to be understood: Conceiving the multi-ethnic public sphere. *Innovation, 9*(2), 205-211.

Husband, C., & Chouhan, J. (1985). Local radio in the communication environment of ethnic minorities in Britain. in T. A. van Dijk (Ed.), *Discourse and communication: New approaches to the analyses of mass media discourse and communication* (pp. 270-294). Berlin: de Gruyter.

Hutter, P. (Ed.). (1978). *Piccole antenne crescono.* Rome: Savelli Editore.

Israels Perry, E. (1994). Image, rhetoric, and the historical memory of women. In A. Sheppard (Ed.), *Cartooning for suffrage* (pp. 3-19). Albuquerque: University of New Mexico Press.

Jacob, M. J. (1995). An unfashionable audience. In S. Lacy (Ed.), *Mapping the terrain: New genre public art* (pp. 50-59). Seattle, WA: Bay Press.

Jakubowicz, K. (1990). Musical chairs? The three public spheres of Poland. *Media, Culture, & Society, 12,* 195-212.

Jakubowicz, K. (1993). Stuck in a groove: Why the 1960s approach to communication democratization will no longer do. In S. Splichal & J. Wasko (Eds.), *Communication and democracy* (pp. 33-54). Norwood, NJ: Ablex.

James, R. (Ed.). (1992). *Cassette mythos.* Brooklyn, NY: Autonomedia.

Jankowski, N., Prehn, O., & Stappers, J. (Eds.). (1992). *The people's voice: Local radio and television in Europe.* London: John Libbey.

Jenkins, H. (1992). *Textual poachers.* New York: Routledge.

Jensen, C. (1997). *20 Years of censored news.* New York: Seven Stories Press.

Jezdinsky, K. (1973). Mass media and their impact on Czechoslovak politics in 1968. In V. V. Kusin (Ed.), *The Czechoslovak reform movement 1968.* Santa Barbara, CA: ABC Clio Press.

Jezer, M. (1982). *The dark ages: Life in the United States 1945-1960.* Boston: South End Press.

Johnston, A. G., & Gilmont, J.-F. (1990). L'imprimerie et la Réforme á Anvers. In J.-F. Gilmont (Ed.), *La réforme et le livre: L'Europe de l'imprimé (1517-1570)* (pp. 191-216). Paris: Les Éditions du Cerf.

Jones, M. C. (1993). *Heretics and hellraisers: Women contributors to the masses, 1911-1917.* Austin: University of Texas Press.

Juhasz, A. (1995). *AIDS TV: Identity, community, and alternative video.* Durham, NC: Duke University Press.

Kahn, D., & Neumaier, D. (Eds.). (1985). *Cultures in contention.* Seattle. WA: The Real Comet Press.

Kaiser, S. M. (1993). The madwomen memory mothers of the Plaza de Mayo. Master's thesis, Film and Media Studies Department, Hunter College, City University of New York.

Kaiser, S. M. (2000, June). The torturer next door: Challenging impunity in post-dictatorial Argentina. Paper delivered at the International Communication Association conference, Acapulco, Mexico.

Kapchan, D. (1996). *Gender on the market: Moroccan women and the revoicing of tradition.* Philadelphia: University of Pennsylvania Press.

Katz, E., & Lazarsfeld, P. (1955). *Personal influence.* Glencoe, IL: The Free Press.

Kawecka-Gryczowa, A., & Tazbir, J. (1990). Le livre et la réforme en Pologne. In J.-F. Gilmont (Ed.), *La réforme et le livre: L'Europe de l'imprimé (1517-1570)* (pp. 417-440). Paris: Les Éditions du Cerf.

Keane, J. (1991). *The media and democracy.* Cambridge, UK: Basil Blackwell.

Keil, C. (1966). *Urban blues.* Chicago: University of Chicago Press.

Kellner, D. (1990). *Television and the crisis of democracy.* Boulder, CO: Westview.

Kellner, D. (1992). *The Persian Gulf TV war.* Boulder, CO: Westview.

Kellow, C. L., & Steeves, H. L. (1998). The role of radio in the Rwandan genocide. *Journal of Communication, 48*(3), 107-128.

Kershaw, B. (1992). *The politics of performance: Radical theatre as cultural intervention.* London: Routledge.

Khosrokhavar, F. (1997). *L'Islam des jeunes.* Paris: Flammarion.

King, D. (1997). *The commissar vanishes: The falsification of photographs and art in Stalin's Russia.* New York: Henry Holt.

Kintz, L., & Lesage, J. (Eds.). (1998). *Media, culture, and the religious right.* Minneapolis: University of Minnesota Press.

Klapper, J. (1960). *The effects of mass communication.* New York: The Free Press.

Kobylinski, A. (1989). *Szesc lat podziemnej poczty w polsce (1982-1988).* Rapposwil, Switzerland: Muzeum Polskiego.

Kogawa, T. (1985). Free radio in Japan. In D. Kahn & D. Neumaier (Eds.), *Cultures in contention* (pp. 116-121). Seattle. WA: The Real Comet Press.

Koljasin, W. (1995). Gastspieler russischer theater in den zwanzigen und dreissigen jahren. In I. Antonowa & J. Merkert (Eds.), *Berlin Moskau 1900-1950* (pp. 173-177). München: Prestel-Verlag.

Komarov, B. (1978). *The destruction of nature in the Soviet Union.* London: Pluto Press.

Konrád, G. (1984). *Antipolitics.* New York: Harcourt Brace Jovanovich.

Kopelev, L. (1969). *No jail for thought.* Harmondsworth, UK: Penguin.

Kouloumdjian, M.-F. & Busato, L. (1987). *L'audiocassette au Brésil: Voix de résistance.* Grenoble: Ellug, Université Stendhal.

Kowalski, T. (1988). Evolution after revolution: The Polish press system in transition, *Media, Culture, & Society, 10*(2), 183-196.

Kubik, J. (1994). *The power of symbols against the symbols of power.* University Park: Pennsylvania State University Press.

Kunzle, D. (1983). Art in Chile's revolutionary process: Guerrilla muralist brigades. In A. Mattelart & S. Siegelaub (Eds.), *Communication and class struggle 2: Liberation, socialism* (pp. 372-381). Bagnolet, France: International Mass Media Research Center.

Laba, R. (1991). *The roots of solidarity: A political sociology of Poland's working class democratization.* Princeton, NJ: Princeton University Press.

Labor and access: A roundtable discussion. (1995). *Community Media Review, 18*(3), 14, 25-28.

Laclau, E., & Mouffe, C. (1985). *Hegemony and socialist strategy.* New York: Verso.

Lacy, S. (Ed.). (1995). *Mapping the terrain: New genre public art.* Seattle, WA: Bay Press.

Lafaye, J. (1985). *Quetzalcóatl y Guadalupe: La formación de la conciencia nacional en México.* Mexico City: Fondo de Cultura Económica.

Land, J. (1999). *Active radio: Pacifica's brash experiment.* Minneapolis: University of Minnesota Press.

Landes, J. (1988). *Women and the public sphere in the age of the French Revolution.* Ithaca, NY: Cornell University Press.

Landry, C., Morley, D., Southwood, R., & Wright, P. (1985). *What a way to run a railroad: An analysis of radical failure.* London: Comedia Publishing Group.

Lasar, M. (1999). *Pacifica radio: The rise of an alternative network.* Philadelphia, PA: Temple University Press.

Latham, J. (1999). *Voices of hate* [On-line]. Available: http://www.rfpi.org/vista/frrr-book1.html

Laughton, B. (1996). *Honoré Daumier.* New Haven, CT: Yale University Press.

Lears, T. J. (1985). The concept of cultural hegemony: Problems and possibilities. *American Historical Review, 90*(5), 567-593.

Lenin, V. I. (1965). *Collected works*(Vol. 5). London: Lawrence & Wishart. (Original work published 1902)

Leuthold, S. (1998). *Indigenous aesthetics: Native art, media, and identity.* Austin: University of Texas Press.

Levine, L. W. (1977). *Black culture and Black consciousness: Afro-American folk thought from slavery to freedom.* New York: Oxford University Press.

Levy, E. (1999). *Cinema of outsiders: The rise of American independent film.* New York: New York University Press.

Lewin, M. (1988). *The Gorbachev phenomenon: An historical interpretation.* Berkeley: University of California Press.

Lewis, B. I. (1971). *George Grosz: Art and politics in the Weimar republic.* Madison: University of Wisconsin Press.

Lidtke, V. (1985). *The alternative culture: Socialist labor in imperial Germany.* New York: Oxford University Press.

Liehm, A. (1977). *Il passato presente.* Bologna: Cappelli Editore.

Lifton, R. J., & Falk, R. (1982). *Indefensible weapons: The political and moral case against nuclear arms.* New York: Basic Books.

Limón, J. E. (1992). *Mexican ballads, Chicano poems: History and influence in Mexican-American social poetry.* Berkeley: University of California Press.

Liperi, F. (1997). La rivoluzione via etere. In M. Bascetta et al. (Eds.), *Millenovecento settanta sette* (pp. 105-114). Rome: Manifestolibri.

Lippard, L. R. (1981). Foreword. In R. Hinz, *Käthe Kollwitz: Graphics, posters, drawings.* New York: Pantheon.

Lloréns, J. A. (1994). Popular media in Peru: Mass media and collective identity. PhD dissertation, Department of Radio-Television-Film, The University of Texas at Austin.

Longo, B. (1978, January-February). I limiti della communicazione "internal." *aut aut, 163,* 18-26.

López Vigil, J. I. (1994). *Rebel radio: The story of El Salvador's Radio Venceremos.* Willimantic, CT and London: Curbstone Press and Latin America Bureau.

Macali, G. (1977). *Meglio tardi che RAI.* Rome: Savelli Editore.

Macpherson, C. B. (1973). *Democratic theory: Essays in retrieval.* London: Oxford University Press.

Maier-Metz, H. (1984). *Expressionismus—Dada—agitprop: Zur entwicklung des Malik-Kreises in Berlin 1912-1924.* Frankfurt am Main: Peter Lang.

Malcolm X. (1968). *The autobiography of Malcolm X.* Harmondsworth, UK: Penguin.

Mallin, P. (1997, October). Marci Lockwood, IGC's new executive director: the NetNews interview. *IGC Netnews* [On-line]. Available: http://www.igc.org/igc/netnews/lockwood.html

Mandela, N. (1973). *No easy walk to freedom: Articles, speeches, and trial addresses.* London: Heinemann.

Manno, J. (1984). *Arming the heavens: The hidden military agenda for space, 1945-1995.* New York: Dodd, Mead.

Marcus, D. (1991). Tales from the tiger den: A history of our deconstruction. In D. Marcus (Ed.), *ROAR! The paper tiger television guide to media activism* (pp. 31-32). New York: The Paper Tiger Television Collective.

Marcus, G. (1989). *Lipstick traces: A secret history of the twentieth century.* Cambridge, MA: Harvard University Press.

Marelli, G. (1998). *L'amére victoire de situationnisme: Pour une histoire critique de l'Internationale situationniste (1957-1972).* Arles, France: Éditions Sulliver.

Martín-Barbero, J. (1993). *Communication, culture, and hegemony: From the media to mediations,* Newbury Park, CA: Sage.

Martínez Victores, R. (1978). *7RR: la historia de Radio Rebelde.* Havana: Editorial de Ciencias Sociales.

Marx, K. (1975). *Contribution to the critique of Hegel's philosophy of law.* In K. Marx & F. Engels, *Collected works* (Vol. 3, pp. 175-187). Moscow: Progress.

Marx, K. (1977). *Capital: A critique of political economy.* New York: International Publishers.

Marx, K., & Engels, F. (1972). *The German ideology.* New York: International Publishers.

Mason, M. (1997, October). IGC fights digital censorship: Basque website attacked by internet mailbombers. *IGC NetNews* [On-line]. Available: http://www.igc.org/igc/netnews/ehj.html

Massachi, D., & Cowan, R. (Eds.). (1994). *Guide to uncovering the right on campus.* Cambridge, MA: University Conversion Project.

Mattelart, A. (1974). *Mass media, idéologies et mouvement révolutionnaire, Chili 1970-1973.* Paris: éditions Anthropos.

Mattelart, A. (Ed.). (1986). *Communicating in popular Nicaragua.* New York: International General.

Mattelart, A., & Siegelaub, S. (Eds.). (1983). *Communication and class struggle 2: Liberation, socialism.* Bagnolet, France: International Mass Media Research Center.

Mattern, M. (1991). Popular music and redemocratization in Santiago, Chile. *Studies in Latin American Popular Culture, 10,* 101-113.

Mayer, V. (1998). For the people and by the people: TV Maxabomba's regeneration of popular cinema. *Studies In Latin American Popular Culture, 17,* 223-232.

McCalman, I. (1988). *Radical underworld: Prophets, revolutionaries, and pornographers in London, 1795-1840.* New York: Cambridge University Press.

McCarthy, P. (1995). *The crisis of the Italian state: From the origins of the Cold War to the fall of Berlusconi.* New York: St Martin's.

McChesney, R. (1993). *Telecommunications, mass media, and democracy: The battle for the control of U.S. broadcasting, 1928-1935.* New York: Oxford University Press.

McChesney, R. (1996). The global struggle for communication. *Monthly Review, 48*(2), 1.

McChesney, R. (1997). Digital highway robbery: Where is the competition the Telecommunications Act is supposed to provide? *The Nation, 264*(15), 22.

McClure, K. (1992). On the subject of rights: Pluralism, plurality, and political identity. In C. Mouffe (Ed.), *Dimensions of radical democracy: Pluralism, citizenship, and community* (pp. 108-125). London: Verso.

McCole, J. (1993). *Walter Benjamin and the antinomies of tradition.* Ithaca, NY: Cornell University Press.

McLaren, P. L., & Lankshear, C. (Eds.). (1994). *Politics of liberation: Paths from Freire.* New York: Routledge.

McLaughlin, L. (1995). From excess to access: Feminist political agency in the public sphere. *Javnost/The Public, 2*(4), 37-50.

McMillan, P. J. (1965). *Khrushchev and the arts: The politics of Soviet culture, 1962-64.* Cambridge: MIT Press.

Medvedev, R. (Ed.). (1978). *Samizdat register I.* London: Merlin.

Medvedev, R. (Ed.). (1982). *Samizdat register II.* London: Merlin.

Mercer, K. (1988). Diaspora culture and the dialogic imagination. In M. B. Cham & C. Andrade-Watkins (Eds.), *Blackframes: Critical perspectives on Black independent cinema* (pp. 50-61). Boston: MIT Press.

Mesquita, M. (1994). Os meios de comunicaçao social. In A. Reis (Ed.), *Portugal: 20 anos de democracia* (pp. 360-405). Lisbon: Círculo De Leitores.

Meyer, R. (1995). This is to enrage you: Gran Fury and the graphics of AIDS activism. In N. Felshin (Ed.), *But is it art? The spirit of art as activism* (pp. 51-83). Seattle, WA: Bay Press.

MIDS (Matrix Information and Directory Services, Inc.). (1997, January). *MN online editorial: State of the internet* [On-line]. Available: http://www.mids.org/mmq/401/pubhtml/ed.html

Mignot-Lefebvre, Y. (1984). Nouveaux média, nouveaux professionels? *Autogestions, 18,* 47-59.

Milkman, P. (1997). PM: *A new deal in journalism, 1940-1948.* Brunswick, NJ: Rutgers University Press.

Minter, W. (1972). *Portuguese Africa and the West.* Harmondsworth, UK: Penguin.

Misztal, B. (1992). Between the state and solidarity: One movement, two interpretations—the orange alternative movement in Poland. *British Journal of Sociology, 43,* 55-78.

Mitchell, C. (1998). Women's radio as a feminist public sphere. *The Public/Javnost, 5*(2), 73-85.

Mlynar, Z. (1980). *Nightfrost in Prague.* New York: Karz.

Mohammadi, A., & Sreberny-Mohammadi, A. (1994). *Small media big revolution.* Minneapolis: University of Minnesota Press.

Molete, M. (1992). La caméra explore les luttes. In N. Thede & A. Ambrosi (Eds.), *Petits écrans et démocratie: Vidéo légère et télévision alternative au service du développement* (pp. 83-91). Paris: Syros-Alternatives

Mouffe, C. (1992a). *Dimensions of radical democracy: Pluralism, citizenship, and community.* London: Verso.

Mouffe, C. (1992b). Feminism, citizenship, and radical democratic politics. In J. Butler & J. W. Scott (Eds.), *Feminists theorize the political* (pp. 369-384). New York: Routledge.

Mueller, R. (1989). *Bertolt Brecht and the theory of media.* Lincoln: University of Nebraska Press.

Münzenberg, W. (1983). Tasks and aims of the international worker-photographer movement. In A. Mattelart & S. Siegelaub (Eds.), *Communication and class struggle 2: Liberation, socialism.* Bagnolet, France: International Mass Media Research Center.

Nader, R., Love, J., & Saindon, A. (1995, July). Federal telecommunications legislation: Impact on media concentration. *Consumer Project on Technology,14* [Internet newsletter].

Nakazawa, K. (1989). *Barefoot gen.* Harmondsworth, UK: Penguin.

Negri, A. (1991). *Marx beyond Marx: Lessons on the Grundrisse.* New York: Autonomedia.

Negt, O., & Kluge, A. (1993). *Öffentlichkeit und Erfahrung* (Public sphere and experience). Minneapolis: University of Minnesota Press. (Original work published 1972)

Nelson, E. (1989). *The British counter-culture, 1966-73: A study of the underground press.* New York: St Martin's.

Network Medien-Cooperative. (1983). *Frequenzbesetzer: Arbeitsbuch für ein anderes Radio.* Hamburg: Rowohlt Taschenbuch.

Network Wizards. (1997, July). *Internet domain survey* [On-line]. Available: http://www.nw.com/zone/WWW/report.html

Neveu, E. (1999). Media and social movements. *La Lettre de la Maison Française 10,* 43-60.

Noriega, C. (Ed.). (1992). *Chicanos and film: Representation and resistance.* Minneapolis: University of Minnesota Press.

Nove, A. (1989). *Glasnost in action.* Boston, MA: Unwin Hyman.

Nowak, J. (1983, April). Poland's resilient underground press. *Washington Journalism Review,* pp. 18-20, 58.

Nwoye, O. G. (1993). Social issues on walls: Graffiti in university lavatories. *Discourse and Society,* 4(4), 419-442.

O'Connor, A. (1990). The miners' radio stations in Bolivia: A culture of resistance. *Journal of Communication, 40,* 102-110.

Orwell, G. (1952). *Homage to Catalonia.* New York: Harcourt.

Ost, D. (1990). *Solidarity and the politics of anti-politics: Opposition and reform in Poland since 1968.* Philadelphia, PA: Temple University Press.

Otzoy, I. (1996). Maya clothing and identity. In E. F. Fischer & R. McKenna Brown (Eds.), *Maya cultural activism in Guatemala* (pp. 141-155). Austin: University of Texas Press.

Painter, N. I. (1996). *Sojourner Truth: A life, a symbol.* New York: Norton.

Paret, P., Lewis, B. I., & Paret, P. (1992). *Persuasive images: Posters of war and revolution from the Hoover Institution archives.* Princeton, NJ: Princeton University Press.

Passerini, L. (1996). *Autobiography of a generation: Italy, 1968.* Hanover, NH: Wesleyan University Press.

Pearson, J. (1999). *Women's reading in Britain 1750-1835: A dangerous recreation.* Cambridge, UK: Cambridge University Press.

Peck, A. (1985). *Uncovering the sixties: The life and times of the underground press.* New York: Pantheon.

Percq, P. (1998). *Les caméras des favelas.* Paris: Les Éditions de l'Atelier.

Philippe, R. (1982). *Political graphics: Art as a weapon.* New York: Abbeville.
Phillips, S. A. (1999). *Wallbangin': Graffiti and gangs in Los Angeles.* Chicago: University of Chicago Press.
Pincus, R. L. (1995). The invisible town square: Artists' collaborations and media dramas in America's biggest border town. In N. Felshin (Ed.), *But is it art? The spirit of art as activism* (pp. 31-49). Seattle, WA: Bay Press.
Pines, J. (1988). The cultural context of Black British cinema. In M. B. Cham & C. Andrade-Watkins (Eds.), *Blackframes: Critical perspectives on Black independent cinema* (pp. 26-26). Boston: MIT Press.
Plant, S. (1992). *The most radical gesture: The situationist international in a postmodern age.* London: Routledge.
Plyushch, L. (1979). *History's carnival: A dissident's autobiography.* New York: Harcourt, Brace, Jovanovich.
Poovey, M. (1984). *The proper lady and the woman writer: Ideology as style in the works of Mary Wollstonecraft, Mary Shelley, and Jane Austen.* Chicago: University of Chicago Press.
Porter, D. (1979). Revolutionary realization: The motivational energy. In H. J. Ehrlich (Ed.), *Reinventing anarchy* (pp. 214-228). London: Routledge & Kegan Paul.
Potash, C. (Ed.). (1997). *Reggae, rasta, revolution: Jamaican music from ska to dub.* New York: Schirmer.
Potel, J.-Y. (1982). *The promise of Solidarnosc.* New York: Praeger.
Price, R. (Ed.). (1973). *Maroon societies: Rebel slave communities in the Americas.* New York: Anchor.
Pringle, P., & Arkin, W. (1983). *SIOP: The secret U.S. plan for nuclear war.* New York: Norton.
Putnam, R. D. (1993). *Making democracy work: Civic traditions in modern Italy.* Princeton, NJ: Princeton University Press.
Quintavalle, C. A. (1974). The development of poster art. In M. Gallo (Ed.), *The poster in history* (pp. 217-230). New York: New American Library.
Raboy, M. (1984). *Movements and messages: Media and radical politics in Québec.* Toronto: Between The Lines.
Radway, J. (1984). *Reading the romance.* Chapel Hill: University of North Carolina Press.
Raina, P. (1981). *Independent social movements in Poland.* London: London School of Economics/Orbis Books.
Ramírez, M. C. (Ed.). (1999). *Cantos paralelos: La parodia plástica en al arte argentino contemporáneo.* Austin, TX: Jack S. Blanton Museum of Art.
Ramus, C. F. (Ed.). (1978). *Daumier: 120 great lithographs.* New York: Dover.
Red Notes. (1978). *Italy 1977-78: Living with an earthquake.* London: Author.
Red Notes. (1979). *Working class autonomy and the crisis.* London: Author.
Red Notes. (1981). *Italy 1980-81: After Marx, jail!* London: Author.
Remington, T. F. (1988). *The truth of authority.* Pittsburgh, PA: University of Pittsburgh Press.
Reporters Sans Frontières. (1995). *Les médias de la haine.* Paris: Éditions La Découverte.

Riaño, P. (Ed.). (1994). *Women in grassroots communication: Furthering social change.* Thousand Oaks, CA: Sage.

Rice, J. (1980-1981). Cable access: Promise of the eighties. In M. L. Hollowell (Ed.), *The cable/broadband communications book* (Vol. 2, pp. 100-117). New York: Industry Publications.

Riggins, S. H. (Ed.). (1992). *Ethnic minority media: An international perspective.* Newbury Park, CA: Sage.

Rips, G. (1981). *The campaign against the underground press.* San Francisco: City Lights Books.

Robberson, T. (1995, February 20). Mexican rebels using a high-tech weapon: Internet helps rally support. *The Washington Post,* pp. A1.

Robinson, G. J. (1977). *Tito's maverick media.* Urbana: University of Illinois Press.

Rodríguez, C. (in press). *Fissures in the mediascape: A comparative analysis of citizens' media.* Cresskill, NY: Hampton Press.

Rodriguez, J. (1994). *Our Lady Of Guadalupe: Faith and empowerment among Mexican-American women.* Austin: University of Texas Press.

Rolston, B. (1991). *Politics and painting: Murals and conflict in Northern Ireland.* Rutherford, NJ: Fairleigh Dickinson University Press.

Rosenberg, T. (1995). *The haunted land: Facing Europe's ghosts after Communism.* New York: Random House.

Rosenfeld, R. (1997). *American aurora: The suppressed history of our nation's beginnings and the newspaper that tried to report it.* New York: St Martin's.

Roszak, T. (1995). *The making of a counter culture* (2nd ed.). Berkeley: University of California Press.

Rothe, N. (Ed.). (1977). *Frühe sozialistische satyrische lyrik aus den zeitschriften "Der Wahre Jakob" und "Süddeutscher Postillon."* Berlin: Akademie-Verlag.

Rowbotham, S. (1975). *Hidden from history: Rediscovering women in history from the 17th century to the present.* New York: Pantheon.

Rowbotham, S. (1981). Beyond the fragments. In S. Rowbotham, L. Segal, & H. Wainwright (Eds.), *Beyond the fragments.* Boston: Alyson.

Rowbotham, S. (1989). *The past is before us: Feminism in action since the 1960s.* London: Pandora.

Rowbotham, S. (1992). *Women in movement: Feminism and social action.* London: Routledge.

Rowland, W. D., Jr. (1982). The illusion of fulfillment: The broadcast reform movement. *Journalism Monograph* (Serial No. 79).

Rozzo, U., & Seidel Menchi, S. (1990). Livre et réforme en Italie. In J.-F. Gilmont (Ed.), *La réforme et le livre: L'Europe de l'imprimé (1517-1570)* (pp. 327-374). Paris: Les Éditions du Cerf.

Ruane, K. (1982). *The Polish challenge.* London: BBC Publications.

Ruggeri, G., & Guarino, M. (1994). *Berlusconi: Inchiesta sul signor TV.* Milan: Kaos Edizioni.

Rumsey, S. (1995). *Re: the situation in Chiapas—update of urgent action* (ICCHRLA Committee Report sent on-line Monday, February 13). Available: gopher://mundo.eco.utexas.edu:70/11/mailing/chiapas95.archive

Ryan, C. (1991). *Prime time activism: Media strategies for grassroots organizing.* Boston: South End Press.

Ryback, T. (1989). *Rock around the bloc.* New York: Oxford University Press.
Sabin, R. (1993). *Adult comics: An introduction.* London: Routledge.
Sabin, R. (1996). *Comics, comix, & graphic novels.* London: Phaidon Press.
Said, G. (in press). *The hamam as a women's public sphere in Morocco.* Dissertation in progress, University of Texas at Austin.
Sakharov, A. (1974). *Sakharov speaks.* New York: Knopf.
Sakolsky, R., & Dunifer, S. (Eds.). (1998). *Seizing the airwaves: A free radio handbook.* Edinburgh and San Francisco: AK Press.
Sakolsky, R., & Koehnline, J. (Eds.). (1993). *Gone to Croatan: Origins of North American dropout culture.* New York: Autonomedia.
Salisbury, H. E. (Ed.). (1974). *Sakharov speaks.* New York: Vintage.
Sampedro Blanco, V. (1997). *Movimientos sociales: Debates sin mordaza—desobediencia civil y servicio militar (1970-1996).* Madrid, Spain: Boletín Oficial del Estado, Centro de Estudios Constitucionales.
Samuelson, F.-M. (1978). *Il Était une fois libé . . .* Paris: Le Seuil.
Samuelson, P. (1996). The copyright grab. *Wired Magazine* [On-line]. Available: http://www.wired.com/wired/whitepaper.html
Saponara, L. E. (1997). Ideology at work: Deciphering the appeal of New Right discourse. Master's thesis, Radio-Television-Film Department, University of Texas at Austin.
Scammell, M. (1984). *Solzhenitsyn: A biography.* New York: Norton.
Scannell, P. (1992). The media and democracy. *Media, Culture, & Society, 14*(2), 325-328.
Schechter, D. (1992). L'expérience de globalvision: Découvrir la couverture. In N. Thede & A. Ambrosi (Eds.), *Petits écrans et démocratie: Vidéo légère et télévision alternative au service du développement* (pp. 135-141). Paris: Syros-Alternatives.
Schell, O. (1994). *Mandate of heaven: A new generation of entrepreneurs, dissidents, bohemians, and technocrats lays claim to China's future.* New York: Simon & Schuster.
Schiller, D. (1981). *Objectivity and the news.* Philadelphia, PA: University of Pennsylvania Press.
Schiller, H. (1995). The global information highway: Project for an ungovernable world. In J. Brook & I. Boal (Eds.), *Resisting the virtual life: The culture of politics and information.* San Francisco: City Lights Press.
Schlecht, N. E. (1995). Resistance and appropriation in Brazil: How the media and "official culture" institutionalized Sao Paulo's *grafite. Studies in Latin American Popular Culture, 14,* 37-67.
Schlesinger, P. (1992). *Putting "reality" together: BBC news* (2nd ed.). London: Routledge.
Schudson, M. (1997). Why conversation is not the soul of democracy. *Critical Studies in Mass Communication, 14*(4), 297-309.
Scott, J. C. (1985). *Weapons of the weak: Everyday forms of peasant resistance.* New Haven, CT: Yale University Press.
Scott, J. C. (1990). *Domination and the arts of resistance: Hidden transcripts.* New Haven, CT, Yale University Press.

Seaton, J., & Pimlott, B. (1980). Media and the Portuguese revolution. In A. Smith (Ed.), *Newspapers and democracy* (pp. 174-199). Cambridge: MIT Press.

Seeger, P. (1992). *American industrial ballads* (Smithsonian/Folkways Recordings). Cambridge, MA: Rounder Records.

Selna, R. (1999, August 3). KPFA transmitter still off-limits to staff. *San Francisco Examiner.* Available: http://www.sfgate.com/cgibin/article.cgi?file=/examiner/archive/1999/08/03/METRO1491 8.dtl.

Semelin, J. (1997). *La liberté au bout des ondes: De coup de Prague à du mur de Berlin.* Paris: Belfond.

Seubert, E. (1987). Native American media in the United States: An overview. In John D. H. Downing (Ed.), *Film And politics in the third world* (pp. 303-310). New York: Autonomedia.

Shamberg, M., & Raindance Corporation. (1971). *Guerrilla television.* San Francisco, CA: Holt, Rinehart & Winston.

Shanor, D. (1985). *Behind the lines.* New York: St Martin's.

Shapiro, A. (1995). Street corners in cyberspace. *The Nation, 261*(1), 10.

Shapiro, A. (1997). Total access. *The Nation, 264*(1), 5.

Sheng, H. (1990). Big character posters in China: A historical survey. *Journal of Chinese Law, 4*(2), 234-256.

Shiva, V. (1996, December 5). U.S. makes exchange of info a crime. *Third World Network Features* [On-line]. Available gopher://mundo.eco.utexas.edu:70/11/mailing/chiapas95.archive

Sholle, D. (1995). Access through activism: Extending the ideas of Negt and Kluge to American alternative media practices. *Javnost/The Public, 2*(4), 21-35.

Shore, E. (1988). *Talkin' socialism: J. A. Wayland and the role of the press in American radicalism, 1890-1912.* Lawrence: University Press of Kansas.

Showalter, E. (1977). *A literature of their own.* Princeton, NJ: Princeton University Press.

Siliato, F. (1977). *L'antenna dei padroni.* Milan: Mazzotta.

Simpson Grinberg, M. (1986a). *Comunicación alternativa y cambio social.* Puebla, México: Premia Editoria de Libros.

Simpson Grinberg, M. (1986b). Trends in alternative communication research in Latin America. In E. G. McAnany & R. Atwood (Eds.), *Communication and Latin American society* (pp. 165-189). Madison: University of Wisconsin Press.

Sinclair, J. (1991). *Images incorporated: Advertising as industry and ideology.* Melbourne, Australia: Methuen.

Sinyavsky, A. (1990). *Soviet civilization: A cultural history.* New York: Arcade.

SIPAZ. (1997). *Servicio Internacional para la Paz / International Service for Peace* [On-line]. Available: http://www.nonviolence.org/sipaz/

Skilling, H. G. (1989). *Samizdat and an independent society in eastern and central Europe.* Columbus: Ohio State University Press.

Slavitsky, A. G., & Gleason, T. W. (1994). Alternative things considered: A comparison of National Public Radio and Pacifica Radio news coverage. *Journalism Quarterly, 71*(4), 775-786.

Smith, D. M. (1997). *Modern Italy: A political history.* Ann Arbor: University of Michigan Press.

Smith, G. S. (1984). *Songs to seven strings.* Bloomington: Indiana University Press.

Smith, R. L. (1970). *The wired nation.* San Francisco: Harper & Row.
Sobel, M. (1979). *Trabelin' on: The slave journey to an Afro-Baptist faith.* Westport, CT: Greenwood.
Solanas, F., & Getino, O. (1983). Toward a third cinema. In A. Mattelart & S. Siegelaub (Eds.), *Communication and class struggle 2: Liberation, socialism* (pp. 220-230). Bagnolet, France: International Mass Media Research Center.
Soley, L. C. (1995). *Leasing the ivory tower: The corporate takeover of academia.* Boston: South End Press.
Soley, L. C. (1999). *Free radio: Electroic civil disobedience.* Boulder, CO: Westview.
Soley, L. C., & Nichols, J. (1987). *Clandestine radio broadcasting: A study of revolutionary and counterrevolutionary electronic communication.* New York: Praeger.
Sparks, C. (1993). Raymond Williams and the theory of democratic communication. In S. Splichal & J. Wasko (Eds.), *Communication and democracy* (pp. 69-86). Norwood, NJ: Ablex Publishing Corporation.
Spechler, D. (1982). *Permitted dissent in the USSR: Novy Mir and the Soviet regime.* New York: Praeger.
Spiegelman, A. (1987). *Maus I.* Harmondsworth, UK: Penguin.
Spiegelman, A. (1992). *Maus II.* Harmondsworth, UK: Penguin.
Sreberny-Mohammadi, A., & Mohammadi, A. (1994). *Small media, big revolution: Communication, culture, and the Iranian revolution.* Minneapolis: University of Minnesota Press.
Staeck, K. (1985). Beware art! Photomontage as political intervention. In D. Kahn & D. Neumaier (Eds.), *Cultures in contention* (pp. 248-261). Seattle: WA: The Real Comet Press.
Stam, R. (1998). *A comparative history of race in Brazilian cinema and culture.* Durham, NC: Duke University Press.
Staniszkis, J. (1984). *Poland's self-limiting revolution.* Princeton. NJ: Princeton University Press.
Starr, S. F. (1983). *Red and hot: The fate of jazz in the Soviet Union, 1917-1980.* New York: Oxford University Press.
Starski, S. (1982). *Class struggle in classless Poland.* Boston: South End Press.
Stebbins, G. R. (1969). *Listener-sponsored radio: The Pacifica stations.* Ph.D. thesis in mass communications, Ohio State University.
Stein, L., & Marcus, D. (1990). *Notes toward a paper tiger television handbook.* Unpublished manuscript.
Sterling, B. (1993). *A short history of the Internet* [On-line]. Available: http://www.unm.edu/~docs/Newsletter/V27n3/Feature_txt/feature_article3.html
Steven, S. (1982). *The Poles.* New York: Macmillan.
Stevens-Fernández, D. (1995). *Afro-Colombian community radio on the Pacific coast.* Master's thesis, Radio-Television-Film Department, University of Texas at Austin.
Streeter, T. (1987). The cable fable revisited: Discourse, policy, and the making of cable television. *Critical Studies in Mass Communication, 4,* 174-200.
Strigaljow, A. (1995). Agitprop—die Kunst extremer politischer Situationen. In I. Antonowa & J. Merkert (Eds.), *Berlin Moskau 1900-1950* (pp. 111-118). München: Prestel-Verlag.

Sullivan, J. D. (1997). *On the walls and in the streets: American poetry broadsides from the 1960s.* Urbana: University of Illinois Press.

Sussman, G. (1997). *Communication, technology, and politics in the information age.* Thousand Oaks, CA: Sage.

Swett, C. (1995, July 17). *Strategic assessment of the Internet* (Pentagon Report, Office of the Assistant Secretary of Defense for Special Operations and Low-Intensity Conflict, Policy Planning). Washington DC: The Pentagon.

Swianewicz, S. (1979). The Katyn affair. *Survey, 24*(1), 188-198.

Switzer, L. (1997). *South Africa's alternative press: Voices of protest and resistance, 1880s-1960s.* New York: Cambridge University Press.

Tarrow, S. (1989). *Democracy and disorder: Protest and politics in Italy 1956-1975.* Oxford, UK: Clarendon.

Thede, N., & Ambrosi, A. (Eds.). (1992). *Petits écrans et démocratie: Vidéo légère et télévision au service du développement.* Paris: Syros-Alternatives.

Thompson, E. P. (1968). *The making of the English working class.* Harmondsworth, UK: Penguin.

Thompson, E. P. (1978). *The poverty of theory and other essays.* London: Merlin.

Thompson, E. P. (1993). *Witness against the beast: William Blake and the moral law.* New York: The New Press.

Tobin, J., & Dobard, R. G. (1999). *Hidden in plain view: The secret story of quilts and the Underground Railroad.* New York: Doubleday.

Tökés, R. (Ed.). (1975). *Dissent in the USSR.* Baltimore, MD: Johns Hopkins University Press.

Tomaselli, K. G., & Louw, P. E. (1991). *The alternative press in South Africa.* Bellville, South Africa: Anthropos.

Tompkins, J. (1985). *Sensational designs: The cultural work of American fiction 1790-1860.* New York: Oxford University Press.

Touraine, A. (1994). *Qu'est-ce que la démocratie?* Paris: Fayard.

Trasatti, S. (1978). Geografia delle radio locali: Linee di tendenza di un fenomeno in atto. In G. Gamaleri (Ed.), *Un posto nell'etere: Le radio locali in Italia* (pp. 55-90). Rome: Edizioni Paoline.

Trend, D. (1993). Rethinking media activism. *Socialist Review, 23*(2), 5-33.

Tsagarousianou, R., Tambini, D., & Bryan, C. (Eds.). (1998). *Cyberdemocracy: Technology, cities, and civic networks.* London: Routledge.

Turner, T. (1992). Defiant images: The Kayapo appropriation of video. *Anthropology Today, 8*(6), 5-16.

Valaskakis, G. (1992). Communication, culture, and technology: Satellites and northern native broadcasting. In S. H. Riggins (Ed.), *Ethnic minority media: An international perspective* (pp. 63-81). Thousand Oaks, CA: Sage.

Van Zoonen, L. (1993). *Feminist media studies.* London: Sage.

Vargas, L. (1995). *Social uses and radio practices: The use of participatory radio by ethnic minorities in Mexico.* Boulder, CO: Westview.

Viénet, R. (1992). *Enragés and situationists in the occupation movement, France, May '68.* New York: Autonomedia.

A vision for Pacifica radio: Creating a network for the 21st century (1997). [On-line]. Available: http://www.pacifica.org/board/docs/avision.html

Walker, J. A. (1983). *Art in the age of mass media.* London: Pluto.

Walker, N. A. (1995). *The disobedient writer: Women and narrative tradition.* Austin: The University of Texas Press.

Wallner, M. (1991). Deep dish: Tigers sprout wings and fly! In D. Marcus (Ed.), *ROAR! The paper tiger television guide to media activism* (pp. 33-34). New York: The Paper Tiger Television Collective.

Watkins, S. C. (1998). *Representing: Hip hop culture and the production of black cinema.* Chicago: University of Chicago Press.

Wechsburg, J. (1969). *The voices.* New York: Doubleday.

Weil, R. (1993). Sometimes a scepter is only a scepter: Pornography and politics in Restoration England. In L. Hunt (Ed.), *The invention of pornography: Obscenity and the origins of modernity, 1500-1800* (pp. 125-153). New York: Zone Books.

Weiler, K. (1994). Freire and a feminist politics of difference. In P. L. McLaren & C. Lankshear (Eds.), *Politics of liberation: Paths from Freire* (pp. 12-40). New York: Routledge.

White, S., & White, G. (1998). *Stylin': African American expressive culture from its beginnings to the Zoot Suit.* Ithaca, NY: Cornell University Press.

Widor, C. (Ed.). (1981). *Documents on the Chinese democratic movement 1978-1980: Unofficial magazines and wall-posters.* Paris: Éditions de l'École des Hautes Études en Sciences Sociales.

Wieck, D. (1979). The negativity of anarchism. In H. J. Ehrlich (Ed.), *Reinventing anarchy* (pp. 138-155). London: Routledge & Kegan Paul.

Willemen, P. (1989). The third cinema question: Notes and reflections. In J. Pines & P. Willemen (Eds.), *Questions of third cinema* (pp. 1-29). London: British Film Institute.

Williams, R. (1977). *Marxism and literature.* London: Oxford University Press.

Wilson, P. L. (1995). *Pirate utopias: Moorish corsairs and European renegades.* New York: Autonomedia.

Winseck, D. (1997). Contradictions in the democratization of international communication. *Media, Culture, & Society, 19*(2), 219-246.

Wollen, P. (1989). Bitter victory: The art and politics of the Situationist International. In E. Sussman (Ed.), *On the passage of a few people through a rather brief moment in time: The Situationist International 1957-1972* (pp. 20-61). Cambridge: MIT Press.

Wood, M. (1994). *Radical satire and print culture 1790-1822.* Oxford, UK: Clarendon.

Woolf, V. (1975). *A room of one's own.* New York: Harcourt, Brace and World.

Worsley, P. (1968) *The trumpet shall sound: A study of "cargo" cults in Melanesia* (2nd ed.). New York: Schocken Books.

Young, I. M. (1990). *Justice and the politics of difference.* Princeton, NJ: Princeton University Press.

Zeltzer, S. (1999, July 15). Union-busting, labor, and Pacifica Radio. *San Francisco Bay Guardian* [On-line]. Available: http://www.superlists.com/kpfa/zelt.html

Zurier, R. (1988). *Art for the masses: A radical magazine and its graphics, 1911-1917.* Philadelphia, PA: Temple University Press.

Index

About the Authors

John D. H. Downing teaches in the radio-television-film department at the University of Texas, Austin. His most recent book, *Internationalizing Media Theory* (Sage 1996), addressed the challenges to media studies posed by media of many kinds in the former Soviet bloc over the Great Transition of 1980-1995. He is currently working on two further books for Sage. One is with Charles Husband on a cross-Atlantic study of media, racism, and ethnicity. The other is the Sage *Handbook of Media Studies,* which he is coediting with Dennis McQuail, Philip Schlesinger, and Ellen Wartella.

Tamara Villarreal Ford is a communications consultant specializing in alternative media, Latino media, and new communications technologies. She has an M.A. from the University of Texas at Austin, where she was an associate with LANIC (the Latin American Network Information Center) conducting Internet research on Latin American/Latino websites and developing a program of computer-assisted education and digital media archives for the Institute of Latin American Studies. She was a 1996 recipient of the Rockefeller Fellowship in Intercultural Collaboration for her work with the ZapNet Collective, a multimedia and website project that traces the Zapatista discourse within emerging public spheres of the Internet. Currently, she is working with the AZ Editorial Collective on a bilingual annotated compilation of "Conversations with Durito," a series of 30 stories by EZLN spokesman Subcomandante Marcos.

Genève Gil is a freelance web developer and research consultant in Austin, where she recently completed a master's degree in Latin American Studies at the University of Texas. She has traveled in Chiapas on four occasions and began researching the Tzotziles and Tzeltales in 1987. Her work has focused on social and political movements in Latin America from the early 1970s to the present, including organized popular resistance in the Southern Cone, Tropicalismo in Brazil, and the Zapatista uprising of the 1990s.

Laura Stein is an assistant professor at the University of San Francisco. She writes about communication law and policy, speech rights, and public communication. She received her Ph.D. at the University of Texas at Austin in 1997.